D1258752

Hypertension Cookbook FOR DUMMIES®

by Rosanne Rust, MS, RD, LDN
and Cindy Kleckner, RD, LD

WILEY

John Wiley & Sons, Inc.

Hypertension Cookbook For Dummies®

Published by
John Wiley & Sons, Inc.
111 River St.
Hoboken, NJ 07030-5774
www.wiley.com

Copyright © 2012 by John Wiley & Sons, Inc., Hoboken, New Jersey

Published by John Wiley & Sons, Inc., Hoboken, New Jersey

Published simultaneously in Canada

No part of this publication may be reproduced, stored in a retrieval system or transmitted in any form or by any means, electronic, mechanical, photocopying, recording, scanning or otherwise, except as permitted under Sections 107 or 108 of the 1976 United States Copyright Act, without the prior written permission of the Publisher. Requests to the Publisher for permission should be addressed to the Permissions Department, John Wiley & Sons, Inc., 111 River Street, Hoboken, NJ 07030, (201) 748-6011, fax (201) 748-6008, or online at http://www.wiley.com/go/permissions.

Trademarks: Wiley, the Wiley logo, For Dummies, the Dummies Man logo, A Reference for the Rest of Us!, The Dummies Way, Dummies Daily, The Fun and Easy Way, Dummies.com, Making Everything Easier, and related trade dress are trademarks or registered trademarks of John Wiley & Sons, Inc., and/or its affiliates in the United States and other countries, and may not be used without written permission. All other trademarks are the property of their respective owners. John Wiley & Sons, Inc., is not associated with any product or vendor mentioned in this book.

LIMIT OF LIABILITY/DISCLAIMER OF WARRANTY: THE PUBLISHER AND THE AUTHOR MAKE NO REPRESENTATIONS OR WARRANTIES WITH RESPECT TO THE ACCURACY OR COMPLETENESS OF THE CONTENTS OF THIS WORK AND SPECIFICALLY DISCLAIM ALL WARRANTIES, INCLUDING WITHOUT LIMITATION WARRANTIES OF FITNESS FOR A PARTICULAR PURPOSE. NO WARRANTY MAY BE CREATED OR EXTENDED BY SALES OR PROMOTIONAL MATERIALS. THE ADVICE AND STRATEGIES CONTAINED HEREIN MAY NOT BE SUITABLE FOR EVERY SITUATION. THIS WORK IS SOLD WITH THE UNDERSTANDING THAT THE PUBLISHER IS NOT ENGAGED IN RENDERING LEGAL, ACCOUNTING, OR OTHER PROFESSIONAL SERVICES. IF PROFESSIONAL ASSISTANCE IS REQUIRED, THE SERVICES OF A COMPETENT PROFESSIONAL PERSON SHOULD BE SOUGHT. NEITHER THE PUBLISHER NOR THE AUTHOR SHALL BE LIABLE FOR DAMAGES ARISING HEREFROM. THE FACT THAT AN ORGANIZATION OR WEBSITE IS REFERRED TO IN THIS WORK AS A CITATION AND/OR A POTENTIAL SOURCE OF FURTHER INFORMATION DOES NOT MEAN THAT THE AUTHOR OR THE PUBLISHER ENDORSES THE INFORMATION THE ORGANIZATION OR WEBSITE MAY PROVIDE OR RECOMMENDATIONS IT MAY MAKE. FURTHER, READERS SHOULD BE AWARE THAT INTERNET WEBSITES LISTED IN THIS WORK MAY HAVE CHANGED OR DISAPPEARED BETWEEN WHEN THIS WORK WAS WRITTEN AND WHEN IT IS READ. SOME OF THE EXERCISES AND DIETARY SUGGESTIONS CONTAINED IN THIS WORK MAY NOT BE APPROPRIATE FOR ALL INDIVIDUALS, AND READERS SHOULD CONSULT WITH A PHYSICIAN BEFORE COMMENCING ANY EXERCISE OR DIETARY PROGRAM.

For general information on our other products and services, please contact our Customer Care Department within the U.S. at 877-762-2974, outside the U.S. at 317-572-3993, or fax 317-572-4002.

For technical support, please visit www.wiley.com/techsupport.

Wiley publishes in a variety of print and electronic formats and by print-on-demand. Some material included with standard print versions of this book may not be included in e-books or in print-on-demand. If this book refers to media such as a CD or DVD that is not included in the version you purchased, you may download this material at http://booksupport.wiley.com. For more information about Wiley products, visit www.wiley.com.

Library of Congress Control Number: 2011941734

ISBN 978-1-118-09513-3 (pbk); ISBN 978-1-118-19481-2 (ebk); ISBN 978-1-118-19483-6 (ebk); ISBN 978-1-118-19482-9 (ebk)

Manufactured in the United States of America

10 9 8 7 6 5 4 3 2

WILEY

About the Authors

Rosanne Rust, MS, RD, LDN, of Meadville, Pennsylvania, is a registered, licensed dietitian and a member of the Academy of Nutrition and Dietetics, formerly known as the American Dietetic Association. She's a nutrition communications consultant who enjoys helping individuals and organizations develop solutions to poor eating habits based on fact, not hype. She coaches clients toward better eating and painless weight loss at www.realliving nutrition.com, an online weight-loss coaching service. Rosanne is the coauthor of *Calorie Counter Journal For Dummies, Restaurant Calorie Counter For Dummies,* 2nd Edition, and *Glycemic Index Cookbook For Dummies,* with Meri Raffetto (all published by Wiley), as well as a regular contributor for *The Meadville Tribune.*

Rosanne is a wife and the mother of three sons. She practices what she preaches by balancing healthy food with regular activity. Her motto: Choose happiness, and enjoy eating for better health. Her website is www.rustnutrition.com, and her Twitter handle is @rustnutrition.

Cindy Kleckner, RD, LD, of McKinney, Texas, is a registered and licensed dietitian, as well as a member of the Academy of Nutrition and Dietetics, formerly known as the American Dietetic Association. For over 30 years, she's been working in the fields of culinary nutrition, weight management, cardiovascular health, and overall wellness. She provides culinary demonstrations to individuals and groups who translate the science of nutrition into practical solutions for consumers, busy executives, and large corporations; she's known for her high-energy presentations that educate, inspire, and entertain. A true advocate that healthy cooking and taste can coexist, Cindy coauthored *What's Cooking at the Cooper Clinic* (published by It's Cooking, Incorporated) and contributed to Dr. Kenneth H. Cooper's *Overcoming Hypertension* (Bantam).

Married to her college sweetheart, she is a proud mom of two sons. She considers her family her master taste testers. When she's not helping others meet their lifestyle goals, Cindy enjoys competitive tennis, travel, fitness, and gourmet cooking. Follow Cindy on Twitter: @clkleck.

Dedication

This book is dedicated to our mothers, Toni and Irene, who gave us an appreciation for the simple things in life: relationships, good food, and food's nurturing powers. Mom's kitchen was always a warm place and a gathering of family and friends where we made strong connections. It was a place to have a good time, make people happy, connect to our roots, and preserve culinary traditions. Teaching us how to prepare wholesome, ethnic food was their greatest gift to us and future generations, a real language of love.

Authors' Acknowledgments

We would like to acknowledge the team that made this book possible.

Our agent, Matt Wagner, whose support and guidance is always timely and helpful; and our acquisitions editor, Erin Calligan Mooney, for bringing this project our way.

A book can't come together without our excellent team of editors. We are truly grateful to our project editor, Heike Baird, for her guidance and exceptional effort through this process. Our copy editor, Christine Pingleton, and the technical reviewer, Desirée de Waal, were invaluable in providing us with a final product that we can be proud of. Our recipe tester extraordinaire, Emily Nolan, helped us fine-tune our recipes. Finally, we truly appreciate the tedious but important task of nutritional analysis provided by Angie Scheetz (with the National Institute for Fitness and Sport) and Patty Santelli.

Rosanne would like to thank her husband, Dave, for his continuous support in allowing her to fulfill her goals and dreams, which often requires his tolerance for her high-energy projects. She also thanks her beautiful sons, Matt, Max, and Marcus, without whose teamwork this book could not have been completed. Rosanne thanks them for emptying the dishwasher, helping with dinner, and entertaining themselves all summer long while she spent days writing.

Cindy thanks her family as well — the people who make life worth living; her deepest love and appreciation to her husband, Barry, for his support and encouragement, and for keeping her centered when she's pulled in a thousand different directions. And to her wonderful sons, Brian and Neil, who outgrew her lap, but never her love and cooking.

Publisher's Acknowledgments

We're proud of this book; please send us your comments at http://dummies.custhelp.com. For other comments, please contact our Customer Care Department within the U.S. at 877-762-2974, outside the U.S. at 317-572-3993, or fax 317-572-4002.

Some of the people who helped bring this book to market include the following:

Acquisitions, Editorial, and Vertical Websites

Project Editor: Heike Baird

Acquisitions Editor: Erin Calligan Mooney

Copy Editor: Christine Pingleton

Assistant Editor: David Lutton

Editorial Program Coordinator: Joe Niesen

Technical Editor: Desirée de Waal, MS, RD, CD

Recipe Tester: Emily Nolan

Nutritional Analysts: Angie Scheetz, RD, in conjunction with the National Institute for Fitness and Sport; Patty Santelli

Senior Editorial Manager: Jennifer Ehrlich

Editorial Assistants: Rachelle S. Amick, Alexa Koschier

Art Coordinator: Alicia B. South

Cover Photos:
© iStockphoto.com / Carolyn De Andaa;
© T. J. Hine Photography

Cartoons: Rich Tennant
(www.the5thwave.com)

Composition Services

Project Coordinator: Sheree Montgomery

Layout and Graphics: Carl Byers, Christin Swinford

Proofreaders: Jessica Kramer, Evelyn Wellborn

Indexer: Estalita Slivoskey

Illustrators: Kathryn Born, Elizabeth Kurtzman

Photographer: T. J. Hine Photography

Food Stylist: Lisa Bishop

Publishing and Editorial for Consumer Dummies

    Kathleen Nebenhaus, Vice President and Executive Publisher

    Kristin Ferguson-Wagstaffe, Product Development Director

    Ensley Eikenburg, Associate Publisher, Travel

    Kelly Regan, Editorial Director, Travel

Publishing for Technology Dummies

    Andy Cummings, Vice President and Publisher

Composition Services

    Debbie Stailey, Director of Composition Services

Contents at a Glance

Recipes at a Glance

Desserts

Lunchtime Meals

Meatless Side Dishes

Salads, Appetizers, and Snacks

Seafood Entrees

Soups, Stews, and Chilis

Vegetarian Entrees

Table of Contents

Introduction

*H*ypertension, or high blood pressure, is a serious health concern affecting millions of people. About one-third of all adults in the United States have hypertension, according to the Centers for Disease Control. Unfortunately, because hypertension often has no symptoms, it may go undetected for years, damaging your heart, blood vessels, and kidneys.

Risk factors for hypertension include the following:

- ✔ Older age
- ✔ Being overweight
- ✔ Lifestyle habits, like smoking and drinking too much alcohol
- ✔ A sedentary lifestyle
- ✔ A high-sodium diet

Treatment for hypertension includes lifestyle change and medication. This book discusses both, but focuses on lifestyle change — particularly, how to cook delicious meals that can help lower your blood pressure.

So what do we mean by *lifestyle change?* A lifestyle geared toward reducing blood pressure incorporates these recommendations:

- ✔ Follow a healthy diet.
- ✔ Be physically active.
- ✔ Maintain a healthy weight.
- ✔ Quit smoking.
- ✔ Manage your stress.

This book shows you how easy lifestyle change can be by helping you create simple meals that support a diet for lowering blood pressure. Have no fear — the recipes are delicious!

About This Book

If you have hypertension, your doctor has probably instructed you to follow a low-salt diet, or perhaps the DASH diet plan. You may often think of "diet" as a negative word that implies deprivation or restrictions. On the contrary, *Hypertension Cookbook For Dummies* neither deprives nor restricts you; instead, it enlightens you to new ways to cook flavorful meals. It's the perfect tool to help you ease into a healthier lifestyle for better blood pressure control.

You don't have to read this book from cover to cover. Instead, you can use it as your personal hypertension guide. You can flip to the chapters with background information on hypertension and your body, or check out the chapters with tips for organizing your kitchen and grocery shopping. If you're eager to get cooking, head straight to check out the recipes, which begin in Chapter 9.

Conventions Used in This Book

In this book, we use the terms "hypertension" and "high blood pressure" interchangeably. The diet and lifestyle recommendations we make come from sources such as the National Heart, Lung, and Blood Institute; Centers for Disease Control; the American Heart Association; and the American Dietetic Association. Our recipes provide a foundation for a blood-pressure-lowering diet.

We've included some recipes that are higher than others in sodium and/ or saturated fat, but we encourage you to balance those recipes with lower-sodium meals and more fruits and vegetables the rest of the day. This book isn't intended to be a substitute for medical care. If you have a family history of high blood pressure or have hypertension, we recommend you see your doctor to determine your personal medical needs, and have your blood pressure monitored by your doctor regularly.

Here are a few ground rules relating to the recipes:

- All oven and cooking temperatures are measured in degrees Fahrenheit; flip to Appendix A for information on converting temperatures to Celsius.
- All eggs are large.
- All onions are yellow.
- For measuring purposes, dry ingredients are lightly spooned into a standard U. S. measuring cup or spoon, and then leveled with a knife.

Liquids are measured in glass, standard U. S. measuring cups. Check out Appendix A if you need help converting to metric measurements.

- All sugar is granulated.

- All flour is all-purpose.

- The term "lightly browned" indicates when the food just begins to change color.

- "One chicken breast" is a half breast. All poultry is skinless unless otherwise noted.

- All herbs are dried unless specified as fresh.

- Lemon and lime juice are freshly squeezed.

- All ground pepper is freshly ground black pepper.

- Some higher-sodium ingredients (Kalamata olives, capers, and Parmesan cheese, for example) are used in very small quantities to enhance the flavor of a recipe. Measure these ingredients carefully to avoid increasing sodium levels significantly.

- References to "percent daily values" or limits on nutrients are based on a daily intake of 2,000 calories.

And then, of course, these are the conventions we use in the rest of the book:

- We use **boldface** to highlight keywords or action steps within lists.

- We use _italics_ to define a word or phrase.

- We use monofont to indicate website addresses.

- The tomato icon to the left of this paragraph appears next to the titles of vegetarian recipes in the "Recipes at a Glance" (see the Table of Contents) and the "Recipes in This Chapter" lists at the beginning of the recipe chapters in Parts III and IV. Exceptions are those chapters that contain _only_ vegetarian recipes — Chapters 11, 12, 21, and 22 — and those categories in the "Recipes at a Glance" that consist entirely of vegetarian recipes (Meatless Side Dishes, Vegetarian Entrees, and Desserts).

What You're Not to Read

Like all _For Dummies_ books, we include gray-shaded _sidebars_ that contain interesting but ultimately nonessential information. You can skip over these sections if you prefer, because the rest of the chapter provides you with the nuts and bolts. You can also skip right over paragraphs marked with a Technical Stuff icon. These details are in the book for inquiring minds that want to know more. While they may inspire interesting conversations at your next cocktail party, you can safely skip them too.

Foolish Assumptions

We assume that you want to fix some meals that keep your heart healthy by following the DASH plan but still tantalize your taste buds. We also assume that you're interested in understanding how diet and lifestyle impact blood pressure because you either have hypertension or are at risk for it. In addition, we assume that you've done some cooking and are familiar with basic cooking terminology and methods, but can benefit from cooking preparation and technique tips. Thus, we've tried to explain the cooking as simply as possible.

How This Book Is Organized

This book is divided into six parts, to help you understand and incorporate the lifestyle changes you need to make to better manage your hypertension.

Part 1: Fighting Hypertension with Healthier Choices

Fortunately, hypertension is a disease that you have some control over. This part helps you understand what hypertension is all about and how you can make lifestyle changes to prevent or control it. We cover the basic facts about the numbers associated with blood pressure and introduce you to the dietary guidelines that lower those blood pressure numbers to within normal range. In addition, you find tips for losing weight and incorporating more physical activity into your weekly schedule.

Part 11: Creating a Low-Salt, Big-Taste Lifestyle

Most doctors recommend that hypertension patients cut back on the salt in their diets. In this part, you find out where sodium may be hiding in your meals and pantry, and how to choose substitutions to replace some of it in your food choices and cooking. This part also takes you step by step through the grocery store, helping you decipher food labels and fill your cart with blood-pressure-lowering foods.

Here you find simple steps to get your kitchen organized so you can put together quick meals and whip up the tasty recipes in this book. We give you tips for using some of our favorite kitchen gadgets, along with some cooking methods that are pretty handy when it comes to adding outstanding salt-free flavorings to your dishes. Finally, this part offers ideas on menu-planning so that special events and busy nights don't add up to unhealthy choices and fast food.

Part III: From Soup to Nuts: Serving Salads, Sides, and Party-Starters

This part kicks off the recipe chapters in the book, providing some bursting-with-flavor salads that are far from a boring bowl of iceberg lettuce. We show you how to create salads that offer more nutrients and more flavor, fulfilling multiple DASH requirements and even incorporating two or three food groups. Soups, chilis, side dishes, and tantalizing appetizers all make an appearance here too, each with flavor to boot and perfect to share.

Part IV: Staying Heart-Healthy through Every Meal

We know you're busy, so we offer solutions to planning balanced menus for every meal throughout the day. We offer ideas for healthy breakfasts, new lunchtime options, and fast (but not fast food) dinners.

If you're going to stick with your hypertension diet, you need to have variety, and that means variety in your protein. We include recipes starring poultry, seafood, beef, and pork, as well as a few vegetarian dishes. In each chapter you find meals you can whip up any night of the week, as well as those you may want to use for entertaining guests.

We also include a special chapter on kid-friendly meals that you'll enjoy, so you can stay healthy and still please the picky (and maybe even expand their horizons).

And what kind of a pathetic cookbook would this be if it didn't include dessert? Your sweet tooth will be happy with our sweet endings to your meals.

Part V: The Part of Tens

For a quick reference point, this part includes go-to tips for adding flavor without salt. You can use these tips for any of your favorite recipes, in addition to the ones you prepare from this book. You also find hassle-free ideas that help you control your blood pressure and keep your heart healthy for the long haul.

Part VI: Appendixes

Appendix A provides information for metric conversion to make measuring a breeze. Appendix B offers ingredient substitution ideas, so you can modify almost any of your favorite recipes by switching out the more problematic ingredients.

Icons Used in This Book

Like any *For Dummies* book, this book features some helpful icons, which are like little guideposts that point out useful information as you read:

Keep your eyes peeled for paragraphs marked with this icon. Those paragraphs highlight the most important actions you can take and facts to keep in mind to beat hypertension.

If a paragraph is marked this way, it means the information is helpful and interesting, but not essential to your basic understanding of hypertension.

Want a tip? Read information with this icon to get helpful hints that save you time and energy while you're cooking.

Halt! Stop! Whoa, Nelly! Watch out! When we place this icon next to a paragraph, it means we want you to pay attention so you don't make a mistake that could impact your health or your recipe.

Where to Go from Here

Which page you turn to next is up to you. Are you hungry for more details about your newly diagnosed high blood pressure and how to combat it? Go to Part I. If you're interested in getting your new, improved, and healthier kitchen in order and getting the lowdown on sodium, go to Part II. Part III is where the cooking begins, so if you want to dive into some tasty new recipes, dig in here. If you don't know where to begin, scan the Table of Contents to find topics of interest or flip to the color photographs of some of our favorite recipes to get an idea of what you may want to cook first.

Part I
Fighting Hypertension with Healthier Choices

The 5th Wave   By Rich Tennant

"I thought it would encourage you to reduce your sodium intake. It's a salt dispenser in the shape of a constricted artery."

In this part . . .

The first step to controlling hypertension is understanding what it means and what's going on inside your body. In this part, we give you the lowdown on hypertension basics, as well as introduce you to the most-recommended diet for preventing and controlling high blood pressure: the DASH plan. We show you how every aspect of your lifestyle can come together for a full-service plan to beat hypertension and heart disease: maintaining a healthy weight, getting more exercise, eating better, and nixing some harmful habits. Finally, we explain some common medications used to treat hypertension and provide tips for staying on track with your treatment regimen.

Chapter 1

Understanding High Blood Pressure

In This Chapter

▶ Discovering how your heart and blood pressure work

▶ Interpreting the top and bottom numbers of blood pressure

▶ Understanding how lifestyle strongly impacts hypertension and heart health

*H*ypertension, otherwise known as high blood pressure, is a serious condition that can lead to damage to the arteries, kidneys, and heart. According to the National Heart, Lung, and Blood Institute (NHLBI), one in three people have hypertension. The good news is, hypertension can be controlled. What you eat plays a big role in both preventing and controlling hypertension, and other lifestyle changes can help keep your heart healthy, too.

In this chapter, you figure out *why* you want to make lifestyle changes for improved heart health and *how* you're supposed to do it. Just because you have hypertension doesn't mean you're doomed to bland, flavorless food forever. On the contrary, you can look at your hypertension in a positive light: It's an opportunity to explore delicious foods, improve your nutrient intake, get fit, and actually be healthier than ever.

Looking at Blood Pressure and Your Heart

Consider blood the life force of your body. It delivers all the nutrients you eat, pumps oxygen into your cells, and brings toxic substances to organs that are responsible for keeping the blood clean and the body healthy. If your blood has trouble moving through your heart's arteries, your heart works extra hard, leading to a weaker heart muscle and potential organ damage throughout the body. In this section, we explore the facts about blood pressure and give you some good reasons to pay attention to it.

Getting up to speed on blood pressure

Blood pressure is a measure of the force at which blood pumps through the arteries in the body (see Figure 1-1). It's recorded as two numbers, the pressure when the heart contracts or beats, known as *systolic* pressure, and the pressure when the heart relaxes, called *diastolic* pressure. (See the section "Decoding the Telltale Heart Numbers" later in this chapter for more on what your top and bottom numbers mean.) This measure represents the amount of blood the heart pumps and the resistance to blood flow in the arteries. A healthy person's blood travels swiftly and steadily through the arteries, allowing adequate oxygen to reach the body's cells and the integrity of the blood vessels to be maintained.

Figure 1-1 shows the arteries of the heart. Blood is pumped through the four chambers (or ventricles) of the heart muscle, so imagine a division through the center of the heart muscle from top to bottom and left to right. Oxygen-poor blood from the body pumps through the superior and inferior vena cava, and flows through the right atrium and ventricle of the heart, where it's then pumped to the lungs via the pulmonary arteries to the lungs. In the lungs, the blood exchanges carbon dioxide for oxygen; then the blood returns to the left atrium. The oxygen-rich blood then passes through the left ventricle, from which it's pumped out to the body via the aorta. This discussion is just a scientific way of saying that the blood does a lot of traveling in your body, so it makes sense that it needs to travel at an appropriate, regulated level for you to stay healthy.

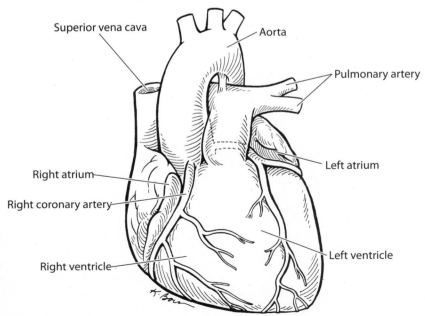

Figure 1-1:
The inner workings of the human heart.

- Superior vena cava
- Aorta
- Pulmonary artery
- Right atrium
- Left atrium
- Right coronary artery
- Right ventricle
- Left ventricle

This process happens quickly. Your heartbeat makes a sort of "lub-*dub*" sound. In the short time between the "lub" and the "dub," your entire blood volume pumps through your heart and circulatory systems.

Why worry about high blood pressure?

High blood pressure indicates that the blood is pumping at a higher-than-normal pressure. When the arteries are narrow, yet the same amount of blood is pumped through the heart, blood pressure rises. You have good reason to be concerned about this. Over time, high pressure takes a toll on the arteries and weakens them, which can lead to health problems that include the following:

- **Heart attack and stroke:** High blood pressure gradually damages artery walls, and this increases the rate of plaque build-up on the artery walls, leading to narrowing or "hardening" of the artery (other factors, such as high blood LDL cholesterol and smoking, also promote narrowing of or damage to arteries). Over time, this blockage can cause a heart attack due to lack of oxygen delivery to the heart, or a stroke (also known as a brain attack) due to lack of oxygen delivery to the brain.

- **Heart failure:** Over time, the heart muscles thicken and have an increasingly difficult time pumping enough blood through the body.

- **Aneurysm:** High blood pressure can weaken blood vessels and form a bulge in a weak area of a vessel. This bulge, or *aneurysm,* can be life-threatening if it ruptures.

- **Kidney damage:** High blood pressure can weaken kidney blood vessels, leading to improper kidney function.

Doctors can tell whether you have hypertension by taking your blood pressure; the numbers don't lie. Check out the section "Decoding the Telltale Heart Numbers" for more. The symptoms of high blood pressure can vary, and sometimes no symptoms occur at all. Only when your blood pressure reaches severely high levels may you experience such symptoms as dizziness, headache, or a nosebleed.

Hypertension affects almost everyone eventually and can develop over years, often without symptoms. Because you may not be aware of hypertension's onset, having routine physicals where your doctor checks your blood pressure is important. If you have a family history of high blood pressure, you should be especially sure to have a physical exam at least every year or two after age 30 to have your blood pressure checked. (Consult with your doctor about how often you should have an exam.) If you discover you have high blood pressure, you should follow your physician's advice.

Decoding the Telltale Heart Numbers

So, you go to the doctor and he tells you that you have hypertension or prehypertension (sometimes referred to as borderline hypertension). But how does he arrive at that conclusion? The answer lies in the systolic and diastolic numbers revealed when your blood pressure is taken. While your doctor may explain the details of what those numbers mean, we give you the lowdown here so you can be sure to play a proactive role in your own health.

Classifying hypertension through systolic and diastolic numbers

An inflatable arm cuff and a pressure gauge are used to measure blood pressure by providing two numbers: a top number and a bottom number. The top number is systolic blood pressure; the bottom one is diastolic pressure. Systolic pressure measures the pressure of blood being carried through the arteries when your heart beats. Diastolic pressure is the pressure in your arteries when your heart relaxes between beats.

Normal blood pressure is usually a reading below 120/80 millimeters of mercury (mmHg), but some doctors recommend 115/75. Once your blood pressure is higher than 120/80, your doctor will likely monitor it. Both systolic and diastolic numbers are important. After the age of 50, however, the systolic pressure is even more important to monitor because systolic hypertension is common at that age. *Systolic hypertension* is when the top number is high (above 120) and the bottom number is normal (below 80).

Like other blood measurements (such as blood sugar and blood fats), blood pressure doesn't stay exactly the same all the time. It's lower when you sleep, rises when you wake up, and escalates even further during exertion. Only when it stays high most of the time are you at risk for health problems. If you have a high blood pressure reading, be sure to follow up with your doctor. Your doctor will probably want to take two or three readings before diagnosing you with hypertension.

For most people diagnosed with hypertension, the cause can't be identified. This type of hypertension is termed *primary hypertension* and develops over the years. *Secondary hypertension* is caused by an underlying condition and is usually discovered suddenly (check out the upcoming section "Sorting out medical issues" for more on how other medical conditions can cause hypertension).

Sometimes just going to the doctor can increase a person's blood pressure. This experience is called *white coat syndrome.* It occurs when a person's blood pressure is elevated at the doctor's office but normal at home or at work. If you're over age 50 and white coat syndrome appears to be at play, your doctor may recommend a 24-hour monitor to determine how your blood pressure changes over a full day. In any case, it's important to follow your doctor's advice and pay attention to your blood pressure numbers.

Check out Table 1-1 for a rundown of how systolic and diastolic numbers correlate to various categories of hypertension, according to the NHLBI.

Table 1-1	Classifications of Hypertension	
Category	*Systolic Reading*	*Diastolic Reading*
Normal blood pressure	< 120	< 80
Prehypertension	120–139	80–89
Stage 1 hypertension	140–159	90–99
Stage 2 hypertension	> 160	> 100

Prehypertension

A systolic reading of 120–139 and a diastolic reading of 80–89 are indicators of *prehypertension.* All levels over 120/80 essentially increase your risk for disease and are likely to lead to Stage 1 hypertension. You can take steps to prevent that — such as planning your meals around the recipes in this cookbook (Chapters 9–22) and following our advice for diet (Chapters 2, 4, and 7) and exercise (Chapter 3).

Mild hypertension

Also called *Stage 1 hypertension,* mild hypertension is a systolic reading between 140–159 and a diastolic reading ranging from 90 to 99. At this point your doctor is likely to consider medication. If you're in this category, you should still continue working on diet, exercise, and lifestyle factors that can reduce your blood pressure.

Moderate to severe hypertension

Severe hypertension or *Stage 2 hypertension* is defined as a systolic reading over 160 and a diastolic reading over 100. At this point, your doctor will prescribe medication to reduce your blood pressure to normal. Even though you're taking medication, you should still reduce the sodium in your diet and move toward a healthier lifestyle to help the medicine do its job.

Your systolic and diastolic numbers may not be elevated to the same degree, thereby placing you in two different categories. Your hypertension is then classified by whichever number is in the highest category. If, for example, you have a blood pressure reading of 160/85, you have Stage 2 hypertension.

If you're being treated for hypertension and your blood pressure is 120/80 or lower, your blood pressure is *controlled,* not cured. You can't quit taking your medication or go back to unhealthy lifestyle choices. A normal reading means that what you're doing is working, so keep on doing it!

Counteracting Hypertension Risk Factors

We've all heard it: Knowledge is power. You need to know your risk factors for hypertension in order to know whether it's possible to counteract them and, if so, how to go about it. In this section, we tell you what you need to do to reduce those risk factors you have power over. But you should also be aware of the risk factors you can't control:

- **Age:** Blood pressure naturally tends to rise with age. Men over 45 and women over 50 should definitely have their blood pressure checked. According to the NHLBI, over half of all Americans over 60 have high blood pressure.

- **Family history:** Because health and disease tend to be hereditary, knowing the disease history of family members helps you understand your risks, allowing you to take the appropriate dietary and positive lifestyle steps. Talk to family members about their current and past health. Ask your parents about your grandparents. Talk to aunts and uncles, too.

- **Gender:** Fewer adult women have hypertension than men; however, women tend to get it later in life, and it's often not as well controlled as it is in men.

- **Race and ethnicity:** Although hypertension can affect anyone, it's more common in African American adults than in Caucasians or Hispanics. African Americans tend to get high blood pressure earlier in life, and it's often more severe. For this reason, early screening and treatment is important in this population.

Following the recommendations in this section adds up to better management of high blood pressure. High blood pressure, like many diseases, is treated with both lifestyle changes and medicines. Sometimes lifestyle change is all that's needed in cases of prehypertension, but a healthier lifestyle benefits anyone with (or without) any level of hypertension, so take the advice in this section to heart.

Losing weight

Weight control is not just about how you look in a pair of jeans. More importantly, it's about maintaining a healthy body, inside and out. Reducing your weight by just 5 or 10 percent can positively impact your hypertension. In addition to helping treat hypertension, losing weight also lowers your risk for other diseases that are complicated by high blood pressure, namely diabetes and heart disease. Make it your goal to attain or maintain a BMI (body mass index) of 19–24. Check out some helpful guidelines for weight loss in Chapters 2 and 3.

Cutting sodium

Consuming a lower-sodium diet is prudent because diets high in sodium have been shown to increase blood pressure in some people. The American Heart Association recommends a daily intake of 1,500 milligrams of sodium. The DASH guidelines we follow in this book (see Chapter 2) suggest 2,300 milligrams daily, but our recommendation is to first begin *reducing* your sodium intake and work gradually toward those goals.

Some people are salt sensitive. A salt-sensitive individual responds to a high salt intake with an increase in blood pressure and a low salt intake with a reduction in blood pressure. People over 50, African Americans, those with diabetes or existing high blood pressure, and overweight people tend to be more salt sensitive and should keep their salt intake at a moderate level (about 1,500 milligrams of sodium daily).

Cutting salt isn't the be-all, end-all way to get hypertension under control. Salt gets a lot of bad press — but keep in mind that you should approach your health from the standpoint of overall well-being, and this includes viewing your diet as a whole, not just food by food. Keeping your daily sodium intake below a certain maximum is only part of the lifestyle change that you should implement for hypertension control.

Generally, the more processing a food undergoes, the more sodium it contains. Where are you getting your sodium? See Table 1-2 to find out. For example, a fast-food fish sandwich has 882 milligrams of sodium. That amount of sodium may be acceptable for an entire, well-balanced meal, but for one little sandwich that probably won't fill you up and doesn't contribute much nutritionally to your diet, 882 milligrams is high indeed. We talk more about cutting sodium in Chapter 4.

Table 1-2	The Amount of Sodium in One Serving of Some Common Foods	
Very Low to Low	*Medium*	*High*
½ chicken breast, 69 mg	Frozen chicken pie, 907 mg	Fast-food fried chicken, 2 pieces,1,500 mg
Cucumber, 7 slices, 2 mg	3-inch sweet pickle, 114 mg	Dill pickle spear, 306 mg
3 ounces pork roast, 59 mg	2 slices bacon, 370 mg	1 hot dog, 584 mg
3 ounces tuna, fresh, 50 mg	3 ounces tuna, canned, 287 mg	Fast-food fish sandwich, 882 mg
¼ cup unsalted peanuts, 8 mg	2 tablespoons peanut butter, 152 mg	¼ cup salted, dry-roasted peanuts, 293 mg

Limiting alcohol

Drinking too much alcohol can raise your blood pressure and also harm your liver, brain, and heart. Many news reports in recent years have touted the benefits of red wine and drinking moderate amounts of alcohol. Moderate alcohol intake, according to the NHLBI, is considered two drinks a day for men and one drink a day for women. Be smart about the facts and warnings about consuming alcohol to excess.

Alcohol provides quite a few calories, leading to unwanted weight gain. A 12-ounce beer, a 5-ounce glass of wine, or 1½ ounces of hard liquor provides 100 to 150 calories each. Drink too much, and you can rack up 500 or more calories a day. In addition, the nutrient-void alcohol may displace other nutrient-rich foods and beverages, causing you to come up short on the important nutrients you need each day.

Excessive alcohol damages the liver and is the root of many other physical and mental health problems. A little bit of alcohol may do you some good, but moderation is important. If you don't drink alcohol, there's no reason to start drinking.

Sorting out medical issues

Several medical issues may cause or negatively impact hypertension:

- ✔ Medical conditions such as kidney disease, thyroid disease, and sleep apnea
- ✔ Medicines such as asthma and cold medicines and corticosteroids

   ✔ Congenital (present at birth) blood vessel defects

   ✔ Illegal drugs, like cocaine or amphetamines

Women should be aware that birth control pills can cause a rise in blood pressure, so women taking birth control should have their blood pressure monitored regularly according to their doctor's orders. Women experiencing menopause and taking hormone replacement therapy (HRT) are also at risk for high blood pressure. HRT may cause only a slight rise in systolic pressure, but if you already have high blood pressure, you should discuss the risks of HRT with your doctor.

If you develop hypertension because of related medical issues, make sure you talk to your doctor about how to best manage all your medications and symptoms.

Managing related lifestyle components

What do we mean by *lifestyle?* Well, lifestyle refers to what you do on a day-to-day basis. Do you have a sedentary job where you sit most of the day, or does your job involve active labor? Do you try to eat right — fitting fruits and vegetables in daily, eating whole grains, and limiting fast food and fried foods? Do you dine out for lunch every day at work? Do you do yard work or housework, and try to get some exercise weekly? Do you smoke? These components of your life have a huge impact on your health and risk for disease.

The bad news: If you ignore your lifestyle and continue with bad habits, you put yourself at risk for hypertension, other heart diseases, and diabetes, to name just a few. The good news: You can control your health destiny! By making a few simple changes, you can gradually reduce your overall risk.

Becoming more active

A sedentary, or essentially inactive, lifestyle is becoming more and more common. The more you move your body, the healthier you are overall. Movement helps condition and strengthen your heart. Because the heart is a muscle, it needs a workout, and exercise helps build heart health. You find out how important exercise is and get tips for squeezing it into your busy schedule in Chapter 3.

Check with your doctor before engaging in any new physical activity. After you get the okay, begin slowly if you haven't been active in a while and gradually increase the amount of time and the intensity of your exercise routine.

Coping with high stress and anxiety

Have you ever heard somebody who's all stressed out complain that someone or something is raising her blood pressure? Stress plays a role in overall health and may impact blood pressure control. Finding ways to cope with daily stress can improve both your physical and mental health.

Consider stress-reduction programs that may be offered through your workplace or health insurance plan. Exercise can also be a terrific stress-buster. Physical activity allows you to move your body, get some fresh air, and clear your head. You can listen to music while you take a walk on the treadmill or outside, or you may consider a new activity such as yoga or tai chi. Look for a class at your local YMCA or fitness center and start exercising some stress away.

Smoking: Kicking the habit

If you smoke or use tobacco, quit. It's that simple. Okay, maybe quitting isn't that simple, but the reasons to quit are clear. Smoking can damage your blood vessels and raise your risk for hypertension (as well as a variety of cancers and other serious diseases). It can also worsen existing health problems. Quitting is a battle, but programs are available to make the transition to nonsmoker easier. Speak with your doctor about smoking cessation plans as well as support groups. Enlist those around you to help you kick the habit.

Chapter 2

Controlling Hypertension through Your Diet

Sure, you picked up this cookbook to dig into some great new recipes to help you lower your blood pressure, but do you know why these recipes work? In this chapter, we help you understand the "why" behind eating certain foods and avoiding others. We don't believe in a one-size-fits-all sort of diet or lifestyle, but keeping weight under control is an important strategy for controlling blood pressure. To that end, we give you some great tips for losing weight and keeping it off in this chapter.

We also give you some tips on cutting the amount of sodium in your diet. Salt, long considered an enemy in the battle against hypertension, is found in abundance in the average American diet. But it doesn't have to ruin yours. Finally, we give you the bottom line on fats and blood cholesterol levels and how they may relate to your overall risk for heart disease. Looking to eat your way toward a healthy heart? This chapter sets you up to do just that!

DASHing into Better Health

Prior to 1997, your doctor may have simply said, "Follow a low-sodium diet" when diagnosing you with high blood pressure. However, recent studies have concluded that it's about more than just the salt. The acronym DASH, which stands for Dietary Approaches to Stop Hypertension, comes from a 1997 clinical trial that tested the effects of nutrients in food on blood pressure (more on the scientific stuff in the next section). The impressive results showed that eating a diet high in fruits, vegetables, and lowfat dairy and low in saturated fat and sodium helps control blood pressure as well as blood cholesterol levels. A DASH diet is now the primary dietary prescription for hypertension, and it works. In this section, we explain the food groups included in DASH and offer a few tips on how to incorporate them into your daily dishes.

Understanding the DASH plan

The DASH diet is proven to lower your blood cholesterol and blood pressure, both big-time risk factors for heart disease. Impressive research from the 1997 clinical study shows the role diet can play in disease.

The study began by feeding 459 subjects with high blood pressure a control diet (low in fruits, vegetables, and dairy products, and of average fat intake) for three weeks. The study participants were then randomly assigned to one of three groups over an eight-week period, to receive either the control diet again, a diet high in fruits and vegetables, or a "combination diet" high in both fruits and vegetables and lowfat dairy products. Both non-control (or *intervention*) diets were also low in saturated fat. Among the 133 participants with hypertension (defined as those whose blood pressure was greater than 140/90 mm Hg [140 over 90 millimeters of mercury]), the combination diet (the one that included dairy) reduced systolic and diastolic blood pressure by 11.4 and 5.5 mm Hg. The diet rich in fruits and vegetables (minus the dairy) also reduced blood pressure, but to a lesser extent. Although the participants were on the DASH diet plan for eight weeks, results of lower blood pressure were evident in two weeks.

This impressive research truly shows the role diet can play in disease, and you'll find that the basic principles of the DASH diet aren't hard to follow: Eat foods that are low in saturated fat and cholesterol, with an emphasis on fruits, vegetables, and lowfat dairy products. The diet also includes whole grains, nuts, fish, and poultry, and reduces the consumption of lean red meats. Added sugars, sweets, and sugar-containing beverages are also limited. Table 2-1 shows the diet at a glance.

Table 2-1	The DASH Diet (Based on 2,000 calories/day)	
Type of Food	*Number of Servings for a 2,000-Calorie Diet*	*Example Serving Sizes*
Grains and grain products	6–8	1 slice bread; 1 cup dry cereal; ½ cup cooked cereal, rice, or pasta
Fruits	4–5	10 grapes, ½ grapefruit, 1 small banana, 2 tablespoons raisins
Vegetables	4–5	1 cup raw, ½ cup cooked
Lowfat or nonfat dairy products	2–3	1 cup milk or yogurt, 1 ounce cheese
Lean meats, fish, poultry	2 or less	6–8 ounces total
Nuts, seeds, legumes	4–5 per week	⅓ cup nuts, 2 tablespoons nut butter, 2 tablespoons seeds
Fats and oils	3–4	1 teaspoon margarine, butter or oil, 2 tablespoons salad dressing
High-fat/High-sugar extras	Less than 2	1 small donut, 1 small muffin, 2 small cookies, 1 "fun-size" candy bar, 8 pieces of gummy-type candy

The preceding guidelines are based on a daily consumption of 2,000 calories. Some people need fewer or more calories, in which case the number of servings noted in Table 2-1 changes accordingly.

The DASH diet is high in potassium, calcium, and fiber, but low in sodium. (See the upcoming section "Avoiding Salt" for more info on sodium.)

The new MyPlate icon, introduced in 2010, depicts food patterns recommended by the U.S. Department of Agriculture's 2010 Dietary Guidelines for Americans. The icon serves as a reminder for healthy eating: filling about half of your plate with fruits and vegetables, less than a fourth of it with protein, and more than a fourth of it with grains, and including a dairy serving, as shown in Figure 2-1.

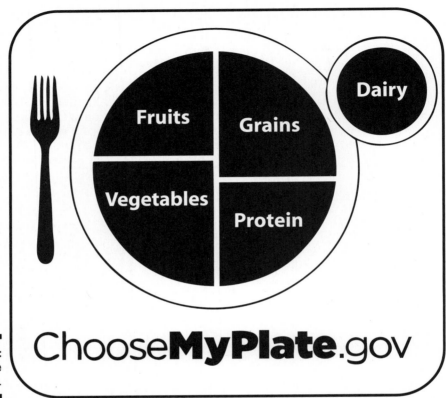

ChooseMyPlate.gov

Figure 2-1: Proper plate portions.

Food is medicine: Adding fruits and vegetables

When embarking on a better diet to treat your hypertension, the biggest change you're likely to encounter is the addition of fruits and vegetables to your day — 4 to 5 servings of each, to be exact. The recipes in Chapters 9 through 11, in particular, can really help you get started in this endeavor; but first, we explain the reasons for making this positive change in your diet.

All fruits and vegetables are valuable sources of nutrients that are important for heart health. In many ways, food can be viewed as medicine because certain plant foods deliver important, damage-fighting substances that help keep your body healthy. Plants contain *phytochemicals,* substances in plants that may have protective properties. (We talk more about phytochemicals in Chapter 7.)

In addition to these phytochemicals, fruits and vegetables also provide a wide variety of important minerals, one of which is potassium. Potassium plays a role in muscle contraction and is crucial to heart function. A diet low in potassium has been associated with an increased risk for hypertension and stroke. Conversely, a diet higher in potassium has been associated with lower blood pressure.

Fruits and veggies are also full of vitamins, several of which are antioxidants. Antioxidants protect against *free radicals,* molecules that damage cells in the body. Vitamins A, C, and E plus beta carotene are all antioxidants, and fruits and veggies are excellent sources. Head to Chapter 7 if you need even more inspiration to take your food-medicine.

Eating good grains

Foods from the bread/grain/cereal group are an important component of the DASH eating plan because they supply fiber. Based on a daily 2000-calorie intake, the DASH plan recommends 6–8 servings of grains. Although you should aim to make at least half of your grain choices whole grains, you can incorporate some refined grains (such as white, Italian, or French breads; regular pasta; and rice or corn cereals) into your diet. Better choices include whole-wheat or oatmeal breads, whole-wheat pasta, brown rice, whole-wheat crackers, whole-wheat cereals, bran cereals, oat bran, and oatmeal.

When choosing whole-grain breads, look for the word "whole." Don't assume that brown-colored "wheat bread" is a great choice. Check the Nutrition Facts label: Whole-wheat flour or another whole-grain flour should be listed as the first ingredient, and the bread should have 2 or more grams of fiber per serving. By comparison, a slice of white bread provides only 0.6 grams of fiber. Refined grains have the bran and germ removed, which eliminates the fiber. The vitamins and minerals taken with it are replaced after the milling process (this is what the term *enriched* means).

DASH suggests eating 6–12 servings of grains per day (based on 1,600–3,100 calories per day), but note the definition of *one serving:* one slice of bread, half a small bun, half an English muffin, ¼ an average bakery bagel, ½ cup pasta or rice, one small waffle or half a Belgian waffle, or one 4-inch pancake. These may be smaller servings than what you're used to, but they're much more in line with what your body really needs.

As you work at improving your diet to lower your blood pressure, consider venturing out into some new grain territory (and check out Chapter 12):

- ✔ Barley
- ✔ Brown rice, wild rice
- ✔ Buckwheat
- ✔ Bulgur (cracked wheat)

> ✔ Oats
>
> ✔ Popcorn
>
> ✔ Quinoa
>
> ✔ Whole-wheat couscous

Choosing lowfat dairy

Adding calcium to your diet is a DASH-certified strategy for reducing high blood pressure. You should consume 2–3 servings of lowfat dairy each day. In addition, studies have shown that drinking lowfat milk helps promote weight loss. If you're overweight, losing weight is important, and choosing lowfat dairy products helps keep calories under control.

The clinical trials showing the greatest reductions in blood pressure were all correlated specifically to an intake of lowfat dairy products.

You can get some calcium from vegetables like broccoli, kale, beet greens, bok choy, or spinach (about 100–200 milligrams of calcium per cup), but an 8-ounce glass of nonfat milk easily provides over 300 milligrams. Chapter 7 offers you more ideas for adding calcium to your diet.

Here are some sample servings of lowfat dairy, with each serving providing about 300 milligrams of calcium:

> ✔ **8 ounces nonfat (skim) or 1-percent milk:** You can drink it with meals or use it in cooking or baking.
>
> ✔ **8 ounces nonfat yogurt:** Look for yogurt that's lightly sweetened or uses a noncaloric sweetener.
>
> ✔ **½ cup part-skim ricotta:** Although it's higher in fat, it's also much higher in calcium than cottage cheese.
>
> ✔ **2 tablespoons light sour cream:** The lighter version adds calcium while controlling the amount of fat in recipes.

Choosing a scoop of nonfat frozen yogurt instead of a scoop of ice cream can save about 8 grams of fat per serving. Additionally, each ½-cup serving provides 100 milligrams of calcium, compared to 60 milligrams in a ½-cup serving of most ice cream brands.

Looking for lean meats, nuts, and legumes

You actually need less protein than most people think: About 6 ounces of lean meat, fish, or poultry daily is all that most people require. Choosing a meal with fish twice a week is a good habit to get into. Most any type of fish is fine, as long as you limit deep-fried fish to no more than once every couple of months. Fish varies in fat content, but fatty fish delivers healthy omega-3 fatty acids and is higher in monounsaturated fat and lower in saturated fat than beef or pork. Most fish is lower in calories as well. Choosing fish that's baked, grilled, or broiled is your best bet.

In the case of poultry, you can choose from a variety of white and dark meats, *without the skin.* Removing the skin trims away more than half the total fat and nearly 70 percent of the saturated fat.

Choosing leaner cuts of beef and pork helps reduce your overall saturated fat intake, which is important for controlling blood cholesterol. In all cases, you can reduce the fat by trimming most of the visible fat from the meat before cooking. Limit your intake of high-fat cuts of beef (such as prime rib and chuck roast) and pork (like bacon, pork ribs, and shoulder) or avoid them altogether. Table 2-2 shows you how to size up lean meat portions. Each trimmed 3–4 ounce portion provides only about 3–10 grams of fat.

Table 2-2	Making Lean Beef and Pork Choices	
Type	*Cut*	*Portion*
Beef	Sirloin	3–4 ounces
	Filet mignon	4–6 ounces
	Eye of round	4–6 ounces
	Loin roast	3–4 ounces
Pork	Tenderloin	4–6 ounces
	Loin chops	3–4 ounces
	Loin roast	3–4 ounces

Don't forget that meat isn't the only food with protein. DASH recommends that you eat 4–5 servings per week of nuts, seeds, and legumes (lentils, beans, peas, and peanuts) for even more protein, folate, and fiber. Nuts and seeds deliver quite a bit of fat, so it's a good idea to eat those only a few times a week or in very small amounts daily. Legumes, on the other hand, are very low in fat and high in fiber and nutrients, so incorporating these into at least one meal a week is a super idea.

We include legume recipes to show you how delicious they can taste. For example, check out the Bean-Tastic Three-Bean Chili in Chapter 10 or our Louisiana Red Beans and Rice in Chapter 21. They're great for both weight control and preventing heart disease!

Controlling portions of high-fat, sugary extras

You probably know that reducing sodium is linked to lowering blood pressure; you may not know that controlling fat and sugar is imperative to DASH, too. Saturated fat in the diet is a risk factor for heart disease and has been linked to raising blood cholesterol, and preliminary research is showing that sugar has detrimental effects on blood lipids (fats) too. Excessive sugar in the diet can raise triglyceride levels in prone individuals. In addition, sugar is high in calories, so consuming large amounts of high-sugar foods easily stacks on the pounds. DASH recommends that you eat fewer than 2 servings of fats and sweets per day. Refer to Table 2-1 for examples.

Fat isn't just present in some meats; it's also hidden in a lot of processed foods like chips, crackers, energy or fiber bars, candy, bakery items, and desserts, many of which are also high in sugar and calories. Make sure you read package labels and eat only one serving. In general, a serving should only amount to about a 100- to 250-calorie portion.

Don't deprive yourself; who doesn't like dessert once in a while? You don't have to completely shun desserts, but take note of the key word in this section's title: portions. We don't promote restrictive diets; we prefer to allow folks to decide how much and how often they treat themselves. But, it's key that "treats" are exactly that — things that are enjoyed infrequently in small portions. The DASH diet guidelines provide you with dietary goals to shoot for in your day-to-day life. They don't pertain to how you may eat during a special occasion, such as on your son or daughter's wedding day!

While you're searching for foods that are either lower in fat naturally or have had the fat reduced, be careful not to do so at the expense of added sugar. Foods like reduced-fat milk are fine, but in some packaged products labeled "lowfat," extra sugar has been added to make up for the flavor lost through the reduction of fat. These foods aren't your best bet. Read package labels carefully (find out more in Chapter 5).

You may be surprised to find out that 37.5 percent of added sugars in the average diet comes from sugar-sweetened beverages. Where are your added sugars coming from? Think about it, and work on consuming less. Sugars add a lot of unwanted calories to the diet, which not only hinders weight control but also adversely affects blood fats.

In general, try to limit added fats like margarine, butter, oils, salad dressing, and mayonnaise to no more than 3–6 teaspoons a day. Other fats, such as sour cream, gravies, cheese sauces or other creamy sauces, should be limited or modified to lower-fat versions.

Losing Weight Using DASH

The DASH diet regime is a healthy way to lose weight, and losing unwanted pounds does wonders for lowering blood pressure. The DASH approach incorporates all the healthiest food choices from each food group, providing variety and balance. It also eliminates or limits choices that are low in nutrients. If you stick to the DASH plan, you can help your body by beating high blood pressure and simultaneously skimming off excess poundage. In this section, we explain exactly how the DASH diet cooperates with your body to help you lose weight.

Peeling off pounds the smart way

Every week, fad diets are promoted on all sorts of media, promising that you'll rapidly lose weight in days or weeks. Guess what? They don't work, and some are simply unhealthy. Sure, you may lose weight by eating only vegetables, drinking some magic potion that sends you to the bathroom frequently, or taking a special berry pill every day; but in spite of what marketers may say, there's simply no long-term benefit to any of these diets. For most people, losing 5 pounds in a week is neither realistic nor sustainable. Even losing 10 or 20 pounds in two or three months is useless if you're 20 or 30 pounds heavier again by the end of the year. Dieters who adhere to fad diets often experience a quick weight loss, only to regain the weight months down the road. A gradual weight loss of no more than 1 to 2 pounds per week has been shown to be most sustainable.

Your goal is to adopt new dietary habits that you can live with for a lifetime, and gradually lose weight so that you can keep it off.

A diet rich in fiber (from beans, whole grains, fruits, and vegetables), adequate in lean protein, and low in saturated fat is the way to go. The DASH lifestyle satisfies these requirements and more. It adds calcium to the diet through lowfat dairy products that help promote weight loss. And those extra fruits and veggies don't just add nutrients like vitamin C and potassium; they also add fiber to the diet, helping you stay full throughout the day. You can actually eat more — not less — when you choose the right foods!

Controlling appetite

Want to know the secret to weight control? Appetite control. If you remain hungry, you'll eat! A key strategy to maintaining a reduced calorie intake for weight loss is choosing the right calories so that you aren't hungry. For example, you'll find that you feel much fuller when you pack a small salad or an apple rather than chips or cookies to go with your lunch sandwich. Losing weight is about getting enough fiber to stay full longer. Adding bulk to your diet helps keep your stomach full and slows how quickly your stomach empties, thereby promoting satiety and prolonging the arrival of hunger cues. The fruit, vegetable, and grain parts of the DASH diet provide the fiber you need. When you aren't hungry as often, you consume fewer calories and lose weight.

Picking proper portions: Calories matter

While you can certainly fill up on the yummy recipes in this book, you still need to be aware of portion size. Almost any food can fit into a diet if it's eaten in the proper portion and frequency. While your goal with the fruit and vegetable group is primarily to increase portions, your goal for most other food groups (like grains and meats) is to control portions. Controlling portions is how you watch your calorie intake. You must balance the amount of energy you're consuming in calorie form with the amount of energy you're really using by moving around. We can't estimate your personal calorie needs because we don't know enough about you and your lifestyle; check out the Mayo Clinic's calorie calculator at `www.mayoclinic.com/health/calorie-calculator/NU00598` for an estimate.

Calories are the body's energy source, and we get them from protein (4 calories per gram), carbohydrate (4 calories per gram), and fat (9 calories per gram). Alcohol provides no nutrients but has 7 calories per gram.

In the section "Eating good grains," we encourage you to eat 6–8 servings of whole grains daily, but that doesn't mean we want you to eat 6–8 heaping plates of pasta, even if it's a whole-wheat variety. Carbohydrates aren't bad, but they do have calories and are easy to overeat. For most people, a portion of a carbohydrate is probably double or triple what it should be (½ cup cooked pasta or rice is the appropriate serving size). For more on what constitutes a good portion of carbs, see the section "Balancing carbohydrate, protein, and fat."

Instead of just helping yourself to what looks like a good-sized portion, note serving sizes on the labels of the foods you eat. The number of calories listed on the label is for the serving size given.

Adding high-fiber foods to your diet makes it easier to keep portions under control. Oversized portions equal too many calories, which result in packing on the pounds — not part of your strategy for fighting hypertension.

Balancing carbohydrate, protein, and fat

As we remind you in the section "Picking proper portions: Calories matter," it's not carbs themselves that are a problem; it's how much of them you consume in relation to protein and fat. Some folks get into a carb binge and end up with an unbalanced diet. Other people consume far too much fat. Table 2-3 shows you how many grams of these three different nutrient groups you should eat daily, depending on how many total calories you're consuming.

Table 2-3	A Well-Balanced Diet		
Calories	*Protein (g)*	*Carbohydrate (g)*	*Fat (g)*
1,600	80	200	53
1,800	90	225	60
2,000	100	250	67
2,400	120	300	80
2,600	130	325	87

When it comes to carbs, remember portion control awareness. The reason a high-carbohydrate diet is often linked to weight gain is that carbohydrates are easy to overeat. Come on, who doesn't love a nice dish of pasta? The pasta isn't the problem; the portion is (and maybe the two slices of fresh bread you add to the meal!).

After your carbohydrate portions are under control (hearken back to "Eating good grains" for what foods should ideally comprise those 200–325 grams), make sure you're getting adequate protein daily and the right types of fat. High-protein diets have been in the news for years now, and although some people are successful with them (simply because they reduce your calorie intake), we don't recommend huge amounts of protein in the diet for controlling hypertension.

How much protein you need depends on your total energy (calorie) needs. Enjoying a small amount of protein at each meal not only balances the meal but also helps satisfy you, helping you to avoid overeating. Fat is important for satiety as well, so although you want to limit saturated fat, you don't need to reduce overall fat drastically. Take a look at Table 2-3 for the breakdown of how much fat and protein you should incorporate in your total calorie count.

Avoiding Salt

Avoiding sodium is a big part of fighting the battle against hypertension. The current recommendation for sodium intake, according to the 2010 Dietary Guidelines for Americans, is 1,500 milligrams daily (the DASH plan encourages 1,500 milligrams, too, though you can talk to your doctor about whether you can add more). In general, the more restrictive the sodium intake, the more successful the DASH diet is at lowering blood pressure.

Excessive dietary salt raises blood pressure in those with hypertension. Rosanne got a kick out of a recent Bill Cosby joke when she saw him live on stage:

> Man: "Can you help me with my high blood pressure?"
>
> God: "Eat less salt."
>
> Man: "But can you cure me?"
>
> God: "Eat less salt."

There's no surer thing to do if you have high blood pressure: Reduce your salt intake!

Peruse your pantry to see how quickly 1,500 milligrams of sodium add up. Try this test: Pick up a few random packages from your pantry and look for sodium in the Nutrition Facts labels. You'll probably be astounded to find out how much sodium is in many packaged foods. A 1-cup serving of canned soup, for instance, contributes 700 to 800 milligrams of sodium, and even "reduced sodium" or "healthy" varieties may contain 400 to 500 milligrams. An ounce of potato chips provides about 150 milligrams, and four crackers provide about 100 milligrams. Besides prepackaged foods, another huge contributor of sodium to the diet is fast-food restaurants: A large fast-food taco may contribute as much as 1,200 milligrams.

Figure 2-2 shows the percentage of sodium that various types of foods contribute to the average American's diet.

Table salt itself adds a lot of sodium to the diet. Just one level teaspoon of salt provides 2,300 milligrams of sodium. Gradually cutting back the amount of salt you use in cooking and removing the shaker from the table will help you gradually reduce your intake. If you're accustomed to using a lot of salt, using less will take some effort, but it's doable. Your palate will adjust.

Some folks like to put their salt in the pepper shaker, which has fewer holes, as a way to cut back as they shake during cooking and while eating.

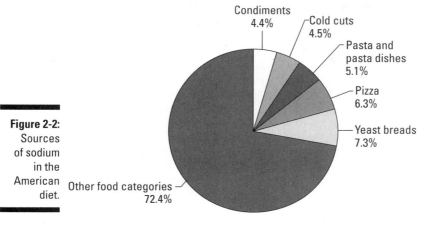

Condiments
4.4%

Cold cuts
4.5%

Pasta and
pasta dishes
5.1%

Pizza
6.3%

Yeast breads
7.3%

Other food categories
72.4%

Figure 2-2:
Sources
of sodium
in the
American
diet.

Another good idea is to replace canned vegetables with fresh or frozen ones. For example, a cup of canned corn can contain 571 milligrams, whereas a cup of frozen corn prepared without salt provides only 2 milligrams. You can remove up to 40 percent of the salt by rinsing the vegetables before you heat them or use them in a recipe — we use this method in this cookbook.

If you're a true-blue salt lover, don't lose heart. When you're on the DASH diet, keep in mind that low sodium doesn't mean no sodium. In fact, most of our recipes in this book contain some sodium. While some recipes may be higher in sodium than others, they represent only one item or meal in your diet. You can balance out a saltier meal with less-salty meals the rest of the day. In Chapters 4 and 6, we give you more techniques for reducing the sodium in your diet. Put them to work, and you won't even miss the salt!

Choosing Good Fat Over Bad Fat

Dietary fat is another key aspect of a diet for reducing high blood pressure. Because your heart is clearly involved in pumping that blood, eating a proper diet to keep your heart and arteries as healthy as possible is important. Fat plays a role in heart health. Choosing foods that are lower in saturated fat and including foods high in healthy unsaturated fats (such as salmon, olive oil, and nuts) contribute to an overall heart-healthy diet.

Recognizing sources of saturated fat

Saturated fat is the bad fat your mother warned you about. If you consume a lot of saturated fat, you're looking at high blood cholesterol levels and hardening of your arteries. Why worry about your arteries? The narrowing of these blood pipes can lead to high blood pressure, which is exactly what you're trying to avoid or reduce.

Chemically speaking, saturated fats are "saturated" with hydrogen. Saturated fats are linked to raising blood levels of low-density lipoproteins (LDLs, which we explain in the section "Keeping Cholesterol in Check"). Practically speaking, saturated fats are solid at room temperature and come mostly from animal fats, which contain cholesterol as well.

Animal fats — the fat on meats (which turns solid when it cools after cooking), butter, lard, cheese, and high-fat (whole and 2-percent) dairy products — are all sources of saturated fat that you want to limit. Palm and coconut oils are plant-based but are also high in saturated fat. Palm oil is found in many candies as well as packaged cookies and crackers. The tricky business with palm and coconut oils is that products using them may be labeled as "trans-fat free" or "cholesterol-free," health claims that may mislead you into thinking they're healthy. *Trans-fats* are fats that have been hydrogenated in processing and have been shown to be just as harmful to blood cholesterol levels as saturated fats. Reading ingredient labels is the way to scout out fat sources; you want to limit products that contain palm, coconut oil, or hydrogenated fats.

Adding good, unsaturated fats to your diet

You've probably heard by now that good fat really does exist. The good stuff is unsaturated fat, which primarily comes from plant products and fish. These fats may help lower your blood cholesterol levels. You want to work at replacing some of the saturated fat in your diet with unsaturated fats.

Sources of good fats include fish, plant oils (but not palm or coconut oils), nuts, and seeds. Salmon, trout, olives, walnuts, avocado, and vegetable oils like soybean, safflower, sunflower, corn, canola, and olive oils are all good choices. Unsaturated fats include both poly- and mono-unsaturated fats, and both of these may help lower cholesterol by raising HDL (see the section "Keeping Cholesterol in Check").

Cooking with healthy vegetable oils, adding nuts to salads and other dishes, and including fish on the menu through the week are some ways to add these good fats in. And we're on your side, too — the recipes we present in this book help you add these healthy fats to your diet. Try the Roasted Mixed Winter Squash with Walnuts in Chapter 11 or our Crusted Pan-Seared Salmon in Chapter 21.

Look for ways to sneak good fats into your breakfast, lunch, or snack routine. Here are a few ideas to get you started:

✔ Add chopped walnuts or pecans to your morning oatmeal.

✔ Use canola oil to make homemade pancakes or muffins.

✔ Try a small handful of almonds for a midday snack.

✔ Enjoy 2 teaspoons of all-natural peanut butter on a banana or apple slices.

✔ Make your own simple salad dressings using olive oil and vinegar.

✔ Slice avocado for a sandwich topping.

✔ Add olives to your tossed salad.

✔ Add nuts to your stir-fry.

Keeping Cholesterol in Check

Every year, more than a million Americans have a heart attack, and half a million die from heart disease. Because high cholesterol, like high blood pressure, is one of the major risk factors for heart disease, staying in tune with your own blood cholesterol levels is a good idea.

The DASH diet is a great approach to lowering not only blood pressure but blood cholesterol levels as well. In addition to diet, several other factors affect blood cholesterol levels, including body weight, physical activity, gender, age, and heredity. As women and men age, their cholesterol levels increase. Premenopausal women typically have lower cholesterol than men of the same age; however, after menopause, women's cholesterol levels typically increase. A family history of high cholesterol increases your risk as well. Of course, you have no control over these factors. Diet, body weight, and exercise, on the other hand, you do have some say in.

If you're overweight, losing excess weight can have a very positive impact on both your blood pressure and your blood cholesterol levels (see the section "Peeling off pounds the smart way"). Exercise can both lower bad cholesterol and raise good cholesterol — not to mention help you lose weight and reduce stress. A win-win! Set a goal to get 30 minutes of physical activity daily.

Knowing your numbers

The National Heart, Lung, and Blood Institute recommends having your blood cholesterol checked every five years after age 20. The best test is a *lipoprotein profile,* which shows your total blood cholesterol, your triglycerides, your LDL (low-density lipoprotein), and HDL (high-density lipoprotein) levels. If a complete profile isn't possible, you may just have your cholesterol and HDL checked.

LDL is the main source of cholesterol buildup and blockage in the arteries, whereas HDL may actually keep cholesterol from building up, so the higher this number, the better. An optimal HDL is greater than 60 milligrams per deciliter (mg/dl); an HDL of less than 40 mg/dl increases your risk. Triglycerides, a blood fat, also raise your risk. An optimal level of triglycerides is less than 150 mg/dl, borderline high is 150–199 mg/dl, and high is greater than 200 mg/dl. Following are the optimal blood ranges for overall cholesterol and LDL.

Category	Cholesterol	LDL
Optimal	< 200 mg/dl	< 100 mg/dl
Near optimal	< 200 mg/dl	100–129 mg/dl
Borderline high	200–239 mg/dl	130–159 mg/dl
High	> 240 mg/dl	160–189 mg/dl
Very high	> 240 mg/dl	> 190 mg/dl

Chapter 3

Doing More to Lower Your Blood Pressure

*F*ighting hypertension is all about making a lifestyle change (head to Chapter 1 for more on what we mean by that). You probably know, because you picked up this book, that your diet is tied to your blood pressure control (flip back to Chapter 2 for diet details). But you can do even more. In this chapter, we show you the important role exercise plays in artery health, and give you lots of tips for how to fit exercise into your schedule. We also briefly explain how to manage the medications you may have to take and talk about monitoring your hypertension on a daily basis.

The changes you implement will not only reduce your risk for hypertension but will reduce your risk for other related diseases as well, such as heart disease and diabetes — not to mention that you'll be able to fit into that long-forgotten suit or pair of jeans in your closet.

Exercising for Heart Health

If you could simply walk away from your health problems, you would, right? It *can* be that easy. Being physically active on a regular basis can lower your blood pressure. What do we mean by physically active? Physical activity is any body movement that involves working the muscles and using energy. Activities like walking, jogging, swimming, dancing, yoga, weight lifting, rowing, housework, and gardening all count. In addition to improving heart health, exercise gives you a sense of well-being and improves your overall strength and balance. Sit less and move more; it's that simple.

Get your doctor's approval before beginning any type of exercise program. Immediately report any discomfort you experience to your doctor's office.

Reaping the benefits

Exercise improves your metabolism over time in several ways:

- You burn more calories when you're exercising than when you're sedentary.
- Your body continues to burn more calories for a short period after your exercise session is completed.
- As you build muscle through exercise, that muscle tissue burns up more calories than the fat tissue in your body.

Because weight control helps reduce blood pressure and lowers your risk for heart disease and diabetes, we can't underestimate the important role physical activity plays in weight loss. Aerobic activity (along with calorie restriction) helps burn fat. Strength training builds muscle. The more muscle and the less fat you have, the faster and more efficient your metabolism is.

Of course, being active isn't just about weight loss but other aspects of metabolic health as well. Regular physical activity reduces your risk of metabolic syndrome and, as a result, type 2 diabetes. *Metabolic syndrome* is a cluster of physiological issues that increase your risk for developing diabetes. These issues include high blood pressure, abdominal obesity, impaired glucose intolerance (the inability to clear glucose from the blood), and high blood lipid (specifically high LDL cholesterol, high triglycerides, and low HDL). People who exercise regularly reduce their risk for all of these symptoms of metabolic syndrome, and therefore also have a lower risk of developing type 2 diabetes.

Most studies show that exercising 120 to 150 minutes weekly gives you the biggest benefit in terms of reducing your diabetes risk; see the section "Doing aerobics and lifting weights" for more specific recommendations for how much you should be working out.

Regular exercise doesn't only improve heart health, lower blood pressure, and aid in weight loss. It also makes you stronger and helps with stress management. In turn, stronger muscles help support bones, which helps keep your bones healthy. Exercise promotes a relaxed, "in-control" feeling, thereby reducing anxiety. With less stress, chances are you'll have lower blood pressure.

Doing aerobics and weight training

Aerobic exercise, sometimes called endurance exercise, increases the rate and depth of your breathing. It raises your heart rate and uses large muscle groups (think brisk walking, cycling, swimming, or running). It also helps your body use up extra fat stores, making it an important component of a weight-loss program.

When you're deciding what kind of aerobics to do, consider these three factors:

- **Intensity:** How hard you work to do the activity. The terms "moderate" and "vigorous" are used to classify the intensity.

  You can use the "talk test" to determine what a "vigorous" cardiorespiratory intensity is for you, and thereby determine whether you're exercising at an intensity that promotes endurance, weight loss, and heart health. In general, if you can barely hold a conversation while you're exercising, you're exercising hard enough, but not too hard.

- **Frequency:** How often you do the activity (twice a week or three times a week, for example).

- **Duration:** How long each session of an activity lasts.

The U.S. Department of Health and Human Services has some recommendations for the intensity, frequency, and duration of your workouts. In their Physical Activity Guidelines for Americans, they suggest the following:

- **Adults ages 18–64** should minimally do 150 minutes a week of moderate-intensity aerobic physical activity or 75 minutes a week of vigorous-intensity aerobic activity. If you exercise five days a week, this recommendation breaks down to 15 to 30 minutes of aerobic activity per session. Sessions should last at least 10 minutes, and aerobic activity should be spread throughout the week.

  As you increase this time, you gain additional health benefits. Doubling the minimum recommendation to five hours of moderate-intensity activity or 2½ hours of intense activity weekly promotes more weight loss, improved cardiorespiratory function, lower blood pressure, and stronger bones.

  In addition to aerobic activity, you should also include some strength-training activities two days a week, such as weight lifting, yoga, or calisthenics (using your body as resistance — lunges, jumps, push-ups, sit-ups, crunches, pull-ups, and calf raises, for example).

- **Adults 65 years of age and older** should also follow the preceding guidelines, if possible. If a chronic condition or your doctor's recommendation makes this impossible, you can still be physically active as your body allows (and your doctor approves). Doing what you can to build muscle and improve flexibility helps with your balance (reducing your risk for a fall) and improves your heart health and overall metabolism.

Strive for at least 30 minutes of moderate activity five days a week, gradually increasing the intensity on some days to include vigorous exercise. If you aren't currently physically active, start by doing whatever you can. After you get started, you'll realize how great exercise makes you feel, and you'll see an improvement. If you stick with it, each week you'll get stronger and faster.

Have you reached a weight loss plateau even though you already get 150 minutes of exercise weekly? It may be time to kick it up a notch. Work toward getting an hour of exercise, five days a week, or replace moderate activities with more vigorous activities (and less time).

If you're currently not working out at all, start by taking a ten-minute walk at a comfortable pace, five days a week. Add two to five minutes each week, and gradually increase your pace. Check out Table 3-1 for a suggested walking plan, as proposed by the National Heart, Blood, and Lung Institute.

Table 3-1	Sample 12-Week Walking Plan			
Week	**Warm-Up**	**Active Session**	**Cool-Down**	**Total Time**
1	Walk slowly 4 min.	Walk briskly 3 min.	Walk slowly 3 min.	10 min.
2	Walk slowly 5 min.	Walk briskly 5 min.	Walk slowly 5 min.	15 min.
3	Walk slowly 5 min.	Walk briskly 7 min.	Walk slowly 5 min.	17 min.
4	Walk slowly 5 min.	Walk briskly 9 min.	Walk slowly 5 min.	19 min.
5	Walk slowly 5 min.	Walk briskly 11 min.	Walk slowly 5 min.	21 min.
6	Walk slowly 5 min.	Walk briskly 13 min.	Walk slowly 5 min.	23 min.
7	Walk slowly 5 min.	Walk briskly 15 min.	Walk slowly 5 min.	25 min.
8	Walk slowly 5 min.	Walk briskly 18 min.	Walk slowly 5 min.	28 min.
9	Walk slowly 5 min.	Walk briskly 20 min.	Walk slowly 5 min.	30 min.
10	Walk slowly 5 min.	Walk briskly 23 min.	Walk slowly 5 min.	33 min.
11	Walk slowly 5 min.	Walk briskly 26 min.	Walk slowly 5 min.	36 min.
12	Walk slowly 5 min.	Walk briskly 30 min.	Walk slowly 5 min.	40 min.

If you're looking for more ideas for getting some aerobic activity, try any of these moderate-intensity activities:

- **Brisk walking:** About 4 miles per hour (mph)
- **Gardening:** Weeding, trimming
- **Leisurely biking:** 8–10 mph
- **Doubles tennis:** Playing with a partner (two teammates per side)
- **Water exercises:** Kick-boarding, leg raises, water aerobics, pool walking using pool weight belts
- **Canoeing or flat-water kayaking:** 4–6 mph

For a more intense workout, try any of these vigorous activities:

- **Power walking, jogging, or running** at a speed greater than 4 mph
- **High-energy aerobic dance**
- **Singles tennis or racquetball** (playing one-on-one)
- **Basketball or soccer** (a one-hour game on full court)
- **Jumping rope** (single hops) for at least 2 minutes, gradually increasing the duration
- **Martial arts**
- **Cycling** at a speed greater than 10 mph (include hills to increase the intensity)
- **Swimming laps**

Although doing aerobics is great for your health, don't neglect weight training. *Muscle-strength training* includes resistance training and weight lifting. These activities cause the body to use muscle groups to lift or move against an applied force or weight via the use of weightlifting machines, free weights (such as dumbbells and barbells), or elastic resistance bands. Ideally, you want to establish a program that engages both upper-body and lower-body muscle groups. As with aerobic activity, the intensity and frequency of your weight training program are important, as is the duration (measured by the number of repetitions you do).

If you've never lifted free weights or used weight machines, setting up a meeting with a qualified, certified personal trainer is a good idea. He or she can show you how to use the equipment, set up a personal program for you, and demonstrate how to do the exercises properly to avoid injuries. You can hire a trainer for just one session to show you how to safely and properly use the machines, or hire a trainer for an extended period of time to coach you through your workouts.

Research findings about health benefits of physical activity

Although this book focuses on *cooking* for hypertension, finding the balance between calories and physical activity is important for a variety of reasons. Although eating well is very important, moving your body more is vital to the equation. Physical activity has many benefits, including reduced blood pressure.

Research has shown that, in most cases, some exercise is better than none. So don't be self-defeating by setting up an unrealistic schedule. Do what you can, when you can. Just be sure to do at least 10 minutes of activity five days a week, and try to increase the duration to 30 minutes on most days. Studies have shown that as intensity and frequency increase, so do the health benefits you reap. Most health benefits occur with at least 150 minutes of moderate exercise a week (that's about 20 minutes a day, or 30 minutes five days a week). Including both aerobic and strength-training exercises seems to be most beneficial.

Exercise helps with arthritis or other rheumatic conditions. Including 2–2½ hours of moderate, low-impact physical activity each week can improve pain management and enhance the quality of life. Including strength training can also help preserve the loss of muscle with aging.

Adults aren't the only ones who benefit from exercise. Studies have shown that children and adolescents in every racial and ethnic group, including people with disabilities, benefit from regular activity. In every case, cardiorespiratory health improves. Cardiorespiratory fitness is the ability of the circulatory (blood-flowing) and respiratory (breathing) systems in the body to supply oxygen to skeletal muscles during activity. The more you use these systems, the stronger they become and the more you can do. So use it or lose it.

Many people use either a three-set or a one-set approach to weight lifting. If you choose to do three sets of an activity, you use lighter weights that allow you to do at least 8–12 repetitions for each of three sets. If you use a one-set approach, you start by lifting the heaviest weight that allows you to do at least 6 repetitions, and gradually increase the weight. Your last two repetitions should be very difficult, sometimes termed *to exhaustion* (as in, you can't do one more without resting).

In addition to muscle building and toning, some exercises benefit your bones. *Bone-strengthening activities* are weight-bearing exercises that exert a force on the bones that promotes bone strength. Examples include jumping jacks, running, brisk walking (also called power-walking), and weight-lifting exercises.

People vary in terms of how much activity they need to lose weight, maintain a healthy weight, or see positive results in terms of other health parameters, such as blood pressure and blood lipids. Some people need more activity than others. If you need to lose a significant amount of weight (more than 5 percent of your body weight) you'll have to reduce calorie intake and may need to include up to 300 minutes of moderate-intensity exercise per week. Creating a 250- to 500-calorie deficit daily (either by reducing calorie intake or adding exercise to burn more calories) results in a weight loss of ½ to 1 pound per week. Ask your doctor to refer you to a registered dietitian to review your dietary goals and create a plan specifically for you.

Weighing yourself weekly is a good way to track the progress of your exercise and eating plan.

Fitting a workout into your schedule

If you aren't currently incorporating regular physical activity into your weekly schedule, you may be wondering how you're going to pack 150 minutes of exercise into your schedule every week. Just as a little bit of planning goes a long way when setting dietary goals, the same goes for exercise: Plan it, and you'll achieve it. Here are a few things to keep in mind as you plan your exercise schedule:

- ✔ **Exercise may be hard sometimes, but it should still be fun.** Enlisting a friend to exercise with makes it a social experience. Doing a variety of exercises (some outdoor, some indoor, some timed, some leisurely) keeps you interested. Listening to music can make the time fly by and even make you move more.

  If it isn't fun, you probably won't stick with it.

- ✔ **Pick a time of the day and week that works for you.** Studies have shown that early morning exercisers are successful, partly because fewer distractions are likely to get in the way so the exercise routine is more likely to get done. Write the day and time you pick into your schedule.

- ✔ **Stick with it.** You may need to adjust your attitude. Some people think of exercise as a luxury or a recreational activity. It's not. It's a health maintenance activity. You wouldn't buy a new car and never take it in for an oil change. Think of exercise as a must-do for health maintenance. Prioritize it, and don't let anything get in its way.

- ✔ **Plan options.** If you choose to exercise outdoors and it's raining when the time rolls around, have an alternative available instead of skipping exercise altogether. Use indoor home equipment, tune in to a TV fitness show or an exercise DVD, or drive to a local gym.

- ✔ **Keep a record:** Using a journal to record what you've done can be very motivating. This process helps you not only log the days and times you exercise, but also track how you're improving. We suggest using the *Calorie Counter Journal For Dummies* (written by coauthor Rosanne and Meri Raffetto and published by Wiley) as a guide to logging diet and exercise.

When you're having a hard time making extra time to work out, find everyday things to do that add to your day's calorie burn:

- ✔ **Keep your house tidier.** Use a broom to sweep the porch each day, vacuum every other day, make extra trips up and down the stairs, carry one load of laundry at a time to bedrooms, or put on some music and dance while you dust.

- ✔ **Walk more.** Park your car downtown and walk to several errands instead of driving to each one. Skip the drive-through windows and walk into the bank, dry cleaner, post office, or coffee shop.

- ✔ **Don't sit too much.** If you find yourself sitting for more than 30 minutes at a time (like book authors do), be sure to check the clock and get up every 20–30 minutes for a stretch, some activity, or to get a glass of water. We like to do 20 jumping jacks.

Fifteen minutes of vigorous activity have the benefit of 30 minutes of moderate-intensity activity. Here are some ways to cut your exercise time by increasing your workout intensity:

- ✔ If you've been walking 3 days a week for an hour, try jogging one of those days. Start slowly by alternately jogging for 2 minutes and walking for 2 minutes, until you can jog the entire 30 minutes. Then work on increasing your pace.

- ✔ Have you been working out with the same 5-pound weights? Try fewer repetitions of heavier weights; then gradually move to using weight machines to lift more weight with fewer reps.

- ✔ Gradually increase the intensity of your moderate-intensity, 60-minute workouts until you're able to do a 30-minute vigorous workout.

Possibly the most important aspect of an effective exercise program is consistency. If you don't exercise at least three to five days a week, you won't reap the rewards. Here are some tips to help you stay motivated:

- ✔ **Buy some comfortable workout clothes and shoes.** Be sure to have clothes for every season so you're comfortable in all weather.

- ✔ **Stay hydrated and nourished.** If you're working toward weight loss, it's important not to overlimit calories. Eat nutritiously using the recipes featured in this book!

- ✔ **Be sure to begin your program gradually.** (Try the walking program we suggest earlier in this chapter.) Do some stretching afterward.

- ✔ **Find an exercise partner whose goals and fitness level are similar to yours.** Exercising with a friend is more fun, and you're more likely to stay on track.

Homeostasis and the amazing machine

Living cells require a specific environment in which to exist. *Homeostasis* involves the mechanisms by which organisms such as the human body maintain this perfect environment (*homeo* means "the same" and *stasis* means "staying"). The body controls blood pressure, blood sugar, body temperature, and respiration by a variety of mechanisms whose goal is to maintain homeostasis, or to keep things constant. Everything you eat and drink and how you live your life can impact this stay-the-same environment. Homeostasis is a fundamental property of life, and lack of homeostasis leads to disease and eventually death.

For instance, if you eat too much, gain weight, and become insulin resistant, your blood glucose (sugar) levels will increase, disrupting the body's homeostasis and eventually developing into diabetes. In the case of blood pressure,

receptors and sensory nerves send messages back and forth from the heart to the brain and central nervous system in order to increase or decrease blood pressure to maintain a normal pressure. High blood pressure is one of the two most common causes of kidney damage because it weakens the small blood vessels in the kidneys over time (the other most common cause is diabetes). The kidneys play an important role in maintaining homeostasis throughout the body. Damaged vessels don't filter waste like they're supposed to, which leads to other health problems.

So you see how important homeostasis is to your health. Eating better and exercising helps your body manage all of these functions every minute of the day. Take care of the amazing human machine!

Adding medication

Cooking healthy meals and getting regular physical activity are important for preventing or lowering high blood pressure, but sometimes they're not enough. In addition to eating well and sticking with an exercise routine, your doctor may recommend that you try medication to lower and stabilize your blood pressure. This decision is completely up to you and your doctor, but you may want to check out some common medicinal terms and some background about how blood pressure medicines work.

Eating well using the DASH diet plan and getting regular physical activity can reduce the amount of medicine you may need.

Becoming familiar with common hypertension meds

There are different categories of hypertension medications (just take a look at Table 3-2). Which category your prescription falls in depends on your medical history and your doctor's evaluation.

Table 3-2	Common Types of Blood Pressure Medicines
Type	*Action*
Thiazide diuretics	Reduce blood volume by stimulating the kidneys to eliminate water and sodium.
Beta blockers	Slow your heart rate and open blood vessels, reducing the workload on your heart. Often combined with a diuretic.
ACE inhibitors	Relax blood vessels by blocking the *formation* of natural chemicals that narrow them.
Angiotensin II receptor blockers	Relax blood vessels by blocking the *action* of the natural chemicals that narrow them.
Vasodilators	Relax the blood vessel walls to open blood vessels, causing pressure to go down.
Calcium channel blockers	Relax the muscles of blood vessels. Some may also slow heart rate. (Grapefruit interacts with some calcium channel blockers, so talk to your doctor or pharmacist about any interaction.)

Take any medicine that your doctor prescribes as directed. If you don't take the medicine properly (taking the right dose at the right times, without skipping any days), it won't help you and will put you at risk. If you experience side effects with a new medicine, call your doctor right away so the issue can be addressed and the medicine adjusted.

No matter which medicine your doctor prescribes, you still need to make the appropriate lifestyle changes of eating better, losing excess weight, exercising, and more (see Chapter 24 for a quick rundown of your long-term lifestyle goals). Medicine alone is usually not the best strategy. As you cook and eat healthier meals and get more physical activity, your body does part of the work so that the medicine can be most effective. You may also be able to reduce the amount of medication you need or prevent the need for additional medications.

The less medicine you need, the better. While medications can be very helpful in keeping your body's systems in homeostasis, too many medicines can eventually wear down your body's systems. Eating well, adding more physical activity, and losing weight go a long way toward keeping your blood pressure down with less or no medication and keeping your whole body healthier.

Keeping tabs on your blood pressure

You want to know whether or not your new exercise program and healthier eating are having positive effects on your blood pressure. To make sure you're staying on top of your blood pressure, you may want to consider monitoring it at home. This self-monitoring helps reinforce that the lifestyle changes you're making and any medication you may be taking are working.

Be sure to keep your appointments with your doctor as well. These visits help confirm that your blood pressure is well controlled and are an opportunity to evaluate the effectiveness of your lifestyle and any medications you're taking.

Check yourself before you wreck yourself: Exploring self-monitoring

Being diagnosed with hypertension is an opportunity to take charge of your health. Checking your blood pressure at home can be helpful in these ways:

- ✓ If you have prehypertension, a home monitor can help diagnose Stage 1 hypertension (see Chapter 1).

- ✓ After diagnosis, self-monitoring can help you track your treatment between visits to your doctor.

- ✓ Knowing what your blood pressure readings are from day to day simply encourages you to be in control. Seeing normal readings offers you positive reinforcement to keep up with your lifestyle program (healthy eating and exercise) and any medications you're taking.

- ✓ If you suffer from "white coat syndrome" (see Chapter 1), it may be helpful to check your blood pressure when you aren't on the doctor's exam table, but in the comfort of your home instead.

You can find blood pressure devices at most pharmacies and medical supply stores, as well as on the Internet. These monitors have an inflatable cuff or strap and a gauge for readouts. Some include a stethoscope, depending on the type of monitor you choose.

Here's a breakdown of what each of the basic parts does:

- ✓ **The cuff:** A nylon cuff wraps around your upper arm and fastens snuggly. It consists of an inner layer made of rubber that fills with air via a tube attached to the cuff when pumped. This pressure squeezes your arm.

The pressure is gradually released from the cuff, and the first sound of blood pulsing indicates the top measurement (systolic). The bottom (diastolic) measurement is the gauge number that appears when that sound disappears.

✔ **The gauge:** Blood pressure monitors are either digital or aneroid. *Aneroid monitors* have a gauge with a dial that points at a number related to your blood pressure. *Digital monitors* have a digital read-out.

✔ **The stethoscope:** Some blood pressure monitors come with a stethoscope. It's used to listen to the sounds your blood makes as it flows through the artery in your arm. However, it really takes proper training to interpret those sounds.

Understanding manual devices

Manual blood pressure monitors use a stethoscope and an inflatable arm cuff connected to a tube that runs to a gauge that records the pressure. To measure your blood pressure, you inflate the cuff by pumping a bulb at one end of the tube. You then listen to the sounds of the blood flowing through the main artery in your upper arm with the stethoscope as the pressure decreases in the cuff. Manual monitors are usually less expensive than digital monitors, but can be more difficult to use because they require training and practice. We recommend digital monitors for home use because there's much less room for error. If you do decide on a manual one, be sure to speak with your doctor or nurse so you can learn how to use it accurately.

Understanding digital devices

Digital monitors have a cuff and a gauge that records the pressure. You touch a button, and the cuff automatically inflates. Digital devices automatically calculate your heart rate and check your blood pressure by measuring the changes in the motion of your artery as the blood flows through the artery while the cuff deflates. They also deflate automatically after a reading is taken.

Digital monitors can be fitted on the upper arm, wrist, or finger. Arm devices are the most accurate. Wrist monitors are an option for people whose upper arm is too large for the arm cuff; finger monitors aren't as accurate.

Keeping your doctor's appointments

Taking any prescribed medication as directed and keeping all appointments with your doctor are both important to your overall blood pressure management. Be sure you know what your blood pressure numbers are and what they mean. Also ask your doctor to write down the name and dose of your medication.

A word about high blood pressure during pregnancy

Women who already have hypertension going into pregnancy tend to have more complications than those who have normal blood pressure, but some pregnant women develop high blood pressure during pregnancy (known as *gestational hypertension*). While the complications may be few and you may deliver a healthy baby, the situation can be dangerous for some women. High blood pressure during pregnancy can cause low birth weight and early delivery. The mother may suffer kidney damage.

Serious cases of gestational hypertension result in *preeclampsia*. Preeclampsia usually surfaces around the 20th week of the pregnancy. It affects the placenta, and, in addition to affecting the kidneys, can impact the liver and brain. The cause is unknown, but it may be impacted by genetic factors, blood vessel problems, or diet. Symptoms may include swelling or rapid weight gain, but these symptoms may also

be part of a normal pregnancy. Kidney problems result in increased protein in the mother's urine. In some cases, no symptoms are apparent. Getting regular check-ups as scheduled throughout the pregnancy helps your doctor keep track of your blood pressure, weight gain, and urine test results.

Women experiencing their first pregnancy and those who are having multiple births (twins or more), are obese, are over age 35, or have a history of diabetes or hypertension are at higher risk. If your doctor diagnoses preeclampsia, you'll be closely monitored throughout the remainder of the pregnancy. You may be asked to be on complete bed rest, drink more water, consume less salt, and visit the doctor more frequently. You may also be asked to self-monitor your blood pressure at home. The condition generally disappears only after the baby is delivered.

When you see your doctor, be sure to ask questions about anything you don't understand. Some sample questions:

- ✔ What is my systolic number? What is my diastolic number?
- ✔ What are my blood pressure goal numbers?
- ✔ What is a healthy weight range for me? What's my BMI?
- ✔ May I see a dietitian to help me set dietary goals?
- ✔ Is it safe for me to begin more physical activity?
- ✔ What time should I take my medicine? Should I take it with food or avoid any particular foods?

What happens if you forget to take your medication? Check with your doctor about that too, but here are some tips to help you remember:

- Take your medicine at the same time daily, as directed.

- Use a pillbox that has seven slots — one for each day. If you take other medications at a different time of day, you may want a pillbox organizer that has 14 slots — one for a.m. and one for p.m.

- Put a "Don't forget!" reminder in a spot that you view frequently — on the refrigerator, the coffeepot, or your bathroom mirror.

- Ask your spouse, a friend, or a family member to remind you or call you about taking your medicine.

- Program a daily reminder into your smartphone or computer.

Part II
Creating a Low-Salt, Big-Taste Lifestyle

The 5th Wave   By Rich Tennant

"It's as easy as replacing the salt with something else — oregano, basil, pencil shavings..."

In this part . . .

Knowing what to do differs from knowing how to do it. This part provides you with the tools and fresh ideas you need to embark on a dietary path to treating or preventing hypertension. Because reducing sodium is a big part of most heart-healthy diets, we list loads of salt-free seasoning ideas that won't have you missing the salt-shaker. We also walk alongside you through the grocery store so you can decipher food labels efficiently and have a well-stocked pantry at the ready.

Of course, having your kitchen stocked won't lead to better eating if you don't know how to prepare the food, so you'll find some "cooking 101" tips here for saving time and bringing out the flavor, and techniques that make cooking easier and tastier. Finally, we can't think of a better way to embark on lifestyle change than involving your family and friends, so we offer some tasty menu plans featuring the recipes in this book. You can party hearty and stay in control of your hypertension while doing it.

Chapter 4

Replacing Sodium

*J*ust about everybody can agree on one thing: Food should taste good. Salty foods can certainly fall into that good-tasting category, but because salt plays a role in high blood pressure, you have to keep your food delicious while making an effort to cut back on sodium. The good news for your taste buds is that less salty doesn't have to mean bland or tasteless. Reducing the salt is only one part of healthier eating; the second part is adding lots of flavor with other ingredients.

In this chapter, we give you a heads-up on where sodium is lurking in your pantry, and we explain how to gradually replace some of the products you use with other, healthier ingredients. We also take a look at some herbs and spices that you may not have tried that can add some much-needed kick to your hypertension diet.

As you read this chapter on finding some replacements for sodium, keep in mind that the other aspects of the DASH eating plan (Dietary Approaches to Stop Hypertension) are still important. Your diet should be about balance, not just cutting out one mineral. Including fruits and vegetables in your meals adds antioxidants and potassium to your diet, both of which are important for controlling blood pressure. So while reducing sodium is important, adding more fruits, vegetables, and lowfat dairy is just as important, if not more so. Be sure to review the details of the DASH eating plan in Chapter 2.

Discovering Where Salt Secretly Lurks

Some salt is important to good health, but if you don't pay attention to where salt secretly hides in your food, you may be consuming way too much. Sodium is a mineral found in salt and in many packaged and processed foods.

The American Heart Association recommends that you limit your sodium intake to no more than 1,500 milligrams per day, while the U.S. Department of Agriculture recommends that you consume less than 2,300 milligrams daily. Your doctor may have a different recommendation for you. Our advice: Reduce.

When you're trying to figure out if something you're about to eat is too sodium-heavy, keep in mind this general rule of thumb: The fresher the food, the lower the sodium content. Similarly, the more processed the food, the higher the sodium.

You'll find sodium tucked away in a variety of common foods:

- **Bottled salad dressings and tomato sauces:** Try making your own salad dressings and tomato sauces to help you cut back on your sodium intake.

- **Breads and cereals:** Some varieties are higher than others in the sodium department, so compare labels before you buy.

- **Canned foods:** Canned goods, including beans and vegetables, are convenient because they have a long shelf life and because all you have to do is heat them up. Unfortunately, sodium is the reason their long shelf life is long. Look for no-salt-added canned foods and rinse all canned beans and vegetables before you eat them to help reduce their sodium content.

- **Cheesy foods, pizza, sausage, hot dogs, bacon, deli meats, ready-to-eat foods, canned soups, canned pasta, boxed dinner mixes, pouch recipe kits, and frozen meals:** Yes, all these foods add convenience to dinnertime chaos, but they also have lots of sodium. Making more homemade foods can help you reduce your intake of these high-sodium culprits.

- **Condiments and sauces:** Indeed, condiments and sauces add zing to dishes, but they can be surprisingly high in sodium. For instance, 1 tablespoon of soy sauce contains 1,800 milligrams of sodium. Use smaller amounts of condiments and sauces or look for low-sodium varieties to reduce the amount of salt you're eating.

- **Flavoring packets that come with foods, such as quick-cooking rice dishes and other packaged "all-in-one" pasta dishes:** If the packet is separate from the rice or pasta, use just half of it to flavor the dish and reduce the sodium.

- **Frozen, processed chicken breasts:** Salt is added as a preservative to many frozen chicken breasts. Check the label and buy fresh chicken breasts instead.

- **OTC (over the counter) medicines, such as antacids:** We bet you never guessed you'd have to worry about getting salt from medicine! Well, think again! Sodium hides in many OTC meds, so check labels before you buy, and talk to your doctor if one of your regular OTCs is pretty high in sodium.

✔ **Restaurant and rotisserie chicken:** In the case of fast-food restaurants, the grilled chicken is often higher in sodium than the burger, so you may be better off with a small burger than a large chicken sandwich. (Check out the *Restaurant Calorie Counter For Dummies,* 2nd Edition, published by Wiley, for nutrient profiles on hundreds of restaurant items; Rosanne coauthored this book with Meri Raffetto.)

Store-bought rotisserie chicken has a higher sodium content than fresh chicken too. If you're in a real pinch to save time, go ahead and use it. Just realize that it's higher in sodium and use fresh whenever possible.

✔ **Spice or herb blends:** Spice blends often aren't labeled with the word *salt* but have salt added anyway. Look for *salt-free* on the front of the package, or read the ingredient list in search of *salt.*

Now that you have a general idea of what types of foods contain hidden sodium, take a look at Table 4-1 for a list of specific foods based on their sodium content. You probably can't realistically eliminate the high-sodium foods altogether, forever, but you need to realize that these products can add significant amounts of sodium to your diet. So be aware of how much you're eating as you measure out portions of them (for more about portion sizes, see Chapter 2) and try to stick with the lower-sodium foods as much as possible.

Table 4-1	Comparing Sodium in Foods		
Food	*Low Sodium*	*Moderate Sodium*	*High Sodium*
Condiments and spices	Herbs, spices, low-sodium mustard, and red pepper sauce	Salted herb/spice blends, barbeque sauce, ketchup, steak sauce, salad dressing, tomato sauce/puree, and Worcestershire sauce	Seasoning salts, soy sauce, teriyaki sauce, dried soup mixes, and bouillon cubes
Grains	Low-sodium breads and crackers, oatmeal (not instant), rice, and pasta	Regular breads and rolls, dry cereals, muffins, instant hot cereals (like oatmeal), pancakes, waffles, pastries, cakes, and cookies	Canned spaghetti, refrigerator biscuit and cookie dough, boxed mixes for pancakes and macaroni and cheese, boxed potatoes, stuffing mixes, and salted crackers, chips, popcorn, or pretzels

(continued)

Table 4-1 *(continued)*

Food	Low Sodium	Moderate Sodium	High Sodium
Fruits and vegetables	Fresh fruit, fruit juices, and fresh or frozen unsalted vegetables; no-salt-added canned vegetables	Canned vegetables	Pickles, olives, pickled vegetables, canned vegetable juice, and frozen vegetables with sauces
Meats, eggs, beans, and nuts	Fresh beef, pork, poultry, eggs, low-sodium canned tuna, and unsalted nuts	Canned beans (rinsed), frozen "healthy" entrees (with less than 500 mg of sodium), fresh fish, deli meats, peanut butter, and low-sodium canned soups	Hot dogs; sausage; bacon; smoked meats; canned soups; frozen dinners; canned tuna, clams, crab, and salmon; and packaged lunchmeats
Dairy	Milk, sherbet, ice cream, and ricotta	Buttermilk, yogurt, aged hard cheeses, feta cheese, Parmesan cheese, cottage cheese, and pudding	Processed cheese (like American) and blue cheese

Putting Down the Salt Shaker

Not all the sodium in your diet is secretly tucked away in a box of cereal or a can of tomato sauce. In fact, a lot of the salt that makes its way into your diet may be right out in the open — in the form of the salt shaker. A salt-restricted diet certainly lowers blood pressure in people both with and without hypertension, and because using less salt will do no harm and probably will only do you good, you should set a goal to avoid using table salt. Here are some tips to help you start cutting back on how often you use the salt shaker:

- Taste food before salting it. If you're in the habit of shaking salt onto your burgers, fries, or other foods before you even taste them, try having a few bites first to make sure additional flavor is really necessary. If you need a little more kick, add some ground black pepper or a dash of red pepper flakes rather than salt.

- Don't shake salt inside the skillet or pan when cooking. Instead, use sodium-free spices and herbs, such as basil, curry, garlic, ginger, mint, oregano, pepper, paprika, rosemary, and thyme to keep food flavorful.

- Instead of salting meats or vegetables when sautéing, add balsamic vinegar or wine to the pan.

- Enjoying some high-fiber popcorn? Hold the shaker! Another way to use less is to load your pepper shaker with salt (it has fewer holes). Try shaking the salt into your hand first to see it; you'll use less this way. You can also find salt-free seasoning powders to add zing to your corn.

- Enjoy the egg recipes in this book. Adding flavor with vegetables and other ingredients encourages you to use less salt — taste the flavors!

- Going out for happy hour with friends? Skip the salted rim on that margarita!

Looking at Salt Alternatives

Table salt is a zesty seasoning, no doubt about it, but you can get that zest without running the risk of raising your blood pressure. You'll find small amounts of salt used in some of the recipes in this cookbook, but using less is a lifestyle change you need to start getting used to. As you use less salt you can maintain or even enhance the flavor of your favorite foods by adding other flavoring agents that don't contribute sodium. In this section, we review a few salt-free options and some other alternatives. Some of them are better than others, but they can all help you meet your goal of reducing your sodium intake. We also touch on this topic in Chapter 6.

Adding flavor the healthy way

One of salt's best features is the flavor it adds to food, but if you could make your food taste just as good without the potential health threat, wouldn't you? Herbs and spices are natural ingredients that can impart a variety of flavors to otherwise bland or boring dishes. The same goes for fruits and veggies, and using them to flavor foods can help you get your daily allowance of these must-haves to boot.

Mixing in herbs and spices

Herbs and spices can add wonderful flavors to a variety of foods. The main difference between the two is that you often add *spices* before or early in cooking, whereas you add *herbs* toward the end of cooking.

While herbs and spices aren't exactly salt substitutes in the traditional sense of the word (like potassium chloride; see the section "Getting to know potassium chloride"), they're salt alternatives in the sense that they provide food with flavor in lieu of salt.

Figuring out which herbs and spices match which foods isn't as complicated as you may think. For one thing, it's a matter of personal taste. Use flavors that you enjoy. If you're looking for some particularly good matches, check out Table 4-2.

Table 4-2	Matching Herbs and Spices to Different Foods
Herb/Spice	*Uses*
Allspice	Add to meats, fish, or cooked fruits.
Basil	Add to tomatoes, egg dishes, salads, pasta, marinades, or herb butter.
Cayenne	Add to soups, sauces, fish, or meats.
Chili Powder	Use in chilis, soups, ground meat, or rubs.
Cilantro	Use in sauces, salads, or salsas with chicken or fish.
Cinnamon	Use on fruits, with pork, or in rubs that include hot spices.
Cumin	Add to salsas, chicken dishes, ground meat, vegetables, or rice dishes.
Curry	Add to soups, vegetables, meats, rice dishes, or sauces.
Dill	Add to fish, eggs, or sauces.
Ginger	Add to curry dishes or Asian-inspired dishes.
Marjoram	Use with meats, poultry, soups, stews, or vegetables.
Mint	Add to salads, lamb, carrots, soups, or sauces.
Oregano	Add to Italian or Mexican dishes, tomato sauces, soups, or poultry.
Paprika	Use with fish, eggs, or sauces.
Rosemary	Add to beef, pork, breads, or pasta.
Sage	Use in stuffing or with poultry or fish.
Thyme	Use in soups, chowders, or sauces and with poultry.

Whether you choose to use fresh or dried herbs is up to you. Fresh herbs provide a more distinct flavor than dried, but they're also more expensive to buy in grocery stores. Basil, dill, thyme, rosemary, oregano, and parsley are just a few herbs that you can purchase fresh or dried.

Grow your own herbs in an outdoor or kitchen garden. You'll save money along with reducing the sodium in your daily meals, and you'll get to enjoy the strong flavor of fresh herbs.

You can purchase dried herbs and spices whole, crushed, or ground (for instance, you can purchase whole dried thyme leaves or ground thyme that's powdered, whole or ground ginger, or whole or ground cinnamon). Similarly, you can purchase whole peppercorns or ground pepper. Try experimenting with grinding different types of peppercorns (red, white, green, or black) to offer a variety of subtle flavors to your food. Black peppercorns have a sharper flavor than white, green, or red ones. Whole peppercorns retain their flavor longer than ground pepper.

Take a quick walk down the spice aisle at your local grocery store, and you're sure to find lots of salt-free herb and spice blends. Many of these easy-to-use blends have labels based on what foods they go best with; for instance, you may see labels like *poultry spice* or *seafood mix.* They may also have labels that specify the region of the world where they're commonly used. For example, you may see a Jamaican or Mexican spice blend or a French or Italian herb blend. Whatever blends you choose, be sure they're salt-free.

Cooking with flavorful fruits and veggies

You may think about fruits and vegetables as side dishes, but you can also use them to add another dimension of flavor to foods. Read on to find out how to use certain fruits and veggies to add a little zest to your meals the sodium-free way.

Garlic

Garlic is part of the *allium* family, which also includes onions, shallots, chives, scallions, and leeks (see the later section "Onions and such"). One clove of garlic provides 4 calories, 1 gram of sodium, and zero fat, making it a perfect food for heart health. It provides wonderful flavor for beef, pork, chicken, fish, or vegetables.

When buying garlic at the grocery store, choose firm bulbs. After you get them home, store them in an open container in a cool, dark place. You can crush, mince, press, or roast garlic before adding it to different dishes. One clove of garlic is equivalent to about 1 teaspoon of chopped garlic or 1/2 teaspoon of minced or crushed garlic. (Check out Chapter 6 for tips on how to use a garlic press.)

Research has indicated that garlic may have anti-cancer properties (due to the mineral selenium that it contains), as well as heart health benefits. Garlic has shown to slow the progression of coronary artery disease by lowering cholesterol. So not only will using garlic in your cooking add unique flavor, but it may also help lower your risk for heart disease. Go ahead, crush a clove into your next dish!

Peppers

Peppers are wonderful flavoring agents. Minced or sliced, cooked or raw, they add flavor and texture to any recipe. Not only do peppers add saltless zest to food, but they're also a good source of vitamins A and C (both of which are antioxidants) and contain those helpful phytochemicals that we describe in Chapter 7.

Peppers come in many varieties and range in flavor from sweet to mild to extremely hot. The four varieties of sweet peppers are

- **Bell:** Green, yellow, orange, or red, they range in size from about 2 to 4 inches in diameter.
- **Banana:** Light green in color, these peppers are thin and about 4 to 5 inches long.
- **Cubanelle:** Available in light green and red varieties, they're thin and about 3 to 4 inches long.
- **Pimento:** These small, round, red peppers are about an inch in diameter.

Surprisingly enough, green and red bell peppers come from the same plant. As they ripen, green peppers turn red and become sweeter. In addition to a sweeter taste, red bell peppers have about twice as much vitamin C as green ones. A half-cup serving provides about 150 percent of the Percent Daily Value.

The most common varieties of hot chile peppers, from the hottest to the least hot are

- **Habanero:** They may be green, red, or orange and are about 2 inches long. Habanero is one of the hottest varieties of chile peppers.
- **Serrano:** A smaller, hotter version of the jalapeño, these peppers are reddish and about 1 to 2 inches long.
- **Jalapeño:** Dark green and small, jalpeños are about 2 to 3 inches long or the size of your thumb.
- **Poblano or ancho:** Deep reddish brown, these peppers are about 4 inches long and have a sweet-hot flavor.

Seeding and mincing a teaspoon or two of hot pepper can really kick up the flavor of a dish. Of course, the more hot pepper you use, the more heat you add. A little can go a long way! By removing the seeds, you remove some of the heat. Just be sure to wear rubber gloves when seeding a very hot pepper;

otherwise, you can cause irritation to the eye if you accidently rub or touch your eye with your hands. (In case you're wondering, *capsaicin,* the active component in peppers, is what gives peppers their hotness factor.)

Onions and such

Onions, like garlic, are part of the *allium* family of plants (see the earlier section "Garlic"). Fortunately for you, the onion family can add loads of flavor and oomph to dishes — without any salt. You can use onions raw in salsas, sauces, relishes, or on sandwiches, or you can add them to meat and other cooked dishes. As onions cook, their sugars become more concentrated, leaving them sweeter and less sharp than when eaten raw. However, high heat makes onions bitter, so we recommend sautéing them (using low-medium heat) to bring out their mild yet deep flavors.

According to the National Onion Association, about 87 percent of the onion crop is devoted to yellow onions, about 8 percent to red onions, and about 5 percent to white onions. Yellow onions can be stored longer than the more delicate white onions. Onions should be kept in a dark, dry, cool place. A cut onion will keep in the refrigerator for about two weeks. If you grow onions, you can store them for months. Just be sure they're dry, placed in a mesh or well-ventilated bag, and kept in a cool place (ideally 40 to 50 degrees, as in a dark cellar or a garage corner). Check out Table 4-3 for the details on these three varieties.

Table 4-3	Onion Facts	
Color	*Character*	*Best Uses*
Yellow	All-purpose, sweet, mellow flavor	Caramelized, raw, sautéed, or grilled
Red	Crisp and mild; nice color	Raw (on sandwiches and salads), grilled, or roasted
White	Slightly pungent	Raw, grilled, or sautéed, especially in Mexican and Southwest cuisine, sauces, or potato dishes

Onions are available at the market all year.

- **Spring-summer onions** tend to have a high water content that can reduce their shelf life. They generally have thin, lighter-colored skins, and they usually range in flavor from sweet to mild. They're available from March through August.

- **Fall-winter onions** have thicker, darker layers and can range from mild to pungent in taste. They're available from August through May.

Regardless of which onions you're buying, look for dry skins and no bruises or wet spots.

 When cooking with onions, cut them right before you use them for best results. Their flavor deteriorates over time if cut too far in advance, and their aroma intensifies — so don't leave chopped onions in your refrigerator for long. When you do chop ahead, be sure to store them in a sealed bag or lidded container.

 Crying over cut onions? You can reduce the tearing up when cutting onions by chilling them for at least 30 minutes prior to cutting. Also, leave the root end intact, because it has the highest concentration of sulfur compounds (which causes the tearing up).

Leeks are part of the onion family, but they have a subtle flavor compared to onions. The edible portion of leeks includes the white bulb, as well as the light green stalk. Generally, you should cut the dark green tops off, because they aren't as tender or flavorful. Leeks are wonderful sautéed and make great additions to soups or stocks.

Chives, scallions, and shallots are also part of the onion family. *Chives* are more delicate, with thin, green stem tops and small bulbs. You can use both the green tops and the white bulb. A pinch of minced chives can turn a plain potato dish from "good" to "wow," adding no salt and few calories. Scallions are larger than chives and are often called green onions. They can be used either raw or cooked to add flavor to salads and vegetable dishes. *Shallots* are almost like a cross between garlic and onion. They're flavorful and mild and work great sautéed in egg, chicken, or fish dishes, as well as in sauces for beef and pork.

Fruits

Adding fruits to meals to reduce sodium may sound a little unorthodox, but it works. For example, you can zest the peels of lemons, oranges, and limes into salad dressings, pasta salads, and potato dishes, or onto fish or poultry to add a tasty punch without adding salt. You can also add dried fruits to stuffing to add new flavors to a stuffed turkey or chicken. When you sauté onions, add some chopped fresh peaches or mango to top baked fish.

You can marinate poultry in the juices of fruits to avoid using salty sauces and store-bought marinades. Soak chicken pieces in ½ cup of orange juice along with your favorite fresh herbs to add flavor and moisture the next time you fire up the grill. Orange juice works well with mild white fish, too. Simply pour about a cup of orange juice over the fish in a glass baking dish, add fresh chives, and bake for 20 to 30 minutes at 350 degrees.

You can make traditional homemade salsas with tomatoes, but try adding some minced seasonal fruit to them too for a sweet-hot flavor. Peaches, nectarines, mango, and pineapple all work well. Or, put the fruit right on the grill. Adding any grilled fruit to beef or pork provides added flavor that helps you cut down on salt. Try grilled peach halves or pineapple slices alongside a small steak or grilled pork loin chop.

Considering some other options

Sea salt, gourmet salts, and potassium chloride are other alternatives to traditional table salt, but they don't carry the health benefits of fruits and vegetables. In the following sections, we give you the lowdown on what these salts are really all about.

Examining sea salt and other gourmet salts

You may have seen the marketing efforts of sea salt and gourmet salt purveyors and wondered whether these fancy varieties are better for you than the traditional old table salt. Grocery store shelves are lined with coarse salt, grinding salt, kosher salt, Italian sea salt, Hawaiian sea salt, regular sea salt, and many more. Unfortunately, just because they have a different name or flavor doesn't mean they're healthy.

The broad term *sea salt* describes salt derived from the ocean or sea. It's harvested by channeling ocean water into clay trays and allowing the sun and wind to evaporate the water, leaving behind salt crystals. As a result, sea salt is generally less processed than table salt. You may notice a subtle difference in flavor, but its nutritional profile is essentially the same. Keep in mind that most table salt is iodized, and you can also purchase iodized sea salt. Iodine is a nutrient essential to normal thyroid function. While iodized salt is the main source, other foods provide iodine as well (kelp, milk, yogurt, fish, seafood, enriched bread, and eggs).

The one benefit to using sea salt may involve table use. If you grind sea salt instead of using refined table salt from a shaker, you may find that you use less because grinding takes more time. Also, table salt pours so easily that you may accidently add too much, so grinding keeps you from overdoing it by accident. Still, the sodium content of each is about the same, so don't add double the salt just because it's sea salt.

Getting to know potassium chloride

Sometimes physicians prescribe *potassium chloride*, a salt composed of potassium and chlorine, to treat low blood potassium levels. Potassium chloride is a salt, like sodium chloride. Although people often think of sodium chloride when they use the term "salt," chemically there are many types of salts (another example is the calcium chloride used to salt roadways in the winter).

You can also find "light" salt mixtures or *salt substitutes* at the supermarket in the salt or spice section. These salt substitutes contain less sodium and often include potassium chloride. Potassium salts taste similar to sodium chloride, but they have a slightly bitter or metallic aftertaste on the tongue. Some salt substitutes may contain potassium and lysine (an amino acid that has a salty taste). A "light" salt may be a mixture of sodium chloride and potassium chloride (thereby cutting the sodium by half).

Don't use a salt substitute without first checking with your physician. Depending on your complete medical history (and especially if you have kidney disease), using a potassium chloride product may be harmful. For this reason, we encourage you to use natural alternatives, such as herbs and spices, rather than salt substitutes.

Chapter 5

Navigating the Grocery Store

*I*f you want to cook healthier meals at home, you have to be a smart grocery shopper first. Grocery shopping may not be your favorite hobby, especially if you have to worry about the health quotients of everything you buy, so this chapter helps make the process as painless as possible. You discover how to quickly scan nutrition and ingredient labels, and you find out which foods to fill your cart with for optimal hypertension success. Once you have your basic list at hand, you'll be on your way to healthier eating and cooking.

Deciphering Nutrition Labeling

Just about every food product on the market is now marked with its nutrition information. This section takes you through each part of the various food labels and explains how to read them. You also get some quick tips that are specific to a diet for lowering blood pressure so that you can get in and out of the store in record time.

The Nutrition Facts label

The *Nutrition Facts label,* a standardized label that's generally found on the back or side of food packaging, is an excellent tool for figuring out what's really in a given food and how much nutrition it provides. This label is required on most packaged foods, but it's voluntary for raw foods (such as produce, fresh meats, and fish). By reading the Nutrition Facts label, you gain information about how much of a particular food constitutes a serving; how many calories, minerals, and vitamins are in each serving; and how much sodium, cholesterol, fat, and so on a serving contains.

As Chapter 2 points out, the DASH diet is based on a few key principles: namely, that your daily diet should be low in saturated fat and sodium, adequate in lowfat dairy, and high in fruits and vegetables. The Nutrition Facts label lists some of the nutrients that can help you decide which foods fit into the DASH diet and how much of them you should eat. The following sections take you through various categories of the label that are important to hypertension management (see Figure 5-1 for an example). For additional information about the Nutrition Facts label, see `www.fda.gov/food/labelingnutrition`.

Figure 5-1:
An example of the Nutrition Facts label shown on most foods.

Nutrition Facts

Serving Size 1 Cup (240mL)
Servings Per Container 2

Amount Per Serving

Calories 120   Calories from Fat 45

	% Daily Value*
Total Fat 5g	8%
Saturated Fat 3.5g	18%
Trans Fat 0g	
Cholesterol 25mg	8%
Sodium 120mg	5%
Total Carbohydrate 11g	4%
Dietary Fiber 0g	0%
Sugars 11g	
Protein 8g	16%

Vitamin A 10%	•		Vitamin C 2%
Calcium 30%	• Iron 0% •	Vitamin D 25%

* Percent Daily Values are based on a 2,000 calorie diet. Your daily values may be higher or lower depending on your caloric needs.

Serving Size

Perhaps the first thing to check out when you look at the nutrition panel is the serving size of the food. If you don't look at the serving size on the label, you may easily consume double, triple, or more of the serving size. Often, what looks like a pretty decent portion is way more than a serving is supposed to be. Most manufacturers attempt to provide realistic serving sizes, but sometimes they're smaller than what may be typical. You don't always have to eat the serving size the package defines, but you do want to be aware of it and account for any extra portion you do eat.

For example, a serving of tortilla chips may provide 140 calories, which doesn't seem like much. But if a serving is only 10 chips, and you start eating them right out of the bag and lose track of how many you've munched, that number climbs quickly. Or, a bottle of sports drink or soda may list "2 to 2.5 servings per package"; however, you're likely to drink the whole thing.

Be sure to do the math. If you eat twice the amount of the serving size listed, then you need to double the amount of calories and all the other nutrients. So looking at Figure 5-1, if you consume 1 cup, you get 120 calories and 120 milligrams of sodium. Two cups, on the other hand, provide 240 calories and 240 milligrams of sodium.

Don't eat out of the box or bag. Use a bowl or plate to help you portion out an exact serving.

Calories and calories from fat

Nutrition Facts labels list how many total calories are in the specified serving size. *Calories* provide a measure of how much energy food provides. Your body needs energy to move and support bodily functions (like respiration, digestion, and so on), and you burn additional calories when your body is active. Unfortunately, many Americans consume more calories than their bodies burn. The calorie information on the Nutrition Facts panel helps you gauge how much of a food can fit into your overall diet in order to maintain a healthy weight.

As you see in Figure 5-1, the panel also shows a "% Daily Value" column, displaying what percentage of a daily calorie intake the food provides. Keep in mind that the % Daily Value is based on a 2,000-calorie intake, which may be more or less than you personally need.

To estimate your personal energy needs, check out the Mayo Clinic's calorie calculator at www.mayoclinic.com/health/calorie-calculator/ NU00598. Set up an appointment with a registered dietitian for a full evaluation of your nutritional needs.

The "Calories from Fat" notation gives you an idea of how high in fat the food is. In Figure 5-1, 45 of the food's total 120 calories come from fat, so this food is pretty high in fat, getting about 38% of its calories from fat. A high-fat food is one that provides more than 30% of its calories from fat, so for a heart-healthy diet, most of the foods you consume should have a % Daily Value of less than 30.

Total fat, saturated fat, and cholesterol

Keeping tabs on your fat and cholesterol intake is important when you're embarking on a diet to lower your blood pressure and cholesterol. Take note of these fats on the nutrition label:

- ✔ **Saturated fat and trans fat** are of particular interest for heart health. Saturated fat comes mostly from animals. A trans fat is an unsaturated (plant-based) fat that has been processed to change its chemical figuration, resulting in a fat that acts like a saturated fat. These two fats are the worst when it comes to raising your blood cholesterol and your risk for heart disease. A good rule of thumb is to look for foods that have 1 gram or less of saturated or trans fat per 100 calories.

   Trans fats are usually hidden in fast food and restaurant foods. See *Restaurant Calorie Counter For Dummies,* 2nd Edition, by yours truly and Meri Raffetto (published by Wiley) for nutrition information to keep your fat intake under control when dining out.

- ✔ **Total fat** shows the total amount of fat per serving. It's composed of the saturated, trans, and unsaturated fats. Although most labels don't include unsaturated fat on the label (because unsaturated fats don't raise blood cholesterol levels), you can estimate it by subtracting the saturated and trans fats from the total fat.

- ✔ **Unsaturated fats** come from plant sources. Polyunsaturated fats actually help lower LDL (bad cholesterol) and monounsaturated fats help increase HDL (good cholesterol). While you want your total fat intake to be low, you want most of the fat you do consume to come from these unsaturated fats. Many of the recipes in this book use vegetable oils, fish, and nuts, which help you achieve this goal.

According to the American Heart Association (AHA) and the National Heart, Lung, and Blood Institute (NHLBI), total fat intake should be about 25 to 30 percent of total calories. Saturated fat should be limited to 7 percent, and trans fats should be limited to less than 1 percent of total calories. For a 2,000-calorie daily intake, this recommendation translates to 55 to 67 grams of total fat, 16 grams or less of saturated fat, and 2 grams or less of trans fats daily. Check out the preceding section for more on daily calorie intake.

A food is considered lowfat if it contains 3 grams or less of fat per serving, and low in saturated fat if it contains 1 gram or less of saturated fat per serving.

While saturated fat has a negative impact on your blood cholesterol levels, dietary cholesterol also plays a role. The food that Figure 5-1 analyzes contains 25 milligrams of cholesterol, or 8 percent of the recommended daily value. The 2010 Dietary Guidelines for Americans recommend consuming less than 300 milligrams of cholesterol daily.

Sodium

Because a lower sodium intake is part of the DASH diet's goals for lowering blood pressure, taking note of the sodium on food labels is important. Sodium is a naturally occurring mineral that's added to foods to enhance flavor or lengthen shelf life (see Chapter 4), but too much of it is detrimental to your heart.

Figure 5-1 provides 120 milligrams of sodium per serving, making it a low-sodium food. Like saturated and trans fats and cholesterol, you want to limit this nutrient. A product is defined as low-sodium if it contains less than 140 milligrams of sodium per serving, but keep in mind as you prepare the recipes in this book that this low-sodium guideline is for individual ingredients you may use, not the sodium in a whole meal (remembering that your total sodium daily should be around 1,500–2,300 milligrams).

Dietary fiber

Unlike fat and sodium, you want to add *more* fiber into your diet. Fiber is important in weight control and can also lower blood cholesterol levels. If you're trying to lose weight on the DASH plan, try to incorporate more fiber into your diet and look for the dietary fiber count on nutrition labels. The food in Figure 5-1 provides 0 grams of fiber per serving.

Rather than consume "fiber-enriched" foods like cereal or granola bars as your primary source of fiber, add fiber to your diet by eating more beans, fruits, and vegetables. Not only do fruits and vegetables provide fiber but also those important phytochemicals. A half-cup serving of a fruit or vegetable provides you with 3–5 grams of fiber. Black beans are an even better source with about 8 grams per serving. If you follow the DASH guidelines of 8–10 servings of fruits and veggies, you easily come up with about 20–30 grams of fiber daily!

Facts Up Front

In 2011, American food and beverage manufacturers released *Facts Up Front,* formerly called *Nutrition Keys,* a new labeling system designed to help you choose healthy foods. This labeling system can serve as a quick reference as you work toward lowering your intake of saturated fat and sodium.

The *Facts Up Front* appear on the front of the package in a rectangular box that includes four main data categories:

- ✔ **Calories:** Limiting the number of calories you consume is important if you're trying to lose weight.

- ✔ **Saturated fat, along with % Daily Value:** See the earlier section "Total fat, saturated fat, and cholesterol" for the lowdown on saturated fat.

> ✔ **Sodium, along with % Daily Value:** See the earlier "Sodium" section for an explanation of why this number is important.
>
> ✔ **Sugar:** While sugar doesn't directly influence blood pressure, reducing the amount you consume generally ensures that you're choosing more nutrient-dense foods.

Some manufacturers may also choose to include the potassium, vitamin A, vitamin C, vitamin D, calcium, iron, protein, or fiber content per serving. *Facts Up Front* let you see at a glance the highlights of what's in a food, so you can compare items in the grocery aisle without picking them up and flipping to the Nutrition Facts on the back or side of the package.

NuVal

NuVal is a new labeling system that uses a score of 1 to 100 to value the overall nutrition of a food, with 100 being the healthiest. The NuVal score is listed on the grocery store shelf right next to the price. The intriguing thing about this system is that it's an independent system developed by a team of medical and nutrition experts. Food manufacturers were not involved in its development, thereby allowing for objectivity in terms of marketing information about foods. This system is being used by select grocery stores across the United States; check out www.nuval.com to find a grocery store near you that uses the system.

NuVal scores may be a handy and easy (though not foolproof) tool for you to use in evaluating the foods you choose at the grocer, but when you're working on dietary goals to treat high blood pressure, looking specifically at a few nutrients on the Nutrition Facts panel — namely sodium, saturated fat, and calories — is still worthwhile.

Choosing Processed Food Wisely

A processed food is defined as livestock or an agricultural product that has been altered to have an extended shelf life. The ingredients used to accomplish this goal are often those substances that need to be reduced in your diet: sodium, sugars, and trans fats. In addition, many processed foods contain additives that are used to enhance the color or flavor of a food or change its texture. Some additives add vitamins and minerals to foods that normally don't contain them (such is the case with calcium-fortified orange juice or iron-fortified cereals).

Some processed foods can play important roles in a healthy diet, particularly for people with food allergies, sensitivities, or digestive diseases. Calcium-fortified items, such as calcium-fortified orange juice, can help those who may be lactose intolerant. Digestive enzymes added to yogurt can help those with gastrointestinal issues. And, being able to keep some foods available on the shelf, limiting spoiling and waste, is a nice advantage for busy families.

Although in general we suggest moving away from processed foods and toward fresh foods, you can still rely on some packaged foods as long as you become an informed shopper. Foods like rice, pasta, canned or frozen vegetables and fruits, boxed cereals, oatmeal, some crackers, and breads are all okay as long as you monitor the info on the nutrition labels. The secret to choosing healthier packaged foods is reading the Nutrition Facts label or using an evaluation system such as NuVal rather than blindly believing what-ever claims the food's advertisers make on the package.

Manufacturers use front-of-package labeling as a way to sell their products. For instance, the front of a package may claim that a product has no high fructose corn syrup (a form of sugar), but although this may be true, the product may still contain several other forms of sugar. "Cholesterol-free" may be proclaimed on products that indeed do not contain cholesterol, but those same products may be very high in trans or vegetable fats (cholesterol is only derived from animal fats). Although regulations are in place for what sort of claims manufacturers can make, we encourage you to use the Nutrition Facts panel and the ingredients list to evaluate products. When you're short on time, take the shortcut and just check the serving size, calories, saturated fat, trans fat, and sodium.

Consider these guidelines as you decide which processed foods to keep on the grocery list and which ones to skip:

- ✔ **Don't assume "all-natural" or "organic" equals the best choice.** These foods can be highly processed as well. Check the labels for excessive salt and sugar.

- ✔ **Remember your daily sodium goal is 1,500–2,300 milligrams per day.** Consider those numbers as you read labels for sodium.

- ✔ **Look for reduced-sodium alternatives.** They're typically available for foods such as condiments, soups, canned tuna, and canned vegetables.

  Rinse canned vegetables under fresh water to remove some of the sodium.

- ✔ **Don't rely on fiber-added processed foods that normally wouldn't con-tribute fiber to your diet.** Fiber added to yogurt, water, or snack foods isn't your best bet. Get your fiber from fresh fruits and vegetables, and whole grains like oats, barley, brown rice, and whole-grain bread.

- ✔ **Check labels for sugar.** Sometimes when a manufacturer lowers fat, it adds sugar. For instance, a "reduced-fat" peanut butter may have only a few less grams of fat, but 2 added grams of sugar. You're better off using a smaller amount of the regular type. Added sugars may have a role in heart health and definitely contribute too many unneeded calories to the diet.

Focusing on Fresh: Gravitating toward Good Groceries

Whether you have hypertension or not, moving toward more good old-fashioned, whole foods and away from packaged foods is a good idea. The more whole foods you eat, the more nutrients — and most likely, the fewer calories — you pack in, and the healthier your dietary intake becomes. This section guides you through the store aisles to help you start filling your cart with the right stuff.

Strolling through the produce aisle

You can't go wrong in the produce section. Each week, choose a variety of fresh fruits and fresh vegetables. Look for specials and sale items, and alternate from one favorite to another. Because some produce items have a longer shelf life than others, plan to make at least one or two trips to the grocery store each week.

You may have asked yourself: Is organic produce worth the higher price? The answer? Sometimes. Even after being washed, many fruits and vegetables have been found to have pesticide residue remaining. An *organic* fruit or vegetable is one that's grown without pesticides or synthetic fertilizers. Farmers must be certified by federal laws in order to label their products "organic." We recommend considering organic choices for those foods that have been found to have the highest pesticide levels. On the other hand, foods that have very low pesticide residue don't warrant a search for organic versions. Table 5-1 shows you which foods belong in each of these categories, from most to least in terms of the amount of pesticide residue they contain.

Table 5-1	Should Your Produce Be Organic?
Yes (Produce with High Pesticide Levels)	*No (Produce with Low Pesticide Levels)*
Apples	Onions
Celery	Corn
Strawberries	Pineapple
Peaches	Avocado
Spinach	Asparagus
Nectarines	Sweet peas

Yes (Produce with High Pesticide Levels)	No (Produce with Low Pesticide Levels)
Grapes	Mangoes
Sweet bell peppers	Eggplant
Potatoes	Cantaloupe
Blueberries	Kiwis
Lettuce	Cabbage
Kale	Watermelon
	Sweet potatoes
	Grapefruit
	Mushrooms

Picking up the right meats

When choosing meats on a hypertension diet, the key words are "fresh" and "lean." Choose lean cuts of beef and pork, and a variety of poultry and fish. Poultry with the skin on is often less expensive, and you can simply remove the skin when you get home (on the other hand, you may be paying for the skin, so compare prices of skin-on versus skinless poultry). Flash-frozen chicken breasts often have added sodium, so a better choice is to buy fresh chicken, clean it, and freeze it yourself.

Lean cuts of beef include sirloin, tenderloin, top sirloin, top round steak or roast, and extra-lean ground beef. Lean pork also includes the loin cuts: tenderloin, top loin chop or roast, and center loin chop or roast. Skinless poultry is considered lean, and all fish counts as lean meat (even fattier types of fish, because their fat content is mostly unsaturated fat).

Skip pre-marinated meats, because they contain large amounts of unnecessary sodium. Chapter 17 offers some great recipes, but here's a basic marinade: Combine ½ cup orange juice, 2 tablespoons white wine or rice wine vinegar, 3 crushed garlic cloves, ½ teaspoon ground cumin, ground black pepper to taste, and ⅛ teaspoon sea salt.

Plenty of sodium is hidden in the deli case. Although you can choose some leaner cuts of deli meat on occasion (such as low-sodium turkey breast, baked ham, and lean roast beef), avoid cuts such as bologna, salami, loaf meats, and pepperoni, which are not only loaded in sodium, but also high in saturated fat. Check out our lunch ideas in Chapter 16 for fresh alternatives.

Buying great grains

You can find grain choices in a few aisles at the market: the bread aisle, the rice/pasta aisle, and the cereal aisle. Your goal is to introduce more whole grains into your diet in all three of these grain categories.

Read labels as you choose products to ensure that the products you choose are 100-percent whole grain. A whole-wheat bread should list "whole-wheat flour" as the first ingredient on the list. Check bread, pasta, and cereal labels for fiber and sugar content too. Include some cereals in your pantry that supply at least 3 grams of fiber and less than 8 grams of sugar. If you can find some with more than 5 grams of fiber and less sugar, so much the better.

It's still okay to consume some refined grains such as white rice, regular pasta, quick-cooking oats, or Italian or French bread. Just try to add some whole grains into the mix and be adventurous. Try something new like quinoa or couscous, which are very simple to prepare. See Chapter 12 for tasty grain recipes.

Chapter 6

Getting Smart in the Kitchen

In This Chapter

▶ Stocking your pantry, refrigerator, and freezer with essential staples

▶ Taking inventory of your kitchen cookware, utensils, and appliances

▶ Using kitchen gadgets and cooking techniques to up the flavor factor

*I*f you don't have what you need in the kitchen, you won't be able to throw a healthy meal together, and getting healthy food in your body is one of the top weapons in your hypertension-fighting arsenal (just see Chapter 2).

This chapter highlights some essential foods to keep in your pantry, fridge, and freezer (the three go-to spots for ingredients). We also list basic cookware pieces that you need to make the recipes in this book (or any cookbook, for that matter). In addition, we want to be sure you have some cooking basics down to make cooking a snap. Simple techniques, such as how to use different knives, make different cuts, zest a lemon, and grill and roast are all covered here. Be prepared to get prepared.

Thinking Like a Chef

You may barely feel like a short-order cook, let alone a chef, but getting some kitchen basics under your belt is a great way to enjoy cooking at home more often. This section helps you determine what you should have on hand almost all the time, so you can prepare a running grocery list. We also tell you about some helpful appliances and utensils that make the most of the time you spend in your kitchen. You'll find that when you master a few basic cooking techniques and have an organized kitchen, home cooking really isn't so hard after all.

Maintaining a well-stocked pantry, fridge, and freezer

One of your dietary goals is to stay away from most prepackaged and high-sodium processed foods by cooking more meals at home. Maintaining an organized pantry puts you closer to that goal. Having cooking staples on hand makes throwing together a meal much easier.

To stay organized, keep a running grocery list. In addition to the day-to-day items you plan to buy, add staples to your list as you run out of them. For instance, when you see that you're starting to get low on olive oil, add it to the list so you remember to buy a back-up bottle and don't risk running out.

Pantry staples

You want to have several recipe ingredients on hand at all times, including the following:

- ✔ **Canned goods:** Although canned vegetables are higher in sodium than fresh or frozen ones, it's okay to keep some on hand for a quick meal. After all, a home-cooked meal is still going to be lower in sodium than most any restaurant meal. Look for low-sodium versions of items like canned tomatoes, beans, broths, and vegetables.

- ✔ **Condiments:** Dijon and other fancy mustards, chutneys, chipotle peppers in adobo sauce, low-sodium soy sauce, capers, and salsa are good flavor boosters to use in recipes. Although these contain more sodium than fresh ingredients or salt-free spices, a small spoonful goes a long way in salad dressing or main dish recipes; that spoonful may be divided among 4 to 8 servings, so your sodium intake is minimal and the flavor is maxed.

- ✔ **Grains and rice:** Quinoa, wild rice, brown rice, Arborio rice, and jasmine rice are all good choices.

- ✔ **Nuts:** Walnuts, pecans, peanuts, hazelnuts, and slivered almonds are great to have on hand at all times. They make wonderful additions to salads, stir-fries, and vegetable dishes.

- ✔ **Olive oil:** You may even consider buying two varieties, a lighter version and an extra-virgin oil (which tends to cost more).

- ✔ **Pasta:** Couscous, penne, spaghetti varieties, bow ties, spirals, and orzo are good go-to's.

- ✔ **Pizza crusts:** Stock a couple of the ready-to-eat, whole-grain variety for quick last-minute meals.

- ✔ **Potatoes:** Sweet and Idaho (any white or yellow-fleshed) potatoes are pantry essentials.

✓ **Seasonings:** Chapter 4 reviews the variety of herbs, spices, and powders that you can use as salt substitutes. Keep these stocked.

✓ **Vegetable oil:** Maintain a stock of soybean, corn, or canola oil. You may also consider a small bottle of peanut oil, which is good for frying. Sesame oil is also great to have on hand — it lends great flavor to Asian-inspired dishes.

✓ **Vinegars:** Buy a couple varieties of vinegar for making marinades and salad dressings. We like keeping apple cider, rice, and balsamic vinegars on the shelf.

Refrigerator staples

Just like your pantry, your refrigerator begs to be consistently stocked with good stuff for your home cooking. Keep these staples in your fridge:

✓ **Apples and pears:** These fruits aren't just healthy snacks, but are also delicious added to salads or stuffing or cooked with pork or poultry.

✓ **Aromatic vegetables:** Onions, garlic, scallions, shallots, chives, and leeks add a distinct flavor and aroma to any food without the addition of sodium.

✓ **Bell peppers:** Like onions, peppers can be sliced or diced into meat, egg, or vegetable dishes or minced into appetizers.

✓ **Butter:** Although butter is higher in saturated fat than liquid vegetable oils, using small amounts in recipes offers great flavor. By reducing the butter in traditional recipes by ½ or ¾, you can achieve the desired flavor with minimal saturated fat.

✓ **Carrots:** Combine them with onions and celery and you have *mirepoix* (French for the combination of these vegetables sautéed), often used in soups, stews, stocks, or sauces.

✓ **Cheeses:** Although high in saturated fat and sodium, a little bit of cheese can go a long way. A small amount of Parmigiano-Reggiano, Gruyère, or mozzarella freshly grated into recipes provides a complex, sharp flavor.

✓ **Citrus fruits:** Lemon, lime, and orange rind help spark the flavor of many dishes. Organic fruit is recommended for the cleanest zest.

✓ **Cream cheese, lowfat (light or Neufchatel):** Cream cheese is useful for lightening up and thickening sauces and spreads.

✓ **Dried fruits:** Apricots, cranberries, and dried cherries are tasty additions to stuffing, salads, and vegetable dishes.

✓ **Eggs:** A staple for both baking and cooking, eggs can also star as the main dish for a quick and easy meal.

✓ **Margarine spread:** Part of a heart-healthy lifestyle, this form of margarine is not only great for spreading on breads, but can also be used in cooking.

- ✓ **Mayonnaise, lowfat:** This staple serves as a base for sauces and toppings.
- ✓ **Milk, 1-percent:** Yes, you can still enjoy creamy sauces by using lowfat milk.
- ✓ **Salad greens:** Whether it's green leaf lettuce, spinach, or Swiss chard, keeping some sort of green in the fridge is a good idea.
- ✓ **Tofu:** A good source of protein for vegetarians, you can use tofu in a breakfast shake or a quick and easy stir-fry.

Freezer staples

Using the freezer to stock up on key ingredients such as meats, poultry, fish, seafood, and vegetables helps save time. If you don't have to run to the grocery store, you can have dinner on the table in a flash. Keep your freezer filled with the following:

- ✓ **Berries:** Frozen strawberries, blueberries, and raspberries often come in handy.
- ✓ **Meats:** Buying a variety of meats and cleaning and prepping them before you freeze them can be a real timesaver when it comes to getting dinner on the table. Be sure to trim the skin from poultry and any visible fat from lean cuts of beef and pork before freezing. Store your meat in any or all of the following ways:
  - Package 2 to 6 portions (depending on the size of your household) in individual freezer bags.
  - Package extra-lean ground beef in 1-pound portions for use in recipes.
  - Cut some meat for use in recipes (strips for stir-fries and fajitas, cubes for stews and soups, and so forth).
- ✓ **Shrimp, precooked:** This item is easy to use and makes a quick meal; shrimp heat in just 2 to 3 minutes.
- ✓ **Vegetables:** Keep frozen corn, a bell pepper and onion mixture, spinach, and peas on hand to mix into recipes.

Brushing up on cookware

To be a successful cook, you have to have some good tools. Good cookware can make a big difference in your end results. If your kitchen isn't already equipped with a few great pots and pans, we encourage you to consider starting a "cookware fund." Look for items on sale or shop at name-brand discount stores to gradually pick up a few pieces.

Here are some must-haves to ensure cooking is a breeze:

- **Sauté pans with lids, 6- and 12-inch sizes:** Use these pans to sauté onions, mushrooms, peppers, garlic, eggs, and more, and to cook chicken or fish.

- **A large stockpot with a steamer insert:** A stockpot is great for cooking soups and big batches of sauces and for boiling water for pasta. You can cook corn on the cob and steam veggies in it, too.

- **Saucepans, 2- and 4-quart sizes:** These pans are good for sauces and small batches of pasta and rice.

- **Nonstick pans, 8- and 10-inch sizes:** These pans have the same uses as sauté pans, but because they're nonstick, you don't need to add much fat to them.

- **A large roasting pan:** A good roasting pan will last for years and is perfect for a large pork or beef roast, as well as a whole chicken or turkey. Look for one with a rack insert; this allows fat drippings from the meat to fall to the bottom of pan, and also allows you to easily remove the roast from the pan.

- **A Dutch oven with a lid:** This pot has a handle on each side and can be used on the stovetop or in the oven. It works well for roasts and stews.

- **A grill pan:** You can use this pan for anything you'd cook on an outdoor grill, such as hamburgers, chicken breasts, steaks, or fish.

- **A steel or plastic colander:** Both work well for draining pasta and rinsing or washing fruits and vegetables.

- **Two or three mixing bowls (small, medium, large):** These are useful for mixing dry ingredients, holding measured and chopped vegetables before cooking, and mixing up meatloaf, among other uses.

- **Glass baking dishes:** You'll find the 8-x-8-inch and 9-x-13-inch sizes come in handy. Glass pans holds up to high temperatures, are easy to clean, and don't warp like metal pans can.

- **Two cookie sheets:** Many times you may need to use two cookie sheets at once, or you may choose to include a smaller one and a larger one in your cupboard.

- **A round pizza pan or a pizza stone:** Either one works well for putting together quick pizzas like the ones in Chapter 21. The advantage of a large rectangular stone is that you can make one large pizza or two smaller round ones on it.

Investing in handy appliances

A few power tools for the kitchen can be very helpful. While some are essential, others may be considered a luxury. For instance, a food processor can save time and provide a very consistent end result (when you're chopping or dicing carrots, onions, or bell peppers, for instance), but a knife will often do the trick. On the other hand, food processors or blenders are very good at blending sauces, dips, and spreads.

Consider these appliances for your kitchen wish list:

- **Blender:** Look for one with at least four speeds. Blenders are often less expensive than food processors. They're also less powerful, but they can do a few of the same jobs. You can use a blender to make smoothies or puree soups.

- **Food processor:** You can purchase a full-size one or a miniature version. Food processors come with a variety of blade cuts, and can be used to dice, chop, slice, or shred. They can also be used to puree or blend foods like dips or soups.

- **Immersion blender:** This handy tool (also called a hand blender) is great for making smooth sauces, soups, salad dressings, spreads, or mixing up smoothies.

- **Slow cooker:** This appliance helps you get dinner on the table when you have a busy week. It's also great for keeping chili, soup, or appetizers warm for a buffet.

- **Stand mixer:** Invest in a heavy-duty mixer if you can, especially if you enjoy baking. A mid-range one will do the trick for basic mixing needs.

Getting a handle on the right knives

A good set of knives is a mainstay in a well-equipped kitchen. Even the most basic cooking methods require food to be sliced, chopped, or diced. Learning to use knives properly not only saves you time, but also saves your fingertips! Although many more types of knives are available than the ones you see listed here, we think these are the bare minimum you need to get through this cookbook and more:

- **Chef's knife, 8-inch:** Use it to chop, slice, or mince vegetables or herbs.
- **Paring knife:** Usually about 3 to 4 inches long, this knife is handy for trimming fruits or vegetables.

✔ **Santoku knife:** The blade of this Japanese-inspired knife works well for mincing and paper-thin slicing.

✔ **Serrated bread knife:** As its name implies, this type of knife is used for slicing bread.

✔ **Steak knives:** Use these knives to cut beef, pork, or chicken. They also work very well for slicing tomatoes!

✔ **Utility knife:** A utility knife is a mid-sized knife, usually from 5 to 7 inches long, that's easy to use for multiple purposes.

Figure 6-1 shows you what a chef's knife, a paring knife, and a serrated knife look like.

chef's knife

Figure 6-1:
Must-have
knives
for your
kitchen.

paring knife

serrated knife

Flip to Chapter 7 (and more specifically, Figure 7-1) to see some of our favorite ways to slice up your fruits and veggies.

Extracting the Most Flavor from Your Food

Low-sodium cooking doesn't have to be tasteless. Finding out how to use some simple tools and techniques allows you to immerse more flavors into your recipes. Salt often takes center stage as a seasoning in the modern palate, but there are many other ways to season and enhance flavor. As we talk about in Chapter 4, using a variety of herbs and spices can offer awesome flavor combinations to foods, and you won't miss the salt. Adding the handy items we tell you about in this section to your kitchen gadget drawer helps you bring out more flavors in your meals.

Demystifying kitchen gadgets

Some easy-to-use tools can be used to add salt-free flavorings to dishes. As you cook with less salt, you'll find that you want to add flavor in other ways. That is, instead of grabbing a large pinch of salt, you'll want to be armed with the knowledge of how to zest a lemon or julienne an onion! Using gadgets like the ones we explain here can help. Here are a few particularly good ones to consider adding to your collection.

The garlic press

A garlic press (see Figure 6-2) makes preparing garlic easy. Pick garlic cloves that are fresh and firm; avoid those with tight skin or green shoots. Put one clove at a time into the press — you don't even need to peel it! Hold the press over a small prep bowl or over the pan you're using and press the handles firmly together. Remove the skin and pulp from the press before inserting another clove. Some presses are self-cleaning, requiring only a quick rinse in hot soapy water; you simply open them, removed the crushed clove, and then close the empty press. A pronged end clamps and clears out any pulp.

Pressing garlic brings out the natural oils in garlic more than chopping or mincing does. Pressing garlic also offers a milder flavor than using whole cloves and allows the flavor to mingle throughout the dish.

Figure 6-2:
A garlic press brings out the most flavor in your garlic.

GARLIC PRESS

The zester, microplane, and grater

The zester and the microplane (see Figure 6-3) make getting consistent flakes of an ingredient safe and easy. A zester is a metal gadget with tiny holes that scrape slim strips from food. You can use a zester with citrus fruits (like lemons or oranges) as well as ginger, hard cheeses, and even chocolate. Zesters work best on firm foods. A microplane is a one-sided, handheld gadget. The microplane also comes in handy for zesting lemons or grating hard cheeses. It provides a fine grating, unlike the zester, which offers a thin strip.

TIP

To make lemon zest with a zester, hold a lemon firmly in one hand on a cutting board. With the other hand, scrape the lemon from top to bottom, at an angle, creating the zest. Rotate the lemon as the yellow zest is removed, until you have the desired amount.

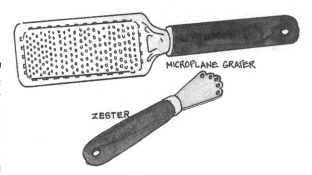

Figure 6-3:
Use a zester and a microplane to add flavor without salt.

Like the zester and microplane, graters provide a safe and quick way to produce a consistently cut ingredient. Grating foods like citrus, fresh ginger, nutmeg, or small amounts of cheese into recipes, can really add oomph to a dish.

Most box graters include four different cutting sides. You may automatically think of grated cheese when you think about grating, but the large-hole and single-cut sides of a box grater can also be used for other foods, such as potatoes, carrots, or cucumbers. Additionally, the large-holed side works well for grating soft vegetables for soups, and the single-cut side is good for slicing hard foods and comes in handy when you need a very large shaving (as for a garnish). The medium-sized holes make smaller shreds that work well for cheeses like cheddar, swiss, or colby. The tiny holes work well for harder cheeses, such as Romano or Parmigiano.

To grate cheese, stand the grater up on a clean cutting board, holding it with your nondominant hand. Grate the cheese by gently pushing it into the grater, from top to bottom. As the piece of cheese becomes small, be careful you don't grate a knuckle!

Spray the grater or zester with a light coating of vegetable cooking spray for easy cleanup. If food does stick, soak the grater in warm, soapy water before cleaning it thoroughly.

A mandoline

A *mandoline* is a tool that helps you produce uniform slices in high volume — no electricity required! Several types are available in specialty kitchen stores and chain department stores. More expensive ones may have prop-up legs and variable blades. You don't have to purchase the most expensive one, but look for one that includes three different blade adjustments, so you can vary the thickness of your slices. You can get a decent one for around $45. A hand guard is also a nice feature for safety purposes. Check out Figure 13-1 in Chapter 13 for an illustration of a mandoline.

Depending on the type you choose, you may have a number of slicing options: matchstick slices, waffle slices, crinkle cuts, or julienne strips. A mandoline is a great tool to have whenever you're preparing vegetables for stir-frys or any dish where you'd like to have uniform slices or strips. It's also great for creating thin strips of potatoes, which you can use in potato dishes or to encrust a piece of fish.

Using lowfat cooking techniques without sacrificing flavor

Microwaving, baking, frying, boiling — these are the cooking methods folks most often turn to for ease, convenience, or just because they're familiar and comfortable. But different cooking methods can actually give the same foods completely different flavors. You can replace salt's flavor-enhancing properties not only with new ingredients but also by trying new cooking methods.

The recipes in this book are bursting with colors and flavors, but they're also low in saturated fat. The cooking methods we use can be considered "light cooking" or "lowfat cooking" techniques. Using lowfat cooking methods doesn't mean sacrificing taste, but it does mean reducing calories. Because every tablespoon of oil provides over 100 calories, the recipes in this book use smaller amounts of oil per serving. Following are some flavorful ways to cook lowfat meals.

Grilling

Sure, lots of people grill; but do they really know how? It's up to you to choose charcoal or gas, but suffice it to say that grilling foods offers a whole new smoky flavor that you can't get by baking. For starters, consider these basics:

- Always use thawed meats on the grill.
- Trim excess fat. You want to do this regardless of the cooking method, but in the case of grilling, it helps keep flare-ups to a minimum.
- When using a sugar-based sauce, such as a traditional honey barbeque sauce, always brush it on toward the end, when the meat is almost completely cooked. Turn the heat to low and brush the sauce evenly on each side, turning the meat a few times.

- Grilling can result in dry, overcooked meat; to avoid this outcome, make sure your heat and timing are right. Don't walk away from the grill!

  For chicken, you generally want to use medium-low heat and grill the meat for at least 30 minutes.

Steaks cook more quickly and require only one turn. Grilling a one-inch cut steak or roast for about 4 minutes per side results in medium-rare doneness. (Keep in mind that your perfect red-meat portion is 4 to 6 ounces of a lean cut.)

✔ When grilling vegetables (such as eggplant, peppers, and squash), lightly brush them with oil before placing them on the grill so they won't stick. You can also place them on a grill pan or wrap them in aluminum foil.

Your oven broiler is essentially an upside-down grill. Use it as you would a grill, but remember that foods cook very quickly here. Keep a close eye on the door to avoid burning.

Roasting

Roasting is a dry-heat cooking method. Roasting, like baking, browns the surface of the food, offering a deep, complex flavor. Keep the following in mind:

✔ Roasting generally requires cooking the food uncovered in an oven set above 300 degrees.

✔ The higher the temperature, the more pronounced the browning and/or caramelization of the food.

✔ Roasted vegetables have a completely different taste and texture compared to steamed vegetables. Roasting is a great way to vary the flavor of your vegetable side dishes. Adding roasted vegetables to a recipe also adds depth to the recipe.

Braising

Braising involves first browning food in a pan, and then finishing it in a covered pot with liquid. Although vegetables can be braised, this method is most often used with meats. Recipes like stews utilize the braising technique. It's a great way to make the most of less tender cuts of meats. Just follow these steps:

1. **Season the meat.**

   You can use fresh or dried herbs, cracked pepper, or a very small pinch of salt (⅛ teaspoon per roast).

2. **Heat 1 to 2 tablespoons of oil in a Dutch oven.**

3. **Sear the meat on all sides, until each side is nicely browned.**

4. **Deglaze the pan.**

   Pour a small amount of liquid (wine or low-sodium stock) into the pan and scrape any bits that are stuck to the bottom.

5. **Add 1 cup of liquid to the pan.**

   You can use water, wine, or low-sodium stock or broth.

6. **Cover and cook over low heat for about 2–3 hours.**

   You can do the cooking on the stovetop or in a preheated 325-degree oven. Cook about 2 to 3 hours until tender or according to your recipe's directions.

Sautéing

Sautéing is a must-have skill for any cook, including beginners. Sautéing is a dry-heat method that's done in a sauté pan (see the section "Brushing up on cookware and utensils") and is often used for vegetables. Using a nonstick pan helps reduce the amount of added fat, although the sauté method does require some fat. Here are a few tips to help you master sautéing in no time:

✔ You need only 1 or 2 teaspoons of fat to provide flavor when using a nonstick pan. You'll see that some of our recipes may use butter, olive oil, or other vegetable oil. The key point: Use only small amounts of fat.

✔ Heat the oil quickly to a high temperature. The fat should move very quickly around the pan when you turn it (the oil almost looks as though it's not touching the pan). If the oil and pan aren't hot enough, the vegetables won't cook quickly and will lose too much water before they're cooked thoroughly.

✔ Add your vegetables when the oil is hot and keep them moving from the start with a wooden spoon. For the most part, vegetables take less than five minutes to sauté.

✔ Lean cuts of meat and fish can also be sautéed. Place small fillets of fish or meat into a hot pan and cook for about 3 to 4 minutes per side until brown.

Chapter 7

Adding Beneficial Foods to Your Diet

In This Chapter

▶ Finding out why a colorful diet matters

▶ Getting your quota of fruits and veggies (and enjoying them!)

▶ Eating enough potassium and calcium

So you know you need to lower your blood pressure, and you know the DASH diet is a great way to do it (flip to Chapter 2 if you're still not convinced). But you may not know just how easy it is to add hypertension-helpful foods to your daily life.

In this chapter, we tell you why and how certain foods impact your health in such a positive way. In addition, we offer some how-to info for meeting the fruit, vegetable, and mineral (specifically, potassium and calcium) goals of DASH.

The Rainbow Effect: Appreciating Phytochemicals

Food comes in every color of the rainbow: Red, orange, yellow, green, blue, and violet. Blue food, you say? Yes, sir, and we're not talking cotton candy. Believe it or not, there are naturally occurring foods that offer every spectrum of the rainbow to your diet. And adding these foods to your diet automatically gives you important nutrients called *phytochemicals*. Scientists are still figuring out all the benefits of a phytochemical-rich diet, but suffice it to say, eating plant foods with these nutrients promotes heart health, helps you retain healthy vision, likely reduces some cancer risk, and even offers anti-aging perks. As you add the rainbow to your diet, consider your next pot of gold to be all-around better health and a younger look and feel. How awesome is that?

Seeing what phytochemicals can do

Several important phytochemicals are present in plant foods. In addition to serving all the purposes listed in the preceding paragraph, many phytochemicals (specifically plant sterols, flavonoids, and sulfur-containing compounds) found in fruits and veggies also act as antioxidants in the body. *Antioxidants* are special substances that protect your body's cells from *free radicals,* cells that may lead to disease and cancer. So you want to eat as many phytochemicals as you can! A few of the best phytochemicals include

- **Carotenoids:** Contained primarily in red and orange foods (but also in some green foods), carotenoids help promote healthy vision and may reduce cancer risk. Lycopene is an example of a carotenoid found in red foods.
- **Flavonones:** Found in citrus fruits and juices, they can lower your risk of gastrointestinal cancer.
- **Flavonols:** Found in red foods like apples, berries, red grapes, and red wine, and also in yellow and green foods such as yellow onions, kale, and broccoli, flavonols promote heart health and may help reduce stroke risk. Flavonols are also present in chocolate and teas.
- **Lutein:** Green and orange foods, including egg yolks, mangos, peaches, sweet potatoes, spinach, romaine lettuce, honeydew, pears, and avocados, contain the antioxidant lutein.
- **Anthocyanins:** Look to blue and purple foods for anthocyanins, which are flavonoids. They've been shown to help with memory and urinary tract health, and they have anti-aging benefits.
- **Allicin:** This sulfur-containing compound is found in garlic and onions, and may be important to heart health due to its antiplatelet (anti-blood-clotting) properties.
- **Indoles/isothoicyanates:** Found in green and white cruciferous vegetables, such as broccoli, cabbage, cauliflower, and kale, they have anti-cancer qualities.
- **Phytosterols:** Whole grains, legumes, and nuts contain phytosterols, which lower cholesterol.

Matching the color with the food

Pop quiz: Which phytochemical promotes healthy vision? Just kidding. You don't really have to remember all those scientific names for various phyto-chemicals. We're just offering up some proof for why it's important to choose more deep-colored plant foods in a variety of colors every week as you work toward getting 5 to 10 servings of fruits and veggies daily. Go ahead; pick out some of your favorites in each color:

- **Red:** Cherries, cranberries, pomegranate, red/pink grapefruit, red grapes, watermelon, beets, red onions, red peppers, red potatoes, rhubarb, and tomatoes

- **Orange and deep yellow:** Apricots, cantaloupe, grapefruit, mangoes, papayas, peaches, pineapples, prunes, carrots, yellow bell peppers, yellow corn, acorn and summer squash, and sweet potatoes

- **Green:** Avocados, apples, grapes, honeydew, kiwi, limes, asparagus, broccoli, green beans, green bell peppers, and especially leafy greens (such as kale, collards, turnip greens, and spinach)

- **Purple and blue:** Blackberries, blueberries, cranberries, plums, concord grape juice, eggplant, purple cabbage, and purple-fleshed potatoes

- **White, tan, and brown:** Bananas, brown pears, dates, white peaches, cauliflower, jicama, mushrooms, parsnips, turnips, white-fleshed potatoes, white corn, nuts, and legumes

 Make sure you add more variety to your diet and eat a few foods from each color group. For example, having a banana every day or putting red tomatoes on your sandwich is great, but you won't be getting the maximum nutritional value from your food if you don't also eat some yellow, green, and bluish foods, too.

Sneaking Fruits and Veggies into Every Meal

Adding more color to your diet is a win-win situation (just read the section "Seeing what phytochemicals can do" for all the pros), but when it comes down to it, eating healthy can seem easier said than done. Have no fear; we have easy suggestions to help you meet your goals of adding more fruits and veggies to every meal! Even if vegetables are on your "don't like it" list or eating spinach at breakfast seems completely weird to you, open your mind to some of our sneaky healthy-eating suggestions in this section and give fruits and veggies another chance.

The first strategy for adding more colorful plant foods to your diet is making sure you have them available. Face it — you won't eat right if all you have in the fridge is junk food. Adding fruits and vegetables to your weekly shopping list is a must. Having easy access to them in the refrigerator is also helpful. When you purchase vegetables, store them in a crisper bin in the refrigerator; they'll last longer and will all be in one place where you can easily grab them. The same goes for fruit: Keep it stored in a fruit bin, and keep fruits that are more likely to perish (bananas, berries) on your running grocery list so you always have them on hand.

Putting your phytochemicals where your mouth is

We're willing to bet that some of our readers have purchased a bag of spinach only to throw it away several days later when they noticed the black, gooey contents of the bag. Many people have good intentions but forget to prepare the healthy produce they purchase. Make an effort to prevent this from happening! Although you may find it easier to add fruit to your breakfast or veggies to your dinner, start thinking out of the box and never waste valuable food again. Here are some ideas:

✔ Cook spinach the night you bring it home, even if you don't eat it then. Cooked spinach lasts a few more days in the refrigerator and is easy to reheat in a microwave or saucepan.

  Spinach only takes about five minutes to cook. Bring a large pot of water to a boil, add the spinach, cover, let simmer for 3 minutes, and drain.

✔ Keep bananas on the counter where you can see them and easily grab one on the go. Eat one each day, before they go brown.

✔ Keep some frozen fruit in the freezer for a quick and economical fruit choice. Hopefully, you'll choose this for a snack instead of the salt-ridden pizza rolls that may have once inhabited that shelf.

✔ Wash and slice strawberries and keep them in a bowl, front and center, on a refrigerator shelf.

✔ Peel and slice your melon and place it in an airtight container in the fridge.

✔ Keep dried fruits like apricots, raisins, and cranberries on a prime pantry shelf for a quick snack or to add to salads and other recipes. Put the chips and croutons out of sight.

✔ Slice or chop vegetables the day you buy them and store them in zipper bags. Vegetables that are prepped are easier to grab and eat or cook with.

  Wash bell peppers, slicing some into thin matchstick strips and dicing others (see the section "Slicing up new shapes"). Bag them separately. Wash broccoli or cauliflower and cut it into small flowerettes. If you're really in a time crunch, purchase some prechopped vegetables. The extra expense is worth a healthy dinner at home.

Keeping fruits and veggies visible and ready for consumption, either on your kitchen counter or in your refrigerator, allows you to easily throw together some quick meals during the week. We present you with some of our favorite tips for sneaking fruits and veggies into meals when you least expect them:

- Add 2 tablespoons of cooked spinach to 2–3 eggs (use no more than 2 yolks and up to 4 whites) to make a quick spinach omelet.

- Dip your eggs in salsa or fill a wheat tortilla with scrambled eggs, salsa, and spinach leaves for a nutrient-packed breakfast wrap.

- Add sliced bananas or a handful of fresh or frozen blueberries to your oatmeal or ready-to-eat cereal.

- Spread peanut butter lightly onto whole-wheat toast and top with sliced bananas.

- Make a yogurt parfait with nonfat vanilla yogurt and fresh fruit.

- Add sliced tomatoes and fresh baby spinach leaves to your sandwich. Try thinly sliced bell peppers or roasted peppers on a sandwich, too.

- Use leftover brown rice to make a quick salad to pack for lunch the following day. Add baby spinach, dried cranberries, and sliced apples and carrots to the rice. Toss with 1 tablespoon of vinaigrette dressing.

- Use carrots and pepper strips instead of crackers or pretzels for dipping. Substitute hummus for cheese as a snack to go with the vegetables and get two vegetables in one (hummus is made from chickpeas).

- Add tomato-based salsa to rice for a quick side dish packed with lycopene.

- Add a side salad to your business lunch. Side salads usually include more vegetables and are always lower in calories than Caesar salads, which really aren't a great choice due to all the croutons, dressing, and cheese.

- Mix up a fruit smoothie for breakfast or for an after-work snack while you're getting dinner together. Take 1 cup of frozen or fresh berries or a banana, and puree in a blender with 4 to 8 ounces of lowfat milk and 3 ice cubes.

- Use more citrus. Using zest from oranges, lemons, or limes really punches up the flavor of a dish. Using the juice from an orange or lemon also offers great flavor to salad vinaigrettes.

Taking shape and size into account

Are you still thinking to yourself: "But I don't like vegetables?" We think one way to make a vegetable more appealing is to cut it into a different shape or size. Whether you eat your vegetables raw or cooked, different shapes and sizes offer different textures as well as a different look. Because we often "eat with our eyes," presenting veggies in a new way can automatically make a dish look more delicious, even before it hits your mouth.

Cutting fruits and vegetables into different shapes and sizes can also make them very appealing to children. When kids see a vegetable cut in a different way, they may view it differently and be more likely to try it.

If you have children, involve them in some of the food prep. You don't want to allow young children to use knives for cutting, but they can place precut fruits and veggies into bowls and help wash the produce in a sink filled with clean water. You can even make things fun by pretending to be on a cooking show, with your child acting as your assistant.

Slicing up new shapes

You can slice and dice vegetables in many ways, but the cuts in Figure 7-1 arm you with some basic shapes that can give your dishes a new look and texture. You don't have to be a chef to cut these shapes.

- ✔ **Chopping** works great for vegetables in salads, stir-frys, or soups.

- ✔ **Cubing** is a larger square cut. It works well for preparing meats and vegetables for stews or cubing fruits for salad. We like cubing a variety of veggies for roasting, too.

- ✔ **Dicing** results in small, uniform cubes of food. A large dice may be about ¾-inch square, whereas a small dice may be ¼-inch square. The idea is to dice the food to a standard size, depending on how big or small you want the bites to be.

- ✔ **Shredding** is cutting very thin, long strips of food. Shred vegetables such as cabbage for slaws or stir-frys. You can also shred carrots for salad or potatoes.

- ✔ **Mincing** requires a very fine chop. A chef's knife (see Chapter 6) is a good mincing knife. After chopping the vegetable, continue to go over it until it's cut into very fine pieces.

- ✔ **Slicing** simply involves cutting through an entire vegetable or meat, resulting in larger pieces than the dicing or chopping methods. A sliced fresh tomato is generally more appealing on a sandwich, for instance, than a diced tomato. Slices can be as thin or as thick as you like. You can slice any vegetable or meat, a technique that works well for stir-frys.

- ✔ **Cutting a matchstick** results in a thin slice about 2–3 inches long and ¼-inch wide, resembling a wooden matchstick. Or, you can cut a julienne, which is similar to a matchstick cut, but thinner, about ⅛ inch. Julienne or matchstick shapes can offer a whole new texture and flavor to cooked vegetables (not to mention how pretty they look in a bowl or on a plate). Using this cutting technique also allows for quicker cooking time.

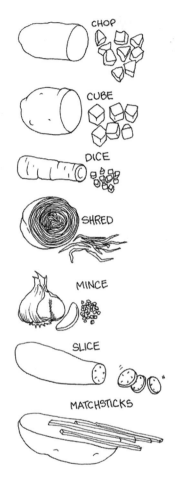

CHOP

CUBE

DICE

SHRED

MINCE

SLICE

MATCHSTICKS

Figure 7-1:
Use a chef's
knife or
mandolin to
create these
shapes.

TIP

For a quick and healthy side dish, cut carrots, zucchini, and red peppers into julienne strips. Heat 1 teaspoon of oil in an 8-inch nonstick skillet. Add the vegetables and stir-fry them until tender, about 4 to 5 minutes.

TIP

After you decide which cut you prefer, get out your chef's knife (see Chapter 6 for an illustration) to make it happen. A chef's knife (or French knife) is one of the most important knives to have in your kitchen. Chef's knives come in sizes generally ranging from 8 to 12 inches. Choose a good knife that feels comfortable in your hand. Grip the handle, using your dominant hand. Your thumb and forefinger should be opposite each other, bracing the top of the handle (just up to the bottom of the blade). Hold the vegetable with your nondominant hand, keeping your fingers curled in a claw-like grip. Cut using a gentle, up and down, rocking motion, while keeping the tip of the knife on the board. When cutting round foods like onions or potatoes, cut them in half first; then lay the flat end on the cutting board in order to keep the food from moving as you cut.

Size matters

You may find that eating vegetables and fruits in smaller pieces is more appealing. The next time you make a salad or a vegetable soup, try using a small dice instead of chunks for the veggies and chicken. And give downsizing your fruits a try; some people simply prefer nibbling on apple slices to eating a whole apple to the core. You can either purchase an apple slicer (a round, metal apparatus that looks like a wheel and cuts through the apple, leaving the core in the middle and slicing around it), or simply use a knife to cut apples or pears into thin slices. Oranges can be cut into sections (who can resist the good ol' "orange teeth" routine?), and grapes are more pleasing when sliced in half for salads. Diced apples are preferable to large chunks in green salads and Waldorf-type salads.

Bringing on the Minerals

When you suffer from hypertension, the two most important minerals you can add to your diet are potassium and calcium. In this section, we bring to your attention some of the foods that give you the biggest bang for your buck; that is, the most potassium or calcium you can get while staying in a healthy calorie range.

And as long as you're adding phytochemicals and potassium and calcium to your life, remember that you want to eat plenty of fiber to keep your appetite at bay. Head to Chapter 2 or Chapter 12 for more on which grains are best.

Eating plenty of potassium

Potassium is abundant in fruits and vegetables, which is one reason the DASH diet promotes getting four to five servings of each into your day. Whereas salt can raise blood pressure, potassium can lower it. Fruits and vegetables contain large amounts of potassium, which is why they're so important to the DASH diet. Nuts, especially almonds, provide potassium, too, so feel free to add them to your daily snack plan (just make sure you get the unsalted variety!).

Potassium may also reduce your body's so-called salt sensitivity by reducing blood pressure response to dietary sodium. The Institute of Medicine's Food and Nutrition Board has set the Adequate Intake (AI) of potassium at 4,700 milligrams (mg) daily for adults, but the average adult consumes only about 49 percent of the AI daily. It's a good idea to try to get all 4,700 mg in, because the Dietary Reference Intakes (DRI) Committee says that this level should help maintain lower blood pressure levels, reduce the adverse effects of sodium chloride (salt) on blood pressure, and reduce the risk of recurrent kidney stones.

People with kidney disease often need to limit potassium, not increase it. Speak with your doctor about any dietary changes you make.

So where do you get all this potassium? It's really pretty easy. Start by slicing a banana into your cereal, sprinkling raisins over your oatmeal, topping your grilled chicken with roasted bell peppers, or adding any other fruits and veggies to your meals. You get about 1,000 mg of potassium from the bread and grain products you eat daily (about six to ten servings). Milk supplies about 380 mg per cup, and yogurt supplies about 530 mg per cup. So between your grain and milk food groups, you should get more than 2,000 mg of potassium. The other 2,700 mg should come from fruits and vegetables. A sweet potato contributes almost 700 mg and ¼ cup of dried apricots provides almost 400 mg. So if you're meeting your DASH guideline to eat eight to ten servings of fruits and veggies a day, you'll have no problem meeting the potassium needs of your diet.

Some fruits and veggies contribute more potassium than others. Fruits that are high in potassium (providing more than 200 milligrams per serving) include:

- ✔ Asparagus
- ✔ Avocado
- ✔ Bananas
- ✔ Brussels sprouts
- ✔ Cantaloupe and honeydew melon
- ✔ Kiwi fruit
- ✔ Mango
- ✔ Mushrooms
- ✔ Oranges, grapefruit
- ✔ Papaya
- ✔ Pears
- ✔ Potatoes (white and yellow)
- ✔ Pumpkin
- ✔ Raisins, dried apricots
- ✔ Sweet potatoes
- ✔ Tomatoes

The following fruits and vegetables offer up a medium amount of potassium (100–200 milligrams potassium per serving):

- ✔ Apples
- ✔ Broccoli
- ✔ Cauliflower
- ✔ Corn
- ✔ Green beans
- ✔ Peaches
- ✔ Peas
- ✔ Strawberries
- ✔ Watermelon

These fruits and vegetables are on the low side in terms of potassium (containing less than 100 milligrams):

- ✔ Applesauce
- ✔ Blueberries
- ✔ Cucumbers
- ✔ Grapes
- ✔ Iceburg lettuce
- ✔ Mandarin oranges

Incorporating a wide variety of fruits and vegetables into your snacks and meals is a sure way to get the potassium you need. In addition, a 3-ounce serving of meat or fish contributes 200–300 milligrams of potassium, and a half cup of beans can provide a whopping 400 milligrams. So you see, eating a balanced diet from the five food groups, in lieu of junk food, surely meets your potassium needs for lowering blood pressure.

Our recipes incorporate lots of ways to add them into your diet in easy, flavorful ways to make reaching this goal enjoyable. For instance, adding bell peppers into a dish adds not just flavor, but potassium too! Instead of a plain egg, make an omelet with potassium-loaded spinach, mushrooms, and onions.

Milking the calcium cow

You may not think about calcium when it comes to high blood pressure, but calcium is an important mineral in heart health. Several studies have concluded that intake of nonfat or lowfat dairy products is associated with reduced risk for diabetes, hypertension, and cardiovascular events. Other studies have shown that calcium can reduce LDL (bad cholesterol) and increase HDL (good cholesterol). In addition, adequate calcium throughout life is important to bone health.

It's important to note that adequate calcium is the goal, not oversupplementation. Adults ages 19–50 need about 1,000 milligrams of calcium daily. After age 51, the National Institutes of Health recommends females up their intake to 1,200 mg daily, whereas most sources say men can maintain 1,000 mg.

Nonfat and lowfat dairy products are the way to go to meet your daily calcium needs. Check out Table 7-1 to see which common foods have the most calcium for the fewest calories. The foods in the table are listed from highest to lowest in terms of their calcium content.

Table 7-1	Calcium and Calories in Common Foods		
Food	*Amount*	*Calcium (mg)*	*Calories*
Yogurt, plain, lowfat	8 ounces	415	155
Cheddar cheese	1.5 ounces	306	180
Milk, 1%	8 ounces	302	100
Yogurt, fruit, lowfat	8 ounces	300	240
Cottage cheese, 1% fat	1 cup	138	160
Spinach, cooked	½ cup	120	40
Frozen yogurt, soft-serve	½ cup	103	120
Kale	1 cup	94	35
Ice cream, vanilla	½ cup	85	200
Broccoli	½ cup	21	25

So if your calcium intake should be 1,000 milligrams per day, perhaps you can try consuming a glass of 1-percent milk with breakfast, a half cup of yogurt mid-morning, a scoop of cottage cheese on your salad at lunch, a side of spinach with dinner, and a scoop of frozen yogurt for dessert.

If you don't enjoy plain milk, it's okay to add some flavoring. Adding 1 to 2 teaspoons of chocolate syrup only adds about 35 calories and still delivers all the calcium in the milk. You can also make an iced mocha or tea drink. Add 4 ounces of nonfat milk to 4 ounces of plain coffee or brewed tea. Shake with ice and enjoy.

Most experts agree that getting your calcium from your diet is your best bet, but you can check with your doctor to see whether supplements are a good option for you. Calcium supplements fall into two categories: calcium carbonate and calcium citrate. Calcium citrate works well for people with reflux who have reduced stomach acid due to taking acid-blockers, whereas calcium carbonate is readily available, well-absorbed, and generally less expensive.

When checking out various supplements, look at the amount of elemental calcium on the Nutrition Facts label. For instance, a 500-milligram calcium carbonate pill may only provide 200 milligrams of elemental calcium (the pill itself isn't pure calcium and only supplies 40% calcium by weight; calcium citrate supplies only about 20 percent calcium by weight). In general, look for the USP seal on a supplement (dietary supplements are poorly regulated, so having the United States Pharmacopeia approval assures quality and standards).

It's probably not necessary to take a supplement that promises more than 100 percent of the daily requirements. Research has suggested that issues may be inherent in oversupplementing with calcium. Keep in mind that a calcium pill is a *supplement* to the dietary calcium you ingest. Check with your doctor before taking any supplements.

Chapter 8

Saving Your Sanity and Health: Low-Stress Meal Planning

In This Chapter

▶ Taking steps now to save time later

▶ Conquering cooking on busy weeknights

▶ Making entertaining a breeze

*I*f you don't have a plan for how you're going to eat your meals according to the DASH plan, falling off the wagon and turning to fast, unhealthy staples is pretty likely. Having a plan saves you the stress of worrying about what to cook, and it means that you'll be eating what's really good for you and not just what's convenient.

One key to low-stress meal planning is being prepared. Making use of your freezer ensures that you have the right ingredients on hand to put together a healthy, enjoyable meal; having some helpful special-occasion menus based on the recipes in this book helps, too. In this chapter, you see how to incorporate the DASH diet into any meal of the day.

One of the great things about cooking your own food is sharing it with others, especially family and close friends. All the meal planning in this chapter not only results in an improved diet for better health, but an enjoyable time with friends and family. After all, the host or hostess deserves to have a good time too!

Saving Time 101: Prepping and Freezing

By getting food ready to use before you store it in your refrigerator, you'll save time later. Chapter 6 makes you aware of what foods to keep in your kitchen; in this chapter, you figure out how to properly prep and freeze those staples to simplify cooking even further.

Spending 30 minutes or so to prep some foods after you bring home your groceries can save you an hour or more when it comes time to cook. Plus, having foods frozen and ready for recipes saves you even more time. When you implement time-saving techniques like prepping and freezing, you're more likely to stay on board with your hypertension diet.

In addition to saving lots of time by prepping and freezing, add one more good habit: Clean as you go. Keep a bowl in your kitchen sink to collect all the scraps and food garbage, saving trips to the garbage can. Empty the bowl when you finish cooking.

Prepping your groceries

A little bit of prep goes a long way, as does cooking a little extra of staple foods. When you work ahead, ingredients become much easier to toss into your recipes on busy nights.

Try these techniques for cutting down on the amount of time you spend each day preparing to cook:

- Wash and core fresh bell peppers when you know you'll be using them within two days. Remove the core, stem, and seeds, and store them in a zipper storage bag in the vegetable bin of your refrigerator. When you need them, you can simply slice or dice them per your recipe.

- Chop a medium-sized onion and store it in either a zipper storage bag or an airtight container in the vegetable drawer of your refrigerator for up to seven to ten days. Having chopped onions on hand saves time on recipes that call for them. If the recipe requires minced onions, you can easily chop them further.

- Take a few minutes in the morning to prep some of the food you plan to have for dinner that night. Chop vegetables and fruit, and make a marinade or salad dressing as needed. Store them in the refrigerator to save time later when you prepare the meal.

- Cook a little extra of staples like meats, veggies, and grains; you can use these in meals over the next couple days. For example, if you're preparing a grilled chicken recipe, grill two extra boneless breasts to save for dinner in a day or two. You'll have cooked chicken ready to go. Make use of our tips for using leftovers and putting quick meals together in Chapters 16 and 20.

- Have vegetables ready for salad fixings or a veggie tray. Clean and slice cucumbers, bell peppers, carrots, and celery so they're ready to munch on before dinner or to use in a salad recipe. Place them in airtight containers or zipper storage bags.

Only you can prevent foodborne illness

Salmonella is a bacterium that lives on food and can make you sick. If you don't follow hygienic kitchen practices, salmonella and other forms of foodborne bacteria can creep onto your table. Make sure you always do the following:

✔ Keep your hands and all surface areas clean.

✔ Designate one cutting board for meat preparation (we prefer plastic over wood) and another for vegetables and dry foods.

✔ Never use a cutting board you've cut raw meat on for anything else before thoroughly washing it.

✔ Don't use the same knife for slicing meat and then veggies. Use a separate knife or thoroughly clean between uses.

✔ Keep foods at the proper temperature. Keep hot foods hot and cold foods cold. Having a buffet? Only hold food for less than 2 hours if it's not refrigerated or kept at the proper temperature.

Freezing for the future

You can use your freezer to help you keep recipe items in stock, saving you additional or more frequent trips to the grocery store. Foods such as meats, fish, poultry, fresh herbs, and vegetables can all be purchased fresh and frozen for later use. When you prepare a homemade tomato, pesto, or other sauce you can also divide and freeze it in sealed, freezer-safe containers.

Purchasing fresh meats, fish, and poultry for same-day preparation is great, but few people's schedules allow for that. Freezing meats is an alternative that can still result in a good product. Most meats can be frozen for up to three months.

Rather than simply throwing the store-bought package straight into the freezer, we recommend opening the package, trimming extra skin or fat, and using zipper bags to prevent freezer burn. Zipper freezer bags are easy to use and come in different sizes, allowing you to divide meats into smaller or larger packages, depending on the number of people you'll be cooking for or the specifications of a given recipe. Be sure to label and date the bags before you place them in the freezer.

To prevent bacterial contamination, don't thaw meats on the counter. Defrost meat, fish, or poultry in either the refrigerator or the microwave, using the defrost function. When defrosting in the refrigerator, be sure the meat is in a sealed bag or container and put it on a bottom shelf to minimize leaks and the chances of contaminating other foods.

Fresh poultry

Poultry pieces with the bones in and the skin on often cost less than their boneless, skinless counterparts. Boning takes some skill and time, but removing the skin is an easy task. After you remove the skin, rinse the pieces under cold water, pat them dry, and freeze them in freezer bags. You can fit two portions in a quart-sized bag or four to six portions in a gallon-sized bag.

To facilitate removing one or two pieces at a time from the freezer, don't place pieces on top of one another when you freeze them, and try to leave a little space between the pieces.

Large boneless chicken breasts may be cut into several smaller pieces. Some breasts are thick enough to cut in half lengthwise, and then again crosswise, making thinner, smaller pieces. Boneless breast meat can also be cut into strips for stir-frys or chunks for chilis, stews, or salads. Thin pieces of boneless breast work well on the grill because they cook more quickly and stay juicier.

Fresh pork or beef

Lean is the key to healthy meats. Trim all visible fat from roasts or steaks before freezing.

Individual steaks can be frozen in a single layer in a freezer bag. You may purchase one large steak at the grocer, but keep in mind that your diet for hypertension requires you to limit the amount of beef and pork you eat. To that end, cut beef and pork steaks or chops into 4- to 6-ounce portions before you freeze them.

Use a large, lean cut, such as beef sirloin, to make strips for stir-frys. Freeze the strips in a single layer in quart-sized freezer bags.

Fish and seafood

You can freeze fillets whole or cut them into 6-ounce portions (about 2–3 inches apiece) before freezing. Use zipper freezer bags that are sized accordingly.

Easier yet, purchase prefrozen fish fillets, shrimp, or scallops. You can find a variety of fish in the seafood freezer section of your grocery store. Fillets are flash-frozen so you can easily take them out of the bag one at a time. Look for weekly sales and stock up.

Fresh vegetables

When vegetables are in season or on sale, you may consider purchasing extras and freezing them for later. When you freeze fresh vegetables, you'll find that they're more flavorful than store-bought frozen veggies. You can even freeze leftover vegetables. For instance, if you steam a batch of fresh peas and have a little bit leftover, place them in a zippered freezer bag and freeze them for use in another recipe. Fresh corn on the cob freezes well also. You can blanch it in boiling water for 3 minutes and then freeze it, or you can cut cooked corn off the cob and freeze it for another recipe in the future.

When freezing any vegetable, blanch it first. To blanch, bring a gallon of water to a boil. Wash and trim fresh vegetables. You can either boil the vegetables in the water or steam them using a steaming basket. Place the vegetables into the steamer or pot and steam or boil them for four to six minutes (steaming usually takes a minute longer, and some veggies will take less time). Plunge the vegetables into ice water immediately or place them in a colander and run cold water over them for a few minutes. Drain well, and then pack them into zippered freezer bags. The quality of the frozen vegetable will be as good as the fresh one.

Out of that ingredient? Keep calm and carry on

Busy people can't run to the store every time they're missing one ingredient in a recipe. If you're cooking according to a recipe and you discover that you're missing an ingredient, don't throw in the towel just yet.

Generally speaking, if you're *baking,* you need to follow a recipe exactly, but when you're

cooking, you have some wiggle room. In most cases, these substitutions can go both ways; in other words, if a recipe calls for yogurt and you only have lowfat sour cream in the fridge, you can make that substitution too.

The next time you're out of something, consider the following substitutions.

Out of This?	*Use This Instead*
Mayonnaise	1 cup plain yogurt + 1 teaspoon Dijon mustard
Lowfat sour cream	Plain lowfat yogurt
1 cup buttermilk	1 cup nonfat milk + 1 tablespoon vinegar
1 whole egg	2 egg whites or ¼ cup commercial egg whites
1 teaspoon baking powder	⅓ teaspoon baking soda + ½ teaspoon cream of tartar
1 teaspoon lemon juice	1 teaspoon white vinegar
1 glove garlic	⅛ teaspoon garlic powder
Boneless chicken breast	Boneless chicken thighs or bone-in breast
Balsamic vinegar	Red wine vinegar
Shallots	White, red, or yellow onions (usually minced)
Dried cranberries	Chopped dried apricots or raisins
Chickpeas	White beans or great Northern beans
1 tablespoon fresh herbs	1 teaspoon dried herbs

Note: If you don't have a specific herb that a recipe calls for, you can really substitute any favorite herb that you do have on hand. The substitution will change the flavor, but if you like it, use it.

You can freeze fresh herbs or peppers without blanching. Because herbs are expensive but offer awesome flavor to recipes, freezing them is a great idea. You may only need a few sprigs for a recipe but many come in larger packages. Place any leftover herb into a freezer bag and just pop it into the freezer for later use. Peppers can easily be frozen also. Simply wash the pepper, cut off the top, and remove the seeds and pulp; then place it into a freezer bag and freeze. Frozen vegetables will keep up to a year.

Putting Good Food on the Table with Ease

Whether you're thinking ahead to your usual weeknights or a big holiday celebration, planning your meal or buffet around the basic food groups and the DASH lifestyle is your goal. Using the dietary goals of DASH (more fruits and vegetables, lean meats, whole grains, lowfat dairy) and MyPlate (see Chapter 2), you can create a balanced meal that is both nutritious and delicious.

Use the MyPlate graphic as a checklist, asking yourself these questions:

- ✔ Am I including enough fruits and vegetables to cover half a plate?
- ✔ Am I including enough lean protein to allow for a 4-ounce portion per person (covering the protein section of the plate)?
- ✔ Am I including enough whole grain to allow for one serving (about ½ cup) per person?

If you can answer yes to these questions, you have yourself a well-balanced meal.

When putting together your menu for any event or meal, consider not only the food groups but also the color combinations of foods. A plate that includes three to four colors is more interesting than one that's brown and white, for instance. In addition to being more pleasing to the eye, a variety of color also ensures a broad source of nutrients and those important phytochemicals (see Chapter 7).

Read through a recipe at least twice before you begin preparing it. Getting the order of doing things straight in your head helps make the process quicker and simpler. Also, set out all the ingredients on the counter before you get started, along with any utensils and cookware you'll need.

Eating well on busy weekdays

Putting together healthy weekday meals is a snap when you have a plan. Use these ideas to put together easy meals that use one recipe and take a few healthy shortcuts.

When it comes to eating your veggies, using bagged lettuce, store-bought chopped veggies, or frozen veggies is better than eating no vegetables at all.

Following are a few weekday meals you can put together in a flash using some of the recipes in this book along with a few shortcuts:

- ✔ When you don't have time for breakfast in the morning, whip up a quick smoothie using 4–6 ounces of plain lowfat Greek yogurt, 2 ounces of fruit juice, and 1 banana or ½ cup of your favorite fruit. Whirl in the blender, pour into a travel cup, and go.

- ✔ Portion out single servings of fresh fruit for the week so you can grab one for breakfast or to pack in your bag before you leave for work. Make up small sandwich bags that each hold ½ to 1 cup of fresh fruit.

- ✔ Portion out ½ cup of quick-cooking oats (not instant) into sandwich bags too. You can then just grab one and take it along with you — all you need is a bowl, a cup of water, a microwave, and two minutes to cook it up. If you have some fruit with you, add it to the oatmeal for a natural sweetener.

- ✔ Make your own breakfast eggwiches and freeze them. Lightly toast a whole-wheat English muffin. Cook an egg or two egg whites and place the egg on the toasted muffin. Wrap each muffin in plastic wrap and place them in a freezer bag. Take one out at a time and microwave for 30–60 seconds on medium high or high (depending on the power of the microwave). Add fresh salsa and enjoy!

- ✔ Fix up our Chicken Soft Tacos (Chapter 20) with Confetti Rice (Chapter 20). Add frozen green beans (microwave for 5 minutes) and sliced watermelon to make a complete meal.

- ✔ Serve the Fit and Fast Steak Salad (Chapter 19) with store-bought whole-wheat dinner rolls.

- ✔ Try Angel Hair Pasta with Shrimp (Chapter 20) accompanied by a tossed salad (use a washed, bagged salad blend) with homemade vinaigrette (see Chapter 9 for quick tips on tossing together a vinaigrette).

✔ Foil pouches make both cooking and cleanup a breeze. See Chapter 19 for foil-pouch-making how-to's and recipes, or try one of these:

- Foil pouch fish: Place 4 fish fillets into 4 foil pouches. Season with 2 teaspoons salt-free Italian herb blend and 1 teaspoon olive oil. Wrap tightly and grill for 15 minutes.

- Foil pouch veggies: Place sliced zucchini, diced bell peppers, and diced onions on a large piece of foil. Add 2 teaspoons olive oil and 1–2 teaspoons (to taste) salt-free Italian herb blend. Wrap up and grill for 20–30 minutes until tender.

Branching out with brunch

If you don't have a lot of experience with entertaining small groups, brunch is a great way to jump in! Brunch menus often feature items that don't have to be cooked or can be prepared ahead of time. For instance, you can simply slice some watermelon or place whole strawberries in an attractive bowl. You can make our Breakfast-on-the-Run Muffins (Chapter 14) or our Cinnamon Apple Cake (Chapter 22) ahead of time and freeze them. Pull them out of the freezer the night before or early in the morning on the day of the brunch.

When planning a brunch, consider these tips:

✔ **Eggs and brunch go together.** To make things easier, prepare a make-ahead egg dish such as the Spinach and Egg Squares (Chapter 14) or the Savory Breakfast Strata (Chapter 15).

✔ **Include one type of fruit juice.** Serve it in small (6-ounce) juice glasses.

✔ **Include a platter of fresh fruit.** Slice cantaloupe and arrange the slices in a single layer on a glass platter. Sprinkle with about a cup of blueberries. Add a few strawberries as well. Fruit platters are easier to put together than a mixed fruit salad, and everyone can take the fruit they enjoy.

✔ **Consider asparagus.** It's available in springtime and works very well on a brunch buffet. You can make it ahead and serve it at room temperature, or try the Grilled Asparagus Panzanella in Chapter 11.

✔ **Offer serve-yourself coffee and tea.** Use urns or a carafe, and put out a variety of tea bags, sugar, and cream. (***Note:*** You can use cream on special occasions, but for day-to-day cooking, 1-percent milk is your best bet. You can also try fat-free half and half for coffee or tea).

✔ **Use paper plates.** Hey, you're doing all the work cooking, so save yourself the trouble of doing dishes and choose a nice set of paper plates. Choosing matching plates and napkins adds color to the table and is pleasing to the eye for your guests, and it's easy cleanup for you.

✔ **Keep it simple.** Too many choices may result in either people overeating or leftover food. Choose one or two main entrees, a fresh fruit, one vegetable, perhaps some sort of rolls or bread, and a dessert.

Psst! Table-setting secrets

Do you remember the proper way to set a table? Forks go on the left of the plate, with a knife on the inside right of the plate and spoon outside the knife on the right. If you're setting a more formal table with multiple spoons and forks, you place the ones that need to be used first (soup, salad) farthest on the outside edge of the plate (the dessert spoon and fork can also go above the plate). The coffee cup goes to the right of the plate, the water or wine glass goes on the top right, and the bread plate goes on the left.

Celebrating family birthdays

Casual birthday celebrations don't have to involve fattening cakes and greasy pizza. Having a few go-to birthday meal plans that can easily be put together makes the day enjoyable for everyone. Following are a few fun and healthy menu suggestions:

✔ **Kid's Birthday Feast**

- Turkey Burger Sliders (Chapter 20)
- Baked Tiger Stripe Fries (Chapter 20)
- Fresh, sliced watermelon
- Favorite Chocolate Pudding Cake (Chapter 22)

✔ **Grownup Birthday Bash**

- Baked Chicken Pesto (Chapter 17)
- Pasta with Herb-Crusted, Roasted Tomatoes (Chapter 12)
- Mixed green salad
- Purchased angel food cake with fresh, sliced strawberries

✔ **Family Birthday Buffet**

- Confetti Vegetable Shrimp Pasta Salad (Chapter 9)
- First-Place Chicken Chili (Chapter 10)
- Homemade cornbread (We couldn't squeeze a cornbread recipe into this book, but try using unsalted butter to reduce the sodium.)
- Baby Spinach Salad with Almonds and Berry Vinaigrette (Chapter 9)

- Very Berry Walnut Crisp (Chapter 22) with vanilla ice cream. (*One scoop* of really good ice cream is worth the splurge.)
- Birthday cake of your choice. (Yes, you can splurge on a small piece of cake once in a while. It's nice to have two dessert options — a healthier one like the Very Berry Walnut Crisp, and a more indulgent dessert option like traditional cake.)

Hosting special — not stressful — holidays

"It's the most wonderful time of the year . . ." except when you get totally stressed out over it. Going overboard is the biggest mistake to avoid when you're planning to entertain a group during the holidays. Instead, keep it simple. The more relaxed the host or hostess is, the more relaxed everyone else is.

When planning holiday gatherings, choosing make-ahead recipes is a life-saver. Setting up a buffet also makes the meal easier to manage. Items can be made ahead or kept warm in the oven until everyone is ready to eat.

You can indulge a bit during the holidays, but you should still keep the DASH plan in mind, whether you're cooking a big holiday meal or deciding what dishes to choose at a friend or family's meal. Include all food groups: lean meat/protein, one or two vegetables, fresh fruit, and one or two grain dishes. A tossed green salad with a basket of whole-grain rolls can even out the meal.

Try this sample menu for a holiday spread:

- Hot Artichoke Bean Dip (Chapter 13)
- Raw carrots and celery
- Fresh fruit plate
- Roast Pork Tenderloin with Apple Stuffing (Chapter 17)
- Sweet Potato Mash (Chapter 12)
- Sautéed Kale with Pine Nuts (Chapter 11)
- Pumpkin Spice Parfait (Chapter 22)

Entertaining outdoors

There's nothing like eating *alfresco* (that's Italian for *fresh air*). The wonderful thing about outdoor entertaining is how relaxed it can be. Just being outside helps soften the tone of the occasion.

One of the best parts about eating outdoors is taking advantage of cooking on the grill. The same rule goes whether you're planning a picnic, an outdoor barbeque, or a weeknight dinner: Include all the food groups to provide a healthy, balanced meal for your guests. Nobody will know you're cooking for high blood pressure.

Mix and match these menu items for your next outdoor soiree:

- Whole-Wheat Couscous with Dried Cranberries and Almonds (Chapter 12)
- Grilled Salmon Fillets with Fresh Fruit Salsa (Chapter 18)
- Barley Pilaf (Chapter 12)
- Haricots Verts with Lemon Dill Dressing (Chapter 11)
- Whole-grain dinner rolls
- Sparkling water
- Beachcomber Smoothie Shooters (Chapter 22)
- Chicken Kabobs with Tzatziki Sauce (Chapter 17)
- Brown rice
- Fresh fruit platter

Having company for cocktails

Cocktail parties are a great way to introduce yourself to the art of entertaining without busting your hypertension diet. All you need are a few great snacks and a few great cocktails. You can make most of the appetizers in Chapter 13 ahead of time.

Provide one or two beverages. Make the first drink for your guests, and then allow them to serve themselves.

If you have high blood pressure, alcohol should be avoided or consumed in moderation. Having more than three drinks in one sitting temporarily raises blood pressure. Doing so on a regular basis can have a permanent effect. Moderate intake is considered two drinks per day for men and one drink per day for women. Follow your doctor's recommendations about alcohol intake.

Our Italian Caprese Skewers, Mediterranean Hummus with Sundried Tomatoes and Feta, and Heavenly Stuffed Mushrooms (all in Chapter 13) are a few of our favorite appetizers. A cocktail party featuring the Thai Fish Cakes with Sweet Chili Sauce, Fresh and Light Roasted Corn and Shrimp Salsa, and

Shrimp Phyllo Tarts (also in Chapter 13) with a nice sauvignon blanc and sparkling water also works well. Just make sure you keep portion control in mind as you munch on these — and any — appetizers.

For a cocktail that also offers one fruit serving, mix up a Pomegranate Martini. Mix 1 ounce citrus vodka, ½ ounce Cointreau liquor (or triple sec), and ¾ cup pomegranate juice in an ice-filled cocktail shaker. Shake vigorously. Strain into a martini glass and garnish with a slice of lemon. To go the nonalcoholic route, try a Pomegranate Splash: Mix equal parts cranberry-pomegranate juice with lime seltzer. Shake over ice and pour into a glass. Garnish with a fresh lime slice.

A simple bowl of nuts can be added to any cocktail spread. Even though they can be high in sodium, they're also high in healthy fats. Stick to small portions, and try unsalted varieties too.

Part III

From Soup to Nuts: Serving Salads, Sides, and Party-Starters

The 5th Wave   By Rich Tennant

"Right now I'm lowering my blood pressure by eating right, exercising, and limiting visits from my mother-in-law."

In this part . . .

Many folks perceive dieting as an on again, off again affair. But to be successful at improving your health through the food you eat, you need to understand that these changes are to become *part of your life*. This means all or most of the time, all or most of your days. The recipes in this part begin introducing you to the idea that eating according to the DASH plan is enjoyable and sustainable.

You won't be sacrificing flavor for salt with these delicious salad, soup, side dish, appetizer, and snack recipes. Each one is bursting with flavor and provides the nutrients you need. The vegetable recipes here make incorporating more veggies into your diet a taste sensation, not a spoonful of medicine. For comfort, nothing is better than soup, and you're going to find our soups, stews, and chili recipes satisfying. And the next time you host a party or take a dish to a potluck, you'll be armed with some awesome appetizers and side dishes that taste impressive and show off your newfound healthy cooking skills.

Chapter 9

Going Lean and Green with Savvy Salads

In This Chapter

▶ Creating new ways to mix greens

▶ Adding more color to your salads

▶ Stirring up fresh, delicious dressings

▶ Bringing salads beyond the first course

*W*e encourage those of you who think that salads are "rabbit food" to take a close look at this chapter. Traditional green salads tossed together using iceberg, leaf, or Bibb lettuce are great, but we offer some new recipes here that will wake up your taste buds.

Adding more colorful foods high in antioxidants and phytochemicals is one of the goals of a diet to manage high blood pressure (flip to Chapter 7 for more on colorful fruits and veggies), and using the salad course is one easy way to meet this goal. A hearty salad can help you meet not only your four to five servings of both fruits and vegetables a day, but also your goal to eat four to five servings of nuts or beans per week — all in one bowl! Three to four food groups in one dish — how's that for savvy and satisfying?

In addition to the awesome salad recipes in this chapter, there's no shame in creating a simple green salad with whatever ingredients you have in your refrigerator drawer. Make sure you always wash your greens thoroughly (you can use a colander or a salad spinner) and dice or julienne your veggies (Chapter 7 gives you the scoop on these terms).

A plethora of bottled salad dressings are on the market, some of which are loaded with sodium. The notion that making your own salad dressing is complicated is a culinary myth. In reality, nothing could be easier.

To make a quick vinaigrette, simply combine the following: ⅓ cup olive oil, 2 to 3 tablespoons vinegar (or a 3:1 ratio of oil to vinegar), 2 teaspoons sugar, and the juice of half a lemon or lime. Mix all the ingredients together with a whisk, and drizzle over your favorite greens and veggies.

Now that you're an expert on basic salad building, we recommend some sensational ingredients that you can add to create some really special salads bursting with color and flavor.

Creating Salads You Won't Want to Skip

We all know that salads up your veggie count. But salads can be both nutritious and filling when they feature the right ingredients, helping you to both decrease your blood pressure and manage your weight. After all, the fuller you are, the less hungry you get, the less you eat, and the more weight you lose. Salads also make quick and easy side dishes, so they fit well into the dinner-planning crunch.

Of course, in order to eat a salad at home, you have to have ingredients on hand, so here are some basic salad tips to consider for your grocery list and meal planning:

- Although purchasing bagged mixed greens is an easy option, they do tend to spoil more quickly than individual greens and cost a smidge more. Consider buying individual greens along with some bagged salads.

- Look for romaine, green leaf, Boston Bibb, and spinach.

- Store greens in a loose bag in your vegetable drawer. Wash them as you need them. Don't chop or tear them until you're ready to use them.

- Keep salad toppers such as dried fruit and roasted, unsalted nuts in your pantry (you may also want to check out prepackaged toppers, but read labels for fat and sodium).

- Keep some veggie salad basics in your fridge: bell peppers, carrots, onions, celery, olives, and cucumbers.

- Have salad dressing staples on hand, like extra-virgin olive oil, red wine, cider vinegars, honey, sugar, and lemons and limes.

Be flexible: Look for sale items of the week to create salads that are not only healthy but budget-friendly, too.

Baby Spinach Salad with Almonds and Berry Vinaigrette

Prep time: 20 min • **Yield:** 4 servings

Ingredients	Directions
Two 10-ounce packages fresh baby spinach, washed and spun	*1* Gently toss together the strawberries and kiwi and place on top of the spinach in a medium serving bowl.
1 pint fresh strawberries, sliced	*2* To make the dressing, whisk the jam together with the vinegar and oil until well blended.
2 kiwi, peeled and sliced	
¼ cup seedless all-fruit strawberry jam	*3* Drizzle the dressing over the salad and sprinkle with the toasted almonds.
¼ cup white wine vinegar	
⅓ cup olive oil	
⅓ cup sliced almonds, toasted	

Per serving: Calories 320 (From Fat 196); Fat 22g (Saturated 3g); Cholesterol 0mg; Sodium 112mg; Carbohydrate 27g (Dietary Fiber 6g); Protein 6g; Potassium 258mg.

Note: All-fruit spreads offer the fresh fruit taste without all the sugar. Another alternative is low-sugar preserves that have 50 percent less sugar than regular preserves. Take a look at what the finished salad looks like in the color section.

Vary It! This can easily morph into a main-dish salad if you add leftover chicken, pork, or even seafood.

Vary It! Substitute raspberries for strawberries and seedless raspberry jam for the strawberry jam. Substitute jicama slices in place of almonds to get the crunch without the extra calories!

Mixed Greens with Hazelnut Goat Cheese and Balsamic Vinaigrette

Prep time: 30 min • **Cook time:** 5 min • **Yield:** 4 servings

Ingredients	Directions
4 baby bella mushrooms One large bell pepper ½ tablespoon olive oil 8 cups mixed salad greens, washed and spun dry One 14-ounce can water-packed artichoke hearts, drained, rinsed, and cut in half 4-ounce log of fresh goat cheese 1 ounce hazelnuts, toasted and minced 6 tablespoons extra-virgin olive oil 2 tablespoons balsamic vinegar 1 garlic clove, minced 2 teaspoons sugar ½ tablespoon Dijon mustard	*1* Preheat a broiler on high. Place the mushrooms on a baking sheet. Cut the bell pepper in half, removing the top and the seeds. Place the pepper halves onto the sheet with the mushrooms and drizzle the vegetables with ½ tablespoon olive oil. Broil for 3 minutes on each side. *2* Remove the mushrooms to cool; then place the pepper back into the broiler and cook until slightly blackened, about 3–5 more minutes. Remove the pepper from the oven and place it into a paper bag, seal it, and set it aside. Slice the mushrooms while the pepper is steaming. Then, remove the pepper from the bag, gently remove the skin, and slice. *3* Divide greens among 4 plates and top with equal amounts of roasted red bell peppers, artichoke hearts, and mushrooms. *4* Slice the goat cheese into 8 equal, thick rounds and roll the edges in minced hazelnuts (check out Figure 9-1 for a simple slicing method). Place two rounds atop each salad. *5* In a small bowl, make the dressing by combining the extra-virgin olive oil, vinegar, garlic, sugar, and mustard and whisking until blended. Drizzle 1 tablespoon of dressing on each salad prior to serving. Refrigerate the leftover dressing for use with other salads.

Per serving: Calories 267 (From Fat 180); Fat 20g (Saturated 7g); Cholesterol 30mg; Sodium 232mg; Carbohydrate 16g (Dietary Fiber 7g); Protein 11g; Potassium 800mg.

Note: Keep in mind that the fat in this salad is a little higher than what you may expect from a salad. However, most of the fat is healthy unsaturated fat, not saturated fat. Balance out the fat in this salad with lower-fat meals the rest of the day.

Note: Mesclun is a salad mix of assorted young salad leaves. The mix traditionally included chervil, arugula, leafy lettuces, and endive. Today, many variations include just about any mix of tender young greens with a variety of color, texture, and flavor from sweet and tender to bitter and crisp to peppery and pungent.

Tip: Besides the broiler method described in the recipe, there are other methods for roasting your own bell pepper, a practice that saves on sodium compared to using prepackaged peppers. Try a gas grill or an open flame on a gas stove. Place a pepper over the open flame until the entire pepper is blistered and charred. The more blackened, the more flavor. Place it in a small paper bag, seal it, and set it aside for 15 minutes. The pepper will steam, making the skin easy to remove under running water.

Tip: Darker green leafy vegetables are nutritional powerhouses. Store leafy greens unwashed in the refrigerator; any added moisture will cause them to spoil more rapidly. Be sure to rinse greens well, even if they're labeled "prewashed." Spin dry using a salad spinner — one of coauthor Cindy's favorite kitchen tools to use when making salads. It dries the lettuce so well that you actually use less dressing.

Vary It! For a quick and flavorful low-cal alternative to fatty processed dressings, try the innovative spray-on salad dressings.

Vary It! You can also use an 8-ounce jar of roasted peppers to save time, but remember that anything that's processed adds sodium.

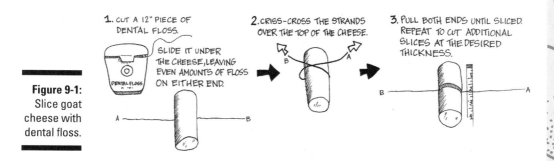

Figure 9-1:
Slice goat cheese with dental floss.

1. CUT A 12" PIECE OF DENTAL FLOSS. SLIDE IT UNDER THE CHEESE, LEAVING EVEN AMOUNTS OF FLOSS ON EITHER END.

2. CRISS-CROSS THE STRANDS OVER THE TOP OF THE CHEESE.

3. PULL BOTH ENDS UNTIL SLICED. REPEAT TO CUT ADDITIONAL SLICES AT THE DESIRED THICKNESS.

Sweet Potato Salad with Mango-Curry Dressing

Prep time: 16–18 min • **Cook time:** 10 min • **Yield:** 4 servings

Ingredients	Directions
1½ pounds sweet potatoes, peeled and cut into ½-inch chunks	*1* In a vegetable steamer, steam the sweet potatoes until tender, about 10 minutes. Do not overcook.
⅓ cup organic Greek nonfat plain yogurt	*2* In a salad bowl, blend the yogurt, mayonnaise, chutney, curry powder, cumin, and pepper.
1 tablespoon reduced-fat mayonnaise	
3 tablespoons mango chutney, finely chopped	*3* Add the sweet potatoes to the dressing along with the celery and onion, and toss gently until well coated.
1½ teaspoons curry powder	
¾ teaspoon cumin	
½ teaspoon freshly ground black pepper	
1 cup diced celery	
⅓ cup minced red onion	

Per serving: Calories 222 (From Fat 14); Fat 1.5g (Saturated 0.2g); Cholesterol 0.4mg; Sodium 122 mg; Carbohydrate 47g (Dietary Fiber 7g); Protein 5g; Potassium 936mg.

Note: Sweet potatoes are ideal for the health conscious — they're highly nutritious, contain huge amounts of beta carotene, and have a low glycemic index — and they're economical, too!

Tip: Purchase mango chutney that blends mangoes, raisins, vinegar, and spices. Use leftover chutney in a shredded chicken salad or as a spread for grilled chicken or chops. Or, mix it with cream cheese and spread on whole-grain crackers or use a small amount as a sandwich spread. A little goes a long way.

Jicama Bell Pepper Salad

Prep time: 10 min • **Yield:** 6 servings

Ingredients	Directions
1 cucumber	**1** Peel the cucumber and cut in half lengthwise. Scoop out and discard the seeds. Cut the cucumber crosswise into ¼-inch slices.
1 jicama	
½ red bell pepper, seeded and cut into 1-inch strips	**2** Peel the jicama with a potato peeler and cut into ¼-inch slices; then cut into matchstick-like pieces.
½ green bell pepper, seeded and cut into 1-inch strips	
¼ cup chopped cilantro	**3** Combine the cucumber, jicama, red bell pepper, green bell pepper, cilantro, and onion and place in a medium bowl.
½ small onion, thinly sliced	
3 tablespoons lime juice	**4** Whisk the lime juice, chili powder, and pepper in a small bowl until well blended. Pour over the salad and refrigerate up to 4 hours. Serve on top of the red leaf lettuce leaves.
¼ teaspoon chili powder	
⅛ teaspoon freshly ground black pepper	
Red leaf lettuce leaves for garnish	

Per serving: Calories 61 (From Fat 2); Fat 0.24g (Saturated 0.1g); Cholesterol 0mg; Sodium 8mg; Carbohydrate 14g (Dietary Fiber 6g); Protein 1g; Potassium 305mg.

Note: The humble jicama (see Figure 9-2), low in starch and calories, offers a crisp texture and a just-sweet-enough taste. Use it like a water chestnut or grate it as a substitute for diakon, a large, mild Asian radish. Like potatoes, jicama can be steamed, baked, boiled, or mashed. Unlike potatoes, jicama can also be eaten raw.

Tip: This side salad (check it out in the color section) pairs nicely with a full-bodied flavorful entree, like a Mexican dish. It cleanses the palate and complements the richness of the meal. Unlike traditional oily dressings, this one offers a fresh twist of lime and spices instead.

Vary It! Substitute seasonal fruit such as orange or grapefruit sections; bite-sized chunks of cantaloupe, honeydew, watermelon, or pineapple; or pomegranate seeds for the bell peppers.

Figure 9-2:
Meet the jicama.

Butternut Squash Salad with Cider-Spiked Vinaigrette

Prep time: 10 min • **Cook time:** 20 min • **Yield:** 4 servings

Ingredients	Directions
1 pound butternut squash, peeled and diced	*1* Preheat the oven to 400 degrees.
2 small sweet potatoes, peeled and diced	*2* Place the diced squash and sweet potatoes on a lined baking pan. Spray the surface of the vegetables with nonstick cooking spray and sprinkle them with pepper (to taste). Toss well. Roast the squash and sweet potatoes for 15 to 20 minutes, turning once during roasting.
Nonstick cooking spray	
Freshly ground black pepper, to taste	
2 tablespoons dried cranberries	*3* Add the dried cranberries to the pan and roast another 5 minutes.
¾ cup apple cider	*4* To make the vinaigrette, bring the apple cider, vinegar, and shallots to a boil in a small saucepan. Cook for 6 to 8 minutes until the cider is reduced to about ¼ cup. Remove from heat and whisk in the mustard, olive oil, and pepper (to taste).
2 tablespoons cider vinegar	
2 tablespoons minced shallots	
2 teaspoons Dijon mustard	
½ cup extra-virgin olive oil	
6 cups mixed salad greens	*5* Divide the mixed greens among 4 salad plates (about 1½ cups each) and add the roasted squash mixture and walnuts. Drizzle vinaigrette over the salad and toss well.
½ cup walnut halves, toasted	

Per serving: Calories 474 (From Fat 345); Fat 38g (Saturated 5g); Cholesterol 20mg; Sodium 89mg; Carbohydrate 33g (Dietary Fiber 6g); Protein 3g; Potassium 804mg.

Note: When coauthor Cindy "builds" a salad, she always thinks about including a variety of flavors and textures. As you're eating healthy, don't worry so much about what foods you have to give up. Instead, focus on adding more variety to your meals to improve your daily nutrition. Roasting caramelizes the squash, giving it a natural sweetness; cranberries add a chewy texture and tartness; vinegar provides a sour feature; and walnuts provide crunchy goodness and omega-3 fatty acids.

Tip: Leave out the walnuts and you save 88 calories but also miss out on the vitamins, minerals, healthy fats, antioxidants, protein, and fiber — the good stuff that promotes meal satiety and reduces hunger levels.

Mixing Up New and Improved Pasta Salads

One of our favorite things to bring to a summer picnic is a great pasta salad. If you're used to that old mayonnaise-type glob, get ready for your mouth to water, because our versions are bursting with flavor. In addition to reducing the fat of normal pasta salads, we also amp up the fiber and antioxidants, again helping you meet the goals for a blood-pressure-reducing diet.

Pasta salads also are a great accompaniment to buffet tables when you're planning a special occasion at home or having a celebration. For instance, Super Bowl Sunday doesn't have to be rife with foods high in sodium, saturated fat, and calories. Balance out the buffet by offering a one-dish pasta salad that can be a meal in itself!

You may have a favorite recipe at home that you want to modify. Here are some tips to help you cut some calories and sodium and add some nutrients:

- ✔ Cut the mayonnaise or salad dressing in half. This trick reduces not only the calorie count but also the sodium content of the dish.

- ✔ Try different pasta shapes and types. A lot of very tasty whole-grain pastas are on the market today. Using these in your salad increases the fiber content of the dish, making the salad more filling and nutritious.

- ✔ Add more veggies! Adding diced bell peppers, cucumbers, zucchini, or carrots adds color, flavor, and nutrients. We prefer a finely diced vegetable in our salads.

- ✔ Add some good fats. Instead of the traditional mayo, use a vinaigrette dressing in a smaller quantity. You can also add sliced olives or slivered nuts for some healthy, monounsaturated fat.

So dive into these updated pasta salad recipes and enjoy more flavor while your keep your blood pressure in check.

Asian Ginger Pasta Salad

Prep time: 25 min • **Cook time:** 10 min • **Yield:** 6 servings

Ingredients	*Directions*
1 pound whole-wheat rotini pasta 3 cups snow peas 4 tablespoons toasted sesame oil 4 tablespoons honey	*1* Cook the pasta in boiling water without salt, according to the package's directions. While the pasta is boiling, blanch the snow peas by adding them to the boiling water for 1 to 2 minutes. Remove the snow peas from the water using a slotted spoon, and place in an ice bath to stop the cooking process. Drain well. When the pasta is cooked, drain and rinse with cold water.
4 tablespoons low-sodium soy sauce 3 tablespoons rice vinegar Juice of 1 fresh lime, or 2 tablespoons lime juice	*2* Make the dressing by combining the sesame oil, honey, soy sauce, vinegar, lime juice, cayenne pepper, garlic, and ginger. Mix well and set aside to allow the flavors to blend.
¼ teaspoon cayenne pepper 5 to 6 medium garlic cloves, minced 1 tablespoon minced fresh ginger	*3* Combine the pasta, peppers, red and green onions, carrots, cucumber, and toasted sesame seeds. Add the dressing and toss well.
2 red bell peppers, seeded and thinly sliced 1 medium red onion, thinly sliced 1 bunch green onions, thinly sliced 5 medium carrots, peeled and julienned 1 large cucumber, unpeeled, cut in half lengthwise and thinly sliced ¼ cup toasted sesame seeds	

Per serving: Calories 515 (From Fat 127); Fat 14g (Saturated 2g); Cholesterol 0mg; Sodium 441mg; Carbohydrate 85g (Dietary Fiber 12g); Protein 14g; Potassium 510mg.

Herb Garden Pasta Salad

Prep time: 20 min • **Cook time:** 12 min • **Yield:** 10 servings

Ingredients	*Directions*
1½ **pounds whole-wheat farfalle pasta**	**1** In a large pot, boil water and cook the pasta as directed on the package without adding any salt. Drain.
3 cups low-sodium, fat-free chicken or vegetable broth or stock	**2** While the pasta cooks, prepare the sauce by heating the chicken or vegetable broth or stock. Add the cheese rind to the broth. Simmer until the broth is reduced to 2 cups.
One 4-inch piece of Parmigiano-Reggiano cheese rind	
4 large Roma tomatoes, coarsely chopped	**3** Strain the broth to remove the rind, and return the broth to the pot. Add the drained pasta to the broth and cook on high until some of the sauce appears thickened.
2 garlic cloves, minced	
½ **cup chopped fresh Italian parsley**	
½ **cup chopped basil**	**4** Combine the tomatoes, garlic, all the herbs, oil, and vinegar with the pasta mixture. Toss until thoroughly combined and adjust the seasoning with pepper, to taste. Top with the shredded cheese before serving.
2 tablespoons chopped fresh tarragon	
2 tablespoons chopped fresh mint	
1½ **teaspoons chopped fresh thyme**	
1 teaspoon chopped fresh sage	
1 teaspoon fresh rosemary	
½ **teaspoon chopped fresh marjoram**	
¼ **cup extra-virgin olive oil**	
2 teaspoons balsamic vinegar	
Freshly ground pepper to taste	
½ **cup shredded Parmigiano-Reggiano cheese**	

Per serving: Calories 329 (From Fat 70); Fat 8g (Saturated 3g); Cholesterol 0mg; Sodium 388mg; Carbohydrate 50g (Dietary Fiber 5g); Protein 18g; Potassium 162mg.

Confetti Vegetable Shrimp Pasta Salad

Prep time: 20 min • **Cook time:** 5 min • **Yield:** 6 servings

Ingredients	*Directions*
1 pound large shrimp, peeled and deveined **1 yellow bell pepper, cut into ¼ -inch cubes**	*1* Boil a pot of water and carefully drop in the shrimp. Cook until just tender, about 1 minute. Drain, rinse under cold water, drain well, and place in a large serving bowl.
3 ripe Roma tomatoes, cut into ½-inch cubes **¼ cup chopped fresh dill** **1 teaspoon dried tarragon** **1 tablespoon chopped shallots**	*2* Add the bell pepper, tomatoes, dill, tarragon, shallots, red pepper flakes, pepper, lemon juice, and olive oil to the serving bowl. Toss well with the shrimp. Cover and refrigerate for an hour to allow the flavors to blend.
¼ teaspoon dried red pepper flakes **½ teaspoon coarsely ground black pepper** **¼ cup fresh lemon juice**	*3* While the shrimp mixture is chilling, bring a large saucepan of water to a boil. Drop in the broccoli and blanch for 1 minute. Remove the broccoli with a slotted spoon and rinse under cold water, reserving the boiled water. Drain and set aside.
2 to 4 tablespoons olive oil **½ head broccoli, cut into small florets** **½ pound whole-wheat vermicelli pasta**	*4* With the same boiling water, cook the pasta according to the package's instructions until just tender. Drain the pasta and rinse under cold water. Toss with the broccoli, and add the shrimp mixture. Serve at once.

Per serving: *Calories 326 (From Fat 88); Fat 10g (Saturated 1g); Cholesterol 115mg; Sodium 128mg; Carbohydrate 38g (Dietary Fiber 5g); Protein 22g; Potassium 379mg.*

Note: The variety of vegetables in this recipe provides you with brilliant colors and flavors, and offers you many vitamins, minerals, and other natural substances that may help protect you from chronic diseases.

Tip: To save time, ask your fishmonger to steam the shrimp or purchase it already steamed.

Staying Healthy with Mouthwatering Main-Dish Salads

More and more restaurants are adding main-dish salads to their menus, so why shouldn't you create some at home? A main-dish salad refers to a salad that includes ingredients beyond just greens, adding some protein to make it a complete meal. By adding some fruit and a hearty roll, you have a great quick supper that includes at least four food groups.

In some cases, you can whip up a main-dish salad in less than 30 minutes, giving you a great ratio of prep time to nutrition and taste (check out the Crabby Louis Salad in this chapter for a filling seafood salad you can whip up in 15 minutes).

Secrets to fast main-dish salads

A secret to putting together quick, healthy meals, is working ahead when you can. This can mean preparing some extra meat or vegetables for later use, or making use of leftovers in the refrigerator to create something completely new. These tips don't just save in the preparation itself, but also in cleanup; for example, if the meat is already cooked, you won't dirty a new skillet. The next time you grill chicken breasts, grill a few extra, slice them into strips, and freeze them in zipper bags. You can defrost them in the microwave or overnight in the refrigerator and have them ready for a quick salad topper.

This trick works with other meats, too: If you have a small piece of baked salmon left over from dinner, mix up a green salad and top it with salmon and some sliced strawberries for your packed lunch the next day.

You can put a new spin on your leftover pasta salad (see the section "Mixing Up New and Improved Pasta Salads" for our recipes) by topping a mixed green salad with it and adding some low-sodium packed tuna.

Besides using leftovers, another secret to fast main-dish salads is keeping items on hand and ready to go. You can always create a stir-fried salad with lean meat and the veggies in your fridge. Stir-fry your sliced meat and vegetables (peppers, onions, and mushrooms work well, but use what you have) in a nonstick pan with 2 teaspoons of canola oil. Top your leafy green salad with the warm mixture, and add 2 tablespoons of vinaigrette dressing.

If you're already going to be spending time cooking, cook extra for another day of the week. This will provide you with a variety of fresh but ready-to-use ingredients to create healthy and filling salads.

Crabby Louis Salad

Prep time: 15 min • **Yield:** 6 servings

Ingredients	*Directions*
½ cup reduced-fat mayonnaise	**1** To make the dressing, combine the mayonnaise with the chili sauce, mustard, and horseradish and mix well. Refrigerate.
¼ cup low-sodium chili sauce	
1 tablespoon Dijon mustard	**2** Toss the crabmeat and shrimp with the almonds and green onions. Refrigerate the dressing and seafood mixture for at least 30 minutes or up to 2 hours to allow the flavors to blend.
¼ teaspoon prepared horseradish	
½ pound fresh crabmeat	
½ pound cocktail shrimp	**3** Line 4 plates with the lettuce leaves and avocado halves (see Figure 9-3 for how to prepare an avocado).
1 cup slivered almonds, toasted	
½ cup sliced green onion	**4** Spoon the crab-almond mixture into the avocado halves. Garnish each plate with tomato wedges and a dollop of dressing.
4 red lettuce leaves	
2 ripe avocados, seeded, peeled, and halved	
2 tomatoes, cut in wedges	

Per serving: Calories 302 (From Fat 162); Fat 18g (Saturated 2g); Cholesterol 91mg; Sodium 657mg; Carbohydrate 18g (Dietary Fiber 7g); Protein 19g; Potassium 902mg.

Note: This recipe is higher in sodium, but chock-full of potassium, a nutrient that the DASH diet (see Chapter 2) highly recommends. Substitute cocktail sauce for the chili sauce to decrease the sodium.

Note: No need to fear shellfish! Low in calories and saturated fats, these delicacies provide a natural source of omega-3 fatty acids; vitamins A, C, and B12; and minerals like zinc and copper and are a low risk for mercury. Enjoy your favorites; just hold the butter.

How to Pit and Peel an Avocado

Figure 9-3: Pitting and peeling an avocado.

Slice avocado in half lengthwise and pull apart.

Firmly strike the pit with a chef's knife.

Lift the pit out with a gentle twist of the knife.

GENTLY scoop out the meat with a spoon.

Chop or slice according to your recipe.

Spinach Salad with Grilled Pork Tenderloin

Prep time: 20 min, plus marinating time • **Cook time:** 10 min • **Yield:** 4 servings

Ingredients	Directions
1½ pounds fresh peaches or thawed frozen peaches, divided	*1* To make the vinaigrette, combine 1 pound of the peaches, the peach nectar, the red wine and raspberry vinegars, the pepper, the jalapeño, and the cilantro in a food processor and pulse until smooth.
½ cup canned peach nectar	
¼ cup red wine vinegar	*2* Marinate the pork tenderloin in ¼ cup of the vinaigrette for at least 3 hours prior to grilling.
2 tablespoons raspberry vinegar	
¼ teaspoon freshly ground black pepper	*3* Preheat a gas grill. Grill the tenderloin for 2 to 3 minutes on each side. Don't overcook, because overcooking will dry out the meat.
1 small jalapeño pepper, seeded	
2 tablespoons chopped cilantro	*4* Toss together the spinach, shallot, remaining thawed peaches, walnuts, and blue cheese. Divide the ingredients among 4 dinner plates. Arrange 3 pork tenderloin medallions on top of each salad.
1 pound pork tenderloin, cut into 12 medallions (1½-inch-thick slices)	
20 ounces baby spinach, washed	*5* Serve with the jalapeño-peach vinaigrette.
1 small shallot, thinly sliced	
½ cup walnuts, toasted	
2 ounces crumbled blue cheese	

Per serving: *Calories 360 (From Fat 144); Fat 16g (Saturated 4g); Cholesterol 73mg; Sodium 517mg; Carbohydrate 18g (Dietary Fiber 5g); Protein 35g; Potassium 787mg.*

Note: Spinach in all its glory is full of essential nutrients, especially iron — Popeye was no dummy! Eating iron with a good source of vitamin C, like peppers or shallots, helps your body absorb the iron.

Tip: This salad is perfect if you have leftover pork (try our Grilled Pork Tenderloin Medallions in Chapter 17). Morph the leftovers into this beautiful and tasty work of art.

Tip: Purchase good-quality frozen peaches for the best flavor. Frozen peaches have more vitamin C than fresh or canned ones because the vitamin C (also known as ascorbic acid) is added to prevent the fruit from turning brown.

Grilled Shrimp Salad with Creamy Mango-Lime Dressing

Prep time: 20–30 min • **Cook time:** 16–18 min • **Yield:** 4 servings

Ingredients	Directions
2 large fresh ripe mangoes, peeled and cut into cubes	*1* To make the salad dressing, place ¼ cup of the mango cubes plus the lime juice, mayonnaise, olive oil, garlic, and sugar in a mini food processor. Add the orange juice, if desired, to thin the dressing. Blend well and set aside.
Juice of 1 small lime, or 2 tablespoons lime juice	
½ cup light mayonnaise	
1 tablespoon extra-virgin olive oil	*2* Peel and devein the shrimp and place in a shallow container with a lid. Add the zesty Italian dressing to coat the shrimp evenly. Cover and marinate on the counter for 10 minutes.
½ teaspoon crushed garlic	
1 teaspoon sugar	
1 tablespoon orange juice to thin (optional)	*3* Roast the pine nuts in a dry skillet over medium-low heat. Watch closely; they brown quickly. Shake the skillet for even browning. When the pine nuts are golden in color, remove them from the heat.
1 pound large shrimp	
2 tablespoons zesty Italian dressing	
⅓ cup pine nuts, toasted	*4* Blanch the asparagus in boiling water for 2 minutes, drain, and refresh in cold water. Drain again and set aside.
1½ cups sliced asparagus, blanched	*5* Divide the mixed salad greens among 4 dinner plates and top with the asparagus, remaining cubed mango, celery, red onion, and pine nuts.
8 cups torn or cut mixed salad greens	
2 celery ribs, sliced	*6* Spray a grill with nonstick cooking spray and heat it to medium. Remove the shrimp from the marinade and place it over direct heat, cooking for 1 to 2 minutes on one side and 30 seconds to 1 minute on the other side. The shrimp is done when the inside is opaque.
¼ small red onion, thinly sliced	
1 to 2 tablespoons chopped fresh cilantro	*7* Arrange the grilled shrimp on top of the mixed greens and sprinkle with cilantro to garnish. Drizzle the mango-lime dressing over the salad and serve.

Per serving: Calories 458 (From Fat 234); Fat 26g (Saturated 3g); Cholesterol 182mg; Sodium 593mg; Carbohydrate 33g (Dietary Fiber 6g); Protein 27g; Potassium 572mg.

Chapter 10

Finding Comfort in Soups, Stews, and Chilis

*N*othing warms your tummy as well as a nice, hot bowl of soup. Because canned soups are so high in sodium, it's a great idea to have some go-to soup recipes you can make at home to satisfy your need for good soup. A nice stew is a one-dish meal that can cover three to four food groups in one bowl. And our chili recipes take you beyond the unhealthy and unnatural chilis that come at you from inside a plastic fast-food bowl. Our chilis offer some new ingredients that provide more nutrients and great flavors to this comforting, easy-to-make-ahead dish.

Comfort Soups: Stewing Over Flavor

In addition to being warm and comforting, soups and stews also provide you with a nutritional bonus. Because all the ingredients are stewed together in one big pot, they retain their full flavor and nutrient value. The beta-carotene in carrots, for instance, isn't lost; it's cooked right into the pot. (Ever notice that when you cook carrots or a green vegetable, the color leaches out into the water? Those colors represent valuable nutrients you're losing!) So in addition to all the fiber and flavor that vegetables and beans provide to soups and stews, the cooking liquid gains the vitamins from these foods, particularly B vitamins, beta-carotene, and vitamin C.

We're sure you'll be pleased with your made-from-scratch, not-from-a-can soups. As you embark upon your new homemade soup venture, keep these cooking tips in mind:

✔ Cooking soups and stews is a great way to clean out your refrigerator. You can add almost any vegetable from your vegetable bin to create a vegetable soup. Frozen veggies work too.

✔ Experiment with the dried, salt-free herbs in your pantry, but be sure they're fresh (see Chapter 4).

✔ Leftover meats work well in soups, too – just finely chop leftover chicken, turkey, or steak into small pieces to add to your soup.

✔ Soups are great make-ahead meals. You can make them on the weekend to enjoy on busy weeknights. They also freeze very well (up to 3 months), so you can save leftovers for a quick weeknight meal next month.

Speaking of poultry, the next time you have roast chicken or turkey, make your own stock. By making your own stock, you reduce the fat and sodium that are in many canned stocks — not to mention end up with a more flavorful stock. You'll also save yourself some money by repurposing a carcass you'd otherwise throw away. Here's how:

1. **Place the entire carcass in a full pot of cold water.**

2. **Add some herbs, citrus fruit, or vegetables (sage leaves, parsley, celery stalks, lemon pieces), and fresh ground pepper.**

3. **Bring to a boil and simmer for about an hour.**

4. **Remove large bones from the pot; then strain the liquid using a fine colander.**

5. **Using your fingers, remove any pieces of meat and save them for soup.**

   You can refrigerate your homemade stock for up to four days, or freeze it for up to two months (now you know exactly what to do with that turkey carcass after Thanksgiving).

Moving along, the following pages offer you step-by-step instructions for some delicious soup recipes.

Velvety Vegetable Soup with Tarragon Cream

Prep time: 15 min • **Cook time:** 60 min • **Yield:** 7 servings

Ingredients	*Directions*
1 yellow onion, peeled and chopped	*1* Place all the chopped vegetables in a Dutch oven.
4 celery ribs, chopped	*2* Pour vegetable stock over the vegetables and add the thyme and bay leaves. Bring to a boil over high heat. Reduce to simmer for about 45 to 60 minutes or until all vegetables are tender.
4 medium carrots, chopped	
2 medium leeks, chopped	
1 rutabaga, peeled and chopped	*3* Remove the bay leaves and puree the soup in a blender in small batches until smooth.
3 large parsnips, peeled and chopped	
6 cups unsalted vegetable stock	*4* Return the soup to the Dutch oven and add pepper to taste. Place the soup over low heat to keep it warm.
1 teaspoon dried thyme	*5* To make the tarragon cream, stir tarragon into the Greek yogurt. Just before serving, place ½ tablespoon of the tarragon cream on top of each bowl of soup.
3 bay leaves	
Fresh ground pepper to taste	
3 tablespoons fresh tarragon, chopped	*6* Sprinkle with extra chopped tarragon as a garnish.
¾ cup organic fat-free plain Greek yogurt	

Per serving: Calories 150 (From Fat 18); Fat 2g (Saturated 0.5g); Cholesterol 0mg; Sodium 107mg; Carbohydrate 28g (Dietary Fiber 7g); Protein 9g; Potassium 657mg.

Tip: Be sure to blend the cooked soup in small batches to avoid a blender explosion — one of the worst kitchen disasters. An immersion blender allows you to blend this soup right in the pot. When purchasing root veggies, choose more regular shapes for ease in peeling. Store the veggies in a cool, dry place.

Note: Often overlooked and underappreciated, root veggies like rutabaga and parsnips are at their peak in the winter months, when their robust flavors come alive. They're nutritional power-houses, versatile, and inexpensive. Roots taste delightful roasted and caramelized for an easy side dish in the winter months, and roasting may be the trick that gets your kids to eat their veggies (it worked for coauthor Cindy!).

French Market Bean Soup

Prep time: 20 min • **Cook time:** 1–1½ hours • **Yield:** 8 servings

Ingredients	*Directions*
1 cup each of any 4 of the following beans:	**1** Wash and drain the beans. Cover them with 6 cups of cold water and soak for at least 8 hours or overnight.

Great Northern beans
   Navy beans
   Black beans
   Red kidney beans
   Garbanzo beans
   Pinto beans
   Black-eyed peas
	2 Rinse the beans and add to a large stockpot or Dutch oven with 5 quarts of water, the smoked turkey, Southwest spice, and the bay leaves. Simmer, covered, for 1 to 1½ hours.

1 to 2 ounces natural smoked turkey breast	**3** Sauté the onions, celery, and garlic in olive oil in a separate skillet. Add to the beans with the chicken and tomatoes. Simmer for 20 minutes. Serve with a few drops of Tabasco sauce and your favorite whole-grain crackers.
1 tablespoon salt-free Southwest spice blend	
2 bay leaves	
1 onion, chopped	
½ cup chopped green onions	
1 cup chopped celery	
4 cloves garlic, chopped	
1 tablespoon olive oil	
1½ chicken breasts, cooked and shredded	
Three 14.5-ounce cans stewed tomatoes, no salt added, undrained	
Tabasco sauce to taste	

Per serving: Calories 182 (From Fat 45); Fat 5g (Saturated 1g); Cholesterol 33mg; Sodium 287mg; Carbohydrate 20g (Dietary Fiber 5g); Protein 16g; Potassium 443mg.

Note: Adding a little smoked turkey breast amps up the flavor without adding too much sodium.

Tip: What to do with the leftover beans? Divide the beans among small jars, tie a colored ribbon around the neck of each jar, and attach the recipe for a nice housewarming gift.

Vary It! Alternately, try quick-soaking the beans when you are pressed for time. Add 6 to 8 cups of water to 1 pound of dry beans and bring to a boil in a Dutch oven. Cover and cook 2 minutes, remove from heat, and let stand for 1 hour. Rinse and drain, then cook according to package directions or add to the recipe as directed.

Autumn Root Vegetable Stew

Prep time: 10 min • **Cook time:** 45–60 min • **Yield:** 4 servings

Ingredients	*Directions*
2 medium carrots, peeled and chopped in 1-inch pieces	*1* Preheat the oven to 400 degrees.
2 cups chopped onions	*2* Combine the carrots, onions, parsnips, turnips, and garlic cloves in a large bowl. Drizzle with the olive oil.
1 parsnip, peeled and chopped in 1-inch pieces	
2 turnips, peeled and chopped in 1-inch pieces	*3* Stir in the tomato paste and flour. Toss to coat the vegetables.
6 whole garlic cloves, peeled	*4* Transfer the vegetables to a large, lined baking pan. Roast for 30 minutes, stirring occasionally, until golden brown.
1 tablespoon olive oil	
1 tablespoon tomato paste, no salt added	
1½ tablespoons whole-wheat flour	*5* Transfer the mixture to a Dutch oven. Add the vegetable stock, bay leaves, and thyme; stir well. Bring to a boil, reduce the heat to a simmer, and cook, uncovered, 15 minutes or until the stew is smooth and slightly thickened.
3 cups unsalted vegetable stock	
3 bay leaves	
½ teaspoon dried thyme	*6* Serve over whole-wheat couscous. Top with Greek yogurt (if desired).
2 cups cooked whole-wheat couscous	
Organic lowfat plain Greek yogurt for topping (optional)	

Per serving: Calories 291 (From Fat 45); Fat 5g (Saturated 0.5g); Cholesterol 0mg; Sodium 198mg; Carbohydrate 55g (Dietary Fiber 10g); Protein 8g; Potassium 541mg.

Note: Roasting root vegetables brings out their best flavor. The high heat locks in the flavors during the caramelization of the outer layers. The vegetables become sweeter, with a melt-in-your-mouth texture.

Tip: Line your pan with parchment paper or a reusable silicon baking mat for easier cleanup. The silicon baking mat has become coauthor Cindy's most trusted kitchen aid, saving money because you can use it multiple times. It also doubles as a nonstick work surface. Clean with a damp cloth to remove any residue or wash in soapy water.

Vary It! Instead of whole-wheat couscous, serve this hearty stew with brown rice or whole-wheat pasta.

Run for the Roses Kentucky Burgoo

Prep time: 30 min • **Cook time:** 2 hrs • **Yield:** 8 servings

Ingredients	*Directions*
1 tablespoon canola oil	*1* Heat the canola oil in a Dutch oven and sauté the chicken and pork in two small batches until browned.
1 pound chicken breast, cut into 1-inch pieces	
½ pound pork tenderloin, cut into 1-inch pieces	*2* Add the water, pepper, and 1 can of stock, scraping the pan and mixing thoroughly. Add the onion, cabbage, and garlic to the pan and bring to a boil. Reduce the heat and simmer low and slow, uncovered, 1 hour or until the meat is tender, stirring occasionally. You can't rush this one!
2½ cups water	
½ teaspoon freshly ground black pepper	
Two 14-ounce cans unsalted chicken stock	*3* Add the remaining can of stock plus the potatoes, beans, corn, and parsley, and bring to a boil. Reduce heat and simmer 30 minutes or until the potato is tender. Stir in the sugar, vinegar, tomato paste, tomatoes, and cayenne pepper; simmer 30 minutes or until the mixture is rich and thick.
1 cup chopped onions	
1 cup chopped cabbage	
3 garlic cloves, minced	
2½ cups diced potatoes	
1 cup frozen lima beans	*4* Sprinkle with additional parsley for garnish and serve with homemade corn bread.
1 cup frozen corn	
1 tablespoon fresh parsley, chopped	
½ tablespoon sugar	
3 tablespoons distilled vinegar	
2 tablespoons unsalted tomato paste	
One 14-ounce can petite diced tomatoes, no salt added, undrained	
1 teaspoon cayenne pepper, or more to taste	
Chopped fresh parsley for garnish	

Per serving: Calories 364 (From Fat 36); Fat 4g (Saturated 0.7g); Cholesterol 52mg; Sodium 225mg; Carbohydrate 23g (Dietary Fiber 4g); Protein 24g; Potassium 774mg.

Roasted Cauliflower Cream Soup

Prep time: 15 min • **Cook time:** 45 min • **Yield:** 4 servings

Ingredients	*Directions*
1 large head cauliflower	*1* Heat the oven to 400 degrees. Remove the leaves and core from the cauliflower. Cut the stem off and discard, and break the flowerettes off into small, bite-sized pieces. Place the flowerettes on a lined baking sheet.
4 cloves garlic	
3 tablespoons olive oil	
16 ounces low-sodium chicken broth	*2* Use a garlic press to crush the garlic cloves. Sprinkle the garlic over the cauliflower. Drizzle the cauliflower and garlic with 3 tablespoons of olive oil.
1 teaspoon herbes de Provence, or 2 teaspoons fresh thyme	
Freshly ground black pepper, to taste	*3* Roast the cauliflower in the oven for 30 minutes or until lightly browned and tender. Remove it from the oven.
8 ounces lowfat (1-percent) milk	*4* Place the cauliflower in a large stockpot. Add the chicken broth, the herbes de Provence or thyme, and the pepper. Heat the mixture to boiling over medium heat. Reduce the heat to low and simmer 15 minutes.
½ cup light sour cream	
	5 In batches, pour the broth mixture into a food processor and process until smooth and creamy; then return to the stockpot over medium-low heat (you can also use an immersion blender, right in the pot). Gradually stir in the milk.
	6 Simmer 5 minutes and then remove the mixture from the heat. Stir in the sour cream. Pour into bowls and garnish with a teaspoon of lowfat sour cream and freshly ground black pepper (if desired).

Per serving: Calories 295 (From Fat 117); Fat 13g (Saturated 3g); Cholesterol 7mg; Sodium 128mg; Carbohydrate 11g (Dietary Fiber 2g); Protein 6g; Potassium 338mg.

Note: Depending on the size of your head of cauliflower, you may need more or less milk. Add the milk gradually to achieve a desirable, creamy consistency.

Tip: Keep a jar of minced garlic in the fridge for easy use. Substitute ¼ teaspoon for one clove.

Vary It! Add some carrots to this recipe for a flavorful twist. Place 1 to 2 cups of baby carrots on the roasting pan with the cauliflower and roast until tender. Proceed through the recipe, pureeing the carrots along with the cauliflower.

Curried Tomato-Lentil Soup

Prep time: 10 min • **Cook time:** 40 min • **Yield:** 6 servings

Ingredients	*Directions*
1 tablespoon olive oil	*1* Heat a large pot and add the olive oil. Add the onion, garlic, and curry powder. Sauté over medium heat until the onion is soft.
½ cup chopped onion	
2 garlic cloves, minced	
1 tablespoon curry powder	*2* Add the lentils and sauté 1 to 2 minutes. Stir in the tomatoes and stock. Bring to a boil. Reduce the heat to low and simmer, stirring occasionally, 40 minutes or until the lentils are tender. Add pepper to taste.
1 cup lentils, rinsed	
6 medium ripe tomatoes, peeled, seeded, and chopped	
6 cups unsalted chicken stock or unsalted vegetable stock	*3* Stir in the lemon juice.
Freshly ground black pepper to taste	*4* Ladle the soup into warm bowls. Serve with a dollop of yogurt and sprinkle with mint, if desired.
1 tablespoon fresh lemon juice	
⅓ cup organic lowfat plain Greek yogurt (optional)	
2 tablespoons fresh mint, chopped (optional)	

Per serving: Calories 199 (From Fat 27); Fat 3g (Saturated 0g); Cholesterol 0mg; Sodium 166mg; Carbohydrate 28g (Dietary Fiber 12g); Protein 15g; Potassium 642mg.

Note: The use of lentils dates back to prehistoric times; they're inexpensive, highly nutritious, and have a distinct pepper flavor. Unlike other dry beans, you don't need to soak them before you cook them, which makes them ideal for a quick meal!

Tip: Curry powder is a mixture of over 20 pungent spices, such as cardamom, chilies, cloves, cumin, fennel seed, and black and red pepper. Don't shy away from this recipe if it sounds too exotic; just use less curry powder in the recipe for just a flavor teaser! If you prefer a thicker consistency, mashing some of the lentils will give the soup more body. And, do consider the yogurt and mint garnish; the mint partners well with the curry.

Rustic Pasta E Fagioli

Prep time: 10 min • **Cook time:** 15–20 min • **Yield:** 4 servings

Ingredients	Directions
1 tablespoon olive oil	**1** Heat the oil in a Dutch oven until hot. Add the rosemary, thyme, bay leaves, onion, carrot, celery, garlic, and pepper. Sauté until the vegetables are soft, about 2 to 3 minutes.
1 tablespoon fresh rosemary, or 1 teaspoon dried	
½ teaspoon dried thyme	
2 dried bay leaves	**2** Add the beans, tomato sauce, water, and vegetable stock, and bring the soup to a rapid boil.
1 cup finely chopped onion	
1 large carrot, finely chopped	**3** Add the pasta, reduce the heat to medium, and cook 6 to 8 minutes until the pasta is cooked.
1 cup finely chopped celery	
2 garlic cloves, chopped	**4** Remove the soup from the heat and add the fresh tomatoes and fresh basil. Ladle the soup into bowls and top with freshly grated Parmigiano-Reggiano cheese before serving.
Freshly ground pepper to taste	
One 15-ounce can cannellini beans, drained and rinsed	
1 cup canned tomato sauce, no salt added	
2 cups water	
4 cups no-salt-added vegetable stock	
1 cup ditalini pasta	
1 cup chopped fresh tomatoes	
¼ cup chopped fresh basil	
1½ tablespoons grated Parmigiano-Reggiano	

Per serving: Calories 378 (From Fat 54); Fat 6g (Saturated 1g); Cholesterol 0mg; Sodium 282mg; Carbohydrate 60g (Dietary Fiber 12g); Protein 17g; Potassium 529mg.

Tip: Serve the soup with hard-crusted, whole-grain bread. The flavor of this soup really develops when refrigerated overnight, so consider making it a day ahead.

Bold and Beefy Slow-Cooker Stew

Prep time: 20 min • **Cook time:** 8–9 hr • **Yield:** 6 servings

Ingredients	*Directions*
1 cup sun-dried tomatoes (not packed in oil)	*1* Rehydrate the tomatoes by placing them in a small glass bowl (a 2-cup glass measuring cup works well) of very warm water and letting them sit for 15 minutes. Drain and coarsely chop.
1½ pounds (or about 10 to 12) new potatoes	
1 medium onion, peeled	*2* Clean the potatoes with water, scrub them, and cut them in half (do not peel). Cut the onion into 1-inch chunks.
1 pound lean beef stew meat	
¼ teaspoon sea salt	*3* Cut the beef into ½-inch cubes. Salt evenly with the sea salt.
One 8-ounce bag baby cut carrots	
2 cups water	*4* Combine the rehydrated tomatoes, beef, potatoes, onions, baby carrots, 2 cups of water, wine, and salt-free herb mixture in a 3½- to 5-quart slow cooker. Cover and cook on low for 8 to 9 hours or until the beef and vegetables are tender.
½ cup dry red wine	
1 tablespoon salt-free Italian herb mixture (a blend of oregano, thyme, garlic powder, and rosemary)	
¼ cup cold water	*5* Stir the flour into ¼ cup of cold water and mix until smooth. Add one ladle of stew broth to the flour mixture. Gradually stir the mixture into the hot stew.
2 tablespoons flour	
	6 Cover, turn the slow cooker to high heat, and continue cooking for about 10 minutes or until slightly thickened.

Per serving: Calories 238 (From Fat 63); Fat 7g (Saturated 3g); Cholesterol 42mg; Sodium 220mg; Carbohydrate 21g (Dietary Fiber 4g); Protein 19g; Potassium 780mg.

Note: Instead of "stew meat," this recipe uses a smaller amount of leaner beef. Purchase a lean cut of sirloin, trim visible fat, and cut into smaller cubes.

Tip: Keep a small, clean jar in the kitchen to use for blending flour and water for sauces. Place water and flour in the jar and shake vigorously until smooth; then pour into your sauce or stew.

Just Chillin' with Zesty Chili

Chili is a great quick supper, and it's also great for serving a crowd. Like soups, chilis are cooked in one pot so they retain all the nutrition of their ingredients.

Chili con carne is the traditional, tomato-based, beef-and-kidney-bean chili that you're probably familiar with. Your family may already have a favorite chili recipe that's a real crowd-pleaser. We have a few tips for modifying your favorite recipe to meet your hypertension goals:

- ✔ **Use lean meat.** If you're using beef, look for the extra-lean (90- to 95-percent fat-free) variety. Brown the beef in your stockpot and drain any excess fat that remains. Try ground buffalo if you can find it; it's very lean.

- ✔ **Move beyond kidney beans.** Try pinto beans, great northern beans, or — our favorite — black beans in your next pot of chili.

- ✔ **Substitute ground venison for beef.** If you have a hunter in the family, use ground venison for an extra-lean chili. While many people feel that venison tastes "gamey," if it's properly butchered, it shouldn't. Using ground venison for chili recipes works well because all the wonderful spices help conceal any gamey flavor your venison may have.

- ✔ **To keep sodium in check, use dried beans and fresh or low-sodium canned tomatoes when possible.** You can use canned beans, but be sure to rinse them thoroughly. Rinsing and draining canned beans has been shown to reduce the sodium content by 36 to 41 percent.

- ✔ **Add fresh herbs.** Adding herbs toward the end of cooking provides a unique, fresh flavor to chilis.

Leftover chili can make a great lunch or a quick dinner. Make a quick bowl of brown rice. Spoon about ⅓ cup of chili and about ¼ cup of brown rice into a whole-wheat flour tortilla. Microwave for one minute. Add fresh chopped tomatoes, minced green peppers, lettuce, and a teaspoon of lowfat sour cream. Wrap burrito-style. Yum!

Chili is a great make-ahead dish. The good news is that the longer it sits, the more the flavors meld and the tastier it gets. You can allow chili to simmer on a warm plate for hours or transfer it to a slow cooker when serving a crowd.

First-Place Chicken Chili

Prep time: 10 min • **Cook time:** 20 min • **Yield:** 9 servings

Ingredients	*Directions*
½ tablespoon ground black pepper	*1* Combine the pepper, thyme, cumin, garlic, chili powder, and flour in a food processor. Add the tortilla pieces a small amount at a time and process until everything is finely ground.
1 teaspoon thyme	
2 teaspoons cumin	
1 teaspoon minced garlic	*2* Heat the canola oil in a Dutch oven. Add the onion, celery, and bell pepper; sauté until the onion is transparent. Add ¼ cup of the chicken stock and cook until the mixture is well-blended.
1 tablespoon chili powder	
¼ cup flour	
12 yellow corn tortillas, torn in pieces	*3* Add the ground tortilla mixture and cook until thick.
½ cup canola oil	
½ cup diced onion	*4* Slowly add the remaining chicken stock, 1 cup at a time, until soup consistency is achieved.
½ cup diced celery	
1 large green bell pepper, diced	*5* Add the chicken pieces and the navy beans. Simmer on low heat just until the flavors are well blended, for about 30 minutes.
8 cups unsalted chicken stock	
3 chicken breasts, cooked and shredded	
One 16-ounce can navy beans, drained and rinsed	*6* Serve in warm soup bowls with grated low-fat cheese, avocado slices, and fresh cilantro and lime wedges (if desired).
¼ cup shredded lowfat cheddar cheese	
1 avocado, cut into 8 to 10 slices	
1 tablespoon fresh cilantro, minced	
Fresh lime wedges (optional)	

Per serving: Calories 567 (From Fat 261); Fat 29g (Saturated 5g); Cholesterol 118mg; Sodium 311mg; Carbohydrate 39g (Dietary Fiber 11g); Protein 36; Potassium 830mg.

Veggie Bean Stew with a Kick

Prep time: 10 min • **Cook time:** 20 min • **Yield:** 6 servings

Ingredients	*Directions*
½ tablespoon olive oil	*1* Combine the oil, chili powder, cumin, cardamom, and mustard seeds in a large Dutch oven. Place over high heat and stir until the spices sizzle, about 30 seconds.
1 tablespoon chili powder	
¾ teaspoon ground cumin	
¼ teaspoon cardamom	*2* Add the onions, mushrooms, salsa verde, and ½ cup of the vegetable stock. Cover and cook until the vegetables are soft. Uncover and stir until the juices evaporate and the vegetables are browned.
2 tablespoons mustard seeds	
½ cup chopped onion	
½ pound pre-sliced baby bella mushrooms	*3* Add the remaining stock, beans, tomato paste, and chipotle pepper and mix well. Cook for 15 to 20 minutes until the flavors are well blended.
2 ounces salsa verde	
3 cups no-salt-added vegetable stock	
Two 14-ounce cans black beans, rinsed and drained	*4* To serve, ladle the chili into warm bowls and garnish with a sprinkling of the cheese and cilantro, a dollop of sour cream, and a lime wedge.
3 ounces tomato paste, no salt added	
1 chipotle pepper in adobo sauce, minced	
1 cup shredded lowfat Mexican-blend cheese	
½ cup chopped fresh cilantro	
½ cup fat-free sour cream	
1 lime, cut into wedges	

Per serving: Calories 228 (From Fat 63); Fat 7g (Saturated 3g); Cholesterol 16mg; Sodium 358mg; Carbohydrate 31g (Dietary Fiber 8g); Protein 15g; Potassium 673mg.

Bean-Tastic Three-Bean Chili

Prep time: 10 min • **Cook time:** 40 min • **Yield:** 6 servings

Ingredients	Directions
1 tablespoon canola oil	**1** Heat the oil in a Dutch oven. Add the onions and sauté until tender.
½ cup chopped onion	
4 cloves garlic, chopped	**2** Add the garlic, cumin, and chili powder, and sauté until fragrant.
1 tablespoon cumin	
1 teaspoon chipotle chili powder	**3** Add the stock, the pumpkin puree, all the beans, and the tomatoes, and simmer for 30 minutes on low heat.
4 cups unsalted vegetable stock	
½ cup pumpkin puree	**4** Ladle into warm soup bowls and garnish with cilantro.
One 15.5-ounce can black beans, rinsed and drained	
One 15.5-ounce can kidney beans, rinsed and drained	
One 15.5-ounce can pinto beans, rinsed and drained	
One 14-ounce can petite diced, low-sodium tomatoes	
½ cup chopped cilantro	

Per serving: Calories 195 (From Fat 36); Fat 4g (Saturated 0g); Cholesterol 0mg; Sodium 487mg; Carbohydrate 33g (Dietary Fiber 9g); Protein 11g; Potassium 631mg.

Note: Beans are delicious, life-sustaining little packages of near perfection. They're versatile and inexpensive, and they contain lots of fiber, iron, folate, magnesium, potassium, and antioxidants. They provide a lowfat, saturated-fat-free and cholesterol-free protein option. Adding pumpkin puree packs a second nutritional punch with the addition of beta-carotene, an antioxidant that may help prevent heart disease and certain types of cancer.

Tip: "Beans, beans, the musical fruit, the more you eat the more you . . . " as the saying goes. The indelicate social consequence of eating too many beans is the result of our body's inability to digest the complex sugars called oligosaccharides. They pass through the digestive tract where they break down and form gasses. Commercial remedies like Beano can provide the necessary enzyme to digest the complex sugars. The reality is the more you eat, the more your body will adjust!

Chapter 11

Think Healthy Is Boring? Trying Scrumptious Vegetable Sides

The mandate to eat more vegetables is almost a running joke. Many a conversation between health professionals and patients goes like this:

Dietitian: "You know what your diet is lacking?"

Patient: "What?"

Dietitian: "You need to eat more vegetables!"

Almost everybody (including some dietitians) needs to work on eating more vegetables. In a world filled with the temptation of easy-to-prepare processed foods, it's no wonder so many people have lost their way when it comes to fixing natural foods. And nothing could be more natural than a vegetable.

Plucked right out of your own garden or purchased straight from the produce aisle of your supermarket, a vegetable with humble beginnings can turn into a tasty, vitamin-packed energy source. (Have you forgotten how good vegetables are for you? Flip to Chapter 7.) And the idea that it takes too much time to cook vegetables is proven incorrect here. Check it out: Veggies are your new, cool friend. (Oh, and did we tell you that eating vegetables helps you feel better and look your sexiest? Oh yeah.)

Fixing Veggies So Tasty You Won't Ask for the Salt

You may have already picked up on a little secret from previous chapters: You can enhance the flavor of foods with very little or no salt in loads of ways. Vegetables are no exception. Seasonings and cooking methods can change and enhance the flavor of a variety of vegetables. Different combinations of ingredients also help create wonderful vegetable recipes.

The following herbs and seasonings are especially handy in making vegetables taste as good as they are for you:

- **Lemon:** Lemon juice and zest are great accompaniments to green veggies like green beans, spinach, asparagus, and broccoli. The acidic nature of lemons enhances the flavor and balances bitterness.

- **Dill:** Dill (dried or fresh) offers a light touch to vegetables like squash, carrots, onions, or string beans.

- **Tarragon, thyme, and rosemary:** These herbs offer unique flavor to mixed vegetable dishes that may include mushrooms, eggplant, onions, or zucchini and other squash.

- **Basil:** This herb lends a mild yet pungent flavor to any dish. It works particularly well with tomatoes, asparagus, and mushrooms.

- **Shallots or onions:** Minced or chopped onions or shallots can really enhance a plain vegetable dish by adding new flavor as well as texture to the dish.

- **Garlic:** Using crushed or minced garlic when grilling or roasting veggies adds a flavor burst as well as some antioxidant properties to your dish.

- **Ground Pepper:** Freshly ground black pepper can replace a lot of the salt you may normally use. Peppered vegetables are delicious. In addition to ground black pepper, you can also add ground red pepper, ground chipotle pepper, or smoked paprika for a little heat.

In this section, we serve up great veggie and flavoring combinations as well as different cooking methods to bring out the taste and texture of vegetables. Far from boring and tasteless, the vegetable recipes in this chapter will make you want to run out to your grocery store's produce aisle or farmer's market today.

Southwest Corn with Chipotle Peppers

Prep time: 10 min • **Cook time:** 10 min • **Yield:** 4 servings

Ingredients	*Directions*
1 tablespoon canola oil **3 medium shallots, peeled and chopped**	*1* Heat the canola oil in a medium skillet. Add the shallots and sauté until tender (about 2 minutes). Add the chopped chipotle peppers and stir for 3 more minutes.
1 tablespoon canned chipotle peppers in adobo sauce, finely chopped **2 cups corn kernels from 3 to 4 ears of grilled corn or thawed from frozen**	*2* Add the corn to the skillet. Add the thyme and cook, stirring frequently, until the flavors are combined (about 5 minutes).
2 tablespoons chopped fresh thyme	*3* Add fresh ground pepper to taste.
Fresh ground pepper to taste **Thyme sprigs for garnish (optional)**	*4* Garnish with thyme sprigs (if desired) and serve at once.

Per serving: Calories 113 (From Fat 36); Fat 4g (Saturated 0g); Cholesterol 0mg; Sodium 21mg; Carbohydrate 19g (Dietary Fiber 2g); Protein 3g; Potassium 212mg.

Note: Check out this flavorful side in the color section. This recipe tastes even better with corn you've grilled rather than thawed or boiled. If you have the will and the way, place the corn cobs directly on the grill and cook for 15 minutes, turning every 5 minutes until the corn is done. Cut the corn from the cob using a sharp knife or mandolin. You can also find frozen grilled corn at specialty grocery stores.

Vary It! Add a 14.5-ounce can of thoroughly rinsed black beans for added flavor, protein, and variety. Serve warm or at room temperature as a dip with unsalted, baked tortilla chips.

Haricots Verts with Lemon Dill Dressing

Prep time: 5 min • **Cook time:** 5 min • **Yield:** 4 servings

Ingredients	Directions
½ pound haricots verts, washed, trimmed, and drained	**1** Fill a large saucepan with an inch of water and bring to a boil.
2 teaspoons fresh dill, chopped	**2** Place a vegetable steamer in the saucepan. Add the haricots verts, cover, and steam until tender-crisp (about 5 minutes). Remove from heat.
1 teaspoon minced shallot	
½ tablespoon olive oil	
½ tablespoon lemon juice	**3** To make the dressing, whisk the dill, shallot, oil, lemon juice, and mustard in a large bowl. Add the steamed haricots verts and toss to coat. Sprinkle with freshly ground black pepper to taste.
½ tablespoon stone-ground mustard	
Freshly ground black pepper to taste	

Per serving: Calories 36 (From Fat 18); Fat 2g (Saturated 0g); Cholesterol 0mg; Sodium 1mg; Carbohydrate 4g (Dietary Fiber 2g); Protein 1g; Potassium 103mg.

Note: The French green beans haricots verts are smaller and slimmer than regular green beans. Their flavor is more intense than regular green beans, and their ends don't require cutting.

Tip: Bean shopping? Choose beans that are deep green, smooth, and crisp.

Vary It! If you can't find haricots verts, you can substitute traditional green beans.

Steamed Broccoli Piccata

Prep time: 10 min • **Cook time:** 6–7min • **Yield:** 4 servings

Ingredients	*Directions*
1 large bunch broccoli, cut into stalks 1 tablespoon butter	*1* Place the broccoli in a steamer basket over 2 inches of water in a large saucepan over high heat. Cover and steam for about 5 minutes.
2 garlic cloves, minced ¼ teaspoon red pepper flakes 1½ teaspoons grated lemon zest	*2* In a small skillet, heat the butter, garlic, and red pepper flakes until the garlic is tender. Add the grated lemon zest.
	3 Drizzle the sauce over the steamed broccoli.

Per serving: Calories 41 (From Fat 27); Fat 3g (Saturated 2g); Cholesterol 8mg; Sodium 33mg; Carbohydrate 3g (Dietary Fiber 1g); Protein 1g; Potassium 130mg.

Tip: Instead of steaming the broccoli, you can microwave it on high for 4 minutes in a large glass baking dish with a tight-fitting lid.

Roasted Mixed Winter Squash with Walnuts

Prep time: 15 min • **Cook time:** 35 min • **Yield:** 8 servings

Ingredients	Directions
1 acorn squash	*1* Heat the oven to 400 degrees.
1 butternut squash	
3 tablespoons extra-virgin olive oil	*2* With a sharp knife, cut both squash in half and scoop out the seeds and pulp. Peel the skin of the butternut squash, using a vegetable peeler. Peel the acorn squash by cutting halves into wedges and then using a knife to cut the skin away. Cube all the squash into ½-inch cubes.
1 large shallot, minced	
⅓ cup walnuts	
1 tablespoon butter	
1 tablespoon finely chopped fresh rosemary, or 2 teaspoons dried	*3* Place the cubed squash on a large baking sheet. Drizzle with the olive oil. Sprinkle the shallot over the squash and roast in the oven for 25 minutes, tossing once.
Freshly ground black pepper	*4* While the squash is roasting, heat a large sauté pan on medium-high heat. Add the walnuts and toss, watching closely to make sure they don't burn. When they're lightly browned and aromatic, remove them from the heat to a cutting board and chop coarsely. Return to the pan.
2 tablespoons freshly grated Romano cheese	
Additional sprigs of rosemary for garnish (optional)	
	5 Add the butter to the walnuts in the pan and heat on medium heat until the butter is just melted. Add the rosemary and ground pepper; toss.
	6 When the squash has finished roasting, add it to the pan and toss gently, browning slightly. Remove from heat and pour into a serving bowl. Sprinkle with Romano cheese. Garnish with additional rosemary sprigs (if desired).

Per serving: Calories 125 (From Fat 90); Fat 10g (Saturated 2g); Cholesterol 5mg; Sodium 28mg; Carbohydrate 9g (Dietary Fiber 2g); Protein 2g; Potassium 277mg.

Vary It!: You can use only one type of squash in this recipe, or add more varieties. The squash is the limit! You can also try substituting thyme for the rosemary, if you prefer. Adding cinnamon or nutmeg provides a slightly sweet tone to the dish.

Tip: For easier cutting, make a slit into a whole squash, microwave for 2 to 3 minutes, and allow the squash to cool slightly before handling. Then, peel and cut.

Grilled Asparagus Panzanella

Prep time: 10 min • **Cook time:** 15 min • **Yield:** 8 servings

Ingredients	Directions
1½ pounds fresh asparagus, trimmed	**1** Preheat the grill. Rinse the asparagus thoroughly under water and snap off the tough ends of the asparagus. Starting at the base of each spear, bend the spear several times and work toward the tip, until you find a place where it breaks easily. Break off the woody base and discard it.
2 tablespoons red wine vinegar, divided	
1 garlic clove, minced	
Freshly ground black pepper to taste	**2** Whisk the vinegar, garlic, pepper, and olive oil in a bowl until combined. Drizzle the asparagus with 1 tablespoon of the vinegar mixture. Save the remaining dressing for the salad.
1 tablespoon olive oil, divided	
6 thick slices day-old sourdough-style bread	**3** Arrange the asparagus perpendicular to the grill grates. Grill 2 to 3 minutes, turn, and cook 2 to 3 more minutes or until the asparagus is crisp-tender, being careful not to burn it.
4 large fresh tomatoes, chopped	
1 tablespoon capers, rinsed and drained	**4** Grill the bread about 1 minute on each side or until slightly charred. Cut each slice into 1-inch cubes. Cut the asparagus into 2-inch pieces and combine the asparagus, grilled bread, tomatoes, capers, and basil in a bowl. Add the remaining vinegar mixture and additional freshly ground pepper (if desired), and serve it up, or let sit for no more than 30 minutes.
8 fresh basil leaves, thinly sliced	

Per serving: Calories 99 (From Fat 18); Fat 2g (Saturated 0g); Cholesterol 0mg; Sodium 159mg; Carbohydrate 17g (Dietary Fiber 3g); Protein 5g; Potassium 347mg.

Tip: Chop your basil like a top chef by cutting a chiffonade. Check out Figure 11-1.

How to Chiffonade !

Figure 11-1: Roll up your basil and cut away.

Mixing and Matching: Dishes with Multiple Servings of Veggies

One reason some people may not be fond of veggies is that they may have only eaten them as supporting side dishes, plain and lonesome on a plate. While serving a veggie as a solo side is just fine, we recommend branching out a bit to enjoy a wider variety of vegetables in your diet. In fact, you can make a whole meal out of some of the recipes in this section.

By combining more than one vegetable, you not only amp up your nutrient intake for the day, but you also may find that a vegetable on your "don't like" list actually deserves a promotion to the "yum" list! Adding small amounts of toppings such as grated cheese or breadcrumbs can raise the yum factor even higher.

One of our favorite ways to make a super-easy, multi-vegetable dish is to fix a mixed roast. Vegetables like zucchini, eggplant, portobello mushrooms, and onions are great for roasting and grilling. The Grilled Summer Vegetable Medley makes a great topping for whole-grain pasta as well.

Cheese is naturally high in sodium (and fat) but offers wonderful flavor. In lieu of salt, a small amount of cheese may be used to enhance the flavor of a vegetable dish.

Toss out the idea that vegetables must be loners, and broaden your plant-based (and phytochemical) horizons. After all, if you don't eat steamed spinach because you don't like it, it can't do you any good. But if you try, say, our Stuffed Summer Squash Zucchini Boats, you may find yourself a new way to enjoy spinach!

Stuffed Summer Squash Zucchini Boats

Prep time: 10 min • **Cook time:** 20 min • **Yield:** 8 servings

Ingredients	Directions
4 large zucchini **One 10-ounce package frozen chopped spinach, thawed** **2 tablespoons olive oil** **½ cup chopped onions** **3 ounces Neufchatel or light cream cheese** **2 garlic cloves, minced** **½ teaspoon black pepper** **Pinch red pepper flakes** **2 tablespoons grated fresh parmesan cheese** **2 tablespoons plain breadcrumbs** **¼ teaspoon dried oregano** **¼ teaspoon dried basil**	*1* Blanch whole zucchini in boiling water for 2 minutes. They'll begin to soften, but will be tender-crisp. Cut them in half lengthwise and remove the seeds with a small spoon. This creates a hollowed-out area for easier stuffing. Place the zucchini cut side up in a 9-x-13-inch baking pan. *2* Drain the spinach well by pressing it between layers of paper towels to remove moisture. *3* Heat the olive oil and sauté the onions until tender. Add the spinach, cream cheese, garlic, black pepper, and red pepper flakes and stir until the cheese melts. Spoon the mixture evenly into the zucchini. *4* Mix together the parmesan cheese, bread crumbs, oregano, and basil. Sprinkle the mixture over the zucchini boats. Bake at 400 degrees for 20 to 25 minutes.

Per serving: Calories 88 (From Fat 54); Fat 6g (Saturated 2g); Cholesterol 9mg; Sodium 121mg; Carbohydrate 4g (Dietary Fiber 1g); Protein 3g; Potassium 178mg.

Tip: Making your own breadcrumbs cuts down on the sodium in this recipe (and saves you money at the grocery store). Stack up a few slices of bread, preferably whole-wheat. Using a serrated knife, cut the bread into ½-inch strips. Cut the strips crosswise into ½-inch cubes. Arrange the cubes in a single layer on a baking pan. Bake the cubes in a 300-degree oven for 10 to 15 minutes, stirring a few times. Let cool. Place the cubes in a Ziploc bag and crush with a rolling pin, or place in a food processor and pulse until finely crushed.

Tomato Basil Spaghetti Squash with Gruyère

Prep time: 10 min • **Cook time:** 1 hr • **Yield:** 4 servings

Ingredients	Directions
1 medium spaghetti squash (2½ to 3 pounds)	**1** Preheat the oven to 350 degrees. Cut the squash in half and discard the seeds. Prick the squash all over with a paring knife. Place in a baking dish cut side down, and bake for 45 to 60 minutes or until soft. Let cool briefly.
2 medium tomatoes, seeded and chopped	
2 tablespoons olive oil	**2** Use a large fork to scrape the flesh and scoop out the spaghetti-like strands of squash into a serving bowl.
¼ cup freshly grated Gruyère cheese	
¼ cup fresh basil, chopped, plus whole leaves for garnish	**3** Mix the tomatoes with the squash and drizzle with olive oil. Toss gently. Grate the fresh cheese on top and add the chopped basil (see the Grilled Asparagus Panzanella recipe for tips on cutting a basil chiffonade).
	4 Garnish with extra basil leaves.

Per serving: Calories 193 (From Fat 99); Fat 11g (Saturated 3g); Cholesterol 9mg; Sodium 79mg; Carbohydrate 22g (Dietary Fiber 1g); Protein 5g; Potassium 466mg.

Note: Spaghetti squash is fun! Its texture is unlike that of any other summer squash. When cooked, the flesh separates naturally into long, spaghetti-like strands. It's low in calories and makes a great substitute for pasta. This dish is pictured in the color section.

Tip: A quick method of cooking the squash is to pierce it with a fork several times, place it on a microwave-safe plate, and cook at full power for 6–8 minutes. Let it sit for another 5 minutes.

Vary It! Instead of Gruyère cheese, add crumbled feta and a few chopped Kalamata olives (but watch the serving size to keep sodium in check).

Vary It! For Southwest flavor, omit the cheese, add 1 cup of rinsed black beans, and substitute fresh cilantro for the basil.

Grilled Summer Vegetable Medley

Prep time: 10 min • **Cook time:** 5 min • **Yield:** 8 servings

Ingredients	Directions
2 tablespoons olive oil	*1* Preheat a gas grill to medium-high.
1 tablespoon balsamic vinegar	*2* Combine the oil, balsamic vinegar, garlic, and thyme in a small bowl.
1 fresh garlic clove, crushed	
1 teaspoon fresh thyme, chopped	*3* Place the cut vegetables in a medium bowl and drizzle with the oil-vinegar mixture.
1 medium red onion, cut into thick slices	
1 pound asparagus stalks, trimmed	*4* Place the vegetables directly on the grill rack and grill for 5 minutes, turning the vegetables occasionally. To prevent vegetables from falling through the gaps of the grate, use a grill basket to cook the vegetables. Remember to stir or turn the vegetables to ensure even grilling.
1 medium zucchini, diagonally sliced	
1 medium yellow squash, diagonally sliced	
1 red bell pepper, sliced	*5* Arrange the grilled vegetables on a platter. Serve immediately.
5 baby portobello mushrooms, cut in half	

Per serving: Calories 64 (From Fat 36); Fat 4g (Saturated 0.5g); Cholesterol 0mg; Sodium 5mg; Carbohydrate 7g (Dietary Fiber 2g); Protein 2g; Potassium 302mg.

Note:. Meat isn't the only thing that tastes great on the grill. Vegetables that hold up especially well to the intense heat of the grill include eggplant, mushrooms, summer squash, peppers, and onions.

Tip: If a grill isn't available, you can roast this dish in a 400 degree oven for 40 to 60 minutes.

Vary It! For a fun and different presentation, make a Vegetable Napoleon: Stack the grilled vegetables in layers on a salad plate with crumbled feta cheese and fresh mint leaves.

Tomato-Stuffed Red Peppers

Prep time: 10 min • **Cook time:** 50 min • **Yield:** 8 servings

Ingredients	Directions
Nonstick cooking spray	**1** Preheat the oven to 375 degrees. Coat a large, shallow baking pan with cooking spray.
4 large red bell peppers	
2 garlic cloves, thinly sliced	**2** Cut the peppers in half lengthwise, removing the seeds but leaving the stem to help the pepper retain its shape after cooking. Place the peppers cut side up in the baking dish.
1 tablespoon chopped Kalamata olives	
4 ripe tomatoes	
2 tablespoons olive oil	**3** Divide the sliced garlic and olives evenly and sprinkle inside the cut side of the pepper halves.
Freshly ground black pepper	
Sprigs of fresh rosemary	**4** Cut each tomato into 8 wedges and put 4 wedges into each pepper half. Drizzle each stuffed pepper with oil and season with pepper.
	5 Place the dish in the oven and roast until the peppers are tender and beginning to brown around the edges, about 50 minutes. Serve immediately with sprigs of fresh rosemary.

Per serving: Calories 62 (From Fat 36); Fat 4g (Saturated 0.5g); Cholesterol 0mg; Sodium 15mg; Carbohydrate 6g (Dietary Fiber 2g); Protein 1g; Potassium 274mg.

Note: Roasting peppers gives them a smoky, rich, sweet flavor. Use roasted peppers as a side dish or an ingredient within a recipe. Roasting browns the vegetables, intensifying the flavor without the sodium or added fat.

Tip: Have leftovers? Make a roasted red pepper puree (coulis) by pulsing the leftover peppers in a food processor or an immersion blender with a few tablespoons of low-sodium vegetable or chicken broth. Use this sauce with your favorite grilled fish, chicken, or pasta.

Bok Choy Stir-Fry

Prep time: 5 min • **Cook time:** 5 min • **Yield:** 4 servings

Ingredients	Directions
1 tablespoon peanut oil 2 tablespoons minced gingerroot 2 large garlic cloves, minced 1 red bell pepper, cut lengthwise into thin strips 2 stalks celery, sliced diagonally 2 large green onions, thinly sliced on a sharp diagonal 1 head bok choy, thinly sliced, green leaf tops only ½ teaspoon sesame oil Toasted sesame seeds (optional)	*1* Heat an electric wok or a heavy wok skillet over high heat. Add the oil and swirl to coat the bottom and sides of the wok. Add the ginger and garlic; sauté 20 seconds. *2* Add the bell pepper and celery, and sauté until crisp-tender, about 2 minutes. *3* Add the green onions and bok choy, and sauté until just wilted, about 2 minutes. Drizzle in the sesame oil. *4* Sprinkle with toasted sesame seeds (if desired) and serve immediately.

Per serving: Calories 78 (From Fat 45); Fat 5g (Saturated 1g); Cholesterol 0mg; Sodium 155mg; Carbohydrate 8g (Dietary Fiber 3g); Protein 4g; Potassium 672mg.

Tip: The trick to perfect stir-frying is to cook using small amounts of food or in batches. It's best not to overcrowd the wok with too many ingredients at once.

Vary It! To make this a vegetarian main dish meal, drain firm tofu and blot with paper towels until much of the liquid is absorbed. Cut the tofu into 1-inch cubes and lightly dust with flour. Prior to cooking the vegetables, heat the wok, add the oil and the tofu, and stir-fry until lightly browned, about 2 minutes. Transfer to a plate and combine with the stir-fried vegetables.

The Other Leafy Greens: Giving Popeye a Run for His Money

When you think about leafy veggies, you probably think of common favorites like lettuce and spinach. We love those green guys (see our salads in Chapter 9 for evidence), but in this section, we introduce you to other leafy greens that deserve a spot in your diet.

For one thing, leafy greens are chock-full of vitamins, particularly folate and vitamins K, C, and A. They're a good source of magnesium and riboflavin too. These greens can work raw in a salad, as a stuffing ingredient, in stir-frys, or on their own, making them quite versatile. Because they cook quite quickly, they make great go-to dishes for those hectic weeknights. Considered nutritional powerhouses, they can be used interchangeably in many recipes.

Some of your new favorite greens may include:

- **Chard:** There are several varieties of chard, the most common being Swiss chard. Chard sports green leaves and a red stem. This leafy vegetable is sweet, mildly bitter, and tender.

- **Kale:** This green, leafy vegetable belongs to the cabbage family and is similar to collard greens. Kale is generally a better choice during the winter months.

- **Napa cabbage:** This green cabbage is great for salads or in cooking. It's very low in calories and high in fiber.

- **Bok choy:** This leafy green is used in Chinese dishes and is slightly sweeter than other cabbages.

When purchasing greens, look for bunches that are firm without any brown or black edges on the leaves. Store greens in a loose bag in the crisper drawer of your refrigerator and plan to use them within a few days of purchase. Don't wash them until you're ready to prepare them.

You'll find that when you cook greens, what first appears to be a huge potful ends up as a mere cupful. This change in volume occurs because as the greens cook, they wilt and take up less space. Six cups of raw greens generally yield about one cup of cooked greens. Keep that in mind, and keep reading for tasty, leafy recipes that would make Popeye jealous.

Curried Swiss Chard

Prep time: 5 min • **Cook time:** 5 min • **Yield:** 4 servings

Ingredients	Directions
1 large bunch red ribbed Swiss chard, washed thoroughly	*1* Remove the stems from the chard and chop the stems into ½-inch pieces.
1½ teaspoons olive oil	
2 to 3 garlic cloves, minced	*2* Stack the chard leaves on top of each other and cut into strips.
½ teaspoon cumin	
½ teaspoon ground ginger	*3* Heat the oil in a large skillet over medium heat. Add the chard stems (not the leaves), garlic, and spices.
½ teaspoon yellow mustard seeds	
⅛ teaspoon pepper	*4* Cover the skillet and cook 5 minutes, until fragrant and tender.
⅛ teaspoon cardamom	
	5 Add the chard leaves and stir just until they reduce in volume. Serve warm.

Per serving: Calories 30 (From Fat 18); Fat 2g (Saturated 0g); Cholesterol 0mg; Sodium 97mg; Carbohydrate 3g (Dietary Fiber 1g); Protein 1g; Potassium 188mg.

Note: Swiss chard, or chard, is a cruciferous vegetable and a member of the beet family. Some call it a vegetable with a PhD because it contains fiber, vitamin C, and magnesium, and it's a low-fat source of vitamins E and K. It contains iron, but the oxalic acid compound in chard may limit the mineral's absorption by the body. The iron is better absorbed when chard is either prepared and eaten with a vitamin C source or heated with olive oil.

Tip: Got leftovers? Use them as a healthy filling for a frittata or omelet.

Vary It! Follow Steps 1–5, but omit all the spices except the minced garlic cloves. Cover and cook until tender and wilted. Drizzle sesame oil and fresh squeezed lemon juice over the chard and serve warm.

Sautéed Kale with Pine Nuts

Prep time: 5 min • **Cook time:** 12 min • **Yield:** 4 servings

Ingredients	Directions
1 large garlic clove, minced	**1** Sauté the minced garlic in olive oil over medium heat; then add the kale and sauté until heated through (about 1 minute).
½ tablespoon olive oil	
1 pound fresh dinosaur kale (Tuscan, black, or cavallo nero), trimmed and chopped	
	2 Stir in the pine nuts. Remove the skillet from the heat.
2 tablespoons pine nuts, lightly toasted	
	3 Sprinkle the kale mixture with lemon juice.
2 tablespoons fresh lemon juice	

Per serving: Calories 104 (From Fat 45); Fat 5g (Saturated 0.5g); Cholesterol 0mg; Sodium 49mg; Carbohydrate 13g (Dietary Fiber 2g); Protein 4g, Potassium 545mg.

Note: This member of the cabbage family has a rich supply of fiber, vitamin C, vitamin B6, beta carotene, and calcium. Eating 2 cups of kale provides 16 percent of the recommended dietary allowance (RDA) for calcium, with only 72 calories. Kale also has a lower oxalic acid content than other greens, making the calcium more easily absorbed by the body.

Tip: Using kale within a day or two of purchase is best because the longer you store it, the stronger the flavor becomes. Dinosaur kale is top-notch, but if you can't find it at your local grocer, you can substitute any variety of kale. If the kale is tough and thick, boil in it a pot of water for about 5 to 10 minutes prior to sautéing.

Note: You may substitute one 10-ounce package of frozen chopped kale, thawed and drained, for fresh kale.

Tip: Use leftover kale as a topping for pizza, a stuffing for poultry, or an ingredient for vegetable soup or potato chowder!

Chapter 12

Seeing a New Side of Potatoes, Grains, and Pasta

Sometimes side dishes seem to be the toughest part of putting a meal together. If you find yourself in a rut, putting plain old potatoes or rice on the table week after week, you're going to love this chapter! We show you how to use a variety of potatoes, introduce you to some different grains, and demonstrate how pasta can be incorporated into healthy side dishes.

Complex carbohydrates are your body's main energy source. Muscles prefer them to protein or fat as an energy source and the brain relies on them over other major nutrients. Starchy carbohydrates like pasta, potatoes (especially white potatoes), and grains have gotten a bad rap over the years. But we assert that "carbs make you fat" claims are unfounded because not all carbohydrates are alike. The wholesome complex carbohydrates supplied by the recipes in this chapter provide an important source of energy, nutrients, and fiber in the diet. Simple carbohydrates like sugar and sweets provide very little nutrition. Portion control, especially of high-sugar foods, is also a large part of the equation in determining how our bodies respond to carbs.

The key to including starchy foods in your diet is knowing how much of them you can eat. Figure 2-1 (go back to Chapter 2) shows how much of your plate should *actually* be filled with *starchy* carbs (like rice, pasta, grains, or potatoes) — only about one-fourth to one-third of your plate. Fill another fourth with lean meat and the remainder of your plate with veggies. This creates balance.

In this chapter, we share tips that show you how to incorporate more fruits and veggies into your grain or pasta dishes. Combining veggies with pasta not only helps you meet your goal of eating eight to ten servings of fruits and vegetables daily, but also adds important antioxidants, nutrients, and fiber to your diet. So dig into these tasty dishes!

Serving Potatoes with Personality

There's nothing wrong with a good old Idaho baked potato. Light and fluffy and full of potassium, vitamin C, and fiber, potatoes make a good side dish. Making a perfect baked potato is a snap: Preheat your oven to 400 degrees. Scrub the potato under cold water and pat it dry. Make a lengthwise slit in the potato, piercing it only about a third of the way through. If desired, brush the potato lightly with oil before placing it directly on the oven rack. Bake for 45 to 60 minutes.

Be sure to choose potatoes that bake well (see the list that follows). Idahos or Russets are great white baking potatoes.

But don't limit yourself to the usual baked potatoes. The recipes we offer in this section help you broaden your potato horizons and keep the cooking easy and nutritious. While all potatoes are good sources of vitamin C and potassium (an average 5-ounce potato gives you 45 percent of your Daily Value for vitamin C and about 600 milligrams of potassium, or 17 percent Daily Value), using a variety of potatoes expands the nutrient profile. Sweet potatoes, for instance, add more beta carotene, whereas white potatoes are higher in vitamin C.

Allow us to pass along some of our favorite hot potato varieties. Here's a handful:

- **Yellow potatoes, such as Yukon Gold:** These potatoes are more golden in color than white potatoes. They work well baked, boiled, or fried.

- **Blue or purple potatoes:** These unique potatoes most likely originated in South America but are now grown in the U.S. They're bluish-purple not only in skin but also in flesh, making them high in healthy flavonoids! They work well baked, mashed, or French fried.

- ✔ **Red potatoes:** These red-skinned potatoes have a white flesh and are well suited for boiling or steaming. They also work well in au gratin dishes.

- ✔ **Fingerlings:** These small, delicate potatoes derive their name from their fingerlike shape. They cook best by boiling, steaming, or baking.

- ✔ **Idaho and Russet:** These white-fleshed potatoes are good for baking and work well for making home fries and potato salads.

Home fries are a quick potato side that offers more va-va-voom than the baked-potato staple. Using a high-quality nonstick pan reduces the fat from frying. Simply cube or thinly slice peeled or unpeeled (but scrubbed) potatoes. Heat 2 teaspoons of vegetable oil in a nonstick pan. Add the potatoes, making sure they're in one layer in the pan. Cover and cook on medium heat for about 5 minutes. Uncover, and gently turn the potatoes to brown the other side. Allow to cook uncovered for another 10 minutes on medium to low heat. Fry up sliced onions and bell peppers alongside the potatoes to increase the vitamin and antioxidant count of this sizzling side.

The following recipes give you a few more ways to jazz up potatoes. Give them a try and broaden your family's horizons while pleasing their tastebuds.

Sweet Potato Mash

Prep time: 2 min • **Cook time:** 45 min • **Yield:** 4 servings

Ingredients	*Directions*
4 medium sweet potatoes, washed **Dash cinnamon, to taste** **Dash ground cloves, to taste** **Dash ground ginger, to taste**	*1* Heat your oven to 400 degrees. Pierce each sweet potato with a fork to allow steam to escape during baking, and place directly on oven rack. Bake 45 minutes or until tender.
	2 Take the potatoes out of the oven and cut a slit in the top of each one. Scoop out the potatoes into a bowl using a large spoon. The potatoes will be hot, so you may prefer to allow them to sit for 5 minutes or use a glove or oven mitt to hold the potato.
	3 Mash the potatoes with a fork to your desired consistency. A perfectly baked potato will mash almost instantly with a fork.
	4 Blend in a dash of cinnamon, cloves, and ginger, to taste.

Per serving: Calories 112 (From Fat 0); Fat 0g (Saturated 0g); Cholesterol 0mg; Sodium 72mg; Carbohydrate 26g (Dietary Fiber 4g); Protein 2g; Potassium 440mg.

Note: Sweet potatoes are one of nature's treasures with their appealing flavor and spectacular nutritional profile. High in fiber, low in calories, and a super supplier of iron, potassium, and vitamins B6, C, and E, one potato provides 100 percent of the daily requirement for beta carotene.

Tip: Baking sweet potatoes provides the richness of roasting and naturally sweet goodness! Another option is to boil sweet potatoes in a saucepan. Peel sweet potatoes and cut them into small pieces. Add them to a small amount of boiling water and cook for 12 minutes or until tender; drain. Mash them with a potato masher, along with your favorite ingredients.

Vary It! To jazz this recipe up for company, drizzle the sweet potato mash with maple syrup, toasted pecans, and toasted coconut, or maple syrup, fresh ginger, and toasted macadamia nuts.

Vary It! Stir plain mashed sweet potatoes into tomato-based pasta sauces. Or, layer mashed sweet potatoes with regular mashed potatoes for a new and tasty treat!

Roasted Cajun Fingerling Potatoes

Prep time: 10 min • **Cook time:** 45 min • **Yield:** 6 servings

Ingredients	Directions
¼ **cup olive oil**	*1* Preheat your oven to 400 degrees.
2 shallots, finely chopped	
1 garlic clove, minced	*2* In a roasting pan, stir together the oil, shallots, garlic, pepper, paprika, and cayenne. Add the potatoes. Mix together to coat the potatoes evenly with the oil mixture.
½ **teaspoon freshly ground black pepper**	
½ **teaspoon paprika**	
½ **teaspoon cayenne pepper**	*3* Roast the potatoes, turning them every 10 minutes until they're tender and golden brown, about 30 to 45 minutes.
2½ **pounds fingerling potatoes, washed and dried**	
2 tablespoons fresh Italian parsley, chopped	*4* Garnish with parsley prior to serving.

Per serving: Calories 215 (From Fat 81); Fat 9g (Saturated 1g); Cholesterol 0mg; Sodium 13mg; Carbohydrate 31g (Dietary Fiber 5g); Protein 3g; Potassium 799mg.

Note: Flip to the color section to see how the finished dish looks. Fingerlings are small, finger-shaped potatoes that are low in starch and rich in vitamin C, fiber, and potassium. Many varieties are grown for flavor and tenderness, including purple Peruvian, yellow-skinned Russian Banana, Ruby Crescent, and orange-skinned French fingerlings.

Tip: Depending on the size of the fingerlings, they may take less time to roast. Be sure to keep an eye on the taters and shake the pan to prevent them from sticking.

Vary It! You can make fingerling potatoes with an entirely different flavor palette. Substitute 1 tablespoon lemon zest and 2 tablespoons each lemon juice, fresh rosemary, and fresh thyme for the garlic, pepper, paprika, and cayenne. Garnish with fresh Italian parsley.

Smashed Potato Medley

Prep time: 40 min • **Cook time:** 20 min • **Yield:** 4 servings

Ingredients	*Directions*
½ **pound red potatoes, peeled, cut into quarters**	**1** Bring 5 quarts of water to boiling in a large stockpot. Put the red potatoes in the pot and allow to continue boiling for about 15 minutes or until the potatoes are fork-tender. Remove the potatoes with a slotted spoon to a medium bowl and set aside.
½ **pound blue potatoes, peeled, cut into quarters**	
2 tablespoons butter, divided	**2** If needed, bring the water back to boiling. Repeat Step 1 with the blue potatoes, placing them in a separate bowl when they're done.
½ **to ¾ cup 1-percent milk, divided**	
¼ **teaspoon salt, divided x 5**	**3** Preheat the oven to 350 degrees. Add 1 tablespoon of the butter to the red potatoes and, using a hand masher, mash lightly but thoroughly. Heat the milk in a microwave-safe measuring cup for 1 minute. Add 3 tablespoons of the sour cream, ¼ cup of the milk, ⅛ teaspoon of the salt, and ¼ teaspoon of the white pepper to the potatoes. Mix until smooth using a wooden spoon. Gradually add more milk if needed to achieve a smooth consistency.
½ **teaspoon ground white pepper, divided**	
6 tablespoons lowfat sour cream, divided	
Cooking spray	
	4 Repeat Step 3 with the blue potatoes in a separate bowl. Again, gradually add more milk if needed to achieve a smooth consistency.
	5 Lightly spray a 3-quart casserole dish with cooking spray. Using a large spoon or an ice-cream scoop, alternately transfer the red and blue potatoes by the spoonful into the casserole dish, ensuring the spoonfuls slightly touch each other. Using a butter knife, cut through the potatoes, going back and forth to achieve a swirl pattern. Bake in preheated oven for 15 to 20 minutes.

Per serving: Calories 174 (From Fat 72); Fat 8g (Saturated 5g); Cholesterol 24mg; Sodium 225mg; Carbohydrate 23g (Dietary Fiber 2g); Protein 4g, Potassium 592mg.

Taking Your Taste Buds on a Grain Adventure

You may have grown up eating refined pastas and white rice, but there's a world of variety waiting for you to discover when it comes to grains. Not only do different grains offer beneficial nutrients and fiber, but they also provide exotic flavors and textures. You'll be the champion chef at the next potluck when you offer up some of these new grains!

In this section we take a look at some options. One is *quinoa* (pronounced "*keen*-wa"), an ancient, grain-like food first harvested by the Incan tribes in South America and now widely available in supermarkets. Use quinoa as the grain in some of your favorite rice dishes (especially pilafs) or pasta salad recipes.

A wide variety of rice is also available, each offering a different texture, color, and flavor to a dish. Here are a few:

- **Brown rice:** This rice has a nutty flavor and is chewier than white rice. It contains 2 grams of fiber per cup.

- **Wild rice:** Actually a grain, wild rice is seeds of wheat grass. These seeds provide a nutty flavor and chewy texture.

- **Converted brown rice:** Brown rice that has been soaked and pre-steamed is called converted rice. It retains most of the nutrients of brown rice, but has a similar taste to white rice.

- **Basmati and jasmine:** Long-grain and sweetly scented, these types of rice have a nutty flavor. Jasmine is slightly stickier than basmati.

- **Arborio:** This rice is used for risotto dishes; the small kernels result in a creamy dish.

In addition to switching up your rice game, try cooking with these grains:

- **Barley** provides 3 grams of fiber per half-cup serving and is mild in flavor. It's a great side or addition to soups, pilafs, or salads.

- **Hominy** is a Native American, corn-based grain. You may be familiar with it in the form of grits, which is hominy that's ground very finely.

- **Bulgur** is made from durum wheat and can be used in soups, pilafs, or as a high-fiber substitute for rice or couscous.

- **Couscous,** actually a tiny pasta but used in recipes like a grain, originated in North Africa and is a popular Moroccan dish. To prepare, mix it with boiling water and let it stand for 5 minutes. Try the whole-wheat kind.

Whole-Wheat Couscous with Dried Cranberries and Almonds

Prep time: 5 min • **Cook time:** 10 min • **Yield:** 4 servings

Ingredients	Directions
½ medium onion, minced 1 tablespoon olive oil	*1* In a medium saucepan, sauté the onion in the oil. Add the couscous and stir together.
¾ cup whole-wheat couscous 1 cup low-sodium vegetable broth	*2* Add the broth and bring to a boil. Cover the pan and remove it from the heat. Let stand until the broth is completely absorbed, about 5 minutes.
2 tablespoons minced fresh parsley ½ cup dried cranberries 2 tablespoons sliced almonds, toasted	*3* Stir in the parsley, dried cranberries, and almonds with a fork. Serve.

Per serving: Calories 155 (From Fat 45); Fat 5g (Saturated 0.5g); Cholesterol 0mg; Sodium 37mg; Carbohydrate 26g (Dietary Fiber 3g); Protein 3g; Potassium 37mg.

Note: Although its tiny grains resemble rice or grits, couscous is really a form of pasta that has been precooked and dried. Originally from North Africa, it's now a staple in many Western homes. A larger type of couscous, called toasted Israeli couscous, requires longer cooking.

Note: This recipe goes well with the Grilled Pork Tenderloin Medallions in Chapter 17 or any plain grilled fish fillet, poultry, or beef.

Vary It! Whole-wheat couscous has a nutty flavor and pairs well with flavored stocks, spices, herbs, veggies, dried fruit, and nuts. Use it as a side dish or as a topping for stews.

Santa Fe Hominy

Prep time: 10 min • **Cook time:** 15 min • **Yield:** 4 servings

Ingredients	*Directions*
1 tablespoon canola oil	**1** Heat the oil in a large skillet and sauté the garlic and onions, stirring over medium heat until the onions are soft.
2 garlic cloves, minced	
1½ cups chopped red onions	
Two 15-ounce cans hominy, rinsed well and drained	**2** Stir in the drained hominy, tomatoes, and both chilies; cover and simmer over low heat for 15 minutes or until all ingredients are well blended and the vegetables are tender.
3 large ripe tomatoes, diced	
2 small poblano chilies, roasted, peeled, seeded, and diced	
1 small jalapeño chili, seeded and minced	**3** Remove the cover and sprinkle the cheese over the hominy. Stir until the cheese is melted. Serve at once.
1 cup lowfat Monterey Jack cheese	

Per serving: Calories 319 (From Fat 108); Fat 12g (Saturated 5g); Cholesterol 18mg; Sodium 614mg; Carbohydrate 41g (Dietary Fiber 7g); Protein 13g; Potassium 413mg.

Note: This recipe is coauthor Cindy's adaptation of posole, her favorite dish from Santa Fe, New Mexico. Posole corn, which is not readily available in all supermarkets, is prepared by soaking hard kernels of field corn in powdered lime and water. After several hours, when the corn kernels have swollen, the liquid is allowed to evaporate and the kernels to dry. The original posole is softer and more bland, thus the need for more flavorful chilies.

Note: To further reduce the sodium content, rinse the hominy and use half the cheese.

Note: While this recipe is made of good-for-you ingredients, it's also slightly higher in sodium, so balance out your meal choices the rest of the day with lower sodium options.

Risotto Primavera

Prep time: 10 min • **Cook time:** 20–30 min • **Yield:** 6 servings

Ingredients	*Directions*
5 to 6 cups plus 1 tablespoon low-sodium vegetable stock	*1* Place the stock in a saucepan and heat until liquid is simmering. Always keep the stock hot so that the risotto stays at a simmer throughout the entire process of cooking.
1 rib celery, finely chopped	
2 medium carrots, finely chopped	*2* Place all the chopped celery, carrots, zucchini, and asparagus in a bowl and mix well.
2 medium zucchini, finely chopped	
½ pound asparagus, trimmed and cut into 1-inch pieces	*3* In a saucepan, heat the olive oil and sauté the garlic and onion until softened.
1 teaspoon olive oil	*4* Add the rice and stir to coat. Add the wine and stir well while allowing the liquid to be completely absorbed.
1 clove garlic, minced	
1 small onion, finely chopped	*5* When all the wine has been absorbed, begin adding 5 to 6 cups of stock, half a cup at a time, stirring well after each addition. Allow the liquid to be absorbed before adding each half-cup of the stock. Halfway through the cooking process and after the addition of about 3 cups of stock, add the vegetables to the risotto mixture and continue simmering. Stir in ½ cup of the parsley.
1¼ cups Arborio rice	
¼ cup dry white wine	
½ cup plus 2 tablespoons chopped parsley, divided	
1 tablespoon plain unflavored yogurt	*6* When all the stock has been added and absorbed, remove the risotto from the heat and add the yogurt, parmesan, and remaining 1 tablespoon of stock, if needed, to make the risotto your desired consistency.
1 tablespoon freshly grated Parmesan cheese	
Freshly ground black pepper to taste	*7* Serve in individual bowls garnished with 2 tablespoons parsley. Add pepper to taste.

Per serving: Calories 101 (From Fat 9); Fat 1g (Saturated 0g); Cholesterol 1mg; Sodium 172mg; Carbohydrate 15g (Dietary Fiber 3g); Protein 3g; Potassium 393mg.

Note: You can't hurry risotto! Although it makes preparation a little more time-consuming, adding the liquid a little at a time releases the starch that thickens the dish and makes it creamier and full of flavor. Risotto is done when it's al dente — firm, but not crunchy. After the stock has been absorbed, get creative and add in your favorite veggies and protein, or a teaspoon of butter or mascarpone cheese if you can afford the calories.

Curried Quinoa with Mango

Prep time: 10 min • **Cook time:** 20 min • **Yield:** 6 servings

Ingredients	*Directions*
1 cup quinoa	*1* Rinse the quinoa thoroughly in a fine mesh strainer. Drain well and transfer to a 3-quart saucepan.
1½ cups cold water	
⅓ cup lowfat plain yogurt	*2* Add the 1½ cups of water; bring to a boil, cover with a tight-fitting lid, and turn the heat down to simmer. Cook for 15 minutes. Remove from the heat and set aside for five minutes with the lid on.
1 tablespoon lime juice	
1 to 2 teaspoons curry powder	
1 teaspoon finely grated gingerroot	*3* While the quinoa is resting, whisk together the yogurt, lime juice, curry powder, ginger, and pepper in a large bowl. Add the oil in a slow stream and whisk until combined.
¼ teaspoon black pepper	
2 tablespoons canola oil	
2 cups firm-ripe mango, cut into small cubes	*4* Toss the quinoa with the yogurt mixture, mango, red bell pepper, carrot, and jalapeño. Serve warm or at room temperature. Garnish with mint and chopped cashews.
1 small red bell pepper, finely diced	
1 carrot, shredded	
1 small fresh jalapeño, seeded and minced	
⅓ cup fresh chopped mint	
¼ cup chopped cashews	

Per serving: Calories 238 (From Fat 81); Fat 9g (Saturated 1g); Cholesterol 1mg; Sodium 27mg; Carbohydrate 35g (Dietary Fiber 4g); Protein 6g; Potassium 472mg.

Note: Quinoa is not a true grain but looks like one. It's actually related to leafy vegetables such as Swiss chard and has been cultivated for over 5,000 years! As it cooks, the external germ around the grain spirals out, forming a tail shape. It provides a pleasant, soft, creamy, and crunchy texture. Its key nutritional advantage is a high level of the amino acid lysine, and it's one of the best sources of plant protein!

Tip: Quinoa should be rinsed thoroughly to remove any powdery residue of saponin, which is a bitter coating said to have contributed to its survival through the years.

Vary It! Quinoa is a complete protein on its own, but if you want to ramp it up a notch, add beans, leftover chicken, or shrimp. You can also substitute bulgur wheat for the quinoa.

Wild Rice, Sweet Potato, and Mushroom Pilaf

Prep time: 10 min • **Cook time:** 20 min • **Yield:** 7 servings

Ingredients	Directions
1½ cups fresh mushrooms, sliced	**1** In a large saucepan, sauté the mushrooms, sweet potatoes, onions, green pepper, and garlic in the oil until crisp-tender, about 5 to 6 minutes.
2 medium sweet potatoes, peeled and diced	
2 medium onions, finely chopped	**2** Stir in the rice. Add the broth, soy sauce, and savory. Cover and simmer for 12 to 14 minutes or until the sweet potatoes are tender.
½ cup chopped green pepper	
1 clove garlic, minced	**3** Toss with almonds (if desired).
2 tablespoons olive oil	
3 cups cooked wild rice	
1 cup low-sodium chicken or vegetable broth	
1 tablespoon low-sodium soy sauce	
½ teaspoon dried savory	
¼ cup sliced almonds, toasted (optional)	

Per serving: Calories 162 (From Fat 36); Fat 4g (Saturated 1g); Cholesterol 1mg; Sodium 132mg; Carbohydrate 27g (Dietary Fiber 3g); Protein 5g; Potassium 335mg.

Note: Contrary to popular belief, wild rice is actually a grass. This pricier but delicious delicacy towers above other grains in the nutrition department with more protein, B vitamins, and folic acid and fewer calories than regular rice. Just 1 serving of wild rice provides 48 percent of the Recommended Daily Intake (RDI) of folic acid for men and 53 percent for women.

Tip: Make sure you rinse wild rice to remove any hulls or storage debris.

Vary It! Thyme or sage can be tasty substitutes for savory.

Vary It! For more color and to keep the cost to a minimum, try combining a cup each of white rice, brown rice, and wild rice. With their varied textures, these rices can really create a symphony in your mouth!

Garlic-Infused Quinoa Cakes

Prep time: 10 min • **Cook time:** 10–12 min • **Yield:** 12 mini-cakes

Ingredients	*Directions*
2 cups quinoa	*1* Rinse the quinoa thoroughly in a fine mesh strainer. Drain well and transfer to a 3-quart saucepan.
1½ cups water	
2 large eggs, beaten	*2* Add 1½ cups of water; bring to a boil, cover with a tight-fitting lid, and turn down the heat to simmer. Cook for 15 minutes. Remove from the heat and set aside for five minutes with the lid on.
3 tablespoons chopped fresh chives, plus chopped chives for garnish	
3 tablespoons fresh chopped Italian parsley, plus sprigs for garnish	*3* Allow the quinoa to reach room temperature, typically about 20 minutes, or refrigerate for 10 minutes until cool.
1 medium shallot, finely chopped	*4* Combine the cooked quinoa and eggs in a medium bowl. Stir in the chives, parsley, shallots, cheese, and garlic. Add the breadcrumbs and stir until the crumbs absorb the moisture.
¼ cup freshly grated Gruyere cheese	
3 garlic cloves, minced	*5* Divide and form the mixture into a dozen 1-inch-thick mini-cakes. If the mixture doesn't bind well, add ½ tablespoon of water to moisten it. If the mixture is too moist, add a few more breadcrumbs.
½ cup lemon-flavored whole-wheat breadcrumbs	
1 tablespoon extra-virgin olive oil	
	6 Heat the oil in a large skillet over medium-high heat. Place half of the quinoa cakes in the pan (don't crowd the skillet). Cover and cook for 8 to 10 minutes until the bottoms are browned. Turn the cakes over with a spatula and brown the second side. Repeat with the remaining quinoa cakes.
	7 Garnish with sprigs of parsley and a few chives and serve immediately.

Per serving: Calories 159 (From Fat 45); Fat 5g (Saturated 1g); Cholesterol 38mg; Sodium 56mg; Carbohydrate 22g (Dietary Fiber 2g); Protein 7g; Potassium 208mg.

Tip: Making your own healthy whole-wheat breadcrumbs is a no-brainer: Preheat your oven to 350 degrees. Pulse 2 slices of whole-wheat bread in a food processor to make coarse crumbs. Spread onto a lined baking pan and bake 10 minutes until the crumbs are golden. Remove from the oven and cool. Use the crunchy morsels as-is, or toss with 1 teaspoon lemon zest. For a zap of garlic, toss your crumbs with ¼ teaspoon garlic powder.

Barley Pilaf

Prep time: 10 min • **Cook time:** 20 min • **Yield:** 4 servings

Ingredients	*Directions*
1 cup quick-cooking pearl barley	*1* Cook the barley according to the package directions. (You usually boil it for about 10 minutes.)
1 tablespoon canola oil	
⅓ cup minced onion	*2* While the barley is cooking, heat the oil in a medium non-stick pan. Add the minced onion and sauté about 2 minutes. Add the pine nuts and continue cooking until the nuts are lightly browned but not burned (watch carefully).
¼ cup pine nuts	
2 teaspoons lemon zest	
2 tablespoons fresh chopped parsley	*3* When the barley is done cooking, drain and transfer it to a serving bowl. Add the onion, pine nuts, and lemon zest, tossing together. Add the parsley and freshly ground pepper, to taste, and lightly toss.
Freshly ground black pepper to taste	

Per serving: Calories 270 (From Fat 90); Fat 10g (Saturated 1g); Cholesterol 0mg; Sodium 6mg; Carbohydrate 41g (Dietary Fiber 8g); Protein 6g; Potassium 221mg.

Vary It! You can add fruit to this pilaf. Try finely chopped dried apricots or dried cranberries. You can also substitute chopped pecans for the pine nuts. This combination is great for pairing with poultry.

Note: When you cook barley, make an extra cup and save it. Add it to a tossed green salad or spinach for a quick, wholesome dish.

Siding with Wholesome Pasta-bilities

Like potatoes and bread, pasta has been getting the "bad carb" rap lately. But we say nothing is wrong with enjoying pasta in your diet. As with any food, the most important thing to be aware of is portion size. Although you can enjoy pasta as a main dish, you do want to be aware of the portion you're eating. Four cups may be too much (unless you're preparing to run a half marathon or do a 40-mile bike race), but a 1- or 2-cup portion is fine when you're eating it as a meal, and ½ to 1 cup works for a side dish.

Like white potatoes, traditional "white" pasta is a healthy choice, but choosing whole-wheat pasta some of the time adds fiber to the diet. Our recipes in this section include some whole-wheat varieties of pasta, but you can substitute regular pasta as well (just remember that the fiber and nutrient content will be reduced). Keep an open mind about whole-wheat pasta — you may need to try a few different brands, but we're sure you can find one you love.

We also include an orzo recipe in this section. Orzo is a rice-shaped pasta that's very versatile and easy to cook. It makes a great pasta salad or addition to tossed green salads.

Pasta salads are wonderful for summer picnics or buffet parties throughout the year. Using a variety of shapes, you can create a pleasing dish that's easy to pick up with a fork. Add fresh vegetables and fresh herbs to make a more nutritious dish by getting in a veggie serving and some added fiber!

Pasta comes in a variety of shapes. The long type can include perciatelli (thick, like spaghetti, but hollow), spaghetti (thick), vermicelli (thinner than spaghetti), spaghettini (thin, but not as thin as cappellini), and cappellini (thin, similar to angel hair). Ribbon-type pastas include linguini (flat and thin) and fettucine (flat and thick). Short, shaped pasta works great for salads, side dishes, and baked dishes. Popular shapes include penne, ziti, rigatoni, rotini, shells, and elbows (and if you look at specialty stores, you may even find bicycles, maple leaves, or pasta shaped like a cluster of grapes!).

Pasta with Zucchini Yogurt Sauce and Walnuts

Prep time: 10 min • **Cook time:** 20 min • **Yield:** 5 servings

Ingredients	*Directions*
1 pound zucchini (about 3 or 4 medium zucchini)	*1* Cut the zucchini into thick slices and place them in a saucepan with a steamer basket over boiling water. Cover the saucepan and steam for 5 minutes.
2 garlic cloves	
2 tablespoons olive oil	*2* Pulse the zucchini in a blender or food processor for 30 to 60 seconds with the garlic, olive oil, yogurt, and pepper.
½ cup plain Greek yogurt	
Freshly ground black pepper to taste	
1 pound whole-wheat penne pasta	*3* Cook the pasta al dente as directed on the package, usually 8 to 10 minutes.
2 tablespoons chopped walnuts, toasted	*4* Mix the pasta with the sauce from the blender and top with the walnuts and cheese.
2 tablespoons freshly grated Parmesan cheese	

Per serving: Calories 215 (From Fat 81); Fat 9g (Saturated 2g); Cholesterol 5mg; Sodium 50mg; Carbohydrate 28g (Dietary Fiber 1g); Protein 9g; Potassium 260mg.

Tip: Zucchini and pasta take on a new flair in this recipe, which is a great way to use zucchini left over from an earlier meal. It goes well with any simple grilled chicken or fish, and can be eaten warm or at room temperature.

Mediterranean Hummus with Sundried Tomatoes and Feta (Chapter 13); Garden-Fresh Gazpacho Shooters with Shrimp (Chapter 13); Italian Caprese Skewers (Chapter 13)

Jicama Bell Pepper Salad (Chapter 9); Grilled Portobello Mushroom Pita (Chapter 16)

Mama Mia Meatball Pizza (Chapter 20); Quick and Easy Veggie Pizza (Chapter 20)

Baby Spinach Salad with Almonds and Berry Vinaigrette (Chapter 9); Morning Muesli with Fresh Fruit (Chapter 14);

© T. J. HINE PHOTOGRAPHY

Roasted Cajun Fingerling Potatoes (Chapter 12); Baby Portobello Burgers (Chapter 21); Tomato Basil Spaghetti Squash with Gruyère (Chapter 11)

© T. J. HINE PHOTOGRAPHY

Southwest Corn with Chipotle Peppers (Chapter 11); Mexi-Chicken Foil Pouches (Chapter 19)

Ginger-Broccoli Beef Stir-Fry (Chapter 17); Chicken Kabobs with Tzatziki Sauce (Chapter 17);

Pumpkin Spice Parfait (Chapter 22) • Grilled Pineapple with Maple Cream Sauce (Chapter 22)

Pasta with Herb-Crusted, Roasted Tomatoes

Prep time: 10 min • **Cook time:** 45 min • **Yield:** 7 servings

Ingredients	*Directions*
Nonstick cooking spray	*1* Preheat your oven to 375 degrees. Spray an 8-x-8-inch glass baking pan with nonstick spray.
4 cups cherub tomatoes, cut in half	
2 tablespoons capers, rinsed well and drained	*2* Combine the tomatoes, capers, garlic, 1 tablespoon of the olive oil, and the pepper (to taste) and place in the pan.
1 garlic clove, minced	
2 tablespoons olive oil, divided	*3* Mix together the breadcrumbs, dried oregano, and basil; then sprinkle over the tomato mixture. Drizzle the top with the remaining tablespoon of olive oil. Bake for 30 to 35 minutes until the top is golden. Cool for 5 minutes.
Freshly ground black pepper to taste	
½ cup plain breadcrumbs	
½ teaspoon dried oregano	*4* Add the pasta to boiling water and stir so it doesn't stick. Cook al dente (firm to bite), about 8 to 9 minutes or according to the package directions (tasting it as it begins to soften). Drain the pasta in a colander, reserving a cup of the pasta water — it comes in handy if the pasta needs moistening.
½ teaspoon dried basil	
1 pound whole-wheat mini-penne	
¾ cup grated Parmesan cheese	*5* Place the drained pasta in a large serving bowl and mix in the cheese. Spoon the tomato mixture onto the pasta and mix until well combined. If the sauce is too thick, add some of the reserved water a few tablespoons at a time. Season with pepper, to taste.
2 tablespoons chopped fresh Italian parsley	
⅛ cup chopped fresh basil	
	6 Garnish with the fresh parsley and basil, and wait for the raves to come!

Per serving: *Calories 182 (From Fat 63); Fat 7g (Saturated 2g); Cholesterol 8mg; Sodium 279mg; Carbohydrate 23g (Dietary Fiber 1g); Protein 8g; Potassium 64mg.*

Note: This recipe offers the great option of a unique tomato sauce in place of traditional pasta sauce from a jar, which is many times higher in sodium. To make your own breadcrumbs, see the Tip accompanying the recipe for Garlic-Infused Quinoa Cakes in this chapter.

Vary It! If you don't have basil and parsley, try rosemary, thyme, or oregano.

Nutty Mac Loaf with Yogurt Sauce

Prep time: 10 min • **Cook time:** 30 min • **Yield:** 6 servings

Ingredients	Directions
Nonstick cooking spray	*1* Preheat your oven to 350 degrees. Spray a large loaf pan with nonstick cooking spray. Line the base and sides with parchment paper and spray the paper.
Parchment paper	
1 cup whole-wheat elbow macaroni	*2* Cook the pasta according to the package instructions or 8 to 10 minutes, just until tender. Drain and cool.
1 cup plain breadcrumbs	
1 cup finely ground cashews	*3* Combine the pasta, breadcrumbs, nuts, both cheeses, raisins, turmeric, cumin, red pepper, eggs, ½ teaspoon of the garam masala, and 2 tablespoons of the cilantro in a bowl and mix well.
1 cup freshly grated Parmesan cheese	
1 cup shredded lowfat cheddar cheese	
2 tablespoons raisins	*4* Spoon the mixture into your prepared pan and smooth the surface. Bake uncovered for about 30 minutes or until firm.
½ teaspoon turmeric	
¼ teaspoon ground cumin	*5* To make yogurt sauce, mix together the yogurt, the remaining 2 teaspoons of the chopped cilantro, and the remaining ½ teaspoon of the garam masala.
1 small red bell pepper, minced	
4 eggs, lightly beaten	
1 teaspoon garam masala, divided	*6* Serve the nutty mac loaf with the yogurt sauce.
2 tablespoons plus 2 teaspoons chopped cilantro, divided	
1 cup lowfat plain yogurt	

Per serving: Calories 402 (From Fat 171); Fat 19g (Saturated 5g); Cholesterol 160mg; Sodium 549mg; Carbohydrate 36g (Dietary Fiber 4g); Protein 25g; Potassium 392mg.

Note: This dish is unique and different with some exotic flavors. Garam masala is a fragrant spice at the heart of most Indian dishes. It contains coriander, cumin, dry ginger, cardamom, cinnamon, and bay leaves.

Note: While this recipe is made of good-for-you ingredients, it's also higher in sodium, so balance out your meal choices the rest of the day with lower-sodium options.

Whole-Wheat Rotini with Spinach

Prep time: 5 min • **Cook time:** 15 min • **Yield:** 6 servings

Ingredients	Directions
10 ounces whole-wheat rotini (spiral) pasta	**1** Cook the pasta in unsalted water according to the package directions. For al dente, this requires only 7 to 9 minutes of cooking time. Drain in a colander.
¼ cup olive oil	
2 cloves garlic, minced, or 2 teaspoons jarred minced garlic	**2** While the pasta is cooking, heat the olive oil over high heat in a large pan for 1 to 2 minutes. Reduce the heat to medium-low and add the garlic. Sauté until aromatic, about 2 minutes. Add the spinach and stir until wilted.
6 cups fresh baby spinach, washed, stems removed, and sliced	
3 tablespoons freshly grated Parmesan cheese	**3** Add the cooked, drained pasta and toss thoroughly so the spinach is evenly dispersed.
Freshly ground black pepper, to taste	**4** Transfer to a serving dish. Add the Parmesan cheese and fresh ground pepper, and serve.

Per serving: Calories 161 (From Fat 90); Fat 10g (Saturated 2g); Cholesterol 2mg; Sodium 82mg; Carbohydrate 14g (Dietary Fiber 1g); Protein 5g; Potassium 7mg.

Vary It! To add protein to this dish, you can toss in some leftover boneless chicken breast chunks or salmon.

Cucumber and Tomato Orzo with Fresh Mint

Prep time: 15 min • **Cook time:** 10 min • **Yield:** 8 servings

Ingredients	*Directions*
12 ounces orzo 3 tablespoons extra-virgin olive oil	*1* Cook the orzo according to the package directions for al dente (firm to bite). Drain and rinse in cool water, and set aside in a medium serving bowl.
1 tablespoon lemon juice 3 tablespoons chopped fresh mint plus fresh mint leaf for garnish (optional)	*2* Mix the olive oil, lemon juice, and mint in a small bowl with a small whisk.
1 large cucumber, peeled, seeded, and cut into small cubes	*3* Add the olive oil mixture to the bowl of orzo. Add the cubed cucumbers and tomatoes to the orzo and mix until combined. Add the feta and toss gently.
4 to 5 ripe plum tomatoes, cut into small cubes 2 ounces feta cheese, crumbled	*4* Serve at room temperature. Garnish with fresh mint leaf, if desired.

Per serving: Calories 239 (From Fat 63); Fat 7g (Saturated 2g); Cholesterol 6mg; Sodium 86mg; Carbohydrate 36g (Dietary Fiber 2g); Protein 7g; Potassium 306mg.

Note: You can make this dish up to 6 hours ahead of time. The flavors will be enhanced, and it also holds up well for a picnic or party buffet.

Note: Orzo is also known as risoni, "big rice," or Italian rice. It's a wheat product traditionally used in soups, but it also makes an awesome side dish or fruit pasta salad. Find it in the supermarket in the pasta aisle; it's so versatile that it can even be substituted for Arborio rice in a risotto recipe.

Tip: To seed the cucumbers, peel the skin, then cut the cucumbers lengthwise in half. Scoop out the seeds with a teaspoon; then slice or cube as desired.

Chapter 13

Serving Smart Snacks
and Appetizers

W ho says that just because you have high
blood pressure you aren't allowed to
party? In this chapter, we offer up some fabulous
party-starters and little nibbles that are easy on
the heart and easy on your schedule. Often, the
word "snack" implies junk food and high-calorie
no-nos, but the recipes in this chapter replace
those greasy fat bullets with colorful, delicious,
and nutritious options that you can enjoy any day
of the week. Pair them with a salad or combine a
few recipes, and you have a light meal.

For instance, the Italian Caprese Skewers and the
Hot Artichoke Bean Dip make a great pairing, as
do the Thai Fish Cakes along with the Heavenly
Stuffed Mushrooms or Mixed Vegetable Skewers.
Just keep in mind the proper plate portions from
Chapter 2 and note the serving sizes per recipe.

We think that the recipes in this chapter are not
only smart because they represent a variety of
food groups and include some vegetables, but
also because they're stress-free, making them a
great option for busy days. Nothing is better than
putting a few simple appetizers together for a
relaxing evening with friends.

Recipes in This Chapter

- Italian Caprese Skewers
- Zucchini Bites
- Hot Artichoke Bean Dip
- Herb-Roasted Chickpeas
- Mixed Vegetable Skewers with Satay Sauce
- Mediterranean Hummus with Sundried Tomatoes and Feta
- Artichoke Nibbles
- Garden-Fresh Gazpacho Shooters with Shrimp
- Thai Fish Cakes with Sweet Chili Sauce
- Shrimp Phyllo Tarts
- Fresh and Light Roasted Corn and Shrimp Salsa
- Jalapeño Flat Iron Sizzlers
- Heavenly Stuffed Mushrooms

The Whole Snackage

Remember being in grade school and getting that oh-so-special time every
day for naps and snacks? If only adults could be so lucky! But you can
still enjoy snacks as a grownup (who happens to be watching her health).

Actually, snacks are a very important part of a healthy eating plan. Snacking helps control hunger, and snacks can also fill in some nutrient gaps (nutrients that you may not get enough of at other meals).

The rules of balanced eating apply to snacking. Keep in mind that you need to control portion size even when you're enjoying a healthy snack. Be aware of your hunger and stop eating when you're full. Eating too quickly can lead to eating too much.

Although we're partial to our recipes in this chapter, you don't always need a recipe to prepare a smart snack. When planning snacks, aim to include at least two food groups per snack (preferably some carbohydrate and a small amount of protein). For most people, a snack should provide about 100–300 calories. Here are some ideas:

- 4 ounces of nonfat fruit yogurt topped with 2 tablespoons of lowfat granola

- 1 sliced apple and 10 almonds

- ½ cup of lowfat cottage cheese mixed with ¼ cup of applesauce and a dash of cinnamon

- 8 ounces of 1-percent milk with a small, homemade muffin (see the recipe for Breakfast-on-the-Run Muffins in Chapter 14)

- 8 baby carrots with 3 tablespoons of hummus dip

While the results are mixed as to whether eating more than three meals a day helps with weight loss, including one or two planned snacks probably does help control hunger through the day. The important factor is to plan ahead, so you don't eat half a bag of chips without even blinking.

Random snacking can get you into trouble. We define random snacking as eating unknown amounts of unknown foods — in other words, not being attentive to what and how much goes into your mouth.

When you're planning a snack, only fill a bowl or a sandwich bag with as much food as you should actually eat. Many of the dips and spreads in this chapter can be made ahead and refrigerated to eat throughout the week, so you can plan an after-work or mid-afternoon snack.

Italian Caprese Skewers

Prep time: 10 min • **Yield:** 10 servings

Ingredients	*Directions*
3 tablespoons balsamic vinegar	*1* To make the dressing, whisk together the vinegar, oil, garlic, and red pepper flakes. Set aside to allow the flavors to blend.
3 tablespoons olive oil	
1 clove garlic, minced	*2* Thread 1 tomato, 1 small basil leaf, and 1 Boconccini on each of 20 small wooden skewers. Place the skewers on a serving dish.
Pinch red pepper flakes	
20 cherry, cherub, or grape tomatoes	
20 small fresh basil leaves	*3* Drizzle the balsamic vinegar dressing over the skewers just before serving.
20 mini fresh mozzarella balls (Boconccini)	*4* Sprinkle with fresh ground pepper to taste.
Freshly ground black pepper to taste	

Per serving: Calories 100 (From Fat 73); Fat 8g (Saturated 3g); Cholesterol 15mg; Sodium 31mg; Carbohydrate 3g (Dietary Fiber 1g); Protein 4g; Potassium 102mg.

Note: Fresh mozzarella is an unripened, as opposed to aged, cheese and was once made only from the milk of water buffalo. Now the cheese is made from mostly cow's milk and some water buffalo milk. Small balls of mozzarella about one inch in diameter are called Boconccini. These delicious skewers are pictured in the color section.

Tip: Boconncini are highly perishable and must be used within 2 to 3 days after opening their vacuum-sealed container. You should also keep these tasty little cheese balls in the water solution they're packed in, which helps maintain their shape and moisture.

Vary It! Do a little searching in your supermarket. You may find the Boconccini already marinated in olive oil and Tuscan spices — you can use these and omit the dressing in this recipe, if desired.

Zucchini Bites

Prep time: 10 min • **Cook time:** 18 min • **Yield:** 24 mini-muffins

Ingredients	Directions
2 tablespoons chopped onion	*1* Preheat your oven to 325 degrees. In a large skillet, cook the onion and garlic in the butter until the onion is tender but not brown. Add the zucchini and stir until crisp-tender, about 2 minutes. Remove from the heat.
1 clove garlic, minced	
1 tablespoon butter	
1½ cups shredded zucchini (about 2 small)	*2* In a large bowl, mix the eggs, cheese, cornmeal, cumin, oregano, and zucchini mixture.
3 eggs, slightly beaten	
1½ cups lowfat shredded Monterey Jack cheese	*3* Coat mini-muffin tins with nonstick spray and spoon a scant 2 tablespoons of the mixture into each muffin cup.
3 tablespoons cornmeal	
¼ teaspoon cumin	*4* Bake in the preheated oven for 15 to 18 minutes or until set. Remove from the pan. Serve hot or at room temperature.
¼ teaspoon dried oregano	
Nonstick cooking spray	

Per serving: Calories 43 (From Fat 27); Fat 3g (Saturated 2g); Cholesterol 32mg; Sodium 53mg; Carbohydrate 2g (Dietary Fiber 0g); Protein 3g; Potassium 61mg.

Note: These faux muffins are a great way to sneak veggies into the diet for picky eaters.

Vary It! Another baking option is to pour all the batter into a greased 8-x-8-x-2-inch baking pan. Bake 20 to 25 minutes or until set. Cut into bite-sized squares.

Vary It! Most summer squash are similar in flavor and texture. Grated yellow crookneck, patty pan, or 8-ball squash can be substituted for the zucchini.

Hot Artichoke Bean Dip

Prep time: 10 min • **Cook time:** 25 min • **Yield:** 24 servings

Ingredients	*Directions*
1½ cups reduced-fat sour cream	*1* Preheat your oven to 350 degrees.
⅓ cup reduced-fat mayonnaise	*2* Place the sour cream, mayonnaise, lemon juice, 1 can (or 2 jars) of artichoke hearts, and the beans in a food processor and pulse until smooth. Add the remaining can (or 2 jars) of artichokes, the Parmesan cheese, 1 tablespoon of the parsley, and the garlic. Pulse until the artichokes are coarsely chopped.
1 tablespoon lemon juice	
Two 14-ounce cans artichoke hearts, well-rinsed and drained, divided, or four 4-ounce jars of marinated artichoke hearts	
One 15.5-ounce can Great Northern beans, well-rinsed and drained	*3* Coat a 2-quart baking dish with nonstick spray. Spoon the mixture into the dish and sprinkle with the remaining tablespoon of parsley and 1 tablespoon of Parmesan cheese.
½ cup fresh grated Parmesan cheese, reserving 1 tablespoon for garnish	
2 tablespoons fresh parsley, divided	*4* Bake at 350 degrees for 30 minutes or until bubbly.
2 garlic cloves, minced	
Nonstick cooking spray	

Per serving: Calories 50 (From Fat 27); Fat 3g (Saturated 1g); Cholesterol 5mg; Sodium 80mg; Carbohydrate 5g (Dietary Fiber 2g); Protein 2g; Potassium 149mg.

Note: Serve this dip with your favorite whole-grain unsalted crackers or bread cubes.

Note: You've no doubt had some yummy artichoke dip at a party or restaurant. The addition of beans to this recipe adds a delicious smoothness and a wonderful source of fiber and protein to the original dip.

Vary It! Canned artichokes offer a calorie savings, but marinated artichokes have less sodium. Choose your poison!

Herb-Roasted Chickpeas

Prep time: 10 min • **Cook time:** 30–40 min • **Yield:** 4 servings

Ingredients	Directions
One 15-ounce can chickpeas (garbanzo beans), well-rinsed and drained	**1** Preheat your oven to 400 degrees. Line a large baking pan with parchment paper or a silicon baking mat.
Nonstick cooking spray	**2** Rinse the beans thoroughly in a colander, drain, and spread them out on a paper towel to dry.
1 teaspoon chopped fresh rosemary	
1 teaspoon thyme	**3** Spread the chickpeas evenly on the parchment paper and spritz them generously with cooking spray. Bake for 30 minutes. Stir every 10 minutes to ensure even baking.
¼ teaspoon cayenne	
	4 Mix together the rosemary, thyme, and cayenne and sprinkle evenly over the beans. Continue to bake for 5 to 10 additional minutes, until the beans are crunchy. Remove the pan from the oven and let cool.

Per serving: Calories 127 (From Fat 9); Fat 1g (Saturated 0g); Cholesterol 0mg; Sodium 191mg; Carbohydrate 24g (Dietary Fiber 5g); Protein 5g; Potassium 187mg.

Note: Cultivated as far back as 7000 B.C., these little gems are versatile and near perfect nutritionally. Chickpeas make an awesome snack because of their protein and soluble and insoluble fiber content, which contributes to satiety, as well as just being really good for you.

Note: Chickpeas are cream-colored, round legumes used commonly in the Mediterranean, India, and Middle East (ever heard of a little dish called hummus? Check out our hummus recipe in this chapter!). They've become more mainstream in the U.S. and are also known as garbanzo beans.

Tip: This recipe is excellent as a crunchy topping for salads, pizza, or stew. Seasoning options for chickpeas are endless, but just be aware that seasonings often add additional sodium. To spice up your chickpeas, try taco seasoning, dry ranch dressing, jerk seasoning blend, or smoked paprika, or use your own creativity!

Mixed Vegetable Skewers with Satay Sauce

Prep time: 15 min • **Cook time:** 5 min • **Yield:** 12 servings

Ingredients	Directions
24 broccoli florets	**1** Place the broccoli, cauliflower, carrots, and zucchini in a steamer basket over boiling water. Cover and steam until tender-crisp, about 5 minutes. Remove from the heat.
24 cauliflower florets	
2 to 3 small carrots, cut into slices	
2 to 3 small zucchini, cut into 12 slices	**2** To make the satay sauce, whisk together the peanut butter, soy sauce, gingerroot, vinegar, sesame oil, garlic, curry, and red pepper flakes in a large bowl until smooth.
½ cup natural peanut butter	
1 tablespoon reduced-sodium soy sauce	
2 tablespoons minced gingerroot	**3** Skewer the broccoli, cauliflower, carrot, and zucchini on small wooden skewers. For a bite-sized version, use wooden toothpicks.
1 tablespoon rice vinegar	
1 tablespoon sesame oil	**4** Serve the vegetable skewers with the satay sauce as a dipping sauce.
1 garlic clove, minced	
½ teaspoon curry powder	
¼ teaspoon red pepper flakes	

Per serving: Calories 100 (From Fat 45); Fat 5g (Saturated 1g); Cholesterol 0mg; Sodium 124mg; Carbohydrate 9g (Dietary Fiber 3g); Protein 5g; Potassium 311mg.

Note: Satay is a traditional Thai sauce that blends sweet and spicy flavors. It's typically made with coconut milk, peanut butter, and red curry paste. Commercially prepared reduced-sodium packages can be purchased that take little or no time to prepare.

Tip: Steaming cooks vegetables without leaching away valuable nutrients and also brings out the vibrant colors of vegetables. As a timesaver, you can purchase veggies already cut up in the produce department of the supermarket.

Vary It! Skewer and grill strips of chicken breast, pork tenderloin, or flat iron steak and serve with the satay sauce for a heartier appetizer.

Mediterranean Hummus with Sundried Tomatoes and Feta

Prep time: 10 min • **Yield:** 8 servings

Ingredients	Directions
One 15-ounce can chickpeas (garbanzo beans), drained and rinsed	*1* Preheat your oven to 350 degrees.
A few drops sesame oil	*2* Place the beans, sesame oil, garlic, lemon juice, and oregano in a food processor and pulse until the consistency is smooth. If the hummus is too thick, add a small amount of olive oil until the desired consistency is reached.
2 tablespoons roasted garlic	
½ tablespoon lemon juice	
½ teaspoon oregano	
2 tablespoons sundried tomato, cut into strips	*3* Place the hummus in a small, deep plate and arrange the sundried tomato strips, feta cheese, and Kalamata olives over the top. Lightly drizzle 1 tablespoon of olive oil around the edges.
2 tablespoons feta cheese	
1 tablespoon chopped Kalamata olives	*4* To prepare pita triangles, use kitchen shears to cut the pita pockets in half crosswise; then split each horizontally. Cut each half into 4 triangles, making a total of 16 triangles per pita pocket. Spread in a single layer on a baking pan and bake for 10 minutes or until crisp.
1 tablespoon extra-virgin olive oil	
5 pita pockets	
	5 Serve the hummus with the pita triangles.

Per serving: Calories 176 (From Fat 31); Fat 4g (Saturated 1g); Cholesterol 2mg; Sodium 326mg; Carbohydrate 30g (Dietary Fiber 3g); Protein 6g; Potassium 148mg.

Note: The mellow and sweet flavor of the roasted garlic gives this recipe its unique quality. Flip to the color section to see this recipe.

Tip: You need roasted garlic in this recipe, but that doesn't mean you have to dirty your stove. You can roast garlic in the microwave, oven, or toaster oven. Try this shortcut: Cut the top off a head of garlic, exposing the cloves. Spray the exposed area with nonstick cooking spray. Wrap the garlic head in a paper towel, cloves facing up, and microwave on high for 1 minute. Turn the garlic head over and microwave on high for another 1 minute to 1 minute 15 seconds, until it feels soft. Squeeze the cloves out of the skin and use in the recipe or spread on bread. Yum!

Artichoke Nibbles

Prep time: 5 min • **Cook time:** 30 min • **Yield:** About 35 servings

Ingredients	Directions
Two 6-ounce jars marinated artichoke hearts	*1* Preheat your oven to 325 degrees.
1 small onion, chopped	*2* Drain the artichokes, reserving the juice, and chop them into fine pieces.
1 garlic clove, minced	
4 eggs	*3* Sauté the onion and garlic in the reserved juice until softened.
⅛ teaspoon pepper	
¼ teaspoon oregano	*4* Beat the eggs in a bowl and add the artichokes and the remaining ingredients.
Dash Tabasco sauce	
2 tablespoons fresh parsley	
¼ cup crushed low-sodium crackers	*5* Coat a 9-x-11-inch baking pan with nonstick spray and spread the mixture evenly in the pan.
¼ cup finely grated Swiss cheese	*6* Bake 30 minutes or until set. Cool; then cut into bite-sized squares. Serve warm or at room temperature.
Nonstick cooking spray	

Per serving: Calories 23 (From Fat 9); Fat 1g (Saturated 0g); Cholesterol 25mg; Sodium 17mg; Carbohydrate 2g (Dietary Fiber 1g); Protein 1g; Potassium 33mg.

Note: Coauthor Cindy's family can't get enough of this dish, and we bet your family will love it, too! Try it as a veggie-based appetizer or snack.

Tip: Fat-free, low-sodium soda crackers offer a significant sodium savings over the regular or unsalted varieties. Be sure to check the labels!

Vary It! The sodium content of cheese varies greatly — from 176 milligrams in 1 ounce of cheddar to 54 milligrams in 1 ounce of Swiss. Cheeses can be used interchangeably in this recipe according to taste preference and sodium allowance.

Party Favors: Keeping Your Friends and Your Blood Pressure Happy

You can incorporate the principles of the DASH diet (see Chapter 2) into all aspects of your lifestyle, including fun times with family and friends. Your goal to add more fruit, vegetables, and whole grains and reduce sodium and saturated fat can be accomplished even when serving food at a party or backyard gathering. Here's our little party trick: Don't ever announce, "This is healthy stuff, everyone!" Sure, you want to offer healthy foods to your guests, but people still seem to associate that "must not taste too good" idea with food deemed "healthy." So keep the secret to yourself.

Whether you're snacking or picnicking, you definitely want to reduce the sodium in what you eat, but don't disregard the importance of keeping your saturated fat intake low as well. By substituting lower-fat ingredients for higher-fat ones, you can significantly reduce overall fat and saturated fat. You'll see that several of the recipes in this chapter include substitutes for full-fat products, such as light or fat-free cream cheese, lowfat or fat-free sour cream, and lowfat mayonnaise.

While you're keeping your blood pressure and heart happy with these recipes, we think your friends will be happy, too, because of the great flavors in these dishes. We enhance flavor by using spices; fresh, aromatic vegetables; herbs; and small amounts of sharp cheese. We also try to help you plan your party by including multiple recipes featuring the same ingredients! A shorter shopping list means less time party planning and more time partying. Have fun!

Easy, peasy recipes

The options for easy appetizers are endless. We couldn't resist giving you a couple more ideas for party snacks that are so easy they don't even need a whole page in this book. Try whipping up some quick veggie kabobs: Skewer grape tomatoes, onion chunks, bell pepper pieces, and small mushrooms onto 6-inch skewer sticks. Brush lightly with vegetable oil and grill until tender. Or, for an easy finger food, beat 4 eggs and 4 egg whites until foamy. Add 2 tablespoons milk, 3 tablespoons grated cheese (your choice!), and 1 teaspoon dry dill, and pour the mixture into 12 mini muffin cups sprayed with vegetable cooking spray. Bake at 350 degrees for 15 minutes, or until set and golden.

Garden-Fresh Gazpacho Shooters with Shrimp

Prep time: 20–30 min, plus chill time • **Yield:** 12 shooters

Ingredients	Directions
1 medium, ripe avocado	*1* To make avocado cream, cut the avocado in half and scoop out the flesh into a food processor. Blend the avocado with the sour cream until smooth. Add the chicken broth, parsley, cilantro, and lime juice and pulse until well-blended.
1 cup lowfat sour cream	
1 cup low-sodium fat-free chicken broth	
3 tablespoons fresh parsley	
3 tablespoons cilantro	*2* To make gazpacho, place the tomato, garlic, cucumber, celery, red bell pepper, onion, vinegar, and olive oil in a food processor and pulse until slightly chunky. Add the tomato juice.
2 tablespoons lime juice	
1 ripe tomato, cut into 4 pieces	
1 garlic clove, chopped	*3* Fill 12 tall shot glasses halfway with avocado cream; then fill the remaining half with gazpacho. Chill for about 1 hour. Prior to serving, top each glass with 2 popcorn shrimp and cilantro leaves.
½ cucumber, peeled, seeded, and chopped	
½ celery stalk, chopped	
¼ cup chopped red bell pepper	
¼ cup chopped onion	
¼ cup red wine vinegar	
1 teaspoon olive oil	
1 cup low-sodium tomato juice	
24 pieces cooked, frozen small shrimp (from a 70 to 90 count bag), thawed	
Cilantro leaves, for garnish	

Per serving: Calories 96 (From Fat 48); Fat 5g (Saturated 2g); Cholesterol 21mg; Sodium 109mg; Carbohydrate 8g (Dietary Fiber 2g); Protein 4g; Potassium 226mg.

Thai Fish Cakes with Sweet Chili Sauce

Prep time: 15 min • **Cook time:** 10–15 min • **Yield:** 8 servings

Ingredients	*Directions*
1 pound white fish fillets (halibut, tilapia, sea bass, or any combination), cut into small chunks	*1* Place all the ingredients in a food processor except for the red bell pepper, lettuce, and chili sauce.
1 blade lemongrass, bruised and chopped	*2* Pulse until the ingredients are well blended and the fish is chunky.
1 clove garlic, minced	
1 teaspoon minced gingerroot	*3* Blend in the red bell pepper with a spoon.
1 teaspoon red curry paste	*4* Using clean hands, form the mixture into 8 small balls. Flatten each into a fish cake about 3 inches in diameter.
1 tablespoon chopped cilantro	
2 tablespoons lite coconut milk	*5* Spray a large skillet with nonstick cooking spray. Sauté the fish cakes approximately 3 to 4 minutes on each side or until the fish is thoroughly cooked. Gently remove from the pan.
Freshly ground pepper to taste	
½ small red bell pepper, minced	
Nonstick cooking spray	*6* Serve over a bed of shredded lettuce or your favorite greens (optional) with a tablespoon of sweet chili sauce.
Shredded lettuce, arugula, or watercress (optional)	
8 tablespoons sweet chili sauce	

Per serving: Calories 91 (From Fat 18); Fat 2g (Saturated 1g); Cholesterol 18mg; Sodium 275mg; Carbohydrate 4g (Dietary Fiber 1g); Protein 12g; Potassium 339mg.

Note: Fish cakes are best when the fresh flavor of the pure ingredients comes through: The lemongrass, fresh ginger, and fresh fish offer quite a party in your mouth!

Tip: Lightly flour your hands while making the fish patties to prevent the fish from sticking.

Vary It! For a simple and lower-calorie accompaniment, serve fish cakes with your favorite greens, chopped cucumber, and a fresh lime wedge, omitting the sweet chili sauce.

Shrimp Phyllo Tarts

Prep time: 10 min • **Yield:** 45 mini-tarts

Ingredients	*Directions*
½ **cup reduced-fat mayonnaise**	*1* In a small bowl, combine the mayonnaise, sour cream, parsley, dill, onion, 1 teaspoon of the lemon zest, and the lemon juice.
½ **cup fat-free sour cream**	
½ **tablespoon chopped fresh parsley**	
2 tablespoons fresh dill	*2* Fill each phyllo shell with 1 teaspoon of the sour cream mixture. Top each shell with two capers and 1 shrimp, tail up.
¾ **tablespoon grated onion**	
1 teaspoon lemon zest plus approximately 4 tablespoons for garnish	*3* Garnish with fresh dill and the remaining lemon zest.
½ **teaspoon lemon juice**	*4* Cover and chill for 30 minutes up to 2 hours.
Three 2.1-ounce packages frozen baked miniature phyllo dough shells (45 total)	
2 tablespoons capers, rinsed well and drained	
45 small cooked, peeled, and deveined shrimp (tails intact)	
Fresh dill sprigs for garnish	

Per serving: Calories 72 (From Fat 2); Fat 2g (Saturated 0g); Cholesterol 11mg; Sodium 142mg; Carbohydrate 11g (Dietary Fiber 0g); Protein 3g; Potassium 28mg

Note: You can make your own phyllo shells, but buying 'em ready-made definitely saves some time. Store-bought shells are low-cal, low-sodium, and quick and easy. If you're in an even bigger party-time time-crunch, you may even be able to find a store-prepared dill dip in the dairy aisle. Just make sure you read the label and keep portion sizes appropriate.

Fresh and Light Roasted Corn and Shrimp Salsa

Prep time: 30 min • **Yield:** About 3 cups dip; 8 servings

Ingredients	Directions
¾ cup frozen corn or 2 cobs of cooked corn	**1** Preheat your oven to 400 degrees to roast the corn and bell pepper. Spread the corn evenly on the cookie sheet. (If you're using fresh ears, scrape the corn from the ears using a mandolin or knife, and then spread on the cookie sheet.)
¼ cup diced green bell pepper	
Vegetable cooking spray	
¾ cup seeded, finely chopped ripe tomatoes	**2** Spread the diced peppers on the sheet with the corn and spray lightly with vegetable cooking spray. Roast in the oven for 15 to 20 minutes or until lightly browned.
¼ cup minced Vidalia onion	
1¼ cup finely chopped fresh cilantro	**3** Combine the tomatoes, onion, cilantro, sea salt, honey, olive oil, and lime juice in a small bowl, tossing together lightly to combine.
⅛ teaspoon sea salt	
2 teaspoons honey	
1 tablespoon olive oil	**4** Place the shrimp in a medium bowl. Add the tomato mixture and the roasted corn and peppers, and stir to combine. Transfer to a serving bowl and refrigerate for at least an hour to meld the flavors.
2 tablespoons lime juice	
1 cup chopped precooked shrimp	

Per serving: Calories 86 (From Fat 18); Fat 2g (Saturated 0g); Cholesterol 55mg; Sodium 101mg; Carbohydrate 10g (Dietary Fiber 1g); Protein 7g; Potassium 210mg.

Tip: Using a mandolin (see Figure 13-1) to take corn from the ear is very efficient. If you don't have this handy tool, you can use a paring knife instead.

Figure 13-1:
A helpful cutting tool called a mandolin.

Jalapeño Flat Iron Sizzlers

Prep time: 10 min • **Cook time:** 4 min • **Yield:** 20 pieces

Ingredients	*Directions*
½ **pound flat iron steak**	*1* Slice the flat iron steak into ¼-inch-thick, long strips, cutting across the grain.
8 ounces fat-free cream cheese	
¼ **cup of your favorite prepared salsa (we recommend Arriba! Mexican Chipotle Salsa)**	*2* Combine the cream cheese and salsa and stuff the mixture inside each jalapeño pepper half.
10 small fresh jalapeño peppers, cut in half lengthwise and seeded	*3* Wrap each filled jalapeño pepper with one strip of steak covering the entire length of the pepper. Fasten with a toothpick.
	4 Grill on a preheated grill rack on low heat for about 4 minutes or until done, turning midway through cooking.

Per serving: Calories 34 (From Fat 9); Fat 1g (Saturated 0g); Cholesterol 7mg; Sodium 106mg; Carbohydrate 1g (Dietary Fiber 0g); Protein 4g; Potassium 93mg.

Note: Flat iron steak is the result of an innovative cutting method from the shoulder of the cow. This cut of beef is perfect for grilling; has a deep, rich flavor; and is a perfect substitute for flank or skirt steak. Serve the sizzlers with additional salsa or reduced-calorie ranch dressing.

Tip: When flat iron is used for other recipes, it's best marinated and cooked only to medium doneness. Some butchers refer to it as top blade steak.

Vary It! Try this recipe with strips of chicken breast for those who prefer white meat.

Heavenly Stuffed Mushrooms

Prep time: 10 min • **Cook time:** 16–18 min • **Yield:** About 22 servings

Ingredients	Directions
Two 8-ounce packages Neufchatel or light cream cheese	**1** Preheat your oven to 350 degrees.
1 package dry ranch dressing	**2** Mix the cream cheese, ranch dressing, mayonnaise, onion, garlic, parsley, and Parmesan cheese.
¼ cup reduced-fat mayonnaise	
2 tablespoons minced onion	**3** Fill the mushroom caps with the cream cheese mixture and place them in a 9-x-13-inch baking pan, filling side up.
1 clove garlic, minced	
1 tablespoon chopped parsley	**4** Blend together the panko breadcrumbs, basil, oregano, and garlic powder. Sprinkle over the top of the mushrooms.
¼ cup fresh grated Parmesan cheese	
2 pounds fresh button mushrooms, cleaned, stems removed	**5** Melt the margarine and lightly drizzle it over the stuffed mushrooms. Bake for 30 minutes.
1 cup panko breadcrumbs	
½ teaspoon dried basil	
½ teaspoon dried oregano	
¼ teaspoon garlic powder	
¼ cup lowfat tub margarine	

Per serving: Calories 103 (From Fat 63); Fat 7g (Saturated 3g); Cholesterol 16mg; Sodium 171mg; Carbohydrate 6g (Dietary Fiber 0g); Protein 4g; Potassium 48mg.

Note: Dry dressing mix is not considered a high-sodium product when used in this recipe in the recommended serving size, although the sodium adds up if consumed in larger quantities.

Tip: You can make your own ranch dressing mix by combining 1 teaspoon dried parsley, ¾ teaspoon ground black pepper, ½ teaspoon garlic powder, ¼ teaspoon onion powder, and ⅛ teaspoon dried thyme.

Part IV

Staying Heart-Healthy through Every Meal

The 5th Wave   By Rich Tennant

"Listed next to the 500 milligrams of sodium is the expiration date. Does that pertain to the product or the person who eats it?"

In this part . . .

Here's where we introduce you to tasty recipes that fit into every meal of the day, from breakfast to brunch to the weeknights. You find simple and healthy breakfast ideas you can use every day — even if it's as you're walking out the door — as well as recipes that offer a new twist to traditional favorites and alternatives to hitting up the greasy breakfast joint. Our lunch recipes provide you with new sandwich and salad ideas you can take to work or enjoy at home. What's for dinner? We guide you through cooking up flavorful dishes with poultry, pork, beef, and seafood. You're crunched for time during the week, so we offer some easy options in this part using foil pouches, your oven, or just one pan so that you can whip up a healthy and delicious weeknight meal in no time — and with easy cleanup.

These recipes encourage everyone, child or adult, to become more healthy and adventurous in making food choices. We finish out the part with a dessert chapter, offering a sweet conclusion to your meals.

Chapter 14

Respecting Breakfast on the Go

*Y*ou've heard it before: Breakfast is the most important meal of the day. Well, we have to agree. "Breaking the fast" after a night's sleep is important in order to get going in the morning. Not only does breakfast fuel your morning activity, but it also engages your metabolism. Studies have shown an inverse relationship between eating breakfast and gaining weight: Those people who eat breakfast gain less weight over time than those folks who skip it. Eating breakfast can impact your overall diet as well. In general, those people who eat breakfast have lower saturated fat intakes and higher fiber intakes, both of which are important to controlling your heart disease risk.

This chapter gives you new reasons to want to eat breakfast: tasty recipes! They're quick and can be made ahead, so there's no excuse for skipping this important chance to fuel your body. As you plan your weekly breakfasts, include whole grains, protein, lowfat dairy, and fruit.

Making Traditional Breakfast Treats Doable

If your idea of a great breakfast involves a quick stop at a donut shop, a coffeehouse, or a fast-food joint for a greasy egg sandwich, you'll be glad to know that you don't have to give up these treats entirely. You can indulge in an occasional donut as long as you balance it with better food choices. If coffee creations or egg sandwiches are your downfall, you can make your own at home, substituting healthier ingredients for the usual diet-busters.

Dealing with donut dilemmas

Carbohydrates have been the subject of a lot of hype, but keep in mind that it's not that the carbohydrate is bad; what's important is the *type* of carbohydrate you're including in your diet, and the portion and frequency. Having donuts for breakfast twice a week isn't in the best interest of your heart or your waistline. But if you tend to crave donuts — or some other less-than-healthy breakfast item — devise a strategy to compensate for it. One idea is to bring two extra pieces of fruit with you on "donut day" and limit yourself to one donut.

Things aren't always as they seem. Muffins often sound like they'd be better for you than donuts, but this isn't always the case. A sugar raised (non-cake) donut has about 190 calories and 9 grams of fat, and a powdered cake donut has about 300 calories and 18 grams of fat. Compare these counts to a large blueberry muffin at 510 calories and 16 grams of fat! Of course, your best bet is to stick to a toasted English muffin with 160 calories and less than 2 grams of fat, but in a donut-craving scenario, choosing one raised donut is better than eating a cake donut or a jumbo bakery muffin.

Keeping coffee calories under control

Your favorite coffee drink could be making you fat and thus increasing your risk for hypertension. Take a look at the calorie content of some of the typical fancy coffees. They can provide anywhere from 150 to 450 calories, or more!

Choosing a heart-healthy margarine

Many margarine spreads are on the market, all claiming to be "light" or good for you. What's a discerning eater to do? The more liquid a fat is, the healthier (or more unsaturated) it is. Using liquid oils as much as possible for your cooking is one way to ensure that you get healthy fats in your diet. Using small amounts of real butter is okay in some cooking, and some of our recipes include it for its unique flavor, but using a margarine spread is another way to keep your daily saturated-fat intake down. For one thing, margarine spreads allow you to use less than stick margarine or butter because of their ease of spreading. They're also lower in calories because of the water that's whipped into them. When choosing one, look for a margarine that provides no more than 2 grams of saturated fat per tablespoon.

Coffee itself is almost calorie-free. You can make a healthier drink at home by using half coffee and half 1-percent milk. Add 1 teaspoon of flavoring and shake or stir over ice for a cold, refreshing treat. Just remember that store-bought coffee syrups are sugary, so use them sparingly.

Making an acceptable egg sandwich

Avoid the pitfalls of the drive-thru and make your own metabolism-boosting, high-protein egg sandwich. Toast one whole-wheat English muffin until lightly browned. While it's toasting, separate 2 egg whites (see Chapter 15 for tips on how to separate an egg). Beat the whites lightly; season them with ¼ teaspoon dried dill. Spray a 3-inch, microwave-safe ramekin with cooking oil. (A ramekin is a small bowl with straight sides. These are perfect for eggs or custards, and can be found at any kitchen supply shop.) Pour the whites into the ramekin, cover them lightly with waxed paper, and microwave for 30 to 45 seconds or until done. Spread 1 teaspoon of a healthy margarine spread (see the nearby sidebar "Choosing a heart-healthy margarine") on one half of the muffin. Slide the cooked egg whites onto the toasted English muffin.

Check out our Yummy Stuffed Eggwiches in this chapter for another egg sandwich idea.

Saying Hello to Healthy, Easy Mornings

If you're like us, your days are chock-full of activity. Sometimes just thinking about what to eat is a drain. But if you get into a healthier new routine, it becomes second nature; no deep thought is required. You may have noticed our two main strategies for healthy eating in this book:

- ✔ **Be prepared.** Shop ahead, keep a running grocery list, stock your pantry, and pre-prep some food.
- ✔ **Keep easy recipes handy.** The more often you make them, the easier they get.

The breakfast recipes in this section are quick, easy, and versatile. After you make our muesli with fresh fruit, you can find other ways to enjoy the muesli itself. Throw a couple of spoonfuls into lowfat vanilla yogurt for a great snack or quick breakfast, for instance. The baked oatmeal can be eaten the next day as well, making it a quick and healthy choice. Freeze our breakfast-on-the-run muffins and take them out of the freezer one at a time as needed. They thaw in no time — for super-fast thawing, place them in a microwave for 45 seconds or in a toaster oven for about two minutes.

Mix up our recipes during the week with these simple, no-cook ideas to get you out the door in a hurry:

- ✔ **Half a peanut butter sandwich and fruit:** Spread 1 slice of whole-grain bread (look for whole-wheat flour as the first ingredient) with 2 teaspoons of nut butter; add a banana or your favorite fruit. Include a glass of 1-percent milk.

- ✔ **A breakfast bar:** Taking a packaged food with you once in a while when you're really rushed is okay. Look for less than 15 grams of sugar, 4 or more grams of fiber, and 5 grams of protein. Don't depend on breakfast bars, however, because they generally have about 250 milligrams of sodium per bar.

- ✔ **Twelve unsalted almonds and an apple:** If you prefer, substitute a cup of unsweetened applesauce for the apple.

- ✔ **Six ounces of lowfat vanilla yogurt and an orange:** You can also mix some chopped nuts and berries into your yogurt.

- ✔ **One-percent or nonfat milk:** Add extra milk to coffee or tea, or just have a glass of milk for the extra protein and calcium boost it provides. You can even mix up a glass of chocolate milk. There's nothing wrong with drinking flavored milk once in a while — unlike other sugary beverages, milk provides protein, calcium, and vitamin D.

Morning Muesli with Fresh Fruit

Prep time: 10 min, plus standing time • **Yield:** 2 servings

Ingredients	*Directions*
½ cup store-bought muesli or **Make Your Own Muesli** (see the following recipe)	**1** Combine the muesli, 1 cup of the yogurt, the grated apple, and the orange juice in a small bowl; stir to blend. Refrigerate at least 1 hour or overnight.
1½ cups organic Greek fat-free plain or vanilla yogurt	
¼ cup grated fresh apple with peel	**2** Serve with the remaining ½ cup of yogurt and the fresh berries.
2 tablespoons orange juice	
½ cup fresh mixed berries: blueberries, strawberries, blackberries, and raspberries	

Make Your Own Muesli

½ cup old-fashioned oats	**1** Mix all the ingredients together in a zip-top bag.
½ cup rolled rye flakes	
½ cup rolled triticale	**2** Divide into ½-cup portions and store in an airtight container.
½ cup rolled wheat flakes	
½ cup dried dates	
¼ cup slivered almonds	
⅓ cup raisins	

Per serving: Calories 237 (From Fat 29); Fat 3g (Saturated 0g); Cholesterol 0mg; Sodium 66mg; Carbohydrate 37g (Dietary Fiber 5g); Protein 19g; Potassium 500mg.

Note: Curious what muesli looks like? Flip to the color section. Coauthor Cindy was first introduced to muesli while living in Sydney, Australia. Muesli is a wonderfully fresh way to get your whole grains in the morning. You can also try it as a super pre-workout meal to fuel your body.

Vary It! For more variety, add other dried fruit and nuts: papaya, dried pineapple, and macadamia nuts, or dried cherries, dried cranberries, and dried blueberries with pecans or walnuts.

Tip: The longer the muesli soaks, the more yogurt it absorbs, giving it a thicker consistency. If you prefer it to be creamier, just add more yogurt.

Baked Oatmeal with Greek Yogurt

Prep time: 5 min • **Cook time:** 30 min • **Yield:** About 4 servings

Ingredients	Directions
¾ cup lowfat milk	**1** Preheat your oven to 350 degrees.
2 teaspoons tub margarine	
1 cup old-fashioned oats	**2** In a 2-quart casserole dish, heat the milk and margarine in the microwave for 2 minutes. Stir in the oats and egg, and set aside.
1 egg, beaten	
¼ cup chopped dried apricots	**3** Mix the apricots, raisins, apple, brown sugar, and cinnamon into the oats until well-combined.
¼ cup raisins	
1 small Honeycrisp apple, shredded	**4** Bake the oats uncovered for 15 minutes. Stir, top with chopped walnuts, and bake for another 15 minutes until the oats are chewy.
1 tablespoon brown sugar	
¼ teaspoon cinnamon	
3 tablespoons walnuts, chopped	**5** Top each serving with 1 tablespoon of Greek yogurt.
¼ cup organic Greek fat-free vanilla yogurt	

Per serving: Calories 251 (From Fat 81); Fat 9g (Saturated 2g); Cholesterol 55mg; Sodium 70mg; Carbohydrate 38g (Dietary Fiber 5g); Protein 9g; Potassium 404mg.

Note: With just 5 minutes of prep time, throw this in the oven as you get ready for work, and it'll be bubbling in the oven before you leave home! Oats are a whole-grain offering and an impressive nutrient package of carbohydrates, soluble fiber, vitamins, and minerals. Oats contain phytochemicals that may help to reduce heart disease, regulate blood sugar, and improve insulin sensitivity for people with diabetes.

Tip: You can purchase oats as regular "old-fashioned," quick-cooking, or instant. In this recipe, you can use either the regular or quick-cooking variety. Instant oatmeal is preprocessed, is higher in sodium, and doesn't provide the same wonderful texture.

Vary It! Consider mashing a very ripe banana into the mixture for a natural sweetness in place of the brown sugar before baking.

Breakfast Smoothie Royale

Prep time: 10 min • **Yield:** 3 servings

Ingredients	*Directions*
2 ripe bananas	*1* Place the bananas, tofu, soymilk, strawberries, honey, and flaxseed in a blender. Pulse until blended.
1 cup soft light silken tofu, drained	
1⅓ cups soymilk	*2* Add the ice cubes and continue to pulse until smooth.
2 cups sliced strawberries	
1 tablespoon honey	*3* Serve with strawberries as a garnish.
1 tablespoon ground flaxseed	
12 ice cubes	
Whole strawberries for garnish	

Per serving: Calories 201 (From Fat 27); Fat 3g (Saturated 0g); Cholesterol 0mg; Sodium 121mg; Carbohydrate 36g (Dietary Fiber 5g); Protein 11g; Potassium 664mg.

Note: Some people are afraid to buy tofu because they don't know what kind to purchase. It's pretty simple, really: Silken tofu has a soft consistency, has the texture of custard, and is perfect for making smoothies, dips, sauces, and desserts. Regular tofu is best used in recipes where you want it to retain its shape, as in stir-fried or grilled dishes. Both kinds of tofu come in soft, medium, firm, and extra firm. Tofu is low in calories, but half of the calories come from fat, so consider reduced-fat tofu, which is equally versatile.

Note: Soymilk is made from soybeans and is available in various flavors. It's a good substitute for people who have lactose intolerance and vegans who eat no animal products. You can substitute lowfat cow's milk in this recipe if desired.

Tip: Be sure to use ground flaxseed to get the most benefit. Whole flaxseeds pass through undigested. Flaxseeds can be ground in a blender or clean coffee grinder. To maintain quality and freshness, store ground flaxseeds in the refrigerator.

Vary It! Substitute your favorite fruits and combinations to vary the flavors: raspberries, peaches, papaya and pineapple, strawberry and kiwi, strawberry and banana, or blueberry. To raise the nutritional bar, consider adding some green vegetables. Spinach is a nutritional powerhouse with a mild flavor, and the fruit trumps the flavor of the greens. A great concept — drink your spinach!

Breakfast-on-the-Run Muffins

Prep time: 10 min, plus cooling time • **Cook time:** 20–22 min • **Yield:** 12 muffins

Ingredients	*Directions*
Nonstick cooking spray	*1* Preheat your oven to 400 degrees. Spritz a 12-cup non-stick muffin tin with cooking spray until well-coated. You can use muffin cups instead, if you prefer.
1 cup whole-wheat flour	
1 cup all-purpose flour	
1 cup quick-cooking rolled oats	*2* Combine the flours, oats, baking powder, baking soda, and pepper in a medium bowl.
2 teaspoons baking powder	
½ teaspoon baking soda	*3* Heat 1 tablespoon of the oil and sauté the green onion, turkey, and green chilies for 2 minutes.
½ teaspoon freshly ground pepper	
4 tablespoons canola oil, divided	*4* Whisk the eggs, buttermilk, and remaining oil in a medium bowl. Fold in the onion, turkey, and chile mixture and the cheese.
4 or 5 green onions, sliced thin	
½ cup diced low-sodium deli turkey	*5* Make a well in the center of the dry ingredients and add the egg mixture; mix until just moistened.
½ cup medium canned green chilies	*6* Pour the batter into the prepared muffin tin and bake until the tops are golden brown, 20 to 22 minutes. Let the muffins cool in the pan for 5 minutes; then loosen the edges and turn the muffins out to a wire rack. Serve warm.
1 egg plus 2 egg whites	
1⅓ cups lowfat buttermilk	
½ cup grated pepper-jack cheese	

Per serving: Calories 187 (From Fat 72); Fat 8g (Saturated 2g); Cholesterol 24mg; Sodium 365mg; Carbohydrate 23g (Dietary Fiber 3g); Protein 8g; Potassium 171mg.

Note: These hearty muffins are a great on-the-run breakfast or a more significant snack. Store any leftover muffins in the refrigerator.

Tip: As a lower-sodium substitute, consider using 1⅓ cups lowfat milk plus 1 tablespoon vinegar or 1 tablespoon lemon juice instead of buttermilk. Let the mixture stand 10 minutes before using.

Deliciosos Huevos Rancheros

Prep time: 15 min • **Cook time:** 15 min • **Yield:** 4 servings

Ingredients	*Directions*
1½ cups shredded romaine lettuce	*1* Preheat your oven to 350 degrees.
1 green onion, sliced	*2* Combine the lettuce, green onion, tomato, cilantro, and lime juice in a small bowl and set aside.
2 tablespoons diced fresh tomato	
1 tablespoon fresh cilantro	*3* Place the tortillas on a baking pan and evenly distribute cheese on each tortilla. Top each with 2 tablespoons of beans. Bake until the beans are heated through and the cheese is melted, about 8 minutes.
1 teaspoon lime juice	
Eight 6-inch corn tortillas	
¾ cup low-sodium sharp cheddar cheese	*4* While the tortillas are baking, heat 1 teaspoon oil in a nonstick skillet and sauté the green pepper. Mix in the eggs and scramble until the eggs are set.
1½ cups canned pinto beans, rinsed well and drained	
1 teaspoon canola oil	*5* To assemble, divide the egg mixture on top of each tortilla and top with the salsa and lettuce mixture.
¼ cup chopped green pepper	
4 large eggs or 2 whole eggs and 4 egg whites, lightly beaten	
¼ cup favorite chipotle salsa	

Per serving: Calories 375 (From Fat 144); Fat 16g (Saturated 7g); Cholesterol 236mg; Sodium 444mg; Carbohydrate 39g (Dietary Fiber 8g); Protein 20g; Potassium 489mg.

Note: Kids and adults alike love this classic Mexican dish. It makes for a quick and filling supper, too! Huevos means eggs in Spanish. You can either fry or scramble them. We love the scrambled huevos so you can control the amount of egg yolk, which is the part of the egg containing cholesterol. We talk more about the nutritional value of eggs in the following section, "Changing Up Old Favorites."

Tip: For a true on-the-go breakfast, whip this up the night before and heat it up in the microwave on your way out the door.

Vary It! In place of the pinto beans, substitute vegetarian refried beans or black beans.

Changing Up Old Favorites

Eggs are traditional breakfast fare, although over the years they've had a bad reputation. Here are the simple facts. Eggs are a healthy food. The white of the egg contains more than half of the egg's protein and is extremely low in fat. Including some protein with your carbohydrate at breakfast and every meal is a great strategy for a balanced diet. One white provides only 16 of the 70 calories in a whole egg. The yolk of the egg provides the other 54 calories and all the cholesterol but also provides choline (which aids brain function) and lutein (an important antioxidant).

The 2010 Dietary Guidelines for Americans suggest that eating one egg a day is okay. Independent of other dietary factors, evidence suggests that one egg yolk daily doesn't result in increased blood cholesterol levels. One yolk contains about 185 milligrams of cholesterol, and your daily cholesterol intake should only be 200 to 300 milligrams per day, so because you're watching your heart health (and cholesterol is related), eating an egg yolk meets the entire day's goal. Enjoy eggs a few times a week, but also eat more vegetables, fruits, and grain-based dishes.

Another traditional favorite in the morning is the breakfast sweet roll or cinnamon roll. Try satisfying your morning sweet tooth with less sugar by trying our German Apple Pear Puff Pancakes or Savory Breakfast Bread Pudding this weekend.

Naturally jazz up your oatmeal for a sweet change of pace. You can easily microwave a half-cup of quick oats with 1 cup of 1-percent milk for 1 to 2 minutes; then just stir in fresh blueberries or banana slices.

Liven up your boring English muffins. Try the whole-wheat or oat bran varieties, and give these ideas a go:

- Toast them and top with a small amount of low-sodium Swiss cheese and a slice of tomato for something different in the morning. Add a fresh basil leaf if you have it.

- For something sweet, add 1 teaspoon of cream cheese to each toasted English muffin half, and top with sliced strawberries.

Yummy Stuffed Eggwiches

Prep time: 10 min • **Cook time:** 15 min • **Yield:** 4 servings

Ingredients	*Directions*
2 eggs, plus 2 egg whites	*1* Beat together the eggs, milk, and hot sauce in a shallow dish.
2 tablespoons lowfat milk	
Dash hot sauce	*2* Mix together the preserves and mustard, and spread ½ tablespoon of the mixture on 1 side of each slice of bread to be on the inside of the sandwich as a condiment.
4 tablespoons all-fruit raspberry preserves with fiber	
2 tablespoons stone-ground Dijon mustard	*3* Complete the sandwiches, layering one slice of chicken breast, one slice of cheese, and a second piece of bread; secure with toothpicks.
8 slices whole-wheat bread	
4 slices roasted chicken breast	*4* Heat a skillet or griddle and melt the butter. Dip each sandwich in the egg mixture using tongs until completely coated, place in the skillet, and cook 3 minutes on each side until golden in color and heated through.
4 slices no-salt-added Swiss cheese	
1 tablespoon butter	
	5 Cut each sandwich into 4 triangles.
	6 Serve with the remaining fruity mustard on the side.

Per serving: Calories 403 (From Fat 163); Fat 18g (Saturated 9g); Cholesterol 146mg; Sodium 420mg; Carbohydrate 68g (Dietary Fiber 6g); Protein 25g; Potassium 256mg.

Note: This stuffed sandwich makes a great breakfast, lunch, dinner, or snack. You can make these sandwiches the night before for a quick heat-up in the morning — and a filling breakfast to boot.

Vary It! Use lower-sodium lean ham along with the chicken breast. Substitute strawberry preserves in place of the raspberry.

German Apple-Pear Puff Pancakes

Prep time: 10 min • **Cook time:** 18–20 min • **Yield:** 8 servings

Ingredients	*Directions*
Nonstick cooking spray	**1** Preheat your oven to 400 degrees. Spritz two 12-cup, nonstick muffin tins with cooking spray.
1 medium apple, cored and thinly sliced	
1 medium ripe pear, cored and thinly sliced	**2** Coat a large nonstick skillet with cooking spray and cook the apple and pear slices until softened, about 4 to 6 minutes. Stir in the brown sugar, cinnamon, and nutmeg and continue to heat until flavors blend, about 2 more minutes. Remove from heat.
1 tablespoon brown sugar	
½ teaspoon cinnamon	
⅛ teaspoon nutmeg	
¾ cup all-purpose flour	**3** Blend together the flours, milk, eggs, and margarine with an electric blender until smooth.
¼ cup whole-wheat flour	
1 cup lowfat milk	**4** Pour the mixture from Step 3 into the muffin tins, filling about ¾ of each muffin cup. Bake 15 minutes or until puffy and golden.
6 eggs or 2 whole eggs and 6 egg whites	
¼ cup melted margarine	**5** Remove the pancakes from the muffin tins while they're still hot. Top with the warm apple-pear mixture. Drizzle with maple syrup or light pancake syrup, if desired, and serve immediately.
Maple syrup or light pancake syrup (optional)	

Per serving: Calories 201 (From Fat 90); Fat 10g (Saturated 3g); Cholesterol 160mg; Sodium 271mg; Carbohydrate 21g (Dietary Fiber 2g); Protein 8g; Potassium 177mg.

Note: These light and airy pancakes are a cross between an omelet and a soufflé. For a dramatic rise (puff), substitute bread flour for the all-purpose and whole-wheat flour. The more traditional large German pancake is made in a cast-iron skillet.

Tip: This recipe works best with regular margarine or butter, not light margarine, which has a higher moisture content.

Vary It! Substitute fresh or unsweetened frozen peaches for the apples and pears.

Savory Breakfast Bread Pudding

Prep time: 10 min • **Cook time:** 40–45 min • **Yield:** 7 servings

Ingredients	*Directions*
Nonstick cooking spray	*1* Preheat your oven to 375 degrees. Spritz an 11-x-7-inch glass baking dish with cooking spray.
4 egg whites	
4 whole eggs	*2* To prepare the custard, whisk the egg whites, eggs, and milk in a bowl. Add the mustard, pepper, and rosemary, whisking until all ingredients are combined.
1 cup evaporated skim milk	
1 tablespoon Dijon mustard	
¼ teaspoon freshly ground pepper	
1 teaspoon fresh rosemary	*3* Combine the cubed bread, spinach, red peppers, and smoked turkey in a large bowl. Add the custard and mix until all ingredients are combined. Pour the mixture into your prepared baking dish. Make a tent using foil to cover the pan. Bake for about 40 to 45 minutes until the custard is set and no longer jiggles.
4 cups (4 to 6 slices) whole-grain bread, cut into 1-inch cubes	
4 cups chopped baby spinach	
½ cup roasted red peppers, chopped	*4* Uncover, sprinkle the cheese on top, and continue to bake until the bread pudding is golden on top and a knife inserted in the middle comes out clean. Transfer to a wire rack and cool for 15 minutes to make it easier to cut individual servings.
½ cup diced smoked turkey	
½ cup shredded low-sodium Swiss cheese	

Per serving: Calories 188 (From Fat 63); Fat 7g (Saturated 3g); Cholesterol 137mg; Sodium 422mg; Carbohydrate 15g (Dietary Fiber 2g); Protein 16g; Potassium 235mg

Note: Bread pudding isn't just a sweet treat — it can be savory as well. Grab a piece for breakfast in a flash; it's great reheated as a leftover.

Vary It! Go gourmet and use some wonderfully wild mushrooms with a pinch of thyme, or roasted chestnuts and grated sweet potatoes. The possibilities are endless. Plus, because you're being frugal and utilizing your stale bread, feel free to splurge (think artisanal cheese or truffles)!

Trying Something New

Keep in mind that as you set a goal to eat a healthy breakfast daily, you don't have to conform to traditional standards. For example, you do *not* have to cook breakfast on a stove, eat it before 7 a.m. (or before you leave for work), or shun egg yolks (see the preceding section for more about eggs). We think if you try some of our newfangled recipes in this section, you'll definitely be motivated to eat your breakfast.

Our breakfast polenta is a nice change of pace. Polenta is a cornmeal-based food that originated in Northern Italy. Often viewed as "peasant food," polenta is inexpensive and easy to prepare. It's eaten either as porridge or sliced from a hard cake form. You can buy polenta coarsely ground or finely ground, as well as instant and precooked in a tube form that's meant to be sliced and heated. The instant and precooked polenta is usually very high in sodium. Cooking polenta from scratch is actually very easy. It can be used at any meal, topped with meat, tomato sauce, or vegetables. At breakfast time it can even be eaten as a cereal, topped with a bit of maple syrup.

Another great idea for a different take on breakfast: Skewers! Using a barbeque skewer, you can use small amounts of breakfast sausages for flavor, and add vegetables and fruits to get some of those 4 to 5 servings of fruits and veggies you need every day. Just follow these steps:

1. Cook breakfast sausage links on the grill until well-done. Remove and cut into bite-sized pieces.

2. Skewer chunks of peaches or pineapple, two pieces of sausage, and bell pepper chunks, and heat on the grill until the fruit and vegetables are tender.

To add another beneficial twist to breakfast, use whole-wheat, buckwheat, or oatmeal pancake mix. Try making your own mix using half whole-wheat flour in your traditional pancake recipe, or purchase a boxed mix. These pancakes work very well topped with fresh fruit and a dollop of vanilla or fruit yogurt. You may prefer to make the batter a bit thinner than usual, so the pancakes turn out light and fluffy.

Breakfast Polenta with Fresh Berries

Prep time: 5 min • **Cook time:** 30 min • **Yield:** 6 servings

Ingredients	*Directions*
2 cups lowfat milk **2 cups water** **1 cup coarsely ground polenta (not instant)**	*1* Bring the milk and water to a boil in a saucepan. Reduce the heat to simmer and carefully pour the polenta in a thin stream, while continuously stirring with a whisk to prevent lumps from forming.
2 tablespoons ground flaxseed **¼ teaspoon cinnamon** **1 tablespoon honey**	*2* Add the flaxseed and simmer for 30 minutes. If the polenta gets too thick, add water ¼ cup at a time to keep the consistency soft and creamy. Turn off the heat, cover, and let stand for 5 minutes.
½ teaspoon vanilla extract **¼ cup slivered almonds, toasted** **2 cups mixed berries: blueberries, sliced strawberries, and raspberries**	*3* Stir in the cinnamon, honey, and vanilla extract. Divide among 4 bowls and top each with 1 tablespoon of toasted almonds and ¼ cup mixed berries. Serve hot.

Per serving: Calories 219 (From Fat 72); Fat 8g (Saturated 1g); Cholesterol 4mg; Sodium 36mg; Carbohydrate 32g (Dietary Fiber 1g); Protein 5g; Potassium 156mg.

Note: This humble and obscure grain of the past has been reincarnated from "cornmeal mush" to a fancy breakfast cereal. Be sure to follow the directions on the package for cooking time; each type of polenta has its own cooking time, texture, and personality.

Tip: To avoid having to continuously stir after adding the polenta, mix the polenta with 2 cups cold water first; then add this mixture to the boiling milk.

Vary It! Consider a polenta bar for your next brunch! Make a large saucepan of cooked polenta and offer a variety of toppings, like toasted nuts (walnuts or pecans), maple syrup, dried fruit, and all-fruit preserves for a sweet delight! And for a savory option, offer chopped fresh herbs, sun-dried tomatoes, and a variety of shredded cheeses.

Spinach and Egg Squares

Prep time: 10 min • **Cook time:** 40 min • **Yield:** 4 servings

Ingredients	Directions
1 to 2 cloves garlic, minced	**1** Preheat your oven to 350 degrees. Sauté the garlic in the olive oil on low heat until softened. Add the spinach, cover, and wilt for about 1 minute. Use paper towels to pat down the spinach and remove any excess liquid.
1 teaspoon olive oil	
One 8-ounce bag baby spinach, rinsed	
5 whole eggs plus 7 egg whites	**2** Beat the eggs and milk in a separate bowl and mix in the pepper and nutmeg.
¾ cup lowfat milk	
¼ teaspoon freshly ground black pepper	**3** Coat an 8-x-8-inch glass baking dish with nonstick cooking spray. Spread ½ of the spinach mixture on the bottom of the dish. Cover the spinach with slices of cream cheese. Top the cream cheese with the remaining spinach mixture.
¼ teaspoon nutmeg	
Nonstick cooking spray	
8 ounces fat-free cream cheese, sliced thin	**4** Spread the sliced mushrooms and onions over the top layer of spinach and pour the egg mixture on top.
8 ounces fresh button mushrooms, sliced thin	
2 tablespoons chopped green onions	**5** Sprinkle the Swiss cheese and cayenne on top and bake for 40 minutes.
¼ cup low-sodium Swiss cheese	**6** Cut into 16 2-inch squares and serve warm or at room temperature.
⅛ teaspoon cayenne	

Per serving: Calories 217 (From Fat 99); Fat 11g (Saturated 4g); Cholesterol 275mg; Sodium 249mg; Carbohydrate 9g (Dietary Fiber 2g); Protein 23g; Potassium 216mg.

Note: Refrigerate leftovers to pack in school lunches or serve as appetizers at your next party!

Tip: Be sure to let the dish sit for 5 to 10 minutes out of the oven for easier cutting.

Chapter 15

Taking Time for Bigger Breakfasts and Brunches

In This Chapter

▶ Planning filling and balanced breakfasts

▶ Enjoying hearty egg breakfasts on the weekend

▶ Finding out why eating in is the new eating out

The nitty-gritty goal of this book is to help you cook homemade meals that reduce your blood pressure and your risk for heart disease. But isn't it wonderful that cooking at home means getting to eat great food? By reducing the processed and restaurant foods you eat and increasing the amount of meals eaten at home, you can automatically reduce the total sodium, fat, and calories in your diet. The secret is including high-quality ingredients.

Enjoying a big breakfast or brunch at home allows you to control portions and ingredients, and also ensure that your meal is balanced, including some fruits and veggies. We tell you all about how to include eggs in your diet in Chapter 14, and we have even more egg dishes for you here, as well as big skillet breakfasts and tasty scrambles.

The recipes in this chapter are properly portioned and well-balanced, yet still full of flavor! Save yourself the trip to the local greasy-spoon breakfast joint, and fix these hypertension-proof and delicious morning or midday meals instead.

Putting Your Eggs in One Basket: Frittatas, Stratas, and More

We're big fans of eggs. Coauthor Rosanne even has hens in the backyard, and her husband gathers fresh eggs every day. (If you're even a little curious, check out *Raising Chickens For Dummies* by Kimberly Willis and Rob Ludlow [Wiley]). The egg is a food that has been around for a long time. We bet your grandmother and great grandmother cooked eggs at least one day a week. Nothing about an egg is artificial or processed. You can use it to make a meal anytime of the day: breakfast, lunch, or dinner. You can enhance the egg with all sorts of savory or spicy flavors, and eggs work very well with vegetables. Eggs have acquired a bad reputation in recent years, but you can still work them into your hypertension meal plan.

One egg white provides only 16 of the 70 calories in a whole egg, and about half the protein (3 of the total 6 grams). The yolk of the egg provides the other 54 calories, 3 grams of protein, and all the cholesterol (about 185 milligrams). Don't forget to use just the egg whites sometimes when you cook. Flip to the section "Whipping Up Restaurant-Style Skillet Scrambles" for the egg-separating how-to.

A *frittata* is a thick, well-cooked omelet that generally has at least two ingredients besides eggs. Unlike the French omelet, the frittata originated in Italy, and you may think of it as more rustic than the formal omelet. While omelets are typically in the shape of a half-circle, frittatas are circular. They can be enjoyed as an easy, hearty comfort food. The main difference between an omelet and a frittata is that, in general, the ingredients for an omelet are gently put into a sauté pan *after* the egg is lightly cooked. With a frittata, the ingredients are mixed into the egg *before* it's cooked. Frittatas are cooked slowly and are sometimes finished in the oven.

A *strata* is another egg dish. It generally includes eggs, cheese, and bread and is baked in the oven. You can also add vegetables and meat, making it an all-in-one meal. Our Savory Breakfast Strata is flavored with a small amount of chicken sausage and uses sun-dried tomatoes, giving it a flavorful punch. You can experiment with all sorts of flavors after you master our egg-cooking techniques.

So how about that? Eggs aren't so bad after all. Believe us when we say that throwing together an egg dish with any or all of the vegetables you have in the fridge is a more economical and healthier option than the drive-thru!

French Market Frittata

Prep time: 15 min • **Cook time:** 10 min • **Yield:** 6 servings

Ingredients	Directions
Nonstick cooking spray	*1* Spritz a 9-inch nonstick skillet with cooking spray until well coated.
1 tablespoon olive oil	
¼ cup chopped green bell peppers	*2* Heat the oil and sauté the green bell pepper, mushrooms, zucchini, onion, red bell pepper, and herbs de Provence over medium heat until the vegetables are tender and the liquid has evaporated.
¼ cup chopped mushrooms	
½ cup chopped zucchini	
½ cup diced onions	*3* Beat the eggs and milk until combined. Add the egg mixture to the vegetables in the skillet. Stir to combine.
½ cup chopped red bell pepper	
½ teaspoon herbs de Provence	*4* Add the cheese, garlic, and pepper. Combine well. As the egg mixture begins to set, lift the edges with a spatula so that the uncooked eggs can flow underneath until the eggs are completely cooked. Cover with a lid and turn the heat on low until the entire frittata is set, 3 to 5 minutes.
6 whole large eggs or 4 whole eggs and 4 egg whites	
¼ cup lowfat milk	
4 ounces lowfat cheese, shredded	
1 clove garlic, minced	*5* To serve, cut in wedges and garnish with fresh sliced tomatoes and fresh basil chiffonade (optional — flip to Chapter 11 for an illustration).
¼ teaspoon freshly ground black pepper	
1 large tomato, sliced	
Fresh basil (optional)	

Per serving: Calories 158 (From Fat 99); Fat 11g (Saturated 4g); Cholesterol 223mg; Sodium 134mg; Carbohydrate 6g (Dietary Fiber 1g); Protein 9g; Potassium 269mg.

Note: The herbs de Provence in this recipe give it a French flair.

Tip: An alternate method of finishing the cooking process is to place the skillet under a broiler 5 inches from the heat until the frittata is solidified (we use the broiler method in the following recipe). An even easier method is to use a specially designed frittata pan to flip the frittata from one side to the other. These are available in gourmet kitchen shops.

Tuna and Sweet Potato Frittata

Prep time: 10 min • **Cook time:** 10–12 min • **Yield:** 3 servings

Ingredients	Directions
1 large sweet potato, peeled and diced	*1* Place the sweet potatoes in a small microwavable container with 2 tablespoons of water and cook 2 minutes on high. Drain and cool to room temperature.
1 tablespoon canola oil, divided	
1 small onion, finely chopped	*2* Heat ½ tablespoon of the oil in a skillet; add the onion and cook until soft. Add the tomato and cook for 3 minutes.
1 large tomato, finely chopped	
One 6-ounce can chunk-style very-low-sodium water-packed tuna, well drained	*3* Place the tomato mixture in a bowl and add the sweet potatoes, tuna, parsley, eggs, and cheese. Stir gently until combined.
2 tablespoons chopped fresh parsley	
2 whole eggs or 1 whole egg and 2 egg whites, beaten	*4* Heat the remaining oil and 1 tablespoon butter in a small skillet and add the tuna mixture. Cook over medium heat for about 3 minutes, gently lifting the edges of the frittata so the liquid runs underneath and the base is cooked.
½ cup grated reduced-fat cheddar cheese	
1 tablespoon butter	*5* Place the skillet under the broiler for about 2 minutes or until golden brown. Cut in wedges and serve.

Per serving: Calories 298 (From Fat 144); Fat 16g (Saturated 6g); Cholesterol 189mg; Sodium 370mg; Carbohydrate 17g (Dietary Fiber 3g); Protein 24g; Potassium 558mg.

Note: Albacore and black fin tuna are used to make "white meat" canned tuna, and yellow fin and skipjack are used in "light meat" tuna. Look for very-low-sodium, water-packed tuna, which has less fat and sodium than tuna in oil.

Savory Breakfast Strata

Prep time: 15 min • **Cook time:** 30–45 min • **Yield:** 8 servings

Ingredients	Directions
Nonstick cooking spray	**1** Spritz the bottom of a 9-x-13-inch glass baking pan with cooking spray. Lay the slices of bread side by side in the pan.
8 slices stale whole-wheat bread, crust removed	
4 ounces loose chicken sausage, browned and crumbled	**2** Sprinkle the cooked sausage, sun-dried tomatoes, shallots, and rosemary over the bread slices. Sprinkle the cheese on top.
¼ cup chopped sun-dried tomatoes, drained	
2 medium shallots, minced	**3** Whisk together the eggs, milk, pepper, and dry mustard and pour over the casserole. Cover and refrigerate overnight.
2 tablespoons fresh rosemary	
1 cup lowfat shredded sharp cheddar cheese	**4** Preheat your oven to 350 degrees. Bring the strata to room temperature; then bake for 30 to 45 minutes or until the eggs are set and the cheese is bubbly.
6 whole eggs or 4 whole eggs and 4 egg whites	
1½ cups lowfat milk	
Freshly ground pepper to taste	
1 teaspoon dry mustard	

Per serving: Calories 253 (From Fat 90); Fat 10g (Saturated 4g); Cholesterol 175mg; Sodium 522mg; Carbohydrate 26g (Dietary Fiber 3g); Protein 17g; Potassium 396mg.

Note: While this recipe is made of good-for-you ingredients, it's also slightly higher in sodium, so balance out your meal choices the rest of the day with lower-sodium options.

Tip: In place of the sun-dried tomatoes, consider making your own oven-dried tomatoes. Core 1½ pounds of plum tomatoes and cut them in half lengthwise. Place on a paper towel cut side down. Preheat the oven to 300 degrees. Arrange the tomatoes on a lined baking sheet, cut side up, and bake for 3½ to 4 hours or until the edges curl. Yield: 1 cup of oven-dried tomatoes.

Spinach, Ham, and Egg Muffins

Prep time: 10–12 min • **Cook time:** 15–20 min • **Yield:** 12 servings

Ingredients	*Directions*
Nonstick cooking spray 12 extra-thin slices lower-sodium ham	**1** Preheat the oven to 350 degrees. Generously spritz two 6-cup large muffin tins with cooking spray.
2 cups chopped fresh baby spinach	**2** Line each muffin cup with one slice of ham large enough for its ends to stick out of the pan.
12 eggs 1 teaspoon Italian herbs 2 cups chopped plum tomatoes	**3** Place spinach in a microwavable dish with 1 tablespoon water. Microwave on high for 2 minutes or until the spinach wilts. Divide the spinach evenly among the muffin cups, layering it on top of the ham.
2 tablespoons chopped chives	**4** Break one egg into each ham-and-spinach-lined cup. Sprinkle the cups evenly with Italian herbs and chopped tomatoes.
	5 Bake approximately 15 minutes or until the egg is completely solidified. Let cool for a few minutes before removing the muffins from the tins. Garnish with fresh chives.

Per serving: Calories 107 (From Fat 54); Fat 6g (Saturated 2g); Cholesterol 221mg; Sodium 240mg; Carbohydrate 2g (Dietary Fiber 0.5g); Protein 11g; Potassium 210mg.

Note: Ham is a high-sodium, but lean, product. Using a small amount can fit into a healthy eating plan. Many delis now carry lower-sodium ham.

Vary It! Instead of ham, you can line the pans with 4 to 5 layers of frozen phyllo dough, alternating with a spritz of cooking spray between layers.

Stuffed French Toast with Apricot-Orange Sauce

Prep time: 10 min • **Cook time:** 15 min • **Yield:** 6 servings

Ingredients	Directions
¼ cup crushed pineapple in juice, drained	**1** Drain the crushed pineapple well, using paper towels to remove excess juice. Blend the pineapple with the cream cheese and set aside.
8 ounces fat-free cream cheese, softened	
10-ounce jar pure-fruit apricot preserves (no sugar added)	**2** To make the sauce, combine the apricot preserves and orange juice and heat in the microwave for 2 minutes until well blended. Set aside and keep warm.
½ cup orange juice	
4 whole eggs or 2 whole eggs plus 4 egg whites	**3** In a shallow bowl, whisk the eggs, milk, vanilla, and ginger.
1 cup evaporated skimmed milk	**4** Cut the bread into 12 equal slices; slice through the top crust of each slice, making a deep pocket.
1 teaspoon vanilla extract	
1 teaspoon ground ginger	**5** Stuff each pocket with 1 heaping tablespoon of the pineapple cream cheese mixture and several small banana slices.
1 French baguette	
2 small ripe bananas, sliced	
Nonstick cooking spray	**6** Heat a large nonstick skillet coated with cooking spray. Dip the entire stuffed bread slices in the egg mixture and cook for 2 to 3 minutes on each side or until golden.
	7 Serve with the apricot-orange sauce.

Per serving: *Calories 408 (From Fat 36); Fat 4g (Saturated 1g); Cholesterol 147mg; Sodium 747mg; Carbohydrate 73g (Dietary Fiber 4g); Protein 22g; Potassium 524mg.*

Note: While this recipe is made of good-for-you ingredients, it's also slightly higher in sodium, so balance out your meal choices the rest of the day with lower-sodium options.

Tip: This recipe works great using different kinds of bread (such as seven-grain, Ciabatta, and Challah) and is a great way to use day-old bread. Many types of bread are high in sodium, however, so check the label (see Chapter 5) and choose lower-sodium brands when you can.

Whipping Up Restaurant-Style Skillet Scrambles

We may sound like a broken record, but we'll say it again: Preparing your favorite dishes at home saves you fat, sodium, and calories, and puts coins back in your pocket. Skillet scrambles are so easy, you don't even need a recipe, and the kids can help. You can also make individual scrambles, allowing family members to be creative and choose their own fillings.

Think about your favorite diner. Sure, the home fries are great, but do you know how much oil, lard, or butter they use? And how much salt is added? You can make some delicious home fries in your own kitchen in no time to satisfy your craving (see Chapter 12 for our Roasted Cajun Fingerling Potatoes, a great alternative to greasy home fries).

Skillet hash is another diner favorite. *Hash* is a dish of finely diced meat or potatoes, vegetables, and seasonings fried together until nicely browned. Hash is another one-dish meal that you can cook up at home with much less fat than the greasy spoon downtown. Our sweet potato hash recipe in this section shows you how to add an egg to the middle of the hash mixture when it's almost done cooking.

No need to confine these scrambles to the morning hours alone. These one-dish meals are perfect as a quick dinner meal before you head out the door for an evening meeting or to take the kids to their soccer game. Have paper plates on hand for those super-rushed evenings. Use a nonstick pan for easy cleanup.

Use egg whites in these skillet recipes instead of the whole egg (two whites equal one whole egg) to cut cholesterol. To separate the white from the yolk, crack the egg over the rim of a small bowl or glass measuring cup. Use your thumbs to gently crack the egg in half. Turn the egg so the yolk remains in one half of the shell. Pour the white into the bowl, and gently transfer the yolk to the other shell half. Continue transferring the yolk back and forth from one shell half to the other until all the white has dripped into the bowl. Here's another way to do it: Crack the egg over a bowl, pour it into your upturned palm, and allow the white to drip through your fingers into the bowl.

Spanish Tortilla Skillet

Prep time: 15–17 min • **Cook time:** 20 min • **Yield:** 6 servings

Ingredients	*Directions*
3 sweet potatoes, peeled and sliced	**1** Combine the potatoes and onions in a bowl.
2 Yukon gold potatoes, peeled and sliced	**2** Heat a large nonstick skillet over medium-low heat, add the oil, and wait for it to get hot enough for its appearance to go from smooth to shimmering (watch closely). Sauté the potatoes and onions in the hot oil and cover for 8 to 10 minutes until the potatoes begin to soften. Sauté over high heat for another 5 to 7 minutes until the potatoes are golden in color. Remove from heat.
1 large onion, diced	
2 to 3 tablespoons olive oil	
8 whole eggs or 4 whole eggs and 8 egg whites	
¼ cup lowfat milk	
Nonstick cooking spray	**3** Whisk together the eggs and milk in a large bowl. Add the potato-onion mixture to the eggs. Wipe any residue from the skillet used for sautéing the potatoes with a paper towel. Spritz the skillet with nonstick cooking spray, and gently pour the egg-potato mixture into the hot skillet over medium heat. Continue cooking over medium heat, stirring until the eggs begin to set. Lift the edges of the egg tortilla with a spatula to allow the uncooked liquid to flow underneath. When most of the eggs have set, cover with a lid until the tortilla has completely cooked. You may have to reduce the heat to medium-low to avoid over-browning.
	4 Cut in wedges and serve warm.

Per serving: Calories 259 (From Fat 103); Fat 11g (Saturated 3g); Cholesterol 284mg; Sodium 99mg; Carbohydrate 27g (Dietary Fiber 3g); Protein 11g; Potassium 512mg.

Note: This is an ideal go-to meal for any time of day when all you have left in the fridge are the basics. Pair it with a mixed green salad fully loaded with fresh vegetables.

Tip: Slicing the potatoes with a sharp knife or mandolin will provide thin and consistent slices and ensure a quick and even cooking rate.

Vary It! You can add leftover steamed or sautéed vegetables, grated low-sodium cheese, and fresh herbs to your Spanish tortilla!

Sweet Potato Hash

Prep time: 10 min • **Cook time:** 10–12 min • **Yield:** 4 servings

Ingredients	Directions
1 tablespoon canola oil	*1* Heat the oil and butter in a nonstick skillet and sauté the sweet potatoes and onions until soft and lightly browned. Add the chili powder and cumin and continue to sauté for a minute longer.
1 tablespoon butter	
1 medium sweet potato, peeled and diced	
1 yellow onion, chopped	*2* Spritz a second nonstick skillet with cooking spray. Break the eggs into the skillet one at a time and sprinkle with ground pepper. Reduce the heat to low and cook for a few minutes until the egg whites are completely set.
½ teaspoon chili powder	
⅛ teaspoon cumin	
Nonstick cooking spray	
4 eggs	*3* Using a wide spatula, gently turn the eggs over so the yolks are down, and continue cooking until the yolks are set.
Freshly ground pepper to taste	
	4 Divide the sweet potatoes among 4 plates and, using a wide spatula, carefully lift the eggs on top of the potatoes.

Per serving: Calories 167 (From Fat 99); Fat 11g (Saturated 4g); Cholesterol 219mg; Sodium 113mg; Carbohydrate 10g (Dietary Fiber 2g); Protein 7g; Potassium 225mg.

Tip: An alternative method for cooking eggs is steam-basting. Break the eggs into the skillet. Reduce the heat and add 1 to 2 tablespoons water; cover and steam for about 3 minutes or until the eggs are set.

Tex-Mex Scramble

Prep time: 10 min • **Cook time:** 15–20 min • **Yield:** 4 servings

Ingredients	*Directions*
1 tablespoon canola oil	*1* Heat the oil and butter in a large nonstick skillet. Add the potatoes and sauté until softened and browned, about 15 minutes. Add the onions, bell pepper, and jalapeño and continue to cook until the vegetables are soft.
1 tablespoon butter	
1 medium Yukon gold potato, peeled and diced into small pieces	
¼ cup diced onions	*2* Add the eggs to the vegetable mixture and cook for 1 minute until the eggs are slightly set. Continue to cook them by gently turning them over until they're completely set.
¼ cup diced green bell peppers	
½ to 1 small jalapeño, seeded and minced	
8 whole eggs or 6 whole eggs and 4 egg whites, lightly beaten	*3* Divide the scrambled egg mixture among 4 plates and sprinkle with cheese. Place under the broiler to melt the cheese. Top with freshly ground pepper to taste.
1 cup shredded lowfat Monterey Jack cheese	
Freshly ground pepper to taste	

Per serving: Calories 316 (From Fat 198); Fat 22g (Saturated 9g); Cholesterol 449mg; Sodium 322mg; Carbohydrate 8g (Dietary Fiber 1g); Protein 21g; Potassium 323mg.

Note: If you feel like a grab-and-go breakfast or anytime sandwich, place the scrambled mixture inside a toasted whole-wheat English muffin.

Grilled Salmon Scramble

Prep time: 10 min • **Cook time:** 5 min • **Yield:** 2 servings

Ingredients	*Directions*
1 teaspoon canola oil	*1* Heat the oil in a nonstick skillet over medium heat. Add the eggs and allow to set for 20 seconds.
3 whole eggs or 2 whole eggs and 2 egg whites, lightly beaten	
1 ounce grilled salmon, cut into strips	*2* Fold the salmon, cream cheese, and chives into the eggs. Gently scramble the mixture just until cooked, about 1 to 2 minutes.
1 ounce reduced-fat cream cheese, cut into 8 pieces	
1 tablespoon chopped chives	
Freshly ground pepper to taste	

Per serving: Calories 182 (From Fat 126); Fat 14g (Saturated 5g); Cholesterol 36mg; Sodium 159mg; Carbohydrate 2g (Dietary Fiber 0g); Protein 14g; Potassium 192mg.

Note: This recipe makes use of leftover salmon. We recommend always fixing more salmon than you need for a meal to make quick and easy scrambles. Smoked salmon is a very high-sodium alternative to using regular grilled salmon, but a few online vendors sell low-sodium smoked salmon.

Scrambled eggs, without the morning scramble

Freshly scrambled eggs are the best, but to make mornings easier, make eggs up ahead of time. This guarantees you a healthier, and probably tastier, choice than what you may pick up through a drive-thru window. The night before, scramble 4 eggs in a nonstick pan, using a bit of 1-percent milk to make them fluffy. Don't overcook; turn the heat off as soon as the eggs are firm but still wet. Place in a container and refrigerate. In the morning, use the eggs to make a quick breakfast wrap or an egg-on-bagel sandwich. You can either microwave it at home or wrap it and take it to work to heat and eat.

Chapter 16

Power Hour: Enjoying Light and Tasty Lunches

Getting caught in the fast-food trap during your lunch hour at work is easy. If you work at home, you may either skip or snack through lunch. Neither scenario is best for your health. Like every meal, a little planning goes a long way at lunchtime. Think ahead. In this chapter, we offer you some new sandwich, salad, and leftover ideas bursting with flavors.

Whatever you do, don't let your deadlines, meetings, or inbox force you to skip lunch. Skipping meals not only means skipping nutrients, but it can also set you up for disaster in terms of calorie control. If you don't eat balanced meals and snacks every four hours or so, you're likely to make poor choices and overeat. Use the quick ideas in this chapter to put together a quick lunch to pack for the office or assemble on Saturdays.

If you don't have one, purchase a sturdy insulated lunch bag. Many types are available for adults. Check your local superstores or office supply stores for a wide selection.

If your mornings are rushed like ours are, put together as much of your lunch as possible while you're cleaning up the dinner dishes the night before. Pack fruit into small snack bags, or simply wash an apple and physically pack it into your lunch bag. You can pack yogurt directly into the bag as well. Use reusable plastic containers for salads or sliced fruit, storing dressings separately. Then refrigerate the whole bag. If a sandwich is on the menu, have chopped veggies ready to go for the fixings, but wait until morning to quickly assemble the sandwich to prevent sogginess. Brown baggin' has never been easier!

Consider lunchtime important to your health. Lunch should make up at least one-third of your nutrient requirements for a day. Make it interesting, delicious, and nutritious; it's a time to take a break, relax, and enjoy a small meal. By breaking for lunch, you give your body the chance to recharge, both physically and mentally.

Crafting Outside-the-Box Sandwiches

Ham and cheese. Turkey. Peanut butter and jelly. Sound familiar and yawn-inducing? It's time to get out of your boring, high-sodium, low-fiber lunch rut and make your lunchbox exciting. Try some new fillings for your bread and some new breads for your fillings.

Sandwiches are a great opportunity to include more vegetables in your diet. As part of the DASH plan (see Chapter 2 for details), you need four to five veggies a day. With the right sandwich, you can easily knock out two or three of these servings, and also add lots of fiber with whole-grain breads. Here are a few of our ideas for incorporating DASH principles in your new, outside-of-the-box lunches:

- ✔ Try a variety of breads, as long as they're whole grain and provide 2 or more grams of fiber per serving; some options are whole wheat, whole rye, and pumpernickel. Substitute whole-wheat pita pockets, whole-wheat flat wraps, or whole-grain tortillas for sliced bread.

- ✔ Use hummus as a filling for small pita pockets or as a spread in place of mayonnaise. Top with spinach, chopped lettuce, alfalfa sprouts, and sliced cucumbers for a great sandwich packed with veggies.

- ✔ Try low-sodium varieties of canned or pouch tuna. Top a tossed green salad with tuna, or make a wrap using a whole-grain tortilla or wrap. Skip the traditional tuna salad recipe. Use just a teaspoon of lowfat mayo and add more veggies, such as minced bell peppers and shredded carrots. Finish off your concoction with ground pepper and tarragon to taste.

Make fresh salsa and keep it on hand, along with some whole-grain tortilla chips, for a healthy side to your sandwich. To make the fresh salsa, combine the following in a small bowl with a lid: 1 small plum tomato, chopped; 1 to 2 tablespoons finely chopped onion; 2 teaspoons seeded and finely chopped jalapeño pepper (use more or less depending on how much heat you desire); and 1 to 2 tablespoons finely chopped fresh cilantro. Refrigerate for up to a week.

Curried Chicken Wrap

Prep time: 10 min • **Yield:** 4 servings

Ingredients	Directions
½ **cup shredded cooked chicken**	**1** Mix all the ingredients except the tortillas together in a bowl until well blended.
¼ **cup diced celery**	
¼ **cup diced red bell pepper**	**2** Divide the mixture atop 4 tortillas. Roll up the tortillas and they're ready to serve.
¼ **cup diced apple**	
2 tablespoons raisins	**3** If you're making the wraps ahead of time, wrap with plastic wrap and refrigerate. When ready to serve, cut each wrap in half diagonally or into bite-sized pieces.
2 tablespoons almonds	
¼ **cup reduced-fat mayonnaise**	
¼ **teaspoon curry powder**	
1 tablespoon lemon juice	
Four 8- or 10-inch whole-wheat tortillas	

Per serving: Calories 243 (From Fat 72); Fat 8g (Saturated 1g); Cholesterol 15mg; Sodium 197mg; Carbohydrate 33g (Dietary Fiber 3g); Protein 10g; Potassium 154mg.

Note: Wraps make great use of leftovers, from rotisserie chicken to vegetables. Including add-ins like raisins and almonds amps up the nutrient value of your wrap. Be creative, and use up all those goodies from your pantry like trail mix, a variety of dried fruit, flaxseeds, and jicama. Let your creativity run wild.

Note: Be on the lookout for low-sodium, low-fat, and whole-grain tortillas now in the supermarket.

Tip: These wraps are easy to pack in lunches or for a quick snack on the road!

Grilled Steak and Onions on Crusty Ciabatta

Prep time: 15–20 min plus marinating time • **Cook time:** 15 min • **Yield:** 4 sandwiches

Ingredients	Directions
¾ **pound flat iron steak, about 1-inch thick**	*1* Marinate the flat iron steak in the Italian dressing for 3 to 4 hours.
2 tablespoons Italian dressing	
1 teaspoon canola oil	*2* Preheat your grill to medium-high.
2 medium onions, thinly sliced	*3* Heat the oil in a skillet on medium heat and sauté the onions until caramelized and softened, about 15 minutes. Add the vinegar and continue cooking for another minute. Keep warm.
1 tablespoon balsamic vinegar	
2 tablespoons reduced-fat sour cream	*4* To make the sauce, mix together the sour cream, mayonnaise, horseradish, and oregano until well blended.
2 tablespoons reduced-fat mayonnaise	
1 teaspoon prepared horseradish	*5* Remove the steak from the marinade and place it on the hot grill. Cook 5 to 7 minutes for rare, 7 to 10 minutes for medium, or to desired doneness. Slice across the grain into even slices.
2 teaspoons oregano	
2 garlic cloves, mashed	*6* While the steak is grilling, cut the ciabatta rolls in half, rub the garlic over the cut sides, and grill the rolls until lightly toasted.
4 ciabatta rolls	
	7 Divide the steak and sautéed onion among the 4 rolls and top with 1 tablespoon of the horseradish sauce.

Per serving: Calories 577 (From Fat 153); Fat 17g (Saturated 5g); Cholesterol 42mg; Sodium 680mg; Carbohydrate 78g (Dietary Fiber 3g); Protein 31g; Potassium 403mg.

Note: While this recipe is made of good-for-you ingredients, it's also slightly higher in sodium, so balance out your meal choices the rest of the day with lower-sodium options.

Note: Welcome back, beef. Beef has a reputation for being high in fat and cholesterol, but many lean beef options are out there. The DASH diet (see Chapter 2) recommends limiting animal protein to 6 ounces a day; choose lean and think of it as a side dish. Flat iron steak is a shoulder top blade steak resembling flank steak. Marinate it for a short time to tenderize.

Grilled Portobello Mushroom Pita

Prep time: 10 min • **Cook time:** 10–12 min • **Yield:** 6 servings

Ingredients	Directions
8 small portobello mushrooms, sliced	**1** Preheat a gas grill to high. Drizzle the olive oil over the mushrooms, rubbing it into the mushrooms to make sure they're coated, and grill for 5 minutes; turn and grill another 5 minutes. Slice the mushrooms into strips and season them with pepper to taste.
2 tablespoons olive oil	
Freshly ground pepper to taste	
½ cup reduced-fat mayonnaise	**2** Mix the mayonnaise with the sweet chili sauce to make a spread.
2 tablespoons sweet chili sauce	
6 whole-wheat pita pockets	**3** Cut the pita pockets in half and lightly spread the inside of each pocket with the spread.
1 cup alfalfa sprouts	
1 small cucumber, sliced thin	**4** Divide the grilled mushrooms, sprouts, cucumber slices, spinach, avocado, and tomatoes among the 12 halves.
1 cup baby spinach	
1 avocado, peeled and sliced	
2 tomatoes, sliced thin	

Per serving: Calories 383 (From Fat 148); Fat 17g (Saturated 3g); Cholesterol 7mg; Sodium 572mg; Carbohydrate 49g (Dietary Fiber 6g); Protein 10g; Potassium 949mg.

Note: While this recipe is made of good-for-you ingredients, it's also slightly higher in sodium, so balance out your meal choices the rest of the day with lower-sodium options.

Note: You can see a photo of this recipe in the color section. Portobello mushrooms come in large, medium, and small. Their meat-like texture and flavor are well suited for grilling whole or sliced. Portobellos are the mature form of crimini mushrooms.

Tip: If you like the kick of chili sauce but want to decrease the sodium, look for a low-sodium chili sauce.

Vary It! Try using your favorite whole-grain bread for a Portobello club sandwich! You can also change the flavor of the sauce by mixing the reduced-fat mayonnaise with any number of ingredients from your fridge, such as basil pesto or sundried tomatoes.

Filling Up on Fresh Luncheon Salads

Chapter 9 includes lots of great, fresh salads to try, and we've put together some additional ones here that pack well for lunch. Flip back to the proper plate image in Chapter 2 to see how important the fruit and veggie count of your daily diet is. Salads are a great way to boost both of these counts. When planning your lunch salad, keep these rules of thumb in mind:

- **Load up on greens:** Include lots of fresh, dark clean greens.

- **Pile on more veggies:** The more raw veggies, the better. Try dicing your vegetables into small pieces for the perfect bite-full.

- **Vary your veggie prep style:** If you prefer, you can roast or sauté veggies for your salads.

- **Add a dose of lean protein:** Cooked chicken, lean beef, lowfat cottage cheese, tuna, chickpeas, or other beans work well.

- **Limit high-calorie toppings:** Skip the extra calories that can sneak in and add up when you include croutons, creamy dressings, high-fat meats, and too much cheese.

- **Expand your (food-group) horizons:** Don't be afraid to include the dairy and fruit groups in your salad. Try a scoop of lowfat cottage cheese or ricotta, an ounce of shredded or chopped low-sodium cheese, dried cranberries, mangoes, or diced apples.

Make sure to include lunch fixings on your grocery list. Keeping fresh produce in the house is a must for lunch to ensure you include fruits and vegetables on the plate. Fresh lettuce or spinach, carrots, onions, celery, tomatoes, and a variety of fruits can serve as the base of any healthy lunch sandwich, salad, or meal. Be sure to keep lowfat dairy products on hand, too, such as lowfat cottage cheese, cheeses, lowfat yogurt, and milk.

Consider growing a small vegetable garden. You can even start with just three or four pots and easily grow your own lettuce, onions, tomatoes, and more. We recommend *Vegetable Gardening For Dummies*, 2nd Edition, by Charlie Nardozzi (Wiley), for all the details on DIY salad fixings.

Quick Shrimp Ceviche Salad

Prep time: 10–15 min • **Yield:** 4 servings

Ingredients	Directions
1 pound frozen cooked small shrimp (from a 70–90 count bag), thawed	**1** Place the thawed shrimp in a bowl. Add the cucumber, onion, tomato, chile, lime and orange juices, orange zest, olive oil, and Tabasco sauce and mix well. Refrigerate the mixture for at least one hour to allow the flavors to blend.
1 small cucumber, seeded and diced	
2 tablespoons minced red onion	**2** Place 1½ cups of the mixed greens on each of 4 dinner plates.
1 large tomato, seeded and diced	
1 serrano chile, seeded and diced	**3** Gently mix the cilantro leaves into the ceviche. Divide among the 4 plates atop the mixed greens and serve with avocado slices and lime wedges.
2 limes, juiced	
2 oranges, juiced	
1 tablespoon orange zest	
2 tablespoons olive oil	
Dash Tabasco sauce	
6 cups mixed greens	
¼ cup chopped cilantro leaves	
1 ripe avocado, sliced	
Lime wedges	

Per serving: Calories 288 (From Fat 117); Fat 13g (Saturated 2g); Cholesterol 221mg; Sodium 313mg; Carbohydrate 21g (Dietary Fiber 7g); Protein 28g; Potassium 680mg.

Note: The acid in the citrus ingredients "cooks" the raw seafood that ceviche is traditionally made with, impeding the growth of microbes. No need to fear — in this recipe, we use only pre-cooked shrimp.

Tip: For a quick lunch, spoon the ceviche on a tostada shell and serve with shredded lettuce and a lime wedge.

Vary It! Along with or as a substitute for shrimp, use your favorite white fish such as grouper, sea bass, tilapia, or even bay scallops. Add fresh chopped citrus fruit and red or yellow chopped bell peppers.

Tuna Nicoise Salad

Prep time: 10 min • **Yield:** 2 servings

Ingredients	Directions
1 teaspoon Dijon mustard	**1** To make vinaigrette, mix together the mustard, garlic, lemon juice, and pepper and blend well. Slowly whisk in the olive oil until emulsified.
1 clove garlic, minced	
Juice of ½ lemon	
Freshly ground pepper to taste	
¼ cup olive oil	**2** To plate up the salad, arrange all the remaining ingredients in small piles divided between two dinner plates and drizzle with the vinaigrette.
One 6-ounce can chunk-style tuna, packed in water	
½ cup haricots verts, blanched for 1 minute	
4 Nicoise olives	
4 whole new potatoes, boiled or roasted	
2 cups mixed greens	
¼ cup thinly sliced red onions	
12 cherry tomatoes	
1 hard-boiled egg, sliced in quarters	

Per serving: Calories 436 (From Fat 315); Fat 35g (Saturated 5g); Cholesterol 136mg; Sodium 485mg; Carbohydrate 12g (Dietary Fiber 3g); Protein 22g; Potassium 524mg.

Note: With so many different ingredients in this salad, from potatoes to tomatoes to tuna, each forkful should be packed with contrasting flavors, textures, and nutrients.

Tip: Lunchtime is new-spin-on-leftovers time, so if you have leftover fingerling potatoes or broccoli piccata, substitute that for some of these ingredients. Using leftovers makes lunch a piece of cake.

Putting a New Twist on Leftovers

There are lots of ways to use leftovers, not only for lunch, but for dinner as well. You can whip up lots of easy lunches using leftovers from the recipes in this book.

Here are some user-friendly leftover ideas:

- ✔ **Leftover beans and rice:** Combine them in a wrap to make a burrito. Add a tablespoon of shredded cheese and heat for 10 seconds in the microwave. You can also add leftover beans or rice to a tossed green salad.

- ✔ **Leftover cooked chicken, pork, beef, or fish:** Use these as a filling for a soft taco lunch or as a salad topping. You can also add leftover meats to soups.

   Turn chicken into chicken salad by adding 3 tablespoons of plain, lowfat yogurt; finely chopped celery, onion, and carrots; and 2 teaspoons of tarragon.

- ✔ **Leftover roasted or grilled vegetables:** These veggies make great sandwich or pasta toppers.

- ✔ **Leftover spinach or asparagus:** Make a veggie omelet.

- ✔ **Leftover chili:** Eat it the next day served over 1 cup of brown rice or a baked potato.

- ✔ **Leftover whole-wheat pasta:** Add it to a green salad for added grains, or top it with roasted vegetables or leftover chicken or fish.

Leftovers make awesome lunch fixings. When cooking dinner, consider how you may use some of the leftovers the next day for lunch. If your family is like ours, some of them may balk at the idea of having Jamaican Jerk Chicken or Roast Pork Tenderloin (both in Chapter 17) two nights in a row, but you can turn those meats into another dish, salad, or special sandwich for lunch and nothing will go to waste.

Go ahead and serve up a healthy new dish. Don't tell anyone you're using leftovers, and they'll never know!

Vegetable Quesadillas

Prep time: 5 min • **Cook time:** 6–8 min • **Yield:** 4 servings

Ingredients	*Directions*
1 large tomato, chopped	*1* To make fresh salsa, combine the tomato, onion, cilantro, and jalapeño. Refrigerate.
2 to 4 tablespoons finely chopped onion	
¼ cup finely chopped fresh cilantro	*2* Heat a medium-sized skillet over medium heat. Spritz one side of a tortilla with cooking spray. Place oil side down in the skillet and sprinkle with ¼ cup of the cheese. Top with the leftover grilled vegetables. Fold the tortilla in half and press gently. Cook for 3 to 4 minutes on one side; turn and cook on the other side until golden.
½ small jalapeño pepper, seeded and finely chopped	
Nonstick cooking spray	
Four 6-inch whole-wheat or corn tortillas	*3* Repeat with each tortilla.
1 cup lowfat Mexi-cheese blend	*4* Serve the quesadillas with the sour cream, avocado, and fresh salsa.
2 cups leftover grilled vegetables	
¼ cup lowfat sour cream	
½ avocado, sliced	

Per serving: Calories 186 (From Fat 72); Fat 8g (Saturated 2g); Cholesterol 12mg; Sodium 52mg; Carbohydrate 24g (Dietary Fiber 6g); Protein 7g; Potassium 599mg.

Note: You can make these into tasty leftovers, as well, by freezing any extras. To defrost, remove from the freezer and place in the refrigerator the day before cooking.

Vary It! We call for leftover veggies as a filling, but utilize whatever leftovers you have. Try your favorite cheese plus any number of combinations: sweet potato hash, black beans and baby spinach leaves; chicken and caramelized onions; grilled pork tenderloin with a mango fruit salsa; or pulled pork with a few drops of barbecue sauce!

Chicken, Spinach, and Fruit Salad Trio

Prep time: 15 min • **Yield:** 4 servings

Ingredients	Directions
2 cups leftover cooked chicken, chopped	*1* Mix the chicken together with the celery, apples, pecans, and mayonnaise until well blended. Set aside.
¼ cup finely chopped celery	
½ cup finely chopped apple	*2* Begin to create your trio-plate. Divide the chicken salad among 4 dinner plates so it constitutes ⅓ of each plate.
2 tablespoons pecans	
¼ cup reduced-fat mayonnaise	
2 cups baby spinach	*3* Divide the spinach among the 4 plates and top with the sliced mushrooms and red bell peppers. Drizzle with ½ tablespoon favorite dressing. This makes up the second third of the trio.
¼ cup sliced mushrooms	
¼ cup red bell pepper	
2 tablespoons favorite dressing	*4* Divide the mixed fruit among the 4 plates, making it the last third of the trio.
2 cups mixed fruit in season: apples, watermelon, strawberries, cantaloupe, oranges, blueberries	

Per serving: Calories 254 (From Fat 99); Fat 11g (Saturated 1g); Cholesterol 60mg; Sodium 317mg; Carbohydrate 15g (Dietary Fiber 3g); Protein 24g; Potassium 395mg.

Note: This is the author's go-to recipe in the summertime . . . for lunch or a quick dinner. You don't really need a recipe, though — just toss together whatever you have left over in your fridge! Substitute your family's favorites to create your very own trio!

Tip: Serve this trio with your favorite dessert bread, such as banana bread.

Asian Chicken Pasta Salad

Prep time: 10 min • **Cook time:** 10–12 min • **Yield:** 4 servings

Ingredients	*Directions*
½ **pound whole-wheat rotini pasta**	*1* Cook the pasta according to the directions on the package. Avoid overcooking.
½ **to 1 tablespoon sesame oil**	
1½ **tablespoons low-sodium soy sauce**	*2* To make dressing, combine the sesame oil, soy sauce, vinegar, and stock. Set aside.
5 **tablespoons rice vinegar**	
5 **tablespoons low-sodium vegetable stock**	*3* Toss the carrots, green onions, snow peas, mushrooms, garlic, ginger, and red pepper flakes together with the pasta. Toss this mixture with the dressing.
½ **cup shredded carrots**	
¼ **cup diagonally sliced green onions**	*4* Add the chopped cooked chicken and garnish with cashews and cilantro. Serve at room temperature or refrigerate before serving.
½ **cup snow peas**	
½ **cup sliced button mushrooms**	
1 **garlic clove, minced**	
½ **tablespoon grated fresh ginger**	
Pinch red pepper flakes	
1 **cup leftover cooked chicken**	
2 **tablespoons chopped, unsalted cashews**	
2 **tablespoons chopped cilantro**	

Per serving: Calories 220 (From Fat 63); Fat 7g (Saturated 1g); Cholesterol 30mg; Sodium 275mg; Carbohydrate 22g (Dietary Fiber 2g); Protein 16g; Potassium 308mg.

Note: This recipe gets even better as it sits in the fridge, allowing the flavors to blend.

Chapter 17

Bringing Flavor to the Table with Poultry, Pork, and Beef

*P*rotein-rich foods like fresh chicken, pork, and beef are naturally lower in sodium and can fit into a hypertension diet perfectly. Because most sodium is added during processing, the pre-packaged, cured, processed choices that you may find at your local deli are the ones to limit. These high-sodium options include salami, cured bologna, loaf meats, beef jerky, sausage links, bacon, ham, meatless breakfast patties, frankfurters, and packaged marinated meats. Your best option is to choose higher quality grades of meat and enjoy a smaller amount. Choice grades of meat may be a better selection than prime, because the quality is excellent and the meat has less fat marbling.

This chapter gives you delicious protein options so that you can include more low-sodium meats, with plenty of flavor, while you limit the high-sodium choices.

Grills Gone Wild: Grilling with Poultry

"Chicken. Again?" If that's the reply you get when you answer "chicken" to the perennial "What's for dinner?" question, have no fear; the grilled chicken recipes in this section will have your family hoping for chicken . . . again. Skinless poultry is a good source of protein and is very low in fat. It's also fairly easy to prepare (especially if you follow our tips in Chapter 8 and have some packaged and ready to cook in the freezer). An added bonus: Poultry is an economical lean protein choice. So why does poultry often take a back seat for many chefs? Fat rules. But because too much fat increases your risk for heart disease, we show you ways to get around the fat by adding flavor instead.

You want bold flavor on the grill, but can you have it without fat? You sure can; rubs and marinades can not only give you the flavor you want, but also help keep poultry moist during the grilling process. So if you've just thrown some chicken on the grill in the past and ended up with a dry, not-so-tasty end result, take a look at the recipes in this section that give poultry new life. Add some wet rub to boneless chicken breasts headed to the grill, and you'll go from boring to bodacious.

In addition to adding flavor and sealing in the juices, rubs help the meat produce a delicious outer coating. So although you're going skinless with poultry, you can still enjoy an "herbal skin" right off the grill.

Here's a quick primer on rubs and marinades:

- **Dry rubs** are dry seasoning blends that are rubbed into the meat. They're often coarse, and they may include a variety of crushed herbs, garlic powder, paprika, and ground pepper.

- **Wet rubs** include herbs and seasonings as well as a wet ingredient, such as vegetable oil, crushed garlic, mustard, or low- sodium Worcestershire or soy sauce.

- **Marinades** are a liquid mixture that often includes an acidic ingredient along with seasonings. Marinades can both flavor and add moisture to meat or poultry. An acidic ingredient (such as vinegar or fruit juice) can be used to tenderize meats and poultry.

Gas or charcoal?

Whether you go for a gas grill or the old-fashioned charcoal method is really up to you. Both have advantages and disadvantages, and they offer subtle flavor differences. Grilling with gas is certainly more convenient and costs very little to fuel, although the grills themselves can be pricy. Charcoal grills are cheaper to purchase and add hints of smoky flavor to your meat, but the charcoal itself can rack up the dough. In either case, grilling involves dry heat, and you can choose whether to use it directly or indirectly. Most grills include a cover — if you leave the cover off, you have no air circulation; if you leave it on, you have warm air circulation (as you do with an oven). Some foods (like steaks) grill best when you place them directly over the flame, whereas other foods (such as slow-cooked roasts, ribs, or chicken pieces) do better with an indirect placement (on an area of the grill that's not directly over the flame) and a closed cover.

Grilled Dijon Chicken with Fresh Blackberry Sauce

Prep time: 10 min • **Cook time:** 10–12 min • **Yield:** 4 servings

Ingredients	Directions
1 cup blackberries 3 tablespoons orange juice 2 teaspoons low-sodium soy sauce 2 teaspoons honey 1 teaspoon sesame oil 2 teaspoons stone-ground mustard Freshly ground pepper to taste 1½ tablespoons olive oil 1 teaspoon lemon juice ½ teaspoon minced garlic ½ teaspoon dried tarragon 4 skinless boneless chicken breast halves Cilantro sprigs	*1* To make the blackberry sauce, mash the blackberries in a small bowl. Add the orange juice, soy sauce, honey, and sesame oil and set aside to blend the flavors. *2* Mix together the mustard, pepper, olive oil, lemon juice, garlic, and tarragon. Place the chicken into a shallow glass dish and pour the mixture over the chicken breasts. Cover and marinate for up to 4 hours in the refrigerator. *3* Preheat the grill on medium-high. Place the marinated chicken pieces on the grill and grill for 6 to 12 minutes or until cooked through, turning frequently to prevent burning. Discard leftover marinade. Transfer the chicken to a plate and cover it with foil to keep it warm. *4* Serve the chicken with a tablespoon of the fresh blackberry sauce and add cilantro sprigs for garnish.

Per serving: Calories 417 (From Fat 135); Fat 15g (Saturated 3g); Cholesterol 157mg; Sodium 237mg; Carbohydrate 9g (Dietary Fiber 2g); Protein 59g; Potassium 573mg.

Note: A staple in just about every culture, chicken is versatile and can be prepared in so many ways. For those dealing with hypertension who need to watch their fat intake, chicken breasts are an excellent source of protein. The breasts are the leanest part of the chicken.

Tip: Place chicken between two pieces of plastic wrap and use a meat mallet to pound the chicken to a similar thickness on all sides so it cooks evenly.

Zippy Grilled Chicken

Prep time: 5 min • **Cook time:** 12–15 min • **Yield:** 4 servings

Ingredients	Directions
3 tablespoons canola oil	**1** Prepare a wet rub by mixing together the oil, garlic, paprika, black and cayenne pepper, and orange zest. Rub the mixture into the flesh of the chicken. Wrap the chicken in plastic wrap and refrigerate for 4 hours or overnight.
3 cloves garlic, minced	
2 tablespoons smoked paprika	
1 tablespoon freshly ground black pepper	
¼ teaspoon cayenne pepper	**2** Preheat the grill; then grill the chicken breasts 4 to 6 minutes on each side. Serve.
1½ tablespoons orange zest	
4 boneless skinless chicken breast halves	

Per serving: Calories 431 (From Fat 171); Fat 19g (Saturated 3g); Cholesterol 157mg; Sodium 138mg; Carbohydrate 5g (Dietary Fiber 2g); Protein 58g; Potassium 584mg.

Note: Rubs are used to season food by adding layers of flavor. If you don't have enough time to let the rub sink in for hours like the recipe suggests, you can just sprinkle the rub on the chicken before cooking to both season and cure the chicken.

Tip: Try serving this chicken dish with your favorite steamed vegetables and a whole-grain side dish.

Chicken Kabobs with Tzatziki Sauce

Prep time: 10 min • **Cook time:** 16–18 min • **Yield:** 4 servings

Ingredients	Directions
3 cups plain Greek yogurt, divided	**1** For the tzatziki sauce, combine 1½ cups yogurt, the minced garlic, 1½ tablespoon lemon juice, 1 tablespoon of the dill, and the cucumber. Mix well, cover, and refrigerate for a few hours to develop flavors.
3 garlic cloves, 1 minced and 2 crushed	
3 tablespoons lemon juice, divided	**2** For the marinade, combine the remaining 1½ cups yogurt, the crushed garlic, 1½ tablespoons lemon juice, the remaining 1 teaspoon dill, and the oregano, tarragon, parsley, and pepper in a large bowl. Set aside.
1 tablespoon plus 1 teaspoon fresh dill, chopped	
1 medium cucumber, seeded and finely chopped	
½ teaspoon oregano	**3** Cut the chicken into 2-inch cubes. Reserve ½ cup marinade. Toss the chicken with the remaining marinade in a shallow glass baking dish, cover, and refrigerate for 1 to 2 hours.
1 teaspoon tarragon	
1 teaspoon parsley	
Freshly ground pepper	**4** Preheat the grill to medium-high. Brush the hot grill with oil to prevent the chicken from sticking. Thread the chicken onto skewers and grill for 8 to 10 minutes. Turn and baste with the reserved marinade during grilling until the chicken is browned and thoroughly cooked. Do not overcook.
4 large chicken breasts, boneless and skinless	
Lemon wedges for garnish	
	5 Serve with tzatziki sauce and the lemon wedges.

Per serving: Calories 245 (From Fat 29); Fat 3g (Saturated 1g); Cholesterol 73mg; Sodium 130mg; Carbohydrate 10g (Dietary Fiber 1g); Protein 42g; Potassium 793mg.

Note: Check out this recipe in the color section. Tzatziki sauce complements beef and lamb well; it can also be used as a dipping sauce for raw veggies. For a creamier tzatziki, pulse the ingredients in a food processor until well combined and smooth.

Tip: If you're using wooden skewers, soak them in cold water for an hour before threading the meat on them to prevent the wood from burning during the grilling process.

Tip: These kabobs pair nicely with our Garlic-Infused Quinoa Cakes in Chapter 12.

Enjoying Saucy — Not Salty — Poultry Entrees

If you think chicken is bland and boring, add a simple sauce to yum it up. Sauces can add wonderful flavors to foods. In fact, in our opinion, the best cooks and chefs are the ones who can make the best sauces.

A good sauce adds richness and moisture to a dish and finishes it by complementing it rather than overpowering it. Some traditional sauces can be time-consuming and involve preparing your own stock or demi-glace. A demi-glace is what chefs use as a sauce base. It's a mixture cooked down from a meat or poultry-based stock, with a flour mixture to thicken it added in. The recipes in this section offer you some quick ideas for creating great sauces with fresh ingredients. Unlike some traditional cream-based or higher fat brown sauces, the options here are light but tasty.

Glazes, another sauce option, are as simple as they are quick to make, but they still add great flavor. You can make a simple chicken glaze by adding about a tablespoon of orange juice to ½ cup of your favorite fruit preserve (such as apricot or peach). Brush the chicken pieces with the glaze about 15 minutes before they've finished cooking in the oven or on the grill.

You don't want to add sugary sauces to poultry early in the cooking process because the sugar will cause the chicken to blacken quickly, leaving you with burnt offerings and, possibly, uncooked poultry.

In this section, you find some tasty chicken sauces that prove you don't have to shop around for fancy, expensive poultry sauces. And if you make extra of these sauces, you can store the leftovers in the refrigerator for later use and your convenience.

Jamaican Jerk Chicken with Cha Cha Salsa

Prep time: 20 min plus marinating time • **Cook time:** 15 min • **Yield:** 6 servings

Ingredients	Directions
3 tablespoons Caribbean jerk seasoning	*1* Combine the jerk seasoning, oil, soy sauce, and cider vinegar and pour the mixture over the chicken breasts. Refrigerate for at least 30 minutes or up to 8 hours.
3 tablespoons canola oil	
2 tablespoons reduced-sodium soy sauce	
1 tablespoon cider vinegar	*2* Preheat your grill on high for 15 to 20 minutes to ensure maximum heat is achieved. Coat the grill rack with cooking spray and place the marinated chicken on the rack. Grill 4 to 6 minutes on each side or until cooked thoroughly. Do not overcook.
6 boneless skinless chicken breasts	
Nonstick cooking spray	
1 ripe mango, peeled, seeded, and diced	*3* While the chicken grills, prepare the salsa. Combine the mango (see Figure 17-1 for how to prepare it), cucumber, onion, cilantro, jalapeño pepper, and lime juice in a small bowl. Serve with the grilled chicken.
½ small cucumber, scrubbed, seeded, and diced	
¼ small red onion, diced	
1 cup chopped fresh cilantro	
1 small jalapeño pepper, seeded and minced	
1 tablespoon fresh lime juice	

Per serving: Calories 419 (From Fat 135); Fat 15g (Saturated 3g); Cholesterol 157mg; Sodium 372mg; Carbohydrate 9g (Dietary Fiber 1g); Protein 59g; Potassium 596mg.

How to Cut a Mango

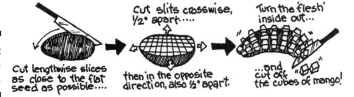

Figure 17-1: Cutting up a mango.

Cut lengthwise slices as close to the flat seed as possible....

Cut slits crosswise, ½" apart.....

then in the opposite direction, also ½" apart.

Turn the 'flesh' inside out...

...and cut off "the cubes of mango!

Baked Chicken Pesto

Prep time: 10 min • **Cook time:** 20–30 min • **Yield:** 4 servings

Ingredients	Directions
4 boneless skinless chicken breasts (6 ounces each)	**1** Flatten the chicken breasts with a meat mallet to achieve a uniform thickness on all sides.
4 teaspoons commercially prepared pesto	**2** Spread 1 teaspoon of pesto on each chicken breast and top each breast with 1 piece of the ham. Fold each chicken breast in half lengthwise and secure each one with a wooden toothpick or skewer.
4 pieces shaved lean ham	
2 tablespoons olive oil	
Freshly ground pepper to taste	**3** Make a marinade by blending together the olive oil, pepper, and garlic. Pour the marinade over the chicken breasts in a baking dish and refrigerate for 1 to 3 hours.
1 large garlic clove, minced	
	4 Preheat your oven to 325 degrees. Bake the chicken for 20 to 30 minutes, or until it's cooked through.

Per serving: Calories 292 (From Fat 108); Fat 12g (Saturated 2g); Cholesterol 157mg; Sodium 250mg; Carbohydrate 2g (Dietary Fiber 0g); Protein 44g; Potassium 642mg.

Note: This chicken also tastes great when grilled on a preheated outdoor grill for 3 to 6 minutes per side, depending on the chicken's thickness.

Tip: To make your own pesto, place 1 cup firmly packed basil leaves, 2 cloves garlic, ⅓ cup olive oil, ⅓ cup parmesan cheese, and ¼ cup pine nuts in a food processor and blend until the mixture is a finely chopped paste.

Tip: Serve over pasta with a light cream sauce using evaporated skimmed milk, fresh tomatoes, and basil.

Glazed Cornish Hens

Prep time: 10 min • **Cook time:** 16–18 min • **Yield:** 4 servings

Ingredients	Directions
½ cup pure apricot preserves, no added sugar	*1* Preheat your oven to 400 degrees.
1 tablespoon apple juice	*2* Combine the preserves, apple and lemon juices, and lemon zest in a small bowl and mix until thoroughly blended.
½ tablespoon lemon juice	
½ teaspoon lemon zest	
Two 1½ pound Cornish hens	*3* To prepare the hens, remove and discard the giblets and necks. Rinse with cold water and pat dry. Trim any excess skin; then split the hens in half lengthwise with a sharp carving knife.
	4 Place the hens in a small roasting pan. Brush half of the mixture over the hens. Roast for 40 minutes, using the remaining mixture to baste the hens every 15 minutes. The hens are completely cooked when the juices run clear, the internal temperature reads 180 degrees, and the skin is brown and crisp.
	5 Remove from the oven and let the hens sit in the roasting pan for 10 to 15 minutes prior to serving.

Per serving: Calories 388 (From Fat 216); Fat 24g (Saturated 7g); Cholesterol 170mg; Sodium 103mg; Carbohydrate 13g (Dietary Fiber 0g); Protein 29g; Potassium 403mg.

Note: If your Cornish hens are frozen, plan ahead: Remove them from the freezer and let them thaw in the fridge for 1 to 2 days. Don't thaw them at room temperature.

Tip: Pair your Cornish hens with couscous made especially for this recipe. Fix your couscous with chicken stock, dried apricots, and toasted almonds with a hint of cinnamon.

Spicy Chicken with Sweet Chili Sauce

Prep time: 20 min, plus marinating time • **Cook time:** 20 min • **Yield:** 6 servings

Ingredients	Directions
4 cloves garlic, minced (about 4 teaspoons), divided	**1** Combine 3 cloves or about 3 teaspoons of garlic, peppercorns, sugar, paprika, turmeric, curry powder, cilantro, and chili paste. Crush these ingredients using a mortar and pestle. Add the peanut oil to make a paste.
1 teaspoon freshly cracked peppercorns	
2 teaspoons sugar	**2** Rub the paste into the chicken breasts and place in a glass covered dish. Refrigerate for 3 hours or overnight.
1 teaspoon hot paprika	
2 teaspoons turmeric	**3** Preheat the grill on medium for 15 to 20 minutes. Cook the chicken on the grill, using indirect heating, and baste with coconut milk halfway through the cooking process. Grill about 5 to 6 minutes on each side or until the chicken is browned and completely cooked.
1 teaspoon curry powder	
1 tablespoon chopped cilantro	
1 teaspoon chili paste	
1 tablespoon peanut oil	
6 boneless skinless chicken breasts	**4** To make sweet chili sauce, mix together the sweet chili sauce, vinegar, and the remaining clove or teaspoon of minced garlic and microwave on medium (50 percent power) for 1 minute.
¼ cup lowfat coconut milk	
2 tablespoons sweet chili sauce	
1 tablespoon vinegar	**5** Serve the chili sauce with the chicken.

Per serving: Calories 383 (From Fat 117); Fat 13g (Saturated 5g); Cholesterol 157mg; Sodium 212mg; Carbohydrate 5g (Dietary Fiber 1g); Protein 58g; Potassium 561mg.

Adding Pork to Your Fork

Some people seem to think that pork can't fit in a heart-conscious diet, but we beg to differ. Pork (and beef, for that matter) supplies more iron than chicken and fish, and you can choose from many lean cuts that fit into a heart-healthy diet. The key with all protein sources is the portion size — enough, but not too much. Enjoying variety in your diet is fantastic — you should like what you eat! Just keep in mind that you still need to balance the saturated fat and sodium in your diet by filling half your plate with fruits and vegetables.

In Table 17-1, you can see how pork and beef compare to chicken and fish, according to the National Pork Board.

Table 17-1	Comparing Chicken, Pork, Beef, and Seafood		
Per 3-Ounce Serving of . . .	*Calories*	*Fat*	*Saturated Fat*
Skinless chicken breast	139	3.1	0.9
Skinless chicken thigh	177	9.3	2.6
Pork tenderloin	120	3.0	1.0
Pork, boneless top loin chop	173	5.2	1.8
Pork, top loin roast	147	5.3	1.6
Beef, top round	169	4.3	1.5
Beef, top sirloin	162	8.0	2.2
Beef tenderloin	175	8.1	3.0
Cod	89	0.7	0.1
Salmon	175	11.0	2.1

"The other white meat" really does fit into your new hypertension-fighting lifestyle. As Table 17-1 shows, a 3-ounce portion of pork tenderloin has even fewer calories than a chicken breast and is barely higher in saturated fat. A 2006 study released by the United States Department of Agriculture (USDA) revealed that pork is leaner than it was prior to the 1990s (16 percent lower in fat and 27 percent lower in saturated fat). In general, lean cuts of pork are comparable to lean cuts of beef. (See the section "Beefing Up Your Plate, Not Your Waistline" for our recipes that let you enjoy beef guilt-free.)

The recipes in this chapter give you some new ideas on how to incorporate pork into your DASH diet (Chapter 2), but round it off with other flavors and even some fruits and vegetables.

When planning to enjoy pork with your meal, follow these tips:

- ✔ Keep in mind that pork is your protein for the meal and, as such, should only comprise one-fourth of your plate. You should be filling up half of your plate with fruits and veggies and one-fourth with grains.

- ✔ Choose the leanest cuts, and check the amount of sodium. When we say eating some pork is okay, we aren't talking about a regular intake of high-fat, high-sodium pork sausage or bacon. Save these meats for special occasions (and enjoy them in small amounts). Ham is lean, but high in sodium, so use it sparingly as a great flavoring to dishes.

- ✔ Because your leanest cuts are from the loin, using marinades rather than extended cooking times to tenderize them is a great idea. These cuts are lean, and you don't want to overcook them, resulting in a dry, tough product.

Despite popular belief, it's normal for properly cooked pork to be slightly pink in the middle. Using a meat thermometer is the best way to ensure that pork is cooked, but not overcooked. A meat thermometer should read 145 degrees for medium-rare, which is still safe. You may then prefer to allow it to rest for at least 3 minutes after removing it from the source of heat (it continues to cook) until the thermometer reaches 160 degrees.

Roast Pork Tenderloin with Apple Stuffing

Prep time: 15–20 min • **Cook time:** 30 min • **Yield:** 7 servings

Ingredients	Directions
1 onion, chopped	**1** Preheat your oven to 425 degrees.
1 tablespoon olive oil	
1 tablespoon butter	**2** To prepare stuffing, sauté the onions in the oil and butter, cooking until the onions are golden. Add the apples and sage and cook until the apples are soft. Remove the pan from the heat.
3 apples, peeled and sliced	
2 tablespoons sage leaves	
2 cups fresh breadcrumbs	**3** Stir the breadcrumbs, milk, and pepper into the apple mixture.
⅓ cup lowfat milk	
Freshly ground pepper to taste	**4** Butterfly the pork tenderloins by cutting a lengthwise slit down the center. Open the tenderloin so it lies flat. On each half, make a lengthwise slit down the center and flatten with a meat mallet to a thickness of ¼ inch.
Two 1-pound pork tenderloins	
	5 Spread the stuffing down the middle of the pork. Roll up the pork jelly-roll style and tie it in place using cotton string at 2-inch intervals. Place any remaining stuffing in a small baking dish that has been coated with nonstick cooking spray. Place in the oven after the pork has been baking for about 12 minutes. Bake for the remaining 15 minutes.
	6 Place the pork on a rack in a shallow baking pan and bake uncovered for 25 to 30 minutes or until the internal temperature reaches 145 degrees. Allow to rest a few minutes, then transfer to a carving board and slice at two inch intervals.

Per serving: Calories 348 (From Fat 72); Fat 8g (Saturated 3g); Cholesterol 67mg; Sodium 560mg; Carbohydrate 37g (Dietary Fiber 5g); Protein 32g; Potassium 900mg.

Note: Loin equals lean! Pork tenderloin is the leanest and most tender cut of pork. To go along with your lean streak, use low-sodium breadcrumbs if they're available. You may also decide to use fewer breadcrumbs.

Vary It! Add pears to the stuffing along with the apples, use rosemary leaves or basil in place of the sage, or use 6 canned or fresh apricots in place of the apples.

Grilled Pork Tenderloin Medallions

Prep time: 10 min, plus marinating time • **Cook time:** 10 min • **Yield:** 4 servings

Ingredients	Directions
One 1-pound pork tenderloin	**1** Slice the tenderloin crosswise into eight ¾-inch thick slices called medallions.
2 tablespoons canola oil	
1 tablespoon lemon juice	**2** Combine the remaining ingredients. Place the pork in a baking dish. Pour the marinade over the pork and marinate 3 to 4 hours.
2 cloves garlic, minced	
1 teaspoon dried basil	
1 teaspoon dried rosemary	**3** When you're ready to cook, preheat your gas grill on high and grill the medallions for 2 to 3 minutes on each side until done. Do not overcook.
1 teaspoon dried thyme	
1 teaspoon Dijon mustard	
Freshly ground pepper to taste	

Per serving: Calories 190 (From Fat 90); Fat 10g (Saturated 2g); Cholesterol 56mg; Sodium 72mg; Carbohydrate 1g (Dietary Fiber 0.5g); Protein 23g; Potassium 617mg.

Note: Cutting the tenderloin into small medallions allows it to cook faster and makes a great hearty appetizer or finger food for a party. Serve it plain or with your favorite sauce.

Pork Teriyaki Lettuce Wraps

Prep time: 10 min • **Cook time:** 10 min • **Yield:** 4 servings

Ingredients	*Directions*
One 1-pound pork tenderloin, cut into thin strips	**1** Heat the peanut oil in an electric wok or a wok skillet on high and stir-fry the pork with the garlic and ginger. Add the minced water chestnuts and green onions and continue stir-frying until the meat is cooked.
1 tablespoon peanut oil	
2 garlic cloves, minced	
1 tablespoon grated fresh ginger	**2** Immediately add the hoisin sauce and sesame oil to the wok and stir quickly until the meat is coated. Remove from heat.
One 8-ounce can water chestnuts, rinsed well, drained, and minced	
3 green onions, sliced thin	**3** Divide the pork mixture among the lettuce cups, spooning an equal amount into each cup. Use the leaves to cradle the pork mixture.
2 tablespoons hoisin sauce	
1 teaspoon sesame oil	
1 head iceberg lettuce or Boston Bibb lettuce, with whole leaves separated	

Per serving: Calories 235 (From Fat 81); Fat 9g (Saturated 2g); Cholesterol 56mg; Sodium 423mg; Carbohydrate 16g (Dietary Fiber 5g); Protein 25g; Potassium 831mg.

Note: This is a fun way to eat lean and tasty pork; it's like a bite-sized salad.

Beefing up Your Plate, Not Your Waistline

Like chicken, beef is a good source of protein, B vitamins, and zinc. Beef even provides a bit more iron than poultry. Chicken provides about 1 to 1.5 milligrams of iron per 3-ounce portion, whereas beef provides about 3 milligrams. Because iron plays an important role in transporting oxygen throughout the body, including some lean cuts of beef in your diet is a good idea.

As with pork, choosing the leanest cuts of beef allows you to benefit from the protein, vitamins, iron, and other minerals sans the fat, so you can still enjoy your favorite comfort foods like meatloaf and burgers or a stay-at-home stir-fry.

A great way to enjoy beef while keeping your portion size under control and reducing fat is to make kabobs or skewers (try our Steak and Vegetable Kabobs). The kabob originated with the Turkish Shish Kabob. Alternate bite-sized pieces of beef and vegetables to create a colorful display. Cherry tomatoes, chunks of bell peppers or onions, and small mushrooms work especially well on kabobs. If you don't marinate before you skewer (though we recommend that you do), you can brush a sauce on your kabobs while they're cooking. Be sure to keep an eye on them and turn them every few minutes. They only take about 15 minutes to cook. We give you a few other ideas for skewers in Chapter 13 and the section "Grills Gone Wild: Grilling with Poultry" in this chapter.

By using a less tender cut of beef and a marinade, you can stretch your food dollars. Make your own marinade and allow the meat to marinate for at least 30 minutes, or even overnight. Pineapple contains a natural enzyme called bromelain, which serves as a natural tenderizer for tough cuts of beef. Alternate chunks of pineapple with small chunks of beef on the skewers, and the result is a flavorful, tender, economical meal! Serve over brown rice.

Savory Meatloaf with Red Wine Mushroom Sauce

Prep time: 15 min • **Cook time:** 60–90 min • **Yield:** About 4 servings

Ingredients	*Directions*
1 pound extra-lean ground beef	*1* Preheat your oven to 350 degrees.
½ cup skim milk	
1 egg	*2* Mix together the meatloaf ingredients: the ground beef, milk, egg, bread, onion, green pepper, carrots, pepper, and catsup. Place the mixture in a meatloaf pan with an insert to drain excess fat. Bake for 60 minutes.
2 slices whole-wheat bread	
¼ cup finely chopped onion	
¼ cup chopped green pepper	
½ carrot, grated	*3* While the meatloaf is baking, prepare the sauce. In a medium skillet over medium heat, melt the margarine and sauté the shallots and garlic for 2 minutes. Add the mushrooms and sauté until tender.
Freshly ground pepper to taste	
1 tablespoon catsup	
1 teaspoon light margarine	*4* Stir in the wine, bring the mixture to a boil, and cook for 1 minute. Dissolve the cornstarch in the beef broth. Stir the broth into the mushroom mixture and continue stirring until the sauce is thickened. Season to taste with ground pepper.
1 small shallot, sliced	
1 garlic clove, minced	
3 cups sliced button mushrooms	
½ cup dry red wine	*5* Serve this rich and nearly fat-free sauce with the meatloaf.
1 teaspoon cornstarch	
½ cup low-sodium beef broth	
One 15-ounce can unsalted petite diced tomatoes, drained	

Per serving: Calories 349 (From Fat 108); Fat 12g (Saturated 4g); Cholesterol 116mg; Sodium 504mg; Carbohydrate 24g (Dietary Fiber 4g); Protein 32g; Potassium 814mg.

Vary It! For a lighter meal, substitute lean ground turkey for the ground beef.

Note: While this recipe is made of good-for-you ingredients, it's also slightly higher in sodium, so balance out your meal choices the rest of the day with lower-sodium options.

Ginger-Broccoli Beef Stir-Fry

Prep time: 10 min • **Cook time:** 16–18 min • **Yield:** 4 servings

Ingredients	Directions
1 pound flank steak, thinly sliced against the grain	*1* Combine the flank steak and 1 tablespoon of the cornstarch in a large plastic bag; shake to coat and refrigerate until ready to cook.
2 tablespoons cornstarch, divided	
½ teaspoon sugar	*2* To make sauce, dissolve the remaining tablespoon of cornstarch in 1 tablespoon of water; then whisk the cornstarch mixture together with the sugar, sherry, chili garlic paste, and stock. Set aside.
1 tablespoon sherry	
1 tablespoon chili garlic paste	
½ cup low-sodium chicken stock	*3* Heat 1 tablespoon of the peanut oil in an electric wok or a wok skillet on high. Add the green onion and ginger and cook for 30 seconds. Add the broccoli and carrots and stir-fry for 1 to 2 minutes. Transfer to a plate.
2 to 3 tablespoons peanut oil, divided	
1 green onion, sliced diagonally	
1 tablespoon minced fresh ginger	*4* Heat 1 to 2 tablespoons of peanut oil on high and stir-fry the flank steak for 2 to 3 minutes. Add the vegetables and sauce back into the wok and simmer for a minute until the sauce thickens and the meat is cooked through.
1 small head broccoli, cut into florets	
½ cup shredded carrots	

Per serving: Calories 266 (From Fat 138); Fat 15g (Saturated 5g); Cholesterol 54mg; Sodium 190mg; Carbohydrate 8g (Dietary Fiber 1g); Protein 23g; Potassium 453mg.

Tip: Serve with brown rice if desired.

Note: We show you this recipe in the color section. Other lean cuts of beef can be substituted for flank: try sirloin, tenderloin, or flat iron.

Tip: Slicing the flank steak thinly against the grain while it's still partially frozen makes it easier to handle.

Vary It! Add or substitute your favorite vegetables. The more color, the higher the nutritional value.

Easy Beef Burgundy with Egg Noodles

Prep time: 10 min • **Cook time:** 3–4 hr • **Yield:** 4 servings

Ingredients	Directions
2 tablespoons canola oil	**1** Preheat your oven to 350 degrees.
1½ pounds stew meat, such as round or chuck	**2** Heat the oil in a Dutch oven and brown the stew meat.
1½ tablespoons flour	
½ teaspoon black pepper	**3** Add the flour, pepper, and thyme and mix to blend well with the meat.
1 teaspoon thyme	
1 cup frozen pearl onions, defrosted and drained	**4** Add the pearl onions, wine, and beef stock and bake for 4 hours. Check after 2 and 3 hours to see whether more liquid is needed; if so, add more beef broth.
1 cup burgundy wine	
1 cup low-sodium beef stock	
12 ounces wide egg noodles, cooked according to package directions	**5** Season the egg noodles with the butter and parsley, and serve with the beef burgundy.
2 teaspoons butter	
Chopped fresh parsley for garnish	

Per serving: Calories 471 (From Fat 126); Fat 14g (Saturated 4g); Cholesterol 110mg; Sodium 124mg; Carbohydrate 28g (Dietary Fiber 2g); Protein 44g; Potassium 601mg.

Note: Stew meat is an inexpensive cut of beef that works well in recipes that require long cooking times. The small pieces of beef are seared and simmered in liquid to produce a very tender meat.

Steak and Vegetable Kabobs

Prep time: 10–15 min • **Cook time:** 12–15 min • **Yield:** 4 servings

Ingredients	Directions
1 pound beef tenderloin, cut into sixteen 1-inch cubes 2 small zucchini, each cut into 4 pieces 4 button mushrooms, cut in half 8 cherry tomatoes 3 tablespoons low-calorie balsamic vinaigrette	*1* Thread 4 beef tenderloin cubes, 2 zucchini pieces, 2 mushroom halves, and 2 tomatoes onto each of 4 metal skewers in an alternating pattern. *2* Preheat your grill to medium-high and grill the kabobs, turning frequently, for 15 to 20 minutes or until cooked through. Baste the kabobs during cooking with the balsamic vinaigrette so the vegetables don't dry out.

Per serving: Calories 321 (From Fat 189); Fat 14g (Saturated 4g); Cholesterol 77mg; Sodium 95mg; Carbohydrate 8g (Dietary Fiber 2g); Protein 24g; Potassium 719mg.

Note: Kabobs are a great way to moderate your intake of animal protein. You don't feel cheated with a small portion because of the variety of low-calorie, colorful vegetables.

Tip: If you decide to use wooden skewers, soak them in cold water for about 30 minutes while you prep the meal.

Vary It! Feel free to substitute any number of vegetables, such as asparagus, sweet potatoes, and green or red onions. If you feel like a meatless dish, use extra-firm tofu, which is meaty and filling. If beef tenderloin isn't in your budget, substitute a lean cut of sirloin.

Chapter 18

Preparing Succulent Seafood Entrees

*W*hen you have hypertension, eating more seafood is a great way to be proactive about your health. Research suggests that consuming about 8 ounces per week of a variety of seafood is associated with reduced cardiac deaths among individuals with and without preexisting heart disease. The 2010 Dietary Guidelines for Americans recommend that we increase the amount and variety of seafood in our diets, choosing it in place of beef or chicken some of the time. Seafood contributes healthy fats, including omega-3 fatty acids, eicosapentaenoic acid (EPA), and docosahexaenoic acid (DHA).

Need a Biology 101 refresher on what kind of seafood is out there? *Seafood* includes fish (such as salmon, tuna, trout, and tilapia) and shellfish (like shrimp, crab, and oysters). *Shellfish* are invertebrate animals with shells that live in water. Shellfish are divided into two subcategories: crustaceans and mollusks. *Crustaceans* have segmented bodies with crust-like shells (think shrimp and lobster). *Mollusks* have soft bodies in whole shells (think clams, scallops, and oysters).

We agree that those fishy scientific names like "crustaceans" and "mollusks" don't sound very appetizing, but the recipes in this chapter are just the opposite. Delightful seafood dishes like Creole Shrimp Jambalaya and Salmon Burgers with Mustard Dill Sauce offer you lots of variety to increase your intake of seafood through the week.

And if you happen to be someone who's protesting, "I don't like fish," we think you should give these meals a try. We've known people who say they don't like fish only because they've never had seafood prepared properly (or purchased properly — fish that isn't fresh isn't tasty!). A lot of cooks out there overcook their fish, which gives it a tough texture. So give it one or two more tries for your heart's health. Please? Just reading through these recipes will make your mouth water.

Delectable Shellfish Made Easy

You may have heard that shellfish is high in cholesterol, which is true to some extent. But even though the cholesterol count is slightly higher than other meats, shellfish is a dieter's dream because it's so low in fat.

Shrimp is an easy-to-cook, lowfat type of shellfish, and while a 4-ounce portion provides about 200 milligrams of cholesterol, it provides no saturated fat and only one gram of total fat. Clams are similar, providing no saturated fat and about 80 milligrams of cholesterol per 4 ounces. Scallops are also very low in fat, cholesterol, and calories.

You can buy either fresh or frozen shellfish. Freshly caught shellfish may be sold in a water tank or stored on ice. Scallops are always sold shucked, but you can buy fresh clams and mussels in the shell. Shells should be closed; if a shell is open, discard it. Scallops sold fresh should be presented on ice (not on that sketchy milky substance). Your best bet is to choose flash-frozen seafood. If you purchase whole shrimp, they'll last longer in the freezer, but keeping some frozen shrimp shelled or even shelled and cooked on hand is a timesaver.

Shrimp-Stuffed Chile Rellenos

Prep time: 10–20 min • **Cook time:** 20 min • **Yield:** 4 servings

Ingredients	Directions
4 large poblano peppers **1 large red bell pepper** **4 ounces medium shrimp, peeled and deveined, cooked, and chopped** **2 ounces goat cheese** **½ cup grated lowfat Monterey Jack or lowfat Mexican-blend cheese** **3 tablespoons chopped shallots, divided** **1 tablespoon chopped fresh cilantro** **1 tablespoon chopped fresh basil** **½ tablespoon olive oil** **1 garlic clove, minced** **1 small jalapeño chile, seeded and minced** **¼ cup lowfat low-sodium chicken broth** **Cilantro sprigs for garnish**	*1* Char the poblano chilies and red bell pepper over a gas flame until blackened on all sides. *2* Enclose the peppers inside a paper bag for 10 minutes. The steam within the bag loosens the skin. Rinse under cool running water; peel off the blackened skin. Slit the poblano peppers along one side and remove the seeds, leaving the stem attached. Set aside the red bell pepper for the sauce. *3* Preheat the oven to 350 degrees. Mix together the shrimp, cheeses, 1 tablespoon of the shallots, the cilantro, and the basil. Divide the mixture and gently stuff each of the 4 poblano peppers, pulling up the sides of the pepper to enclose the filling. Place the stuffed peppers in a glass baking pan. *4* In the preheated oven, bake the peppers uncovered until they're heated through and the cheese melts, about 20 minutes. *5* While the poblano peppers are in the oven, make the red bell pepper sauce. Chop the charred red bell pepper. In a small skillet, sauté the remaining 2 tablespoons of shallots, the garlic, and the jalapeño chile in the olive oil until all are tender. *6* Blend the red bell pepper and shallot mixture using an immersion blender or a mini food processor. Add the chicken broth and puree until the mixture has a smooth consistency. *7* To serve, spoon red bell pepper sauce onto each plate and place a stuffed poblano pepper on top of the sauce. Garnish with cilantro sprigs.

Per serving: Calories 191 (From Fat 81); Fat 9g (Saturated 4g); Cholesterol 71mg; Sodium 317mg; Carbohydrate 12g (Dietary Fiber 1g); Protein 15g; Potassium 442mg.

Seared Scallops with Pistachio Sauce

Prep time: 10 min • **Cook time:** 10 min • **Yield:** 4 servings

Ingredients	Directions
1½ pounds large sea scallops	*1* Dry the scallops well with paper towels, removing as much water as possible. Heat ½ tablespoon of the olive oil on high in a large nonstick skillet.
1 tablespoon extra-virgin olive oil, divided	
Freshly ground black pepper to taste	*2* Add half of the scallops and sauté without turning them until they're well browned, about 2 minutes. Turn the scallops and cook until the sides are firm and the centers are opaque.
¼ cup chopped unsalted pistachios	
1 tablespoon unsalted butter	
	3 Transfer the scallops to a plate and loosely tent them with foil (fold a piece of aluminum foil in half, and loosely cover the plate). Repeat with the remaining oil and scallops. Transfer to the plate.
	4 Add the chopped pistachios and butter to the skillet and cook until the butter is lightly browned. Pour the sauce over the scallops and serve.

Per serving: Calories 289 (From Fat 108); Fat 12g (Saturated 3g); Cholesterol 98mg; Sodium 451mg; Carbohydrate 2g (Dietary Fiber 1g); Protein 41g; Potassium 889mg.

Tip: Don't crowd the pan with too many scallops at once. The scallops should sizzle when they hit the pan.

Note: This recipe is delicious served with our Sweet Potato Mash in Chapter 12.

Classic Steamed Mussels

Prep time: 10 min • **Cook time:** 10 min • **Yield:** 4 servings

Ingredients	*Directions*
¼ cup olive oil	*1* Heat a Dutch oven over high heat. When the pot is hot, add the olive oil, shallots, and garlic and cook for about 1 minute.
6 tablespoons minced shallots	
1 tablespoon minced garlic	
2 pounds blue mussels or green-lipped mussels	*2* Add the mussels, wine, Old Bay Seasoning, lemon juice, butter, half of the parsley, and half of the cilantro. Place a lid on the Dutch oven and shake the pot.
½ to ¾ cup dry white wine	
1 teaspoon Old Bay 30% Less Sodium Seasoning	*3* Cook, shaking the pot often, until the mussels open, about 4 minutes. The larger the mussels, the longer they take to cook.
Juice of 1 lemon	
2 teaspoons butter	*4* Reduce the heat to medium-high. Reduce the liquid by one-third and then turn off the heat. Divide the mussels and sauce among four large soup plates.
⅓ cup chopped fresh parsley, divided	
⅓ cup chopped fresh cilantro, divided	*5* Garnish with the remaining parsley and cilantro, and serve immediately.

Per serving: Calories 381 (From Fat 189); Fat 21g (Saturated 4g); Cholesterol 69mg; Sodium 668mg; Carbohydrate 12g (Dietary Fiber 0g); Protein 28g; Potassium 811mg.

Note: While this recipe is made of good-for-you-ingredients, it's also slightly higher in sodium, so balance our your meal choices the rest of the day with lower-sodium options.

Note: Purchase mussels that are tightly closed or just barely open. They should smell like the sea breeze. If they smell fishy, they're past their prime. To store fresh mussels, place them in a bowl, cover the bowl with a damp towel, and then refrigerate them in the coldest part of the refrigerator. They'll keep for up to 2 days stored this way. Never freeze them.

Note: Old Bay Seasoning is a seafood flavor-booster that the company now offers in a 30-percent-less-sodium package. It's available nationwide, and you can also order it online from www.oldbay.com.

Creole Shrimp Jambalaya

Prep time: 10–15 min • **Cook time:** 45 min • **Yield:** 6 servings

Ingredients	Directions
1 teaspoon canola oil	**1** Heat the oil in a skillet and sauté the onion, pepper, celery, and garlic until translucent.
1 large onion, chopped	
1 large green pepper, chopped	**2** Add the tomato sauce, tomatoes, water, bay leaf, basil, thyme, paprika, and chipotle pepper. Bring to a boil and add the rice. Reduce the heat and simmer, covered, for 45 minutes. Stir a few times during the cooking process.
1 celery stalk, chopped	
2 garlic cloves, chopped	
Two 8-ounce cans low-sodium tomato sauce	
One 28-ounce can unsalted crushed tomatoes	**3** Add the shrimp and cook, uncovered, until they're pink and firm, about 5 minutes. Don't overcook the shrimp. Remove the bay leaf prior to serving.
1 cup water plus more if mixture appears too dry	
1 bay leaf	
1 teaspoon dried basil	
1 teaspoon dried thyme	
1 teaspoon paprika	
⅛ teaspoon ground chipotle pepper	
1 cup uncooked basmati rice	
½ pound small shrimp, shelled and deveined	

Per serving: Calories 291 (From Fat 18); Fat 2g (Saturated 0g); Cholesterol 57mg; Sodium 253mg; Carbohydrate 54g (Dietary Fiber 8g); Protein 14g; Potassium 905mg.

Note: A traditional jambalaya includes shrimp, sausage, and chicken. We've modified the ingredients here, but the ingredient possibilities for jambalaya are countless: beef, pork, chicken, duck, shrimp, oysters, crayfish, sausage, and so on! Using shrimp in your jambalaya gives you an excellent source of protein while keeping your fat and saturated fat intake low.

Tip: The secret to perfect shrimp is to be sure you don't overcook it. Cook only until the shrimp have just become firm and turned pinkish-white.

Vary It! Try using Fresh Homemade Tomato Sauce (see Chapter 19) in place of the canned low-sodium tomato products.

Fish with Benefits

The whole point of adding fish to your hypertension diet is twofold: You get less saturated fat and more omega-3 fatty acids. EPA and DHA are two forms of omega-3s that are beneficial to heart health. Omega-3s may slow plaque formation inside arteries, lower blood pressure, positively affect heart rhythm, and reduce heart rate and blood triglycerides.

Because fish are so beneficial to your heart health, you probably want to know which types of seafood contain the healthiest acids. Check out Table 18-1 for the answers, and enjoy consuming a variety of fish to get all its benefits.

Table 18-1 EPA and DHA Content of Various Types of Seafood	
Type of Seafood	*Milligrams of EPA and DHA per 4 ounces*
Salmon	1,200–2,400
Mackerel, Atlantic and Pacific (not King)	1,350–2,100
Bluefin and albacore tuna	1,700
Halibut	500–1,250
Rainbow trout	1,000–1,100
Canned albacore tuna	1,000
Yellowfin tuna	150–350
Tilapia	150
Shrimp	100

Mercury is a heavy metal present in some types of seafood. Purchase your seafood from a variety of sources; you're more likely to get too much methyl mercury if all your fish comes from the same source. Types of seafood that contain higher levels of methyl mercury include lobster, trout, mackerel, herring, cod, albacore tuna, and catfish. Salmon, shrimp, tilapia, and clams have lower levels. Still, consistent evidence shows that the health benefits of consuming a variety of seafood in the amounts recommended outweigh the health risks associated with methyl mercury.

Halibut with Grilled Lemon

Prep time: 5 min • **Cook time:** 5 min • **Yield:** 4 servings

Ingredients	Directions
Four 4-ounce halibut fillets, or other favorite white fish	*1* Preheat your grill. Lightly coat the fish fillets with olive oil and pepper.
4 teaspoons olive oil	
Freshly ground black pepper to taste	*2* Place the fish on the grill rack, cover, and grill 4 minutes on one side. Turn the fish to cook the other side. Place 4 lemon halves on the grill and cook for 4 minutes. The fish is done when it flakes easily with a fork.
2 lemons, cut in half	
Fresh parsley, chopped, for garnish	*3* Serve the fish with the grilled lemon halves. Garnish with a sprinkling of fresh parsley.

Per serving: Calories 175 (From Fat 63); Fat 7g (Saturated 1g); Cholesterol 36mg; Sodium 63mg; Carbohydrate 6g (Dietary Fiber 3g); Protein 24g; Potassium 589mg.

Note: Lemon is the new salt! On the grill, it provides a wonderfully tart flavor. You probably won't even miss the salt.

Tip: For grilling, choose fish that's firm with a meaty texture to prevent the fish from falling apart. Another option is to use a hinged wire basket or flat metal plate with holes to keep the fish from breaking apart during cooking.

Vary It! Try spearing the fillet, like you would with a skewer, with a long piece of lemongrass before grilling to infuse the flavor into the fish. When grilling lemon, substitute Meyer lemons for regular lemons for a sweet-tart flavor.

Grilled Salmon Fillets with Fresh Fruit Salsa

Prep time: 5 min • **Cook time:** 10 min • **Yield:** 4 servings

Ingredients	Directions
½ **small papaya, peeled, seeded, and chopped**	*1* To make a fruit salsa, combine the papaya, peach or nectarine, jalapeño pepper, and your choice of rosemary, basil, or thyme. Cover and chill thoroughly.
1 small ripe peach or nectarine, pitted and chopped	
1 fresh jalapeño chili pepper, seeded and chopped	*2* Preheat your grill on high; then lower the temperature to moderate heat. If desired, lightly brush the surface of the fish with olive oil. Place the fish skin-side-down on the grill and cook for 10 minutes per inch.
1 tablespoon rosemary, basil, or thyme	
Four 4-ounce salmon fillets with skin on	*3* Serve with the chilled fruit salsa.
Olive oil (optional)	

Per serving: Calories 270 (From Fat 132); Fat 13g (Saturated 3g); Cholesterol 76mg; Sodium 80mg; Carbohydrate 8g (Dietary Fiber 2g); Protein 27g; Potassium 627mg.

Note: Salmon is the top source of some seriously good-for-you essential fatty acids. It's so versatile you can prepare it in many ways, from basic grilling to sautéing or stir-frying.

Tip: If you're buying fresh salmon, ask your fishmonger to cut the fillets into individual portions. The presentation will be cleaner and the portions better controlled.

Tip: Grilling fish with the skin on prevents the flesh from burning. The skin should be crisp but not burnt. Covering the grill causes the fish to cook from the top down, and you don't even have to turn it! Remove the fish from the grill using two metal spatulas to prevent the fish from breaking apart.

Vary It! Use your favorite fruit for the salsa. Another great flavor combination is fresh chopped pineapple, papaya, jicama, chopped red bell pepper, and Serrano chile with grated ginger and cilantro.

Crusty Crab-Topped Grouper

Prep time: 20 min • **Cook time:** 20 min • **Yield:** 4 servings

Ingredients	Directions
Four 4-ounce grouper fillets	**1** Preheat your oven to 300 degrees.
4 tablespoons fresh breadcrumbs	**2** Lightly coat the fish fillets with the breadcrumbs and pepper. Melt the butter in a large skillet and sauté the grouper until done, about 4 minutes per side. Place in a single layer in a baking pan coated with cooking spray.
Freshly ground pepper to taste	
2 tablespoons unsalted butter	
Nonstick cooking spray	
½ cup chopped green onions	**3** In the same skillet, sauté the green onions, mushrooms, and almonds. Gently stir in the crabmeat. Divide the mixture into 4 portions and layer it over the fish fillets.
1 cup sliced button mushrooms	
2 tablespoons sliced almonds	**4** Cover with foil and bake for about 10 to 12 minutes. Remove the foil and bake another 5 minutes until the top is golden.
4 ounces fresh lump crabmeat	
1 or 2 limes, cut into 8 wedges	**5** Serve with lime wedges and parsley sprigs.
Parsley sprigs for garnish	

Per serving: Calories 227 (From Fat 72); Fat 8g (Saturated 4g); Cholesterol 55mg; Sodium 534mg; Carbohydrate 15g (Dietary Fiber 2g); Protein 25g; Potassium 662mg.

Note: While this recipe is made of good-for-you-ingredients, it's also slightly higher in sodium, so balance our your meal choices the rest of the day with lower-sodium options.

Note: Crabmeat can be purchased raw, cooked, frozen, pasteurized, and tinned. Lump crabmeat is from the center of the crab's body and is the most desirable. Dungeness crabs, stone crabs, and Kona crabs are the most eco-friendly crabs, according to the Monterey Bay Aquarium Seafood Watch Program. This organization is a useful resource for learning more about fishing practices, sustainability, and how to make the best choices when purchasing seafood.

Vary It! You can substitute mahi-mahi for grouper.

Salmon Burgers with Mustard Dill Sauce

Prep time: 10 min • **Cook time:** 10 min • **Yield:** 4 servings

Ingredients	Directions
1 tablespoon reduced-fat mayonnaise	**1** To make the mustard dill sauce, combine the mayonnaise, yogurt, mustard, dill, lemon juice, and pepper. Set aside.
1½ tablespoons nonfat plain Greek yogurt	
1 tablespoon honey mustard	**2** Place the salmon in a food processor and gently pulse until the salmon is roughly chopped.
1 tablespoon fresh dill	
1 teaspoon lemon juice	**3** In a large bowl, combine the fish, green onions, egg, ginger, parsley, and sesame oil. Shape the mixture into 4 salmon burgers. The mixture will appear loose, but will hold together when cooked.
Freshly ground black pepper to taste	
1 pound salmon fillet, skinned	
2 green onions, chopped	**4** Spritz a skillet with olive oil cooking spray, add the salmon burgers, and cook for 4 minutes. Gently turn and continue cooking until the burgers are firm and the fish is cooked through.
1 egg, lightly beaten	
2 tablespoons minced fresh ginger	
2 tablespoons chopped parsley	**5** Serve on your favorite whole-grain sandwich buns with the baby spinach, sliced tomato, and mustard dill sauce.
1 teaspoon sesame oil	
Olive oil cooking spray	
4 whole-grain thin sandwich buns	
1 cup baby spinach	
4 tomato slices	

Per serving: Calories 350 (From Fat 108); Fat 12g (Saturated 2g); Cholesterol 115mg; Sodium 369mg; Carbohydrate 32g (Dietary Fiber 8g); Protein 31g; Potassium 358mg.

Note: Salmon is versatile and a great choice for novice seafood cooks. Due to its higher fat content, the fish stays moist when prepared by any cooking method. Remember, salmon provides you with lots of healthy fats and those almighty omega-3 fatty acids.

Fish Tacos with Baja Crème and Fresh Salsa

Prep time: 15–20 min • **Cook time:** 10 min • **Yield:** 4 servings

Ingredients	Directions
Fish Rub (see the following recipe)	**1** Brush the fish fillets with 1 tablespoon of the canola oil and generously rub the Fish Rub into the fish on both sides.
Salsa (see the following recipe)	
Baja Crème (see the following recipe)	**2** Heat the remaining tablespoon of oil in a large skillet and sauté the fish on each side about 5 minutes, or place the fish in a grill basket and grill on high heat.
1 pound cod or tilapia fillets	
2 tablespoons canola oil, divided	**3** Place the tortillas between damp paper towels and microwave on high for 10 to 12 seconds until soft and pliable.
Eight 6-inch corn or whole-wheat tortillas	
2 cups shredded lettuce or green cabbage	**4** Place the cooked fish inside the tortillas along with the shredded cabbage, Salsa, and Baja Crème. Serve with the lime wedges.
2 small limes, cut into 8 wedges	

Fish Rub

1 teaspoon sugar	**1** Mix together the sugar, oregano, garlic powder, allspice, chipotle chile powder, and cumin.
1 teaspoon oregano	
¾ teaspoon garlic powder	
¼ teaspoon allspice	
¼ teaspoon chipotle chile powder	
1 teaspoon cumin	

Salsa

2 ripe tomatoes, seeded and chopped	*1* Combine the tomatoes, onion, jalapeño, and cilantro.
4 tablespoons minced red onion	*2* Squeeze fresh lime juice over the salsa. Set aside.
1 small jalapeño, seeded and minced	
2 tablespoons chopped fresh cilantro, or to taste	
Fresh lime	

Baja Crème

1 ripe avocado, cut into chunks	*1* Combine all ingredients in a small food processor.
1 tablespoon reduced-fat mayonnaise	*2* Pulse until well-blended. Refrigerate.
2 tablespoons fat-free sour cream	
1 teaspoon cumin	
¼ teaspoon chipotle chile powder	

Per serving: Calories 386 (From Fat 154); Fat 17g (Saturated 2g); Cholesterol 45mg; Sodium 193mg; Carbohydrate 38g (Dietary Fiber 8g); Protein 24g; Potassium 806mg.

Note: The best type of fish is the freshest fish. Tilapia has a mild flavor and a firm texture, is readily available year-round, and can be prepared many different ways.

Tip: When sautéing fish, turn it only once during the cooking process to prevent it from falling apart.

Vary It! You can substitute other types of fish for the cod or tilapia, such as sole or flounder.

Chapter 19

Making the Most of Your Time with Easy Weeknight Meals

In This Chapter

▶ Creating easy, flavorful meals

▶ Getting dinner on the table in a flash

▶ Saving time and maximizing flavor with aluminum foil

This chapter may well be our favorite one, and we hope it comes in handy for you on a jam-packed weeknight. After all, those busy weeknights are the biggest challenge for working families. How can you possibly get a meal together when you walk in the door hungry and tired at 6 p.m., with games, practices, meetings, and other activities soon to follow?

In this chapter, we help you get a healthy meal on the table in a flash — without ever hitting up a fast-food place. We even give you some do-ahead tips and show you some new cooking methods that the whole family can help out with. You may also want to refer to Chapters 5, 6, and 8 to be sure your kitchen and pantry are organized and you have what you need in the freezer. Cooking on weeknights doesn't have to be a nightmare; for example, by having onions chopped in the refrigerator, batch-cooking extra chicken, or having meats cut and frozen and ready to defrost, you can throw a healthy meal together easily. (In addition, Chapters 15 and 16 offer quick breakfast and lunch recipes that can easily sub for dinner one night a week. Go ahead. Break the rules!)

Keeping It Simple with One-Dish Wonders

One way to get dinner on the table without breaking a sweat is to make a one-dish meal. Every ingredient goes into one pan or oven dish. Getting a meal into a slow cooker, sauté pan, or the oven usually takes only about 10 to 15 minutes of prep time. Not only is a one-dish meal easy to cook, but cleanup is easier too. The recipes in this section definitely keep things simple, and keeping it simple helps to keep you eating wholesome food at home instead of relying on convenience foods or frequenting restaurants.

When you have high blood pressure, eating at home is almost always healthier than eating too many meals out. Restaurants pack more sodium into their meals than you'd ever include yourself at home (not to mention loads more calories). Even if you use some convenience items at home to put your meal together, like a quality jar of spaghetti sauce or canned beans, you'll still end up with less fat and sodium than most restaurant meals.

You don't have to limit yourself to the recipes in this chapter. You can create your own one-dish meals with a little imagination and whatever ingredients you have on hand.

When planning your own unique one-dish meals, follow this simple guideline: Include a protein, vegetables, and a grain (rice, whole-wheat tortillas, or whole-wheat pasta are best).

Check out these general suggestions for even more stovetop one-dish meals to keep your family healthy, even on a hurried evening:

- **Whole-wheat pasta with veggies and protein:** Pasta itself only takes 8 to 10 minutes to cook, and whole-wheat pastas pack added flavor, texture, and even fun shapes into your meal. You can add leftover diced chicken and vegetables right to the pot, or you can quickly sauté some spinach and mushrooms to toss with the cooked pasta.

- **Jambalaya:** Add your own healthy spin to this Louisiana tradition by using lowfat chicken sausage (not all chicken sausages are low in fat, so read the labels) and adding more tomatoes and peppers to the rice (see Chapter 18 for our Creole Shrimp Jambalaya).

- **Stir-frys:** What do you get when you mix a nonstick pan with sliced chicken or lean beef and 2 cups of sliced vegetables? Dinner! Using about 2 teaspoons of oil in the pan, cook the meat first, and then add the vegetables. Serve over a cup of whole-grain rice.

And, hey, don't neglect the oven! While it may take the Thanksgiving bird three or four hours to cook, your oven can cook lots of easy meals quickly. You can get an entire dinner on the table with just one oven dish.

Some larger pieces of meat do take some time to roast in the oven, but ease still comes into play. All you have to do is put the meat in a baking dish, season it with pepper and fresh herbs, and slide it into the oven. Then you can go take a run and grab a shower or just enjoy a little downtime while dinner cooks itself.

When you're making your own oven-roasted creation and you're in doubt about what temperature to set your oven to, go with 350 degrees. You'll need a higher temperature for roasting vegetables (400 degrees), but 350 is always a safe bet for meat. With the exception of 3-to-5-pound (or larger) meat roasts, most items take 45–60 minutes to cook.

Using smaller cuts of meat, such as pork tenderloin or chicken breasts, reduces the roasting time. For instance, a pork tenderloin cooks in the oven at a rate of about 25–30 minutes per pound. (Therefore, a 1½-pound tenderloin takes 40–45 minutes to cook.) You can use your oven to cook larger, lean cuts of beef as well. A 2-pound sirloin roasts in about 45 minutes and can be made into multiple meals (slice it thinly and serve it with a vegetable and roast potato one day; use it on a salad or in a stir-fry the next).

Don't forget to preheat your oven to the desired temperature. Cooking times are based on a preheated oven.

Enjoy all the time you save with the recipes in this section, and don't forget to plan ahead for the next busy night. When preparing chicken recipes, cook an extra batch of chicken for another night later in the week. Do the same with vegetables. If you're chopping onions for our Oven-Roasted Fish with Vegetables or Boneless Pork Loin Roast with Glazed Apples, chop some extra onion and store it in a small container or zippered bag for another night. You'll save a step in the future.

Spiced Chicken Tagine

Prep time: 10 min • **Cook time:** 30–40 min • **Yield:** 5 servings

Ingredients	Directions
½ tablespoon olive oil	**1** Heat the oil in a tagine or Dutch oven and sauté the onion and garlic.
1 medium onion, thinly sliced	
2 cloves garlic, minced	**2** Add the chicken pieces and sauté until browned. Add the ginger and cinnamon and cook for 1 minute.
4 boneless skinless chicken breast halves, cut into bite-sized pieces	
½ teaspoon ground ginger	**3** Combine the honey, lime juice, vinegar, and chicken stock and pour over the chicken. Season with pepper to taste, cover, and simmer for 30 to 40 minutes.
1 teaspoon ground cinnamon	
2 tablespoons honey	
2 tablespoons lime juice	**4** When the chicken is tender, add the raisins and almonds.
1 tablespoon red wine vinegar	
1 cup low-sodium fat-free chicken stock	
Freshly ground black pepper to taste	
⅓ cup raisins	
⅓ cup whole blanched almonds	

Per serving: Calories 395 (From Fat 117); Fat 13g (Saturated 2g); Cholesterol 125mg; Sodium 126mg; Carbohydrate 21g (Dietary Fiber 2g); Protein 49g; Potassium 571mg.

Note: This Moroccan-inspired recipe uses traditional cookware called a tagine. Tagine is also the name of the most common dish served in Morocco.

Tip: Serve this recipe with quinoa or your favorite whole grain.

Fresh Homemade Tomato Sauce

Prep time: 10 min • **Cook time:** 20 min • **Yield:** 4 servings

Ingredients	*Directions*
2 tablespoons olive oil	*1* Heat the olive oil in a Dutch oven for a few minutes. Add the minced garlic and onion and sauté until fragrant but not brown.
2 small bulbs garlic, peeled and minced	
¼ cup minced onions	
6 cups chopped plum tomatoes, peeled and seeded, juice reserved	*2* Add the tomatoes, juice, and basil and bring to a boil. Reduce the heat and simmer for 20 minutes or until the liquid evaporates.
¼ cup minced fresh basil	
Freshly ground pepper to taste	*3* Add black pepper to taste and red pepper flakes, if desired.
¼ teaspoon red pepper flakes (optional)	

Per serving: Calories 162 (From Fat 63); Fat 7g (Saturated 1g); Cholesterol 0mg; Sodium 180mg; Carbohydrate 21g (Dietary Fiber 3g); Protein 4g; Potassium 69mg.

Note: This hearty sauce can be used in any recipe calling for canned tomato sauce or spaghetti sauce without all the extra sodium that comes along with processed tomato products! Make a double batch to save yourself time on another day.

Tip: Serve this sauce with your favorite pasta. Reserve some of the cooking liquid to mix in with the pasta and sauce.

Tip: To make peeling tomatoes an easier task, cut an X on the bottom of each tomato. Place the tomatoes in a pot of boiling water for up to a minute. Remove them from the boiling water and place them in a container of ice water to stop the cooking. You can then easily remove the skin.

Vary It! After this basic sauce is made, you can add leftover grilled vegetables, chicken, or grilled seafood to create a complete one-dish meal.

Sichuan-Style Shrimp with Snow Peas

Prep time: 15 min • **Cook time:** 5 min • **Yield:** 4 servings

Ingredients	Directions
1 tablespoon peanut oil	**1** Heat the peanut oil in an electric wok and stir-fry the shrimp in batches until cooked, or about 1 minute. Remove the shrimp from the wok. Set aside.
1 pound medium shrimp, peeled and deveined	
1 tablespoon sesame oil	**2** Heat the sesame oil and stir-fry the garlic and ginger to flavor the oil. Add the snow peas and scallions and gently stir-fry for 2 to 3 minutes.
2 cloves garlic, minced	
½ teaspoon finely chopped ginger	
½ pound snow peas	**3** Combine the soy sauce, vinegar, chili paste, sugar, and chicken stock and add to the snow peas. Stir to combine. Add the shrimp and cook for 1 minute.
2 scallions, sliced diagonally	
1 tablespoon low-sodium soy sauce	
1 tablespoon rice vinegar	**4** Combine the cornstarch and water to make a paste. Add the paste to the sauce and simmer until thickened.
1 tablespoon garlic chili paste	
½ teaspoon sugar	
3 tablespoons low-sodium chicken stock	
2 teaspoons cornstarch	
2 tablespoons water	

Per serving: Calories 220 (From Fat 81); Fat 9g (Saturated 1g); Cholesterol 172mg; Sodium 355mg; Carbohydrate 8g (Dietary Fiber 2g); Protein 25g; Potassium 354mg.

Note: Cooking with a wok is fast-paced, so have everything you need chopped, measured, and ready to go when you turn on the heat. Searing the food at high temperatures preserves its natural juices and makes for a quick and painless meal. You can even buy everything prechopped at the grocery store.

Tip: Four key wok tips to remember: Heat the wok for a few minutes before adding oil, cut food into bite-sized pieces, don't overcrowd the wok, and keep tossing the ingredients with a spatula.

Vary It! Substitute bite-sized chicken pieces or reduced-fat firm tofu for the shrimp.

Oven-Roasted Fish with Vegetables

Prep time: 10 min • **Cook time:** 30–35 min • **Yield:** 4 servings

Ingredients	*Directions*
¾ **cup baby carrots, scrubbed**	*1* Preheat your oven to 450 degrees. Line a large baking pan with parchment paper or a nonstick baking liner.
½ **pound haricots verts, trimmed**	
1 small red onion, cut into quarters	*2* Combine the carrots, haricots verts, red onion, and potatoes in a large bowl. Drizzle the olive oil over the vegetables and toss until well coated. Place the vegetables on the prepared pan.
½ **pound fingerling or small red potatoes, cut into halves**	
1 tablespoon olive oil, divided	*3* Roast in the middle of the oven for 15 minutes. Take the pan out of the oven and stir the vegetables with a spatula, moving them to one side of the pan. Place the salmon on the same pan alongside the vegetables. Lightly drizzle with olive oil to prevent the fish from drying out.
Four 4-ounce salmon fillets	
Coarsely ground black pepper to taste	
Chopped fresh rosemary to taste	*4* Sprinkle the vegetables and fish with coarsely ground black pepper and fresh rosemary to taste. Return the pan to the oven for an additional 15 to 20 minutes or until the salmon flakes with a fork. Check the fish after 10 minutes for doneness.

Per serving: Calories 265 (From Fat 99); Fat 11g (Saturated 2g); Cholesterol 62mg; Sodium 220mg; Carbohydrate 16g (Dietary Fiber 3g); Protein 25g; Potassium 972mg.

Note: This lowfat way to cook a one-dish meal couldn't be easier. Selecting vegetables with contrasting colors and textures makes an appetizing, quick meal.

Tip: For more flavor, use a garlic-flavored oil to roast the vegetables. Garnish each serving with chopped fresh mint leaves and grated lemon zest.

Vary It! Substitute your favorite vegetables, such as broccoli, red or yellow bell pepper, zucchini, or asparagus, for the veggies in the recipe.

Boneless Pork Loin Roast with Glazed Apples

Prep time: 15 min • **Cook time:** 1½ hr • **Yield:** 8 servings

Ingredients	*Directions*
2 teaspoons cornstarch	*1* Preheat your oven to 325 degrees. To make the glaze, mix the cornstarch, cinnamon, apple juice, and water in a small saucepan. Cook over medium-low heat, until thickened. Set aside.
¼ teaspoon cinnamon	
2 tablespoons apple juice	
2 tablespoons water	
3-pound boneless pork loin, fat trimmed	*2* Place the pork loin onto a rack in a roasting pan. Rub the sage over the pork, and grind pepper onto the pork to taste. Add quartered apples around the roast, and pour a few spoons of glaze over the pork and apples. Roast in the oven for 30 minutes. Open the oven and brush the pork roast and apples with the glaze using a basting brush; do this about every 20 minutes (you may or may not use all the glaze). Continue roasting for 45 to 60 minutes, or until a meat thermometer reaches 145 degrees.
1 teaspoon ground sage	
Freshly ground black pepper to taste	
4 medium apples, peeled, cored, and quartered	
	3 Remove from the oven and allow to rest for 15 to 20 minutes. Remove to cutting board and slice. Place the sliced pork on a serving platter, placing the apples around the roast.

Per serving: Calories 358 (From Fat 170); Fat 19g (Saturated 7g); Cholesterol 105mg; Sodium 76mg; Carbohydrate 11g (Dietary Fiber 1g); Protein 35g; Potassium 600mg.

Vary It! Substitute fresh peaches or nectarines for the apples. You can also use an apricot jam instead of glaze. Simply heat ¼ cup jam in a small saucepan, adding a small amount of water if necessary to thin; brush it onto the pork and fruit.

Pulled Pork Sandwiches

Prep time: 5 min • **Cook time:** 6–8 hr • **Yield:** 8 servings

Ingredients	*Directions*
Two 1-pound pork tenderloins 6 ounces favorite low-sodium barbecue sauce ½ cup water 8 whole-wheat buns	*1* Place the pork roast in a slow cooker. Pour the barbecue sauce and water over the roast. Cover and cook on your slow cooker's low setting for 6 to 8 hours. The meat will fall apart when it's done cooking. Use a fork to "pull" the meat into shreds.
	2 Serve on buns.

Per serving: Calories 216 (From Fat 45); Fat 5g (Saturated 1g); Cholesterol 56mg; Sodium 437mg; Carbohydrate 17g (Dietary Fiber 3g); Protein 26g; Potassium 666mg

Note: Nothing is finer than walking in the door and having dinner ready. Using a regular barbeque sauce in place of a low-sodium variety will increase the overall sodium of the dish. You can reduce the sodium further by thinning with water, which will cook down as the sauce heats.

Tip: Be sure to trim the excess fat from the roast before cooking, and skim the fat off the sauce after cooking.

Tip: Balance out this old-time favorite with some healthy sides. Sliced watermelon and a tossed green salad with light dressing on the side balance the meal well. Also consider some out-of-the-box toppings such as chopped green bell peppers, alfalfa sprouts, or thinly sliced cucumbers.

Vary It! You may choose to roast the pork in a 300-degree oven for 6 to 7 hours or until the meat falls apart.

Fit and Fast Steak Salad

Prep time: 10 min • **Cook time:** 10 min • **Yield:** 2 servings

Ingredients	*Directions*
Vegetable oil spray 5 to 6 ounces lean sirloin steak 4 cups mixed greens, such as spring mix	*1* Heat a nonstick pan over medium heat. Spray the pan with vegetable oil and place the steak in the pan. Cook the steak until medium-rare, about 3 minutes per side. Remove from the pan to a cutting board; let rest.
2 tablespoons chopped red onion ½ small cucumber, seeded and sliced 2 or 3 plum tomatoes, sliced	*2* Prepare a salad on each of two large dinner plates. Place the greens, onion, and cucumber on the plates; then add the sliced tomatoes.
3 tablespoons crumbled blue cheese	*3* Slice the steak crosswise into thin slices. Divide the meat between the salad plates. Sprinkle with the blue cheese.
2 tablespoons olive oil 1 tablespoon balsamic vinegar 1 teaspoon minced parsley 1 teaspoon sugar Freshly ground black pepper to taste	*4* Mix the oil, vinegar, parsley, and sugar with a whisk in a small bowl. Divide the dressing evenly between the salads. Finish with a sprinkling of ground pepper to taste.

Per serving: Calories 323 (From Fat 189); Fat 21g (Saturated 6g); Cholesterol 50mg; Sodium 304mg; Carbohydrate 17g (Dietary Fiber 4g); Protein 24g; Potassium 782mg

Note: You can use leftover steak or leftover roast beef or chicken for this salad. If you're using chicken, substitute 2 teaspoons of coarsely grated Romano cheese for the blue cheese.

Vary It! Use any fresh herbs that you have on hand to give the dressing a variety of flavors. You can also substitute red wine or apple cider vinegar for the balsamic vinegar.

Fab Fish Tacos

Prep time: 10 min • **Cook time:** 15–20 min • **Yield:** 4 servings

Ingredients	Directions
12 ounces mild, white fish such as tilapia or cod **1 tablespoon lemon salt-free seasoning blend** **Vegetable cooking spray** **Fresh lime juice, to taste** **8 warmed small corn tortillas** **1-ounce jar fruit salsa (such as mango or pineapple)** **1 cup chopped romaine lettuce** **2 or 3 plum tomatoes, seeded and chopped** **4 tablespoons light sour cream (optional)**	*1* Heat a medium-sized nonstick skillet on medium-high heat for 2 minutes. Sprinkle the salt-free seasoning on the fish. Spray the pan with cooking spray. *2* Place the fish fillets in the pan. Allow to sear for 3 minutes per side or until cooked, squeezing fresh lime juice on both sides of the fish while it's cooking. *3* Remove from the heat. Break the fish apart (fish is cooked when it flakes easily) with a spatula or fork. *4* Place the warmed tortillas on a serving plate. Divide the shredded fish among the tortillas. Top each serving with a spoonful of salsa, lettuce, and tomato. Garnish with light sour cream, if desired.

Per serving: Calories 207 (From Fat 27); Fat 3g (Saturated 1g); Cholesterol 43mg; Sodium 102mg; Carbohydrate 26g (Dietary Fiber 5g); Protein 21g; Potassium 557mg

Note: Warm tortillas by placing 2 or 3 at a time between two paper towels and microwaving for 20 to 30 seconds on high. You can also wrap them all in foil and heat them in a warm (200 degrees) oven for 15 minutes.

Tip: You may choose to grill the fish using a grill pan.

Vary It! Substitute grilled shrimp for the fish. Add additional vegetable garnishes such as minced bell peppers, onions, or even sautéed zucchini. Try sliced avocado as a garnish as well.

Wrapping Up Dinner Fast with Foil

This section offers up a new way to get dinner on the table quickly: foil pouches. Using a foil pouch is a great way to cook a meal, whether you purchase foil bags or make aluminum-foil pouches yourself at home. Meats and poultry stay moist and vegetables cook quickly using this method.

This easy cooking technique is a great way to get the children involved: They can help assemble the pouches. Use either heavy-duty foil or doubled-layered standard foil. Cut a 12- to 15-inch square of foil for each pouch, making the pouches big enough to allow air space to surround the food. Always spray the foil with cooking spray to keep food from sticking to it. Place the food onto the center of the foil square. Taking opposite ends, fold up each side so the edges meet at the top. Fold the top over two or three times until it almost meets the food. Fold in each open side until the pouch is well sealed.

We have a few ideas to help you fill your pouches like a pro:

✔ Add protein (chicken, fish, or beef) and season with herbs. Add chopped or sliced fresh vegetables such as zucchini, onion, mushrooms, carrots, or bell peppers.

For chicken pouches, try a mixture of 2 tablespoons honey and 2 teaspoons brown mustard per four servings. Glaze the chicken and vegetables before wrapping up the pouch.

✔ Make fajitas by combining sliced lean beef, sliced green bell peppers, and slices of onion. Make a seasoning mixture using ½ teaspoon each of garlic powder, cumin, and cayenne pepper; and 1 tablespoon each of paprika and sugar. Sprinkle the seasoning on the beef and vegetables in the pouch. Cook for 15 minutes. Wrap the contents in whole-wheat tortillas.

Whether you're making the recipes in this section or blazing the trail by coming up with your own ideas, always seal the foil by folding the ends together so no steam will escape. Place your pouches on a grill plate and cook them for 15 minutes. Alternately, you can place them on a baking pan and cook them in a 375-degree oven for 20 to 25 minutes.

Use big oven mitts to remove the pouches from the grill or the oven. Metal turners may rip the foil, and then you'll have a mess on your hands. Keep the pouches sealed until you're ready to eat so the food stays hot. Foil pouches work great for camping trips, too!

Mexi-Chicken Foil Pouches

Prep time: 10 min • **Cook time:** 12–15 min • **Yield:** 4 servings

Ingredients	Directions
4 sheets heavy-duty aluminum foil	**1** Heat a gas grill to high.
Nonstick cooking spray Four 4-ounce boneless skinless chicken breast halves	**2** Spritz 1 square of aluminum foil with cooking spray. Place 1 chicken breast half in the center of the foil. Top with ¼ cup beans and 2 tablespoons salsa.
1 cup canned pinto beans, rinsed and drained well ½ cup low-sodium chunky salsa	**3** Bring the opposite edges of the foil together. Double-fold the foil at the top. Crimp the edges of the pouch on the sides in a tight seal. This seal allows the steam to cook the chicken and preserves the juices.
½ cup low-sodium cheddar cheese	**4** Repeat with the other 3 chicken breast halves.
Fresh cilantro sprigs for garnish	**5** Place the pouches on the preheated grill, close the grill's cover, and cook for 12 to 15 minutes. When done, open each pouch slightly to allow steam to escape; sprinkle with cheese and garnish with cilantro sprigs.

Per serving: Calories 249 (From Fat 70); Fat 8g (Saturated 4g); Cholesterol 77mg; Sodium 424mg; Carbohydrate 13g (Dietary Fiber 3g); Protein 30g; Potassium 500mg.

Tip: Serve with your favorite Spanish rice and avocado slices.

Note: We show you what the finished pouches look like in the color section. Foil pouches can also be baked for 15 to 18 minutes in an oven preheated to 425 degrees.

Balsamic- and Maple-Infused Salmon Pouches

Prep time: 5 min • **Cook time:** 18–20 min • **Yield:** 4 servings

Ingredients	Directions
2 tablespoons orange juice	**1** Preheat the gas grill to high. To make a glaze, combine the orange juice, maple syrup, balsamic vinegar, and garlic in a small bowl.
2 tablespoons maple syrup	
3 tablespoons balsamic vinegar	
1 garlic clove, minced	**2** Wilt the spinach by adding 2 tablespoons of water in a pan with the spinach. Turn the heat to high and gently mix until the spinach has wilted.
One 10-ounce bag baby spinach	
Nonstick cooking spray	**3** Spritz 4 large pieces of aluminum foil with cooking spray. Divide the wilted spinach among the 4 pieces of foil. Place a salmon fillet in the center of each foil square. Top each fillet with ½ cup tomato halves and 1 to 2 tablespoons of the glaze.
4 sheets heavy-duty aluminum foil	
Four 4-ounce salmon fillets	
2 cups cherry tomatoes, cut in half	**4** Double fold each foil square at the top and crimp the side edges of the foil in a tight seal. This seal allows the steam to cook the salmon and preserves the juices.
	5 Place the pouches on the grill, close the grill's cover, and cook for 18 to 20 minutes. When the fish is cooked, open each pouch slightly to allow steam to escape.

Per serving: Calories 235 (From Fat 63); Fat 7g (Saturated 1g); Cholesterol 62mg; Sodium 112mg; Carbohydrate 16g (Dietary Fiber 3g); Protein 25g; Potassium 821mg

Note: These pouches are easy, flavorful, and colorful — the perfect nutritious meal. Serve with a wild rice pilaf, whole-wheat couscous, or our Garlic-Infused Quinoa Cakes from Chapter 12.

Tip: Have your fishmonger cut the fish fillets to your specifications to make your prep time easier.

Vary It! For an even easier way to flavor the salmon, use a commercially prepared salad dressing spray in place of the orange juice mixture.

Chapter 20

Pleasing the Picky: Meals for Kids or Kids at Heart

*1*f you're a parent, you've probably experienced a funny face at the dinner table at one time or another. A turned-up nose, a scrunched-up face, or the worst: the "Yuck!" exclamation, which may have you throwing up your arms.

If you're also suffering from hypertension, you have the additional challenge of keeping your salt and fat intake low while feeding the kids something they won't push away because it tastes too bland, too boring, or too healthy. Let this chapter be your guide to kid-friendly recipes and helpful tactics to encourage your child to become a well-balanced eater. Of course, these recipes appeal not only to kids, but also to any adult who's a kid at heart.

No Whine with Dinner

First off, there's a difference between being "picky" and being "choosy." We all have various taste preferences, and children are no different. In fact, children have more heightened taste buds than older adults (we lose taste buds beginning at around age 40 or 50). Avoiding strong flavors or rough textures is normal for young children. As a parent, your job is to provide a variety of healthy foods, and your child's job is to decide what and how much to eat.

Keep these tips in mind:

✔ **Involve children and teens in the cooking and table-setting.** Even young children can gather flatware and place napkins on the table. Allow them to help toss salad or shuck corn. Show your teens some easy recipes and give them tasks such as chopping, mixing up the salad dressing, sautéing vegetables, preparing skewers, or getting food out of the oven or off the grill.

✔ **Encourage trying new foods by serving some that are similar to foods your child already likes.** If your child loves breaded chicken, try the same breading on fish.

✔ **Give funny names to healthy foods.** Coauthor Rosanne used to call broccoli "dinosaur trees" in her house to entice her son to try them. It worked! Coauthor Cindy called pumpernickel bagels "chocolate bagels" and won her sons over.

✔ **Insist on good table manners.** The first time a child utters "yuck" or a similar adjective at the table, let him know that won't be tolerated. Saying "no thanks" is okay, but using negative language about food isn't.

Nutrition accumulates over the course of the day and week, not all at one meal. If your child says "no thank you," don't worry about it. Never force a child to eat or clean her plate. Offer a small portion and allow her to take seconds if she likes it.

The recipes in this section contain some kid favorites that you can enjoy guilt-free; for example, our chicken fingers are made from fresh chicken, and we're sure they have less salt and saturated fat than the "chicken" bites you'll find on any kids' menu.

Finger-Lickin' Chicken Fingers

Prep time: 10 min • **Cook time:** 12–15 min • **Yield:** 10 servings

Ingredients	*Directions*
1 cup cornflake crumbs or panko breadcrumbs	*1* Preheat your oven to 400 degrees.
½ teaspoon garlic powder	*2* Mix together the crumbs, garlic and onion powders, parsley, pepper, and paprika.
½ teaspoon onion powder	
½ teaspoon parsley	*3* Combine the egg whites, mustard, and oil in a medium bowl and soak the chicken pieces in this mixture.
¼ teaspoon freshly ground black pepper	
¼ teaspoon paprika	*4* Drain a few pieces at a time and roll them in the crumb mixture. Place the chicken tenders on a lined baking pan and place the pan in the oven for 12 to 15 minutes. Turn halfway through the baking process.
2 egg whites	
½ teaspoon Dijon mustard	
½ teaspoon canola oil	
1 pound chicken tenders	

Per serving: Calories 144 (From Fat 72); Fat 8g (Saturated 2g); Cholesterol 19mg; Sodium 228mg; Carbohydrate 11g (Dietary Fiber 1g); Protein 8g; Potassium 100mg.

Note: For cost savings, purchase whole chicken breasts and cut across the grain in 1-inch strips.

Tip: If you prefer thinner chicken tenders, place the strips between two pieces of heavy-duty plastic wrap and gently pound them with a meat mallet to the desired thickness.

Better than Fish Sticks

Prep time: 10 min • **Cook time:** 10–15 min • **Yield:** 10 servings

Ingredients	Directions
½ cup all-purpose flour	**1** Mix together the flour, pepper, garlic powder, and parsley in a shallow plate. Pour the milk in a second shallow dish.
¼ teaspoon freshly ground black pepper	
¼ teaspoon garlic powder	**2** Dip the fish in the milk, drain, and then dredge in the flour mixture (lightly coat by dragging the fish through the flour, turning to coat both sides). Shake off any excess and repeat the process. Repeat the procedure with all the fish sticks.
½ teaspoon parsley	
½ cup lowfat buttermilk	
1 pound firm white fish, cut into ¾-inch sticks	
1 tablespoon butter	**3** In a nonstick skillet, melt the butter and sauté the fish over medium-high heat, turning to cook on both sides until golden brown.

Per serving: Calories 90 (From Fat 27); Fat 3g (Saturated 1g); Cholesterol 31mg; Sodium 41mg; Carbohydrate 5g (Dietary Fiber 0g); Protein 10g; Potassium 233mg.

Note: The best firm fish to use are halibut, pollock, or cod.

Tip: To prevent your hands from becoming too sticky to handle the dredging, use one hand for the wet dredge and one hand for the dry ingredients.

Vary It! You may choose to bake these in the oven. Skip Step 3 and place the fish sticks on a baking sheet coated with cooking spray. Bake them at 350 degrees for 20 to 25 minutes, until golden brown.

Medallions of Beef

Prep time: 15 min • **Cook time:** 20 min • **Yield:** 4 servings

Ingredients	*Directions*
3 teaspoons olive oil, divided **Four ¾-inch- to 1-inch-thick pieces of beef tenderloin (about 4 ounces each)** **⅛ teaspoon sea salt** **Freshly ground black pepper to taste** **1 small onion, thinly sliced** **2 cloves garlic, sliced** **¼ cup low-sodium chicken stock** **¼ cup light sour cream**	**1** Heat 2 teaspoons of the oil in a nonstick skillet over medium-high heat. Sprinkle the salt and pepper on the beef. Place the beef in the hot skillet. Cook for 2 minutes per side for medium rare, or up to 4 minutes per side for medium to medium-well. Remove the beef from the pan to a platter, keeping it warm. **2** Add the remaining teaspoon of oil to the pan and heat. Add the onions and garlic; sauté until clear and lightly colored. **3** Add the chicken broth and bring to a boil. Reduce the heat and simmer 2 minutes. Then remove the pan from the heat and stir in the sour cream. **4** Serve the sauce with the beef medallions.

Per serving: Calories 344 (From Fat 234); Fat 22g (Saturated 7g); Cholesterol 81mg; Sodium 71mg; Carbohydrate 4g (Dietary Fiber 0.5g); Protein 23g; Potassium 425mg.

Tip: Serve the sauce on the side the first time. Allow children to choose the amount they like or just taste it. Serve this dish with a side your child enjoys: Smashed potatoes, green beans, or peas.

Chicken Soft Tacos

Prep time: 15 min • **Cook time:** 15 min • **Yield:** 6 servings

Ingredients	*Directions*
3 teaspoons olive oil, divided 1 pound sliced skinless boneless chicken breast 1 tablespoon salt-free Mexican blend seasoning (or use our Fajita blend in Chapter 19)	**1** Heat 2 teaspoons of the oil in a nonstick skillet. Sprinkle the seasoning onto the chicken. Place the chicken in the hot skillet and cook over medium-high heat for 3 to 5 minutes or until it's no longer pink and juices are clear. Remove from the pan and transfer to a small serving bowl. Keep warm.
1 small sweet onion, diced 1 small bell pepper, diced 12 small whole-wheat flour tortillas	**2** Add the remaining teaspoon of oil to the pan and heat. Add the onions and peppers; sauté until the onions are clear and the peppers are tender. Transfer to a small serving bowl.
1 cup shredded lettuce 4 ounces shredded cheddar or colby-jack cheese	**3** Set up a "taco station" and set out the tortillas, chicken, onion/pepper mixture, shredded lettuce, and shredded cheese, allowing everyone to make his own tacos.

Per serving: Calories 521 (From Fat 144); Fat 16g (Saturated 6g); Cholesterol 89mg; Sodium 669mg; Carbohydrate 54g (Dietary Fiber 5g); Protein 39g; Potassium 344mg.

Note: While this recipe is made of good-for-you-ingredients, it's also slightly higher in sodium, so
balance out your meal choices the rest of the day with lower-sodium options.

Note: Look for fresh salsa in the deli. It's usually lower in sodium.

Tip: Allow children to garnish their own tacos. "Plain" is a start!

Tip: Try garnishing each soft taco with 2 teaspoons of light sour cream and 1 tablespoon salsa. Serve with sliced fresh watermelon.

Turkey Burger Sliders

Prep time: 15 min • **Cook time:** 20 min • **Yield:** 8 servings

Ingredients	Directions
1 pound lean ground turkey breast	**1** Mix the ground turkey with the egg, onion, steak seasoning, and Worcestershire sauce. Blend together well and divide into 6 balls. Form a patty from each ball.
1 egg, beaten	
¼ cup minced sweet onion	
2 teaspoons salt-free steak seasoning	**2** Spray a grill with vegetable cooking spray. Heat the grill to medium-high heat. Place the burgers on the grill and cook 2 to 3 minutes per side.
1 teaspoon Worcestershire sauce	
Vegetable cooking spray	**3** Serve the burgers on slider buns with lettuce and tomato.
8 whole-wheat slider buns	
6 lettuce leaves	
6 plum tomato slices	

Per serving: Calories 177 (From Fat 18); Fat 2g (Saturated 0g); Cholesterol 54mg; Sodium 284mg; Carbohydrate 23g (Dietary Fiber 6g); Protein 19g; Potassium 34mg.

Note: Look for lean ground turkey breast that has less than 2.5 grams of fat per serving. You can find this info on the package label.

Tip: Sliders are the perfect size for kids and adults! A 2- or 3-ounce burger is just right. Round off this meal with a tossed green salad and corn on the cob.

Vary It! Try different spices with the ground turkey — cumin for a Tex-Mex flare or oregano for an Italian flavor. Or, use extra-lean ground beef or even bison to make beef sliders.

Expanding Your Youngster's Horizons

The recipes in this section are a bit more sophisticated but have been hits with our kids for many years. Offering your child different foods from time to time helps expose him to variety, and even if he doesn't try them the first time, he just might next time.

The Crusted Pan-Seared Salmon is appealing because your children probably enjoy batter-fried fish, and this salmon gives you an outer crunch and an appearance that children may be familiar with from eating fish sticks and chicken fingers. After enjoying this recipe, they may eventually adapt to other grilled or baked salmon recipes.

Grow a small kitchen herb garden with your child. When the herbs grow, ask your child to pick them as you cook. This involvement may eventually turn your child into an adventurous eater, and teaching your child at an early age to flavor food with herbs and spices instead of salt is a big win for her health.

It can take a child up to 20 exposures to eventually enjoy a food. This is why it's so important to offer variety and expose your child to all sorts of fruits, vegetables, grains, fish, and types of meat. The more often a child sees a food, the more likely he is to try it. Looking at it, smelling it, and then tasting it are all part of the process. Encourage your child to taste new foods, and allow him to politely spit the food out into a napkin if he doesn't like it. This encourages a key step to eventually liking a new food: Putting it into the mouth! But if he really doesn't like it, you don't have to force him to swallow it. Instead, praise him for trying, adding an encouraging, "Maybe next time you'll like it!" You don't want to create power struggles over food.

It's never too early to introduce positive messages about making good choices to prevent obesity, diabetes, and heart disease. Showing your child how to cook more fresh foods; enjoy nature through cultivating small gardens, a fruit tree, or a shrub; and limit packaged snacks will help her develop an appreciation for a wholesome diet.

Crusted Pan-Seared Salmon

Prep time: 20 min • **Cook time:** 15 min • **Yield:** 4 servings

Ingredients	Directions
¼ cup flour (more if needed)	**1** Place the flour and breadcrumbs on 2 separate plates. Mix the lemon-herb seasoning into the breadcrumbs until well combined. Place the eggs in a small bowl. Dredge the salmon fillets in the flour (lightly drag the fish through the flour to coat both sides), then the eggs, and finally the breadcrumbs, and set them on a clean plate.
½ cup unseasoned plain breadcrumbs	
1 tablespoon salt-free lemon-herb seasoning blend	
2 eggs, lightly beaten	
4 skinless salmon fillets (each about 2 x 4 inches and 3 to 4 ounces)	**2** Heat the oil in a nonstick skillet over medium heat. Place the salmon in the hot skillet and cook 3 to 4 minutes on each side or until golden brown. Remove from the heat and serve.
2 tablespoons peanut oil	

Per serving: Calories 303 (From Fat 15); Fat 21g (Saturated 1g); Cholesterol 76mg; Sodium 147mg; Carbohydrate 15g (Dietary Fiber 2g); Protein 27g; Potassium 1,117mg.

Note: Depending on the size of your fillets, you may need a few more breadcrumbs than what we've specified here. Just add a few more to the plate.

Tip: Peanut oil is good for frying due to its low smoke point. You can also use vegetable oil.

Angel Hair Pasta with Shrimp

Prep time: 10–12 min • **Cook time:** 10 min • **Yield:** 4 servings

Ingredients	Directions
2 large garlic cloves, minced	**1** In a large nonstick skillet, heat 2 teaspoons of olive oil and sauté the vegetables and garlic for a minute or two, just until the vegetables are tender crisp; add the remaining olive oil to the pan and sauté the shrimp just until they heat through, about a minute.
3 tablespoons olive oil	
2 cups assorted julienne vegetables: carrots, yellow squash, zucchini, red bell pepper, mushrooms, red cabbage	
20 medium cooked frozen shrimp (about ¾ pound)	**2** Pour the cooked, drained pasta into a serving bowl (being sure to reserve ¼ cup liquid). Toss the cooked shrimp and vegetables with the cooked pasta and the water saved from cooking. Blend in the fresh herbs before serving. Garnish with Parmesan.
½ pound angel hair pasta, cooked according to package directions without salt; save ¼ cup cooking water	
1 tablespoon chopped fresh basil	
½ tablespoon chopped fresh thyme	
2 tablespoons grated Parmesan cheese	

Per serving: Calories 349 (From Fat 111); Fat 12g (Saturated 2g); Cholesterol 48mg; Sodium 96mg; Carbohydrate 45g (Dietary Fiber 3g); Protein 16g; Potassium 302mg.

Note: This recipe is shown in the color section.

Vary It! You can add a variety of herbs to this recipe. Fresh chopped parsley, basil, or mint taste great. Children may or may not be accustomed to the herbs, so we kept this recipe simple. You can always offer to toss in fresh herbs at the table.

Confetti Quesadillas

Prep time: 10 min • **Cook time:** 10 min • **Yield:** 8 servings

Ingredients	*Directions*
Nonstick cooking spray Eight 8-inch corn tortillas or fat-free flour tortillas	*1* Heat a griddle on medium heat. Spritz nonstick cooking spray lightly over a tortilla. Place the tortilla sprayed side down in the hot skillet.
1 cup shredded Mexi-blend cheese 1 cup frozen corn, thawed ½ cup minced red bell pepper ½ cup minced green bell pepper ½ cup fresh salsa	*2* Top the tortilla with ⅛ of the cheese, corn, and peppers and heat for 30 seconds. Fold over the tortilla, gently press it down with a spatula, and continue to heat until golden brown. Flip over and heat the other side until golden and cheese is melted.
	3 Repeat the process with the remaining tortillas.
	4 Cut each folded tortilla into 4 equal pieces and serve with your favorite salsa.

Per serving: Calories 203 (From Fat 54); Fat 6g (Saturated 3g); Cholesterol 15mg; Sodium 158mg; Carbohydrate 31g (Dietary Fiber 3g); Protein 6g; Potassium 93mg.

Note: Quesadillas are the new grilled cheese sandwich. Using a griddle instead of a skillet to cook the quesadillas allows you to make four at the same time.

Tip: Quesadillas are the perfect way to use up leftovers — veggies, meat, seafood, and even fruit — and nothing is better than grilled apple and cheddar.

Plating Spunky Side Dishes

Some health-conscious parents get overly concerned with what a child *won't* eat, instead of focusing on all the foods they *will* eat, especially when it comes to side dishes like vegetables. As we explain in the preceding section, children often take a while to decide to try new things, and they do have their own taste preferences. Kids and picky eaters may grow to love many of the side dishes from Chapters 11 and 12, but in this section, we give you a trio of side dishes that are sure to please everyone from the get-go.

While you want to continue to offer your children a variety of veggies — they should see vegetables on the dinner table each night — whether to take a spoonful is ultimately the child's choice. You can improve the odds by serving veggies in ways that up their appeal from a kid's perspective:

 ✔ **Pair a few veggies with a popular starch.** Sneaking veggies into rice, for example, is a good way to incorporate good nutrition and variety.

 ✔ **Dice and slice your way to success.** How you slice or dice a vegetable can make a difference, especially to children. A smaller chop makes veggies less daunting — try serving them minced or julienned.

 ✔ **Take advantage of color's charisma.** We like using orange, red, and yellow bell peppers for their bright colors and sweet, mild flavor.

 Let your child pick out a colorful serving bowl to purchase at a discount store for serving veggies!

Our recipe for Confetti Rice incorporates all three strategies: The bell peppers are minced, paired with rice, and it's a colorful dish.

Another way to be sure your children are getting the nutrients and fiber they need is to give them the option of a fruit side they enjoy along with a vegetable. For example, offer applesauce, sliced strawberries, or orange slices with the meal. This way, your children can choose a healthy side (that's not much work for you to prepare and serve) and still benefit from watching others eat their vegetables . . . one day, they'll surprise you and take some all on their own!

The following recipes are based on two universal kid favorites, rice and potatoes, and pair well with the main-dish entrees in this chapter. For example, the Baked Tiger Stripe Fries go well with the Turkey Burger Sliders, and the Confetti Rice is great with the Crusted Pan-Seared Salmon, Better than Fish Sticks, Confetti Quesadillas, or Finger-Lickin' Chicken Fingers.

Perfect Smashed Potatoes

Prep time: 10 min • **Cook time:** 15 min • **Yield:** 4 servings

Ingredients	Directions
4 medium baking potatoes, peeled and cut into 1-inch cubes **2 to 3 garlic cloves, minced** **½ cup lowfat milk, heated** **1 tablespoon butter** **Freshly ground black pepper to taste**	*1* In a 3-quart saucepan, cover the potato cubes with cold water. Add the minced garlic. Bring to a boil and simmer gently for 15 minutes or until the potatoes are tender. Drain in a colander. *2* Return the peeled potatoes to the hot pan and cook over medium heat for a few minutes to absorb any excess moisture. Remove from the heat. Mash well with a potato masher until the desired consistency is achieved. *3* Add the butter and hot milk, beating continuously until the potatoes are smooth. Add pepper to taste, and stir well.

Per serving: Calories 209 (From Fat 27); Fat 3g (Saturated 2g); Cholesterol 9mg; Sodium 45mg; Carbohydrate 41g (Dietary Fiber 3g); Protein 6g; Potassium 942mg.

Tip: Cut potatoes into uniform cubes so they cook evenly. For a more rustic feel and more fiber and nutrients, leave the skin on the potatoes.

Note: Using hot milk, as specified in this recipe, instead of cold results in creamier mashed potatoes.

Vary 1t! Swap extra-virgin olive oil for the butter or infuse the potatoes with chives or your favorite cheese.

Confetti Rice

Prep time: 10 min • **Cook time:** 35–45 min • **Yield:** 6 servings

Ingredients	*Directions*
1 tablespoon olive oil ¼ cup minced red bell peppers ¼ cup minced green bell peppers ¼ cup minced yellow bell peppers One small onion, minced 1 cup brown or converted rice, uncooked 2½ cups low-sodium chicken broth	*1* Heat the olive oil in a medium stockpot. Add the minced red, green, and yellow bell peppers and the onion to the pan and sauté until tender, about 4 minutes. *2* Add the rice and broth to the pot, bring to a boil, cover, and cook as directed. *3* Transfer to a serving bowl, fluffing with a fork.

Per serving: Calories 83 (From Fat 27); Fat 3g (Saturated 1g); Cholesterol 2mg; Sodium 61mg; Carbohydrate 12g (Dietary Fiber 1g); Protein 3g; Potassium 109mg.

Vary It! If you're out of stock and broth, you can substitute water and add a very small pinch of salt and ground black pepper.

Tip: If you're short on time during the week, you can purchase an already-minced bell pepper trio in the produce section.

Vary It! You can use any finely chopped vegetable in a simple rice dish, bumping up the nutritional value of your grain. For example, try rice with finely cubed zucchini, onion, and mushrooms.

Tip: Brown rice increases the cooking time, so be sure to read the package directions.

Baked Tiger Stripe Fries

Prep time: 10 min • **Cook time:** 30–40 min • **Yield:** 4 servings

Ingredients	*Directions*
2 large Yukon gold potatoes, peeled	*1* Preheat the oven to 400 degrees. Line a large baking pan with parchment paper or a silicon baking mat.
2 large sweet potatoes, peeled	
Olive oil cooking spray	*2* Cut the potatoes into ¼-inch wedges and line them up in a single row (without overlapping) in the baking pan. Generously spray the potatoes with the cooking spray and dust them lightly with pepper, paprika, and garlic powder.
Freshly ground black pepper to taste	
Paprika to taste	
Garlic powder to taste	*3* Bake the potatoes for 30 to 40 minutes or until they're tender, turning midway through the baking time.

Per serving: Calories 237 (From Fat 2); Fat 0g (Saturated 0g); Cholesterol 0mg; Sodium 21mg; Carbohydrate 54g (Dietary Fiber 6g); Protein 5g; Potassium 389mg.

Note: Coauthor Cindy recommends baking with a silicon baking mat, a durable pan liner that replaces the need for parchment paper and oil. Nothing sticks to it, even when the baking temperature is very high. Cleaning up the mat is simple; just use some hot, soapy water.

Getting the Pizza Party Started

Who doesn't like pizza? Kids and grownups alike love pizza night, so dig into these recipes and have a family affair. The great thing about making homemade pizzas is that everyone can choose the perfect amount of sauce and cheese and his favorite toppings; plus, the pizzas in this section contain only half the sodium of takeout pizza and are much lower in fat. Pizza is also a great way to introduce new foods. Does your child turn up her nose at chicken? Try barbecue chicken chunks on a pizza!

The combinations are endless, so use your imagination to make gourmet pizzas at home. You can purchase frozen pizza dough from your grocer, or you can make your own to use that day or freeze for later. Pizza dough is easy and quick to make (just see the nearby sidebar "Rolling in the dough"). And check out the sidebar "Throwing a secretly healthy make-your-own-pizza party" to make an event of it.

Try something new. Use your grill to cook up some crunchy crusts! Heat the grill on medium-high heat. Make your pizza as usual, and then grill for about 4 minutes, watching it closely to make sure the bottom doesn't burn. You can even grill a dessert pizza. Try a s'more pizza by spreading your dough with a hazelnut chocolate spread (like Nutella), and then adding miniature marshmallows and one crushed graham cracker. Grill for 4 minutes and serve.

Rolling in the dough

Making your own pizza dough is cheap, quick, and better for you.

To prepare pizza dough, lightly spoon one cup whole-wheat and one cup white flour into a measuring cup and level with a knife. Pour the flour into a large bowl. Add 1 package of dry, quick-rise yeast and ¾ teaspoon of salt. Blend 1 cup of hot (120–125 degrees) tap water, 1 tablespoon of vegetable oil, and 1 tablespoon of honey or granulated sugar in a glass measuring cup. Add the liquid to the flour mixture and stir by hand until all ingredients are well blended (about 3 minutes), forming a soft, round ball of dough. Cover the dough with plastic wrap and let it rise until double in size (about 10–15 minutes; check package directions on the yeast).

Punch down the dough; then press it onto a greased 15-x-10-x-1-inch jelly-roll pan or a 12- to 14-inch pizza pan. Press the dough to cover the bottom of the pan and up the sides to form a rim. Add the pizza sauce of your choice and your favorite toppings. Bake for 15 to 20 minutes in a preheated, 425-degree oven or until the crust is golden brown, or, if you're using a pizza recipe, according to its directions.

Throwing a secretly healthy make-your-own-pizza party

Whether you have kids or not, a great way to bring together friends is to host a pizza party. Ordering pizza for delivery may be easy, but it also gets boring, so skip the high-sodium, high-fat boxed pizza and make a party out of putting together your own. It's a fun way to involve the kids in dinner preparations with their friends or neighbors, and even the adults will have a blast!

Just follow these simple steps to host a great pizza party:

1. Have some healthy munchies out when guests arrive, because you'll be cooking the pizzas while they wait. Put out a platter of fresh fruit like grape clusters, sliced melon, berries, and apples. Place skinny, unsalted, dry breadsticks in a pretty, tall container or glass. You may even want to make our Italian Caprese Skewers (see Chapter 13) sans the mozzarella (because you'll be adding cheeses to your pizzas).

2. Indulge in some good red wine. Resveratrol in red wine is an antioxidant that may help prevent blood-vessel damage and reduce HDL ("bad") cholesterol. Having a glass as you get the pizzas ready will relax both you and your guests, so everyone will have a good time.

3. Put out a variety of toppings in separate, small serving bowls: sliced mushrooms, chopped peppers, roasted eggplant, and shredded part-skim mozzarella are only the beginning. You may want to sauté the mushrooms or peppers ahead of time — we prefer to place them on the pizza lightly cooked rather than raw. Offer a bowl of cooked chicken chunks or sliced meatballs as toppings too. Have a ladle in the tomato sauce for guests to use. You can also offer a small bowl of pesto sauce or herbed olive oil so guests can put together a "white pizza."

4. Preheat the oven to 425 degrees and sprinkle cornmeal onto 2 large cookie sheets.

5. Portion out small mounds of dough (double the recipe in the sidebar "Rolling in the dough" to make 8 to 10 small, single pizzas). You can make these ahead of time and wrap them in plastic wrap if you like. Keep in mind these will be free-form personal pizzas, so a ball of dough about the size of a baseball is enough. Give each guest one ball of dough to work with, and have a clean surface available for two or three guests to work on at a time. Allow guests to spread the dough into circles, place them on a cookie sheet, and top them with sauce (flip back to Chapter 19 for our personal tomato sauce recipe) and the toppings of their choosing. You'll probably fit three personal pizzas on one cookie sheet.

6. Bake for 10 to 15 minutes until the crust is golden and the cheese is melted.

If you don't have time for a full-on pizza, give this quick snack a try. (The youngsters can even help with the toppings!) Preheat your oven or toaster oven to 375 degrees. Spread whole-wheat English muffin halves with 2 to 3 teaspoons of pizza sauce apiece. Sprinkle 2 teaspoons of cheese over the sauce. Place the pizzas on a baking sheet and bake until the cheese is bubbly. Sneak in some veggies like sautéed sliced mushrooms and diced green peppers.

Quick and Easy Veggie Pizza

Prep time: 10 min • **Cook time:** 5–10 min • **Yield:** 4 servings

Ingredients	Directions
Nonstick cooking spray	**1** Preheat the oven to 450 degrees.
1 small zucchini, thinly sliced	
2 small button mushrooms, sliced	**2** Coat a small skillet with nonstick cooking spray. Sauté the zucchini, mushrooms, and onions until soft. Add the thyme and stir to blend it with the vegetables.
½ cup sliced red onions	
½ teaspoon thyme	**3** Spread 1 tablespoon pesto on each of the pizza crusts. Divide the sautéed veggies between the two pizzas.
2 tablespoons prepared pesto	
1 package of two 8-inch whole-wheat thin pizza crusts	**4** Top each pizza with half of the provolone and half of the gruyere cheese.
¼ cup provolone cheese	
¼ cup gruyere cheese	**5** Bake for 5 to 10 minutes until golden brown. For a crispier pizza, bake the pizza longer at a higher temperature. Slice with a pizza cutter.

Per serving: Calories 317 (From Fat 121); Fat 13g (Saturated 7g); Cholesterol 20mg; Sodium 557mg; Carbohydrate 37g (Dietary Fiber 7g); Protein 15g; Potassium 293mg.

Note: While this recipe is made of good-for-you-ingredients, it's also slightly higher in sodium, so balance out your meal choices the rest of the day with lower-sodium options.

Note: Flip to the color section for a picture of this pizza to make your mouth water.

Tip: If you have teenagers, keep a couple pizza crusts on hand for quick meals when hunger strikes.

Vary It! Substitute Focaccia bread, pita bread, or whole-wheat English muffin halves for the pizza crusts. Use Italian-blend shredded cheese in place of the provolone and gruyere.

Mama Mia Meatball Pizza

Prep time: 10 min • **Cook time:** 8–10 min • **Yield:** 4 servings

Ingredients	*Directions*
1 package of two 8-inch whole-wheat thin pizza crusts	*1* Preheat the oven to 450 degrees.
4 tablespoons prepared pizza sauce	*2* Spread 2 tablespoons pizza sauce on each of the pizza crusts. Divide the meatballs between the two pizzas.
1 cup frozen Italian-style meatballs, thawed and halved	
¼ cup shredded provolone cheese	*3* Blend the two cheeses together and top each pizza with half of the cheese mixture.
¼ cup shredded gruyere cheese	*4* Bake for 8 to 10 minutes until golden brown. Slice with a pizza cutter or a pair of kitchen shears (see Figure 20-1).

Per serving: Calories 343 (From Fat 124); Fat 14g (Saturated 7g); Cholesterol 46mg; Sodium 619mg; Carbohydrate 38g (Dietary Fiber 7g); Protein 19g; Potassium 230mg.

Note: While this recipe is made of good-for-you-ingredients, it's also slightly higher in sodium, so balance out your meal choices the rest of the day with lower-sodium options. Flip to the color section for a photo of this pizza.

Tip: Kitchen shears are useful for cutting a variety of ingredients. Use them to more easily cut salad greens, herbs, and pizza, as shown in Figure 20-1.

Figure 20-1: Kitchen shears are highly versatile.

Tico Taco Pizza

Prep time: 20 min • **Cook time:** 20 min • **Yield:** 4 servings

Ingredients	*Directions*
½ small onion, minced	**1** Preheat the oven to 350 degrees. Brown the ground turkey and onion in a skillet for 5 to 8 minutes or until the meat is thoroughly cooked. If necessary, drain the meat in a colander to remove excess fat; then transfer the meat back to the skillet.
6 ounces lean ground turkey	
⅓ cup favorite salsa	
4 tostada shells	
½ cup shredded lowfat cheddar cheese	**2** Stir the salsa into the turkey mixture.
½ cup shredded lettuce	**3** Place the tostada shells on a lined baking sheet. Divide the meat mixture evenly among the 4 shells. Sprinkle each tostada with cheese and bake for 10 minutes or until the cheese is melted.
1 small tomato, chopped	
4 tablespoons light sour cream	
	4 Top the pizzas with the lettuce, tomatoes, and a dollop of sour cream.

Per serving: Calories 185 (From Fat 72); Fat 8g (Saturated 3g); Cholesterol 38mg; Sodium 350mg; Carbohydrate 13g (Dietary Fiber 2g); Protein 15g; Potassium 236mg.

Tip: Save cooked lean ground beef or ground turkey from other recipes and freeze it for an even quicker taco pizza.

Vary It! Substitute shredded rotisserie or grilled chicken breasts for the ground turkey.

Chapter 21

Enjoying Hearty and Heart-Healthy Vegetarian Entrees

In This Chapter

▶ Maximizing the taste factor with new vegetable dishes

▶ Creating luscious main-dish vegetable entrees

▶ Flipping vegetable-based burgers packed with flavor and nutrients

Okay, we admit it; this is one of our favorite chapters. "Big surprise," you say. "Two dietitians love vegetables." But the recipes here aren't your grandmother's soggy vegetable dishes. These dishes burst with flavor and are so hearty that you won't miss the meat.

For those of you out there in the "I hate vegetables" club, we challenge you to give at least two of these recipes a try. We bet that once you do, you'll be cooking up all the recipes in this chapter in no time.

When you eat more high-flavored vegetables and reduce animal protein, you're likely to lose weight, automatically lowering your blood pressure and improving your health. The extra fiber, potassium, and magnesium and the decreased sodium and fat in a vegetarian meal all fit in perfectly with the DASH plan (see Chapter 2). Tweak your diet by adding a few new vegetable dishes over several weeks and months to give yourself a chance to adapt to vegetarian dishes.

One Dish, No Meat, All Flavor

Cooking up a meatless entree at least once a week helps you reduce your overall saturated fat intake. It also adds important antioxidant nutrients and fiber to your diet, meeting more of your DASH diet goals (for more info on the DASH diet, see Chapter 2). Meatless dishes can still be satisfying and filling, while retaining lots of flavor. Having a meatless dish in place of meat at a meal doesn't mean going without protein. You can take care of that by including protein in the form of beans, legumes, tofu, or nuts.

When you consider vegetarian food, do you suffer from tofu-phobia? Tofu is an awesome food to add to your diet for high blood pressure because it's low in salt, high in protein, cholesterol-free, and low in calories. Even better, it's quick to cook. Its mild flavor is enhanced by whatever foods you choose to pair it with, so give it a try in your favorite meat recipes or with your favorite flavorings.

If you need a little background information, tofu is a soy product made from soymilk. Tofu is to soy what cottage cheese is to cow's milk. It's the curd.

There are different types of tofu: silken and regular. Silken tofu has a softer consistency than regular tofu. Both silken and regular tofu come in soft, medium, firm, and extra-firm. The latter two are best used when you want tofu to retain its shape in stir-fry dishes.

Be sure to try the Stir-Fry Tofu with Mushrooms in Sichuan Sauce in this section if you haven't tried tofu yet. You can make the veggie dishes in this section in just one dish, but you won't find a casserole in sight.

Roasted Vegetable Moussaka

Prep time: 20 min • **Cook time:** 75 min • **Yield:** 5 servings

Ingredients	Directions
1 large eggplant, peeled and sliced 2 large zucchini, sliced 2 onions, sliced 2 red bell peppers, seeded and chopped Nonstick cooking spray Freshly ground pepper to taste 2 garlic cloves, minced 1 whole egg and 2 egg whites, beaten 1¼ cups nonfat plain Greek yogurt ¼ teaspoon nutmeg One 14-ounce can chopped tomatoes in juice, no salt added, drained ½ teaspoon thyme ½ teaspoon dried oregano ½ teaspoon dried rosemary ¼ teaspoon cinnamon Pinch red pepper flakes 2 ounces feta cheese, crumbled Fresh parsley, minced, for garnish	*1* Preheat your oven to 425 degrees. Place the eggplant, zucchini, onions, and peppers on a lined baking pan. Spritz the vegetables with nonstick spray, gently toss, and sprinkle with freshly ground pepper to taste. Roast the vegetables for 15 minutes. *2* Toss the vegetables again, add the minced garlic, and roast for another 15 to 20 minutes or until the vegetables are tender. Remove from the pan and set aside. Reduce the oven temperature to 350 degrees. *3* Combine the beaten eggs with the yogurt and mix well. Add the nutmeg and fresh ground pepper to taste, stirring until well blended. *4* Place half of the vegetable mixture in the bottom of a glass baking dish. Mix together the tomatoes, thyme, oregano, rosemary, cinnamon, and red pepper flakes. Set aside ¼ cup to top the dish. *5* Pour the remaining tomatoes over the vegetable mixture; then add a second layer of vegetables. Spread the yogurt mixture over the vegetables. Sprinkle the crumbled feta atop the yogurt. Bake for 45 minutes or until golden brown. *6* Sprinkle with minced parsley and drizzle extra chopped tomato mixture on top, if desired.

Per serving: Calories 141 (From Fat 18); Fat 2g (Saturated .5g); Cholesterol 44mg; Sodium 203mg; Carbohydrate 24g (Dietary Fiber 7g); Protein 10g, Potassium 645mg.

Stir-Fry Tofu with Mushrooms in Sichuan Sauce

Prep time: 10 min • **Cook time:** 15 min • **Yield:** 4 servings

Ingredients	Directions
12 ounces extra-firm tofu, drained and cut into cubes	**1** Drain the tofu well, using paper towels to soak up the extra liquid. Lightly dust with cornstarch.
1 tablespoon cornstarch	
2 tablespoons low-sodium catsup	**2** In a small bowl, combine the sauce ingredients: the catsup, rice vinegar, sugar, soy sauce, sesame oil, and chili paste. Set aside.
2 teaspoons rice vinegar	
1 teaspoon sugar	**3** Heat an electric wok or stir-fry pan over high heat. Add 1 tablespoon of the peanut oil and stir-fry the mushrooms until golden; then add the garlic and green onions for a few seconds. Add the bean sprouts and carrots and toss quickly in the hot oil until crisp tender.
2 teaspoons reduced-sodium soy sauce	
1 teaspoon sesame oil	
1 tablespoon chili paste	
2 tablespoons peanut oil	**4** Remove the vegetables from the wok and set aside. Add the remaining tablespoon of peanut oil and the tofu, and stir-fry until the tofu begins to brown.
4 ounces button mushrooms, cut in half	
2 cloves garlic, minced	**5** Add the stir-fry sauce and cook until it's bubbly. Return the vegetables back to the wok and toss all ingredients until completely covered with the sauce and heated through.
2 green onions, sliced	
4 ounces bean sprouts	
4 ounces shredded carrots	

Per serving: Calories 175 (From Fat 90); Fat 10g (Saturated 2g); Cholesterol 0mg; Sodium 352mg; Carbohydrate 14g (Dietary Fiber 2g); Protein 9g; Potassium 429mg.

Tip: Tofu browns more easily when excess liquid is removed.

Vary It! Use your favorite veggies in this stir-fry and clean out the vegetable bin in the fridge.

Butternut Squash Enchiladas with Avocado Cream

Prep time: 20 min • **Cook time:** 50–60 min • **Yield:** About 6 servings

Ingredients	Directions
2 small butternut squash, peeled and cut into small cubes (about 3 to 4 cups)	**1** Preheat your oven to 425 degrees. Toss the butternut squash with the pepper, cumin, and chili powder. Spritz with nonstick cooking spray. Place on a lined baking sheet and roast for 30 minutes, tossing once during the cooking process. When roasting is completed, reduce the oven temperature to 350 degrees.
Freshly ground pepper to taste	
½ teaspoon cumin	
½ teaspoon chili powder	
Nonstick cooking spray	**2** Sauté the onion and garlic with the olive oil in a large skillet until tender. Add the squash and corn to the onion mixture. Set aside.
1 tablespoon olive oil	
½ small onion, chopped	
2 garlic cloves, minced	**3** To soften the tortillas, wrap them in a paper towel and place in the microwave on high for 30 seconds to 1 minute. Divide the squash mixture evenly among the tortillas, placing the veggies in the center of the tortillas.
½ cup frozen corn, thawed	
Twelve 6-inch-diameter corn tortillas or whole-wheat fat-free tortillas	
2 cups lowfat shredded Mexi-blend cheese	**4** Top each with a tablespoon of cheese, roll 'em up, and arrange them side by side in a 9-x-13-inch glass baking dish. Pour the salsa verde over the enchiladas and sprinkle the remaining shredded cheese on top. Bake until the cheese is bubbly, about 20 minutes.
One 16-ounce jar salsa verde	
8 ounces lowfat sour cream	
1 ripe avocado	**5** While the enchiladas are baking, mash the avocado until smooth and creamy. Blend in the sour cream and 2 tablespoons cilantro.
¼ cup finely chopped cilantro	
	6 To serve, top the enchiladas with the avocado cream and the remaining fresh cilantro.

Per serving: Calories 542 (From Fat 126); Fat 14g (Saturated 4g); Cholesterol 32mg; Sodium 300mg; Carbohydrate 84g (Dietary Fiber 10g); Protein 20g; Potassium 578mg.

Sweet and Savory Garbanzo, Orzo, and Broccoli Salad

Prep time: 15 min • **Cook time:** 30 min • **Yield:** 6 servings

Ingredients	Directions
6 dried apricots	**1** Heat your oven to 450 degrees. Soak the apricots in hot water for about 10 minutes. Drain the beans and rinse thoroughly. Spread the beans on a baking sheet.
One 7-ounce can garbanzo beans	
2 tablespoons plus 4 teaspoons olive oil, divided	**2** Sprinkle the beans with 2 teaspoons of the olive oil. Sprinkle half the cumin and turmeric over the beans, tossing to coat. Roast for 10 to 15 minutes or until popped and lightly browned. Transfer to a medium serving bowl and set aside.
½ teaspoon ground cumin, divided	
¼ teaspoon ground turmeric, divided	
¼ cup orzo pasta	**3** While the beans are roasting, bring unsalted water to boil for the pasta. Cook the orzo for 9 minutes or according to package directions. Drain, rinse with cold water, and set aside. While the orzo is cooking, slice the apricots into thin slices. Set aside.
1 teaspoon orange zest	
3 tablespoons orange juice	
2 tablespoons apple cider vinegar	**4** Mix 2 tablespoons of the olive oil with the orange zest, orange juice, vinegar, and pepper. Whisk until blended. Add the onion and the sliced apricots.
¼ teaspoon freshly ground pepper	
¼ cup Vidalia onion, diced	**5** Place the broccoli on the same baking sheet the beans were roasted on. Sprinkle with the remaining 2 teaspoons of the olive oil, ¼ teaspoon cumin and ⅛ teaspoon turmeric and toss to coat. Roast in the oven for 15 to 20 minutes, until tender and lightly browned.
3 crowns broccoli, trimmed into small flowerettes (about 5 to 6 cups)	
½ cup diced tomatoes, unsalted	**6** Add the orzo to the beans in the serving bowl. Add the tomatoes. Pour half of the olive oil-orange dressing over the beans and toss lightly. Add the broccoli and the remainder of the dressing and toss until mixed.

Per serving: Calories 158 (From Fat 63); Fat 7g (Saturated 1g); Cholesterol 0mg; Sodium 136mg; Carbohydrate 21g (Dietary Fiber 5g); Protein 5g, Potassium 393mg.

Meatless Mondays, for a good cause

During World War I, President Hoover asked the American people to help in the war effort by eating less meat and wheat products to aid the war effort. He declared Meatless Monday and Wheatless Wednesday as a way to conserve food staples. The effort was successful in saving tons of meat each week. In 2003, the Johns Hopkins Bloomberg School of Public Health established a new Meatless Monday campaign, which has been endorsed by over 20 schools of public health across the nation. The goal? Help Americans cut back on meat, reducing saturated fat intake and thereby reducing the risks of preventable disease, like heart disease, cancer, and diabetes.

Cooking Mighty Meaty Veggies

Creating a meal without meat doesn't have to imply a giant tossed salad or heaps of green beans and carrots — or hearing your stomach growl an hour after dinner. You can create a vegetable-based meal in such a way that you won't miss the meat and will be just as satisfied.

A few of our best tips to make sure you get your fill while eating vegetarian include the following:

- **Use beans.** Try black beans, garbanzo beans, cannelloni beans, or kidney beans.
- **Choose hearty vegetables.** Squash, eggplant, and Portobello mushrooms hold up well in baked dishes.
- **Substitute a vegetable or tofu where a starch or meat would be used.** Instead of using traditional pasta sheets for lasagna, use slices of grilled eggplant. Instead of adding ground meat to chili, add three varieties of beans.

Rice and beans are meatless meal staples. When you cook up a batch, consider doubling the recipe so you can use it in another meal or snack later in the week. It keeps for 3 to 4 days, and is great served in a burrito or wrap, on top of a tossed salad, or as a side dish.

Weighing in on vegetarianism

As you add more vegetables and grains to your diet, you may find them to be quite enjoyable. The vegetarian lifestyle has several benefits. Many studies have shown a reduction in obesity, diabetes, high blood pressure, and heart disease with a vegetarian diet. A vegetarian diet is a healthful way to eat, as long as meals are carefully planned. As with any diet, adequate (not excessive) calories and protein are important, as well as a balance of other nutrients.

There are several different types of vegetarians. *Vegans* eat absolutely no animal products. *Lacto* vegetarians include milk products and *lacto-ovo* vegetarians include both dairy and eggs, but both eliminate all poultry, fish, and meat. Vegetarians who don't consume dairy products can get calcium from green leafy vegetables (such as spinach and kale) as well as foods fortified with calcium (such as juices and cereals).

Protein is a particular concern when looking at vegetarianism. Plant proteins are just as beneficial as animal proteins. To get enough protein, you should include vegetables, rice, pasta, whole-grain breads, beans, nuts, seeds, and tofu in your diet. Variety is important.

A few key vitamins and minerals are also worth noting:

- ✔ **Iron:** This mineral is found in red meats and liver, but it's also available in beans and spinach. Be sure you include iron-rich plant foods to replace the iron lost from meat. You can also find other iron-enriched products like breads and cereals. Read package labels to find foods with added iron.

- ✔ **Zinc:** Nuts and grains are a good source of zinc (also present in meats).

- ✔ **Vitamin B-12:** Naturally present only in animal products, this essential vitamin needs to be added to the diet either by supplement or by including fortified breakfast cereals or fortified soy beverages.

To find out more, visit the Vegetarian Nutrition Dietetic Practice Group of the American Dietetic Association at `http://vegetarian nutrition.net/`.

You don't have to become a vegetarian to enjoy the health benefits of avoiding meat now and then. Adding some of the meals in this section to your diet and seeking out additional vegetarian dishes once in a while helps you meet some of your DASH diet goals: lowering intake of saturated fat and salt, and increasing intake of fiber and antioxidants — both with a potential side effect of weight loss. So, relax; it's all good!

Louisiana Red Beans and Rice

Prep time: 10 min plus soaking time • **Cook time:** 2 hr • **Yield:** 10 servings

Ingredients	*Directions*
1 pound red beans, washed and drained	*1* Place the beans in cold water in a 4-quart pot and soak overnight.
1 large onion, chopped	
4 green onions, chopped	*2* Drain and rinse the beans, and place them back in the pot. Add water to 1 inch above the beans. Add the remaining ingredients except the brown rice, bring to a boil, lower the heat, and simmer for 1 hour, covered. Stir several times during cooking.
1 small green pepper, chopped	
1 clove garlic, minced	
1¼ teaspoons cayenne pepper	
1¼ teaspoons black pepper	*3* Cook uncovered for an additional hour, continuing to stir to prevent the beans from sticking to the bottom of the pot.
¼ teaspoon thyme	
1 teaspoon celery flakes	
¼ teaspoon oregano	*4* Serve over steaming brown rice.
1 tablespoon Worcestershire sauce	
2 to 5 drops hot pepper sauce	
6 ounces no-salt-added tomato paste	
5 cups cooked brown rice	

Per serving: Calories 48 (From Fat 0); Fat 0g (Saturated 0g); Cholesterol 0mg; Sodium 120mg; Carbohydrate 10g (Dietary Fiber 3g); Protein 3g; Potassium 175mg.

Note: Red beans and rice is a Louisiana creole classic typically made with sausage, smoked meat, or pork bones; we left those out to reduce the sodium content and keep it simple. This recipe makes an easy and yummy meal.

Vary It! Make this recipe even easier by tossing the ingredients into a slow cooker and cooking the mixture on low for 7 hours. If you can be a little more flexible on your sodium counts for this meal, substitute two 15-ounce cans of pinto beans, well-rinsed and drained, in place of the dried beans.

Baby Portobello Burgers

Prep time: 10 min • **Cook time:** 16–18 min • **Yield:** 4 servings

Ingredients	*Directions*
4 small Portobello mushroom caps, stems removed	*1* Marinate the mushrooms, smooth side up, in 3 tablespoons of vinaigrette dressing at room temperature for 10 to 15 minutes.
4 tablespoons sweet and sour balsamic vinaigrette, divided	
2 tablespoons reduced-fat mayonnaise	*2* To make the horseradish sauce, combine the mayo, sour cream, and horseradish and refrigerate until ready to use.
2 tablespoons light sour cream	
½ to 1 teaspoon prepared horseradish	*3* Preheat a gas grill on high. Grill the mushrooms caps until tender, about 5 minutes per side, basting occasionally with the extra tablespoon of vinaigrette.
4 whole-grain burger buns	
4 red leaf lettuce leaves	*4* Spread 1 tablespoon of the horseradish sauce on one side of each bun. Place one grilled mushroom on each bun and layer with the lettuce leaves and red onions.
4 slices red onion	

Per serving: Calories 227 (From Fat 72); Fat 8g (Saturated 1g); Cholesterol 2mg; Sodium 447mg; Carbohydrate 28g (Dietary Fiber 3g); Protein 11g; Potassium 638mg.

Note: Portobello mushrooms have a steak-like texture that stands up to strong flavors like balsamic vinegar and horseradish. You may want to lightly toast the buns. Open up the color section to see these baby burgers in action.

Tip: Leftover mushrooms are great as a grilled topping for salads, a filling for quesadillas, or a topping for pizza.

Vary It! For an appetizer or small meal, consider substituting cremini mushrooms and whole-wheat, two-bite "slider" buns.

Tofu Parmesan

Prep time: 15 min • **Cook time:** 20 min • **Yield:** 5 servings

Ingredients	*Directions*
Two 14-ounce blocks extra-firm tofu, each cut into 8 slices	*1* Drain the tofu slices by placing them on top of several layers of paper towels and covering them with more layers. Place a cast-iron skillet or another heavy object on top to absorb all the moisture, about 3 minutes.
¼ cup olive oil, divided	
1 tablespoon dried basil	
1 teaspoon rosemary	*2* Combine 2 tablespoons of the olive oil with the basil, rosemary, oregano, chili pepper flakes, garlic, and freshly ground pepper (to taste), and rub the mixture on the drained tofu. Let sit for 30 minutes so the tofu absorbs the flavors. Preheat your oven to 350 degrees.
1 teaspoon oregano	
Pinch chili pepper flakes	
2 teaspoons minced garlic	
Freshly ground pepper to taste	*3* Place the flour in a shallow dish. Beat the eggs in another shallow dish. Place the breadcrumbs in a third shallow dish. Dip the tofu slices in the flour, shake off excess, dip them into the egg bath, and then press them into the breadcrumbs.
2 tablespoons all-purpose flour	
1 whole egg and 1 egg white	
1 cup panko breadcrumbs	
¾ cup shredded provolone	*4* Heat the remaining olive oil in a nonstick skillet and sauté the tofu slices until golden brown. Transfer to a parchment-lined baking sheet. Mix the parmesan and provolone cheeses together. Top each slice of tofu with 1 tablespoon marinara sauce and 1 tablespoon of the cheese mixture.
½ cup grated Parmigiano-Reggiano cheese	
1 cup marinara sauce	
	5 Bake for 20 minutes or until the cheese is melted.

Per serving: Calories 528 (From Fat 270); Fat 30g (Saturated 8g); Cholesterol 64mg; Sodium 689mg; Carbohydrate 31g (Dietary Fiber 5g); Protein 30g; Potassium 289mg.

Note: While this recipe is made of good-for-you-ingredients, it's also slightly higher in sodium, so balance out your meal choices the rest of the day with lower-sodium options.

Note: For a lower-sodium option, use the Fresh Homemade Tomato Sauce in Chapter 19 in place of the marinara sauce.

Black Bean 'n' Slaw Sliders

Prep time: 20 min • **Cook time:** 20 min • **Yield:** 6 servings

Ingredients	*Directions*
2¼ cups bagged coleslaw mix with carrots	*1* Combine the coleslaw mix with the lime juice, canola oil, honey, and chipotle peppers and refrigerate for 30 minutes to let the flavors blend.
2 teaspoons lime juice	
1 teaspoon canola oil	
½ teaspoon honey	*2* Mash the beans with a fork and mix together with the egg, onions, breadcrumbs, garlic, cumin, coriander, chili powder, and cilantro. Shape the bean mixture into 6 small patties. Set aside on a well-oiled, flat grill basket.
½ tablespoon chipotle peppers, minced	
One 15-ounce can black beans, rinsed well and drained	
1 egg white, beaten	*3* Preheat the grill and cook the patties until heated through, about 3 to 4 minutes on each side.
½ cup minced red onion	
¼ cup whole-wheat panko breadcrumbs	*4* Serve on whole-wheat buns with the slaw.
1 large garlic clove, minced	
1 teaspoon cumin	
½ teaspoon coriander	
½ teaspoon chili powder	
3 tablespoons fresh cilantro, chopped	
6 whole-wheat slider buns	

Per serving: Calories 212 (From Fat 27); Fat 3g (Saturated 0g); Cholesterol 4mg; Sodium 451mg; Carbohydrate 42g (Dietary Fiber 10g); Protein 10g; Potassium 321mg.

Note: If you prefer, you can broil the burgers for 3 to 4 minutes on each side rather than grilling them.

Tip: You can eliminate using the egg white in this recipe by simply moistening your hands with water or oil to shape the burgers. Handle the burgers with care when turning them on the grill.

Vary It! In place of the coleslaw mixture, peel and shred jicama and red onion for a nice variety of flavors.

Chapter 22

Don't Desert Dessert: Savoring Sweet Endings

*W*ho doesn't love dessert? Having high blood pressure doesn't have to stop you from enjoying dessert. Keeping fat content and portion size in check allows you to incorporate a dessert into your diet with no problem.

Many desserts are high in fat and sugar, and therefore pack in the calories, too. Because one of your goals for blood pressure control is to achieve and maintain a healthy body weight, you want to keep calories in check while sampling something sweet. Desserts are also often high in saturated fat due to ingredients like butter, cream, and shortening. In this chapter, we offer you some lower-fat alternatives to traditional desserts. You can whip these up at home to satisfy your sweet tooth. We also give you some tips on how to enjoy a higher-fat dessert item now and then. The recipes in this chapter are not only delicious but also nutritious enough to justify eating dessert first!

Satisfying Your Sweet Tooth with Fruit

Just as you can substitute fragrant herbs and sharp spices for the salt in your main-dish cooking, you can switch out the less-heart-healthy components of your desserts for fruit and other ingredients. The more flavors you combine, the more mouthwatering the end result. For example, pairing maple with sweet pineapple is so much tastier than just eating a bowl of pineapple.

Grilling is a great technique to use with fruit. Grilling brings out the fruit's juices and intensifies its flavor, making it way more exciting than your average raw produce. Try grilling a whole peeled pineapple using the rotisserie attachment on your grill, or fresh peaches, pears, and bananas cut in half. Alternately, you can skewer smaller pieces of fruit and make grilled kabobs.

Using a pastry brush, coat the fruit with a little melted butter or vegetable oil to prevent the fruit from sticking to the grill. Add a touch of ground cinnamon or another favorite spice to the oil for a flavor punch. Cook your fruit over medium heat, turning once.

Simple sauces, like the one we use in Grilled Pineapple with Maple Cream Sauce, can also enhance the fruit and become part of the dessert itself. Using lowfat yogurt as a base, you can quickly create a tasty fruit sauce that's not only light but also adds calcium to your diet. As we note in Chapter 2, including two to three servings of dairy in your diet daily helps lower your blood pressure. Using yogurt along with fruit is double-happiness when it comes to hypertension.

To one cup of plain lowfat yogurt, add ½ teaspoon of cinnamon, ¼ teaspoon vanilla, 1 tablespoon honey, and ¼ teaspoon of nutmeg. Stir it all together and serve with assorted fruit as a dip, or pour over strawberries with a slice of angel food cake.

When you think dessert, do you crave pie? A one-crust pie contains half the fat and calories of a regular pie. Use your favorite fresh fruit to cover your baking dish as the bottom of the pie, and use only strips of the crust as the top latticework on the pie. You save all the calories from the bottom crust and still get to enjoy a crusty, baked dessert.

Pumpkin Spice Parfait

Prep time: 10 min • **Cook time:** 6–8 min • **Yield:** 4 servings

Ingredients	Directions
One 4-ounce box French vanilla cook-and-serve pudding	**1** Cook the pudding on the stove according to the instructions on the box using lowfat milk. Cool to room temperature.
2 cups lowfat milk	
One 14-ounce can prepared pumpkin pie filling	**2** Fold the pumpkin pie filling and brandy, if desired, into the cooked pudding. Chill.
1 tablespoon brandy or brandy extract (optional)	**3** Place the graham crackers or gingersnap cookies in a food processor. Pulse on and off until the crumbs are your desired consistency.
1 cup gingersnap cookies or graham crackers	
1 pint vanilla frozen yogurt	**4** In a parfait glass or small wine goblet, build layers of pumpkin custard, crumbs, frozen yogurt, and nuts (optional). Top with a small dollop of whipped topping and crystallized ginger, if desired.
1 cup chopped pecans (optional)	
8-ounce container light whipped topping	
Crystallized ginger for garnish (optional)	

Per serving: Calories 234 (From Fat 26); Fat 3g (Saturated 2g); Cholesterol 5mg; Sodium 314mg; Carbohydrate 47g (Dietary Fiber 4g); Protein 6g; Potassium 276mg.

Note: This sweet favorite is pictured in the color section. Each ½-cup serving of cook-and-serve pudding provides a savings of 269 milligrams of sodium versus instant pudding.

Tip: Wondering how to make a cup of cookie crumbles for the crunchy filling? Fourteen graham crackers make 1 cup of graham-cracker crumbs; 20 gingersnaps make 1 cup of gingersnap crumbs. If you don't want to get out the food processor, you can also prepare crumbs by placing crackers or cookies in a plastic bag and using a rolling pin to crush them to the desired consistency.

Very Berry Walnut Crisp

Prep time: 15 min • **Cook time:** 30 min • **Yield:** 8 servings

Ingredients	Directions
1 pint blackberries	*1* Preheat your oven to 350 degrees. Wash the fruit and drain it well.
1 pint raspberries	
1 pint blueberries	
1 quart strawberries, washed well and sliced	*2* Mix together all the berries and spread in the bottom of a 13-x-9-inch glass baking pan.
¼ cup Splenda Brown Sugar Blend	*3* In a small bowl, combine the Splenda, flour, walnuts, oats, nutmeg, and cinnamon. Add the margarine and blend together with your fingertips until small clumps form. Sprinkle over the top of the fruit.
½ cup whole-wheat flour	
¼ cup chopped walnuts	
½ cup old-fashioned oats	
¾ teaspoon nutmeg	*4* Bake approximately 30 minutes or until the crumble topping is golden and the berries are bubbly. Cool for 5 to 10 minutes.
¾ teaspoon cinnamon	
⅓ cup soft tub margarine (not light version)	*5* Serve with your favorite frozen yogurt or Greek yogurt, if desired.
Lowfat frozen or Greek yogurt (optional)	

Per serving: Calories 242 (From Fat 99); Fat 11g (Saturated 2g); Cholesterol 0mg; Sodium 103mg; Carbohydrate 34g (Dietary Fiber 8g); Protein 4g; Potassium 312mg.

Note: If you prefer to use regular brown sugar, use ½ cup. Regular brown sugar adds an additional 50 calories or so per serving.

Vary It! Substitute 4 cups fresh sliced and peeled or frozen (thawed) peaches in place of the berries. Peaches are naturally sweet.

Easy Fruit Kabobs Kissed with Strawberry Cream

Prep time: 10 min • **Cook time:** 20 min • **Yield:** 4 servings

Ingredients	Directions
1 cup fresh pineapple, cut into 16 chunks	*1* Thread the fruit onto 16 wooden skewers. Place in the refrigerator until ready to serve.
2 medium unpeeled Granny Smith apples, cut into sixteen 1-inch chunks	*2* To prepare the strawberry cream, combine the cream cheese, yogurt, and whipped topping and blend well with a wooden spoon. Cover and chill for at least an hour. This can be made ahead and stored for a few days.
2 small bananas, cut into 16 slices	
16 seedless red grapes	
16 fresh strawberries	*3* Serve each fruit kabob with a heaping tablespoon of strawberry cream.
½ cup reduced-calorie cream cheese, softened	
½ cup lowfat strawberry yogurt	
¼ cup light whipped topping	

Per serving: Calories 240 (From Fat 54); Fat 6g (Saturated 4g); Cholesterol 24mg; Sodium 157mg; Carbohydrate 43g (Dietary Fiber 5g); Protein 4g; Potassium 541mg.

Note: These fruit kabobs are a great way to add more fruit to your day, and the assembly makes it easy to get the kids involved.

Tip: If you're not going to eat the fruit right away, brush the fruit chunks with unsweetened orange juice to prevent the fruit from oxidizing.

Vary It! Add a few cubes of leftover angel food cake or pound cake to make this dessert a little more filling. Enjoy changing up the kinds of fruit you use on the kabobs to match what's currently in season where you live.

Roasted Figs and Plums with Greek Yogurt and Walnuts

Prep time: 15 min • **Cook time:** 20 min • **Yield:** 4 servings

Ingredients	*Directions*
2 tablespoons walnuts **3 Black Mission or Brown Turkey Figs, cut in half**	*1* Preheat the oven to 350 degrees. Place the walnuts on a lined baking pan and toast for 5 to 6 minutes. When cooled, coarsely chop the walnuts.
3 ripe dark plums, cut in half and pitted **Nonstick olive oil spray**	*2* Place the figs and plums cut side up on a lined baking pan and spritz with nonstick olive oil spray. Drizzle with honey or agave nectar.
1 tablespoon honey or agave nectar **½ cup nonfat vanilla-flavored Greek yogurt**	*3* Place in preheated oven and bake for 15 to 20 minutes until the fruit is soft and warm.
	4 Divide the fruit among 4 dessert dishes and serve warm from the oven, topped with yogurt and a sprinkling of walnuts.

Per serving: Calories 105 (From Fat 27); Fat 3g (Saturated 0g); Cholesterol 0mg; Sodium 12mg; Carbohydrate 19g (Dietary Fiber 2g); Protein 4g; Potassium 184mg.

Note: This recipe is like a warm fruit pie without the crust. Figs are an extraordinary fruit that's luscious eaten plain and fresh. They have a quick growing season, so look for them in early summer and in late summer through fall.

Tip: When toasting nuts, be sure to watch them closely because they burn very quickly. If you prefer, you can toast them in a dry skillet over medium heat rather than in the oven. Stir constantly for 1 to 2 minutes until toasted.

Vary It! Substitute peaches, nectarines, or even ripe pears when figs and plums are out of season. These fruits are perfect served with any type of nuts and aged cheese. If you want to splurge on calories, substitute mascarpone cheese or crème fraiche for the yogurt.

Grilled Pineapple with Maple Cream Sauce

Prep time: 10 min • **Cook time:** 4–8 min • **Yield:** 6 servings

Ingredients	Directions
¾ cup Greek vanilla yogurt	**1** Preheat your grill to high heat.
¾ tablespoon pure maple syrup	
½ cup unsweetened light coconut milk	**2** To make maple cream, mix together the yogurt and maple syrup. Refrigerate until ready to use.
2 tablespoons sugar	**3** Pour the coconut milk in a shallow bowl. Combine the sugar and cinnamon in a small cup.
¼ teaspoon ground cinnamon	
1 ripe pineapple, peeled, cored, and sliced	**4** When the grill is ready, be sure to oil the grill grates or spray them with nonstick cooking spray to prevent the pineapple from sticking. Dip each pineapple slice in the coconut milk bath and shake off excess milk.
Sprigs of fresh mint for garnish	
	5 Sprinkle lightly with the cinnamon sugar. Repeat for all of the slices. Arrange the pineapple slices on the hot grate and cook until grill marks appear; gently flip and grill on the other side. Transfer the pineapple to a dessert plate.
	6 Add 2 tablespoons of the maple cream sauce to each pineapple slice and garnish with mint sprigs.

Per serving: Calories 94 (From Fat 13); Fat 2g (Saturated 1g); Cholesterol 0mg; Sodium 17mg; Carbohydrate 18g (Dietary Fiber 1g); Protein 3g; Potassium 212mg.

Note: This simple yet special dessert is wonderful, whether it's served hot, cold, or at room temperature; check it out in the color section. The grilling caramelizes the sugars to intensify the flavors.

Tip: When choosing a fresh pineapple, look for a deep golden color and a slightly sweet smell. It should be soft to the touch, and when you pull the leaves from the top, they should come out without too much resistance.

Beachcomber Smoothie Shooters

Prep time: 5 min • **Yield:** 18 servings

Ingredients	*Directions*
1 small banana	*1* Combine the bananas, sliced strawberries, pineapple, and orange juice in a blender and puree until smooth.
½ cup sliced strawberries, hulled and rinsed well	
1 cup unsweetened crushed pineapple	*2* Add the skim milk, vanilla and coconut extracts, yogurt, and ice and blend until smooth and thick.
¼ cup orange juice	
¼ cup skim milk	*3* Pour 1½ ounces into each of 24 standard shot glasses or demitasse cups. Garnish each glass with a fresh strawberry.
Dash vanilla extract	
¼ teaspoon coconut extract	
½ cup nonfat plain or vanilla yogurt	
1 cup ice	
18 whole small fresh strawberries	

Per serving: Calories 31 (From Fat 0); Fat 0g (Saturated 0g); Cholesterol 0mg; Sodium 7mg; Carbohydrate 7g (Dietary Fiber 1g); Protein 1g; Potassium 67mg.

Tip: In the winter months when fresh fruit isn't as readily available, you can use any of your favorite frozen fruits with no added sugar.

Vary It! Experiment with any number of your favorite fruits and vary them with the seasons!

Indulging Your Cravings

How many times have you read this advice?: "If you want something sweet, have a piece of fruit." In theory, this is a grand idea, but in our book, fruit may not always cut it when a craving for cake or chocolate really hits. So thank goodness you have our book and can dive into these awesome desserts that (for your heart's sake) will add a bit of fiber and vitamins to your plate and also tantalize your taste buds and satisfy that sweet tooth. The preceding section shows you how to turn plain old fruit into real desserts; this one offers you some more traditional ideas with a healthy twist.

If you're going to satisfy your craving for cake, make your own. Unlike the gummy super-sweet cakes you may find in grocery stores, baking your own is worth the time once in a while. If you don't have time to whip one up, look for one in a good bakery and serve it with fresh sliced peaches or berries.

Keep in mind that while desserts may be lower in sodium, they are high in fat and sugar, and thus not friendly to your waistline if overindulged in.

Favorite Chocolate Pudding Cake

Prep time: 20 min • **Cook time:** 20 min • **Yield:** About 15 servings

Ingredients	*Directions*
½ cup soft tub margarine (not light) 1 cup all-purpose flour 1 cup finely chopped pecans	*1* Preheat your oven to 350 degrees. Combine the margarine, flour, and pecans and press into a 13-x-9-inch glass baking pan. Bake for 20 minutes. Remove from the oven and cool completely.
One 8-ounce package light cream cheese or Neufchatel 1 cup powdered sugar	*2* Blend the cream cheese, powdered sugar, and 1 cup of the thawed whipped topping with a wooden spoon. Gently spread the mixture over the cooled crust.
One 8-ounce container frozen light whipped topping, thawed 1 small package chocolate instant pudding	*3* Whisk together the pudding mixes with the milk and blend until thick. Pour over the cream cheese filling. Top with the remaining whipped topping.
1 small package vanilla instant pudding 2 cups very cold nonfat milk Grated chocolate (optional)	*4* Top with grated chocolate, if desired. Chill for at least 1 hour or up to a few days before serving.

Per serving: Calories 274 (From Fat 171); Fat 19g (Saturated 6g); Cholesterol 27mg; Sodium 480mg; Carbohydrate 23g (Dietary Fiber 1g); Protein 4g; Potassium 164mg.

Vary It! Substitute your favorite flavor of instant pudding. For an island treat, try coconut cream flavored pudding, and garnish with a few tablespoons of toasted coconut. Don't substitute nonfat cream cheese for the light or Neufchatel, though.

Cinnamon Apple Cake

Prep time: 10 min • **Cook time:** 35–60 min • **Yield:** About 14 servings

Ingredients	*Directions*
Nonstick cooking spray	*1* Preheat your oven to 350 degrees. Prepare a 13-x-9-inch cake pan or Bundt pan with nonstick cooking spray and a dusting of flour.
4 cups peeled, diced apples (1 cup of each variety — Granny Smith, Braeburn, Gala, and Rome)	
1¼ cups sugar	*2* Mix together the apples, sugar, flour, cinnamon, and baking soda with a wooden spoon.
2 cups flour	
1½ teaspoons cinnamon	*3* Pour the wet ingredients — the canola oil, eggs, and vanilla — over the dry ingredients and mix well.
2 teaspoons baking soda	
½ cup canola oil	*4* Pour the batter into your prepared cake pan and bake in the oven for 35 to 45 minutes for a 13-x-9-inch cake pan or 45 to 60 minutes for a Bundt pan. Serve warm or at room temperature.
2 eggs, beaten	
2 teaspoons vanilla	

Per serving: Calories 160 (From Fat 24); Fat 3g (Saturated 0g); Cholesterol 27mg; Sodium 165mg; Carbohydrate 32g (Dietary Fiber 1g); Protein 3g; Potassium 57mg.

Note: You can use your favorite apples — most any will work. If you have any of this cake left, it will become moister as time goes on.

Note: Good news: You don't have to pull out the mixer! This one is done by hand.

Tip: Scrub the apples and remove the cores but leave the peel intact for more fiber.

Vary It! Add 1 cup chopped walnuts or pecans for variety. Serve warm with vanilla frozen yogurt for an added treat!

Cappuccino Granita

Prep time: 10 min • **Cook time:** 20 min • **Yield:** 4 servings

Ingredients	Directions
4 cups skim milk	**1** Stir together the milk, coffee, and sugar until all ingredients are dissolved. Blend briefly in a blender to speed up the process.
2 tablespoons coffee crystals or instant espresso	
6 tablespoons sugar	**2** Pour into a 13-x-9-inch freezer-safe plastic container. Cover loosely. Freeze for 4 hours or overnight.
Cinnamon or chocolate curls for garnish (optional)	
	3 To serve, use an ice cream scoop. When served, this granita looks like light brown shaved ice.
	4 Garnish with a sprinkling of cinnamon or chocolate curls, if desired.

Per serving: Calories 163 (From Fat 0); Fat 0g (Saturated 0g); Cholesterol 5mg; Sodium 104mg; Carbohydrate 32g (Dietary Fiber 0g); Protein 9g; Potassium 478mg.

Note: A granita is a light, refreshing Italian dessert. In Italy, coffee granita is served at breakfast on hot summer days.

Tip: Granitas can be made using any liquid, such as champagne, pomegranate juice, applesauce, and even carrot juice. The fruity ones are light and refreshing and can serve as a perfect palate cleanser between courses at dinner. Granitas can be frozen up to two weeks.

Part V
The Part of Tens

The 5th Wave   By Rich Tennant

"He's lost 12 pounds on the DASH diet.
Now if I can just get him to lose that hat."

In this part . . .

You can't oversimplify a plan to reduce hypertension as just eating low-sodium or lowfat. In this part, we remind you that managing your hypertension is about living a healthy, enjoyable life by eating well, staying active, and modifying whatever risk factors you can. Some risk factors for heart disease (such as gender or age) are out of your control, but you can do your part to help your body. In this part, we offer some quick tips for adding flavor to dishes without salt, as well as modifying whatever lifestyle behaviors you can in order to better manage your high blood pressure.

Chapter 23

Ten Ways to Add Flavor without Salt

*O*ne of the overarching goals of the DASH lifestyle (see Chapter 2) is to reduce your dietary sodium. Salt contributes flavor to foods, but it contributes a lot of sodium, too, and you can easily add flavor without it. There are many ways to replace salt — not only with herbs and spices, but via cooking techniques as well. This concept is called *flavor-building*. It involves using multiple, complimentary flavors to create new flavors in a dish, and it makes your food so tantalizing that you don't feel the need to add salt to make your food palatable. Most times, you want to add some seasoning before you cook and some during cooking. Flavor-building just takes a bit of practice and is worth the learning curve.

Check out our top ten ways to build flavor without salt here. Decide what your favorite flavors are and find out how to adjust recipes accordingly. If you're going to maintain a lower-sodium diet for the long haul, you have to enjoy what you eat!

Sautéing, Grilling, and Roasting

Sautéing, grilling, and roasting are cooking methods that bring out the natural caramelizing properties in foods and really seal in the natural flavors and juices of meats and vegetables. Learning to do a quick sauté is a versatile skill to master in the kitchen. Sautéing simply involves using a sauté pan to cook foods at high temperatures for short periods. When you sauté chicken, for instance, you brown the chicken on both sides in a small amount of vegetable oil, add some flavoring (perhaps garlic or shallots), and then add some liquid (wine or low-sodium chicken broth) to finish cooking.

Grilling doesn't have to dry out your meats and veggies. Seasoning foods properly and then refrigerating them for one or more hours before grilling can create moisture and allow more flavor to be absorbed into the food. Grilling sears in flavor, creating a "crust" on the outside that keeps juices in. Grilling is generally a quick-cook method, so keeping an eye on the food or using a meat thermometer to avoid overcooking is key.

Roasting is generally done in an open pan in the oven. It involves beginning at a higher temperature to promote exterior browning (caramelizing), and then reducing the temperature for the remainder of the cooking time. Slower roasting times for meats or vegetables promote tenderness and allow more flavors to develop. To keep meats moist when you roast them, be sure to add cooking liquid (even just water, which allows the meat to create its own juice) throughout the cooking process.

Adding Herbs, Spices, and Pepper

Herbs and spices can add great flavor to your dishes. The important thing is to use the ones you really love. For instance, say you're not fond of oregano and a tomato sauce recipe calls for two teaspoons of it. Guess what? You can skip the oregano and substitute another herb that you do enjoy! Basil or rosemary may work, as may parsley. Salt-free herb blends can be purchased at the store, or you can mix up your own blends with various jarred herbs you have in the pantry. Try mixing up 3 tablespoons dried parsley, 1 tablespoon powdered sage, 2 tablespoons dried rosemary, and 1 tablespoon garlic powder in a small bowl. Use immediately or store in an airtight jar for a week.

To bring out the aroma of dried herbs, such as rosemary, thyme, and oregano, crush them between your fingers before adding them to a dish.

Squeezing in Citrus

The way a bit of lemon or orange zest can make the flavors of a dish come alive is amazing. Citrus juices can also add intense flavor when reduced or combined with other spices. We recommend fresh corn on the cob with lime chili butter instead of teaspoons of salt, and orange juice reduced to an orange oil as an addition to salad dressings and sauces instead of added sodium.

Including Onions, Peppers, Garlic, and More

Aromatic vegetables such as onions, garlic, scallions, shallots, leeks, and chives add a distinctive flavor and aroma whether sautéed, roasted, or raw. Use them to build flavors by adding the sweetness of caramelizing, the pungency of raw onion, or the earthiness of roasted garlic.

A small amount of garlic (one clove) can enhance the flavor of a variety of foods from pork and beef to vegetables (especially green beans, spinach, eggplant, and squash). Garlic also has heart-health benefits, providing those important phytochemicals and antioxidants. When in doubt, add a clove of crushed garlic!

Using Fresh Ginger and Horseradish

Fresh ginger adds a flavor punch that can't be matched. Fresh gingerroot is available in the produce section of your grocery store and is easy to store and use. Store it in a brown paper bag and keep it in the vegetable bin of your refrigerator. Or, you can use ginger to give oil a mild ginger flavor: Cut a small, coin-like piece of ginger (you don't have to peel it) and place it in hot oil. Cook it for a few minutes, taking care not to burn it; then remove and discard the ginger.

Horseradish is an underused flavor agent. You can purchase it fresh or jarred. A little bit goes a long way, adding heat and punch to a sauce or stew. It also makes a great condiment — add it to mayonnaise to make a sandwich spread.

Cooking with Oils and Flavored Oils

Add extra-virgin olive oil or walnut oil to a garden-fresh salad mix, or top off a stir-fry with a dash of sesame oil. Neutral oils, such as canola, safflower, and grapeseed oils, can be infused with spices and herbs to give them unique flavors as well. These additions not only boost flavor, but also give you another way to add heart-healthy fats to your diet.

Pouring in Vinegars and Wine

Flavored vinegars can really wake up your taste buds without added salt. You can choose a wine vinegar (made from red wine, white wine, rosé wine, champagne, rice wine, or sherry), cider vinegar (made from apples), or balsamic vinegar. Infused vinegars may be flavored with roasted garlic, chili peppers, herbs, vegetables, and fruit. Wine and spirits can be used as flavor builders too. Use them in a sauce or as a flavoring. Two to try: sherry in a cream sauce and amaretto with cooked carrots.

Trying Vegetable Sauces

Using vegetables to make a puree, coulis, or salsa is a great way to infuse flavor into a dish. These wonderful alternatives replace high-fat and high-salt sauces, and they add not only flavor but color and nutrition too! For a delicious vegetable coulis, blend a roasted red bell pepper with a small amount of homemade stock. Salsas and relishes are generally chunky mixtures made from a variety of vegetables or fruits, with the addition of one or two intense flavors, such as chili peppers or cilantro.

Making Rubs and Marinades

A rub or marinade can be used as a seasoning as well as a tenderizer. Dry or wet rubs can provide flavor profiles that vary from sweet and hot (try a Jamaican jerk) to full-bodied (like a garlic rub). A dry rub is a combination of spices and herbs that are blended together and rubbed right into the meat. A wet rub is a combination of spices and herbs blended with liquid ingredients — usually oil — and rubbed over the surface of the meat. You can adjust a homemade rub to have as much heat as you desire by adding in more or less cayenne, freshly ground pepper, jalapeños, and so on. Marinades are liquids that contain an acidic ingredient to tenderize tough meat or add flavor. Wine, citrus juice, and yogurt can serve as the base of a marinade, dressed up with herbs, spices, and even fruit.

Sprinkling on a Wee Bit of Cheese

Small amounts of sharp, pungent white cheeses such as Romano, Parmesan, or Asiago can really boost the flavor of a dish. Just one or two tablespoons add tons of flavor while you're skipping the extra salt. Better yet, this flavor booster may help you consume more veggies. For instance, a teaspoon of Parmesan may make the spinach go down with delight, and adding a tablespoon of shredded mozzarella to sautéed zucchini may tempt even the most hesitant of vegetable eaters.

Chapter 24

Ten Long-Term Tips to Beat Hypertension

In This Chapter

▶ Discovering the best ways to live a low-blood-pressure lifestyle

▶ Finding out what you need to eat more of

▶ Living well and having fun with family and friends

Hypertension can be serious when not treated properly (check out Chapter 1 for more on the medical issues that can surface because of high blood pressure). Unfortunately, no quick fixes exist to cure your hypertension for good. Instead, you need to look at setting new, long-term goals that can improve your lifestyle and reduce your high blood pressure. In this chapter, we give you the ten best lifestyle changes you can make in your battle against hypertension. In addition to what you see here, check in with your doctor regularly. Beating hypertension doesn't happen overnight, but you can make progress by following these ten tips.

Lose Weight and Keep It Off

Weight loss is the number-one treatment for hypertension. Being overweight strains your body, and losing even 10 percent of your body weight is practically guaranteed to improve your blood pressure control. So, get to it — start losing the weight by using the healthy recipes and tips in this cookbook, as well as exercising (flip to Chapters 2 and 3 for more how-to's on losing weight). After you've lost the weight, the key is to keep it off. Don't think that because you've lost some weight, you can return to an unhealthy lifestyle and remain at your ideal weight. To maintain a weight loss, you must maintain the lifestyle changes: eating the right amounts of the right foods (lean meats, vegetables, fruits, grains, less salt, and smaller portions of treats) and exercising four to five times per week. Sticking to lifestyle changes often means continuously setting new goals to avoid a setback. A great tool to help you set diet and exercise goals — and stick to them — is *Calorie Counter Journal For Dummies* by coauthor Rosanne and Meri Raffetto (Wiley).

Develop an Exercise Routine

Along with eating right, regular exercise keeps your weight under control, improves your cardiovascular health, and reduces your stress level, all of which help you beat hypertension in the long run. *Regular* is a key word here: You need to exercise regularly for it to work its magic. Scheduling a 20- to 30-minute walk five days a week is a great way to begin moving regularly. Do whatever you can at first, and then add minutes each week. Once you're up to 30 to 45 minutes of walking, gradually increase your pace until you can walk a mile in 15 to 20 minutes.

Weight-bearing exercise is important too, especially as you age because muscle loss occurs at a more rapid rate. Adding workouts with weights or weight machines two or three times a week to your aerobic activity is a great plan. Consider meeting with a certified personal trainer initially to begin a program that works for you.

If you haven't been getting any exercise, check with your doctor for any health limitations that you should be aware of before beginning your exercise regime; then start a simple program. Check out Chapter 3 for more on working exercise into your schedule.

Stick to DASH

While one of the goals of DASH (Dietary Approaches to Stop Hypertension; see Chapter 2) eating is to reduce sodium, saturated fat, and cholesterol in the diet, this diet plan is more about what to *add* as opposed to what to *limit*. Fruits and vegetables, for instance, are very important sources of potassium and magnesium, which help lower blood pressure, and fiber, which helps keep cholesterol in check. This diet also encourages you to include more monounsaturated fats and lowfat dairy products. Following the DASH dietary guidelines has been proven to lower hypertension. Enjoy the recipes in this book, which all incorporate aspects of the DASH plan (see Chapters 9–22), and check out Chapters 3, 4, and 7 for even more information on what to eat.

Eat Less Salt

A high-salt diet has been shown to raise blood pressure in some people, so reducing your intake of high-sodium foods and the amount of salt you use in cooking is a good idea. The first strategy is to put down the salt shaker or shake a lot less. Secondly, read food labels and reduce your consumption of highly processed or salty foods. Sodium is a component of salt. The recommended intake of sodium is 1,500–2,300 milligrams per day. You'll find loads of tips throughout this book for reducing salt in your diet, especially in Chapters 4 and 5.

Add Good Fats to Your Diet

Because hypertension is a risk factor for heart disease, consuming heart-healthy fats is a good idea in order to avoid another risk factor for heart disease: high blood cholesterol. Vegetable oils such as olive, canola, and peanut are high in monounsaturated fat. Other vegetable oils are high in polyunsaturated fat. Although polyunsaturated fats aren't harmful, research has shown that monounsaturated fats seem to have a positive effect on blood lipid levels (whereas polys have a neutral effect — see Chapter 1 for more details). Adding nuts, seeds, and the aforementioned oils to your diet is a good idea. Try walnuts in salads and stir-fries or have a small handful as a snack. Nuts can be a nutritious snack as long as you don't overindulge. Eating about 15 to 20 nuts is sufficient to get the good nutrients you need.

Avoid Drinking Excessive Alcohol

Although a glass of red wine or an alcoholic beverage a day may be beneficial to your circulation and heart health, overindulging is not. Moderate alcohol intake can increase your HDL (good cholesterol) and has a mild anticoagulant effect (which keeps blood from clotting), but drinking more than two drinks a day can lead to heart damage. The Centers for Disease Control and Prevention (CDC) define heavy drinking as more than two drinks daily for men and more than one drink daily for women. One drink is equivalent to a 5-ounce glass of wine, a 12-ounce beer, or 1½ ounces of 80-proof liquor. So keep your alcohol intake moderate for heart health — and if you don't drink alcohol, don't start. Make other heart-healthy lifestyle choices instead, such as proper eating and exercise.

Don't Use Tobacco Products

Smoking causes coronary heart disease, which is the leading cause of death in the United States. It also narrows the blood vessels in the body, putting smokers at risk for *peripheral vascular disease* (obstruction of the large arteries in the arms and legs, resulting in pain and possible tissue death).

Smoking increases blood pressure, so it's an important lifestyle habit to address. It also causes coronary artery disease, and if your arteries aren't strong and healthy, your blood pressure and overall heart health is impacted. Chewing tobacco also raises blood pressure, just as smoking cigarettes or cigars does. Of course, smoking also causes lung cancer and is linked to many other cancers, and according to the CDC, smokeless tobacco contains 28 cancer-causing agents.

Smokers' risk of heart disease and stroke is two to four times greater than that of nonsmokers. All nicotine products cause a temporary rise in blood pressure. The bottom line? Don't smoke or chew tobacco.

Stress Less

Although there may not be definitive evidence that stress causes high blood pressure or heart disease, it definitely plays a role. Work, family, health, and your personal life may impact your overall stress level. Finding ways to manage stress helps you cope with day-to-day life and simply makes you feel better. You can reduce stress in a number of ways — one is to engage in regular exercise. Even simple breathing exercises can help. Try taking long, slow breaths: Inhale to a count of four; then exhale to a count of eight.

Enlist Your Family and Friends

Whether the goal is weight loss, a diet for hypertension, or a diet for diabetes, everyone has more success when they have support. Making lifestyle changes is tough, and enlisting your family and friends can be a huge help. Talk to your family about your dietary and health goals. Let them know how important it is that you make these changes, and emphasize that you need their help and positive support. Ask a friend to meet you for a walk to the gym so you can maintain a regular exercise program. Having support helps keep you on track and turns eating well and exercising into pleasant experiences.

Follow Your Doctor's Orders

If you've been diagnosed with hypertension, be sure to follow your doctor's advice and keep regular appointments, including an annual physical exam. If you're over 40, you should have at least a biennial physical checkup. Take any prescribed medications as directed. If you have any concerns about the medication or treatment your doctor recommends, ask questions.

Part VI
Appendixes

The 5th Wave   By Rich Tennant

"Oh, I have a very healthy relationship with food. It's the relationship I have with my blood pressure that's not so good."

In this part . . .

The appendixes in this part go over lots of useful information to help you as you cook. Appendix A includes metric conversions for those who may be translating U.S. recipes to metric measures (and don't like doing the math). If the idea of converting ounces to grams raises your blood pressure just thinking about it, please hurry over to Appendix A.

Because you probably want to cook other recipes besides those you read in this book, Appendix B details some options you can substitute to keep other favorite recipes lowfat and low-sodium. This appendix is a helpful, general resource to cooking with better ingredients when a recipe calls for something a bit less healthy.

Appendix A

Metric Conversion Guide

* *

*N*ote: The recipes in this book weren't developed or tested using metric measurements. There may be some variation in quality when converting to metric units.

Common Abbreviations	
Abbreviation(s)	*What It Stands For*
cm	Centimeter
C., c.	Cup
G, g	Gram
kg	Kilogram
L, l	Liter
lb.	Pound
mL, ml	Milliliter
oz.	Ounce
pt.	Pint
t., tsp.	Teaspoon
T., Tb., Tbsp.	Tablespoon

Volume

U.S. Units	Canadian Metric	Australian Metric
¼ teaspoon	1 milliliter	1 milliliter
½ teaspoon	2 milliliters	2 milliliters
1 teaspoon	5 milliliters	5 milliliters
1 tablespoon	15 milliliters	20 milliliters
¼ cup	50 milliliters	60 milliliters
⅓ cup	75 milliliters	80 milliliters
½ cup	125 milliliters	125 milliliters
⅔ cup	150 milliliters	170 milliliters
¾ cup	175 milliliters	190 milliliters
1 cup	250 milliliters	250 milliliters
1 quart	1 liter	1 liter
1½ quarts	1.5 liters	1.5 liters
2 quarts	2 liters	2 liters
2½ quarts	2.5 liters	2.5 liters
3 quarts	3 liters	3 liters
4 quarts (1 gallon)	4 liters	4 liters

Weight

U.S. Units	Canadian Metric	Australian Metric
1 ounce	30 grams	30 grams
2 ounces	55 grams	60 grams
3 ounces	85 grams	90 grams
4 ounces (¼ pound)	115 grams	125 grams
8 ounces (½ pound)	225 grams	225 grams
16 ounces (1 pound)	455 grams	500 grams (½ kilogram)

Length

Inches	Centimeters
0.5	1.5
1	2.5
2	5.0
3	7.5
4	10.0
5	12.5
6	15.0
7	17.5
8	20.5
9	23.0
10	25.5
11	28.0
12	30.5

Temperature (Degrees)

Fahrenheit	Celsius
32	0
212	100
250	120
275	140
300	150
325	160
350	180
375	190
400	200
425	220
450	230
475	240
500	260

Appendix B

Substitution Guide

When you have hypertension, you may want to make some ingredient substitutions as you're cooking to reduce the sodium, cut some fat, or simply make your meals a little lighter and more DASH-friendly (head to Chapter 2 for more on what those four letters mean). We have you covered.

In this appendix, we offer some substitutions that make any recipe you cook a bit healthier. We also offer substitutions for a few different kinds of alcohol because consuming alcohol in moderation, rather than in excess, helps reduce blood pressure. For ideas on how to sub ingredients when you don't have something on hand, flip to Chapter 8.

When you bake, don't get too freewheeling with ingredient substitution or change the amounts of the given ingredients. Cooking, however, is another matter; feel free to tweak ingredients when you cook.

The next time you're cooking using these ingredients, consider swapping them for their healthier alternatives:

- ✔ **Amaretto:** For two tablespoons of amaretto, substitute ¼ to ½ teaspoon of almond extract.
- ✔ **Beef or chicken broth:** For 2 cups of broth, make your own low-sodium broth by using 1 beef or chicken bouillon cube plus 2 cups of water (or look for low-sodium beef or chicken broth).
- ✔ **Beer:** Substitute an equal amount of low-sodium chicken broth.
- ✔ **Breadcrumbs:** Replace breadcrumbs with an equal amount of salt-free cracker crumbs or ground oats.
- ✔ **Buttermilk:** Try this lower-fat ratio: If a recipe calls for 1 cup of buttermilk, add 1 tablespoon of lemon juice or vinegar to 1 cup of lowfat or nonfat milk.
- ✔ **Cream cheese:** Substitute light cream cheese.
- ✔ **Egg:** Instead of 1 whole egg, try 2 egg whites. If a recipe calls for more eggs, you can use some yolks. For example, instead of 3 eggs, use one whole egg and 4 egg whites.
- ✔ **Fats used in baking:** For 1 cup of vegetable oil, butter, shortening, or margarine, use ⅔ cup of fruit puree.

- ✔ **Grand Marnier:** For two tablespoons of Grand Marnier, substitute 2 tablespoons of orange juice concentrate.

- ✔ **Ground beef:** Replace regular ground beef with either 90-percent-lean ground beef or 93-percent-lean ground turkey.

- ✔ **Heavy cream:** Whisk two tablespoons of flour into 1-percent milk to use in place of heavy cream for sauces.

- ✔ **Coffee-flavored liqueur:** For 2 tablespoons of coffee-flavored liqueur, try using 2 tablespoons of strong brewed coffee plus 1 teaspoon of sugar.

- ✔ **Pork sausage:** Substitute a lowfat chicken sausage to reduce the saturated fat content of the recipe.

- ✔ **Rum or brandy:** For 2 tablespoons of rum or brandy, use ½ to 1 teaspoon of rum extract.

- ✔ **Salt:** Boy, do we have some ideas for you. A whole chapter, in fact. Rather than repeat ourselves, head to Chapter 4 for some salt-substitution ideas you may not have tried.

- ✔ **Sherry or bourbon:** Replace 2 tablespoons of sherry or bourbon with 1 to 2 teaspoons of vanilla extract.

- ✔ **Sour cream:** Substitute an equal amount of light sour cream or lowfat plain yogurt for regular sour cream.

- ✔ **White flour:** Add some fiber by substituting whole-wheat flour for half of the white flour in a baking recipe. For instance, if the recipe calls for 2 cups of flour, use 1 cup of whole-wheat flour and 1 cup of white flour.

- ✔ **Whole milk:** In sauce recipes calling for whole milk, add 1 to 2 tablespoons of light cream cheese to nonfat or 1-percent milk; heat and stir until thickened.

Keep in mind the following tips, too, which offer you some alternate cooking habits to improve the health quotient of whatever comes out of your kitchen:

- ✔ Choosing fresh, instead of processed, ingredients whenever possible almost always results in less sodium, more flavor, and more nutrients.

- ✔ Using high-quality, nonstick pans makes it much easier to use smaller amounts of fat in cooking. Do choose healthy fats, however — olive oil, canola oil, or peanut oil, for instance (see Chapter 2).

- ✔ Oven-baking or pan-frying many traditionally fried foods (think fried chicken) uses much less oil, thereby significantly cutting the fat and the calories.

- ✔ Using smaller amounts of really good ingredients can make a big difference. Sometimes just a tablespoon of an imported cheese (versus a cup, which has loads more sodium) or a garnish of high-quality chocolate is all it takes to kick the flavor up a few notches.

Index

• *W* •

• *Y* •

Apple & Macs

iPad For Dummies
978-0-470-58027-1

iPhone For Dummies,
4th Edition
978-0-470-87870-5

MacBook For Dummies, 3rd
Edition
978-0-470-76918-8

Mac OS X Snow Leopard For
Dummies
978-0-470-43543-4

Business

Bookkeeping For Dummies
978-0-7645-9848-7

Job Interviews
For Dummies,
3rd Edition
978-0-470-17748-8

Resumes For Dummies,
5th Edition
978-0-470-08037-5

Starting an
Online Business
For Dummies,
6th Edition
978-0-470-60210-2

Stock Investing
For Dummies,
3rd Edition
978-0-470-40114-9

Successful
Time Management
For Dummies
978-0-470-29034-7

Computer Hardware

BlackBerry
For Dummies,
4th Edition
978-0-470-60700-8

Computers For Seniors
For Dummies,
2nd Edition
978-0-470-53483-0

PCs For Dummies,
Windows
7 Edition
978-0-470-46542-4

Laptops For Dummies,
4th Edition
978-0-470-57829-2

Cooking & Entertaining

Cooking Basics
For Dummies,
3rd Edition
978-0-7645-7206-7

Wine For Dummies,
4th Edition
978-0-470-04579-4

Diet & Nutrition

Dieting For Dummies,
2nd Edition
978-0-7645-4149-0

Nutrition For Dummies,
4th Edition
978-0-471-79868-2

Weight Training
For Dummies,
3rd Edition
978-0-471-76845-6

Digital Photography

Digital SLR Cameras &
Photography For Dummies,
3rd Edition
978-0-470-46606-3

Photoshop Elements 8
For Dummies
978-0-470-52967-6

Gardening

Gardening Basics
For Dummies
978-0-470-03749-2

Organic Gardening
For Dummies,
2nd Edition
978-0-470-43067-5

Green/Sustainable

Raising Chickens
For Dummies
978-0-470-46544-8

Green Cleaning
For Dummies
978-0-470-39106-8

Health

Diabetes For Dummies,
3rd Edition
978-0-470-27086-8

Food Allergies
For Dummies
978-0-470-09584-3

Living Gluten-Free
For Dummies,
2nd Edition
978-0-470-58589-4

Hobbies/General

Chess For Dummies,
2nd Edition
978-0-7645-8404-6

Drawing
Cartoons & Comics
For Dummies
978-0-470-42683-8

Knitting For Dummies,
2nd Edition
978-0-470-28747-7

Organizing
For Dummies
978-0-7645-5300-4

Su Doku For Dummies
978-0-470-01892-7

Home Improvement

Home Maintenance
For Dummies,
2nd Edition
978-0-470-43063-7

Home Theater
For Dummies,
3rd Edition
978-0-470-41189-6

Living the
Country Lifestyle
All-in-One
For Dummies
978-0-470-43061-3

Solar Power Your Home
For Dummies,
2nd Edition
978-0-470-59678-4

Available wherever books are sold. For more information or to order direct: U.S. customers visit www.dummies.com or call 1-877-762-2974.
U.K. customers visit www.wileyeurope.com or call (0) 1243 843291. Canadian customers visit www.wiley.ca or call 1-800-567-4797.

Internet

Blogging For Dummies,
3rd Edition
978-0-470-61996-4

eBay For Dummies,
6th Edition
978-0-470-49741-8

Facebook For Dummies,
3rd Edition
978-0-470-87804-0

Web Marketing
For Dummies,
2nd Edition
978-0-470-37181-7

WordPress
For Dummies,
3rd Edition
978-0-470-59274-8

Language & Foreign Language

French For Dummies
978-0-7645-5193-2

Italian Phrases
For Dummies
978-0-7645-7203-6

Spanish For Dummies,
2nd Edition
978-0-470-87855-2

Spanish
For Dummies,
Audio Set
978-0-470-09585-0

Math & Science

Algebra I
For Dummies,
2nd Edition
978-0-470-55964-2

Biology For Dummies,
2nd Edition
978-0-470-59875-7

Calculus For Dummies
978-0-7645-2498-1

Chemistry For Dummies
978-0-7645-5430-8

Microsoft Office

Excel 2010 For Dummies
978-0-470-48953-6

Office 2010 All-in-One
For Dummies
978-0-470-49748-7

Office 2010 For Dummies,
Book + DVD Bundle
978-0-470-62698-6

Word 2010 For Dummies
978-0-470-48772-3

Music

Guitar For Dummies,
2nd Edition
978-0-7645-9904-0

iPod & iTunes For
Dummies, 8th Edition
978-0-470-87871-2

Piano Exercises
For Dummies
978-0-470-38765-8

Parenting & Education

Parenting For Dummies,
2nd Edition
978-0-7645-5418-6

Type 1 Diabetes
For Dummies
978-0-470-17811-9

Pets

Cats For Dummies,
2nd Edition
978-0-7645-5275-5

Dog Training For Dummies,
3rd Edition
978-0-470-60029-0

Puppies For Dummies,
2nd Edition
978-0-470-03717-1

Religion & Inspiration

The Bible For Dummies
978-0-7645-5296-0

Catholicism For Dummies
978-0-7645-5391-2

Women in the Bible
For Dummies
978-0-7645-8475-6

Self-Help & Relationship

Anger Management
For Dummies
978-0-470-03715-7

Overcoming Anxiety
For Dummies,
2nd Edition
978-0-470-57441-6

Sports

Baseball
For Dummies,
3rd Edition
978-0-7645-7537-2

Basketball
For Dummies,
2nd Edition
978-0-7645-5248-9

Golf For Dummies,
3rd Edition
978-0-471-76871-5

Web Development

Web Design
All-in-One
For Dummies
978-0-470-41796-6

Web Sites
Do-It-Yourself
For Dummies,
2nd Edition
978-0-470-56520-9

Windows 7

Windows 7
For Dummies
978-0-470-49743-2

Windows 7
For Dummies,
Book + DVD Bundle
978-0-470-52398-8

Windows 7 All-in-One
For Dummies
978-0-470-48763-1

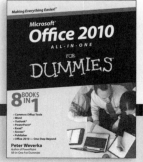

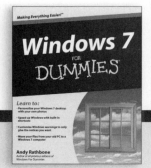

Available wherever books are sold. For more information or to order direct: U.S. customers visit www.dummies.com or call 1-877-762-297.
U.K. customers visit www.wileyeurope.com or call (0) 1243 843291. Canadian customers visit www.wiley.ca or call 1-800-567-4797.